# 12th European Workshop on Natural Language Generation 2009

# (ENLG 09)



## Athens, Greece
## 30-31 March 2009

ISBN: 978-1-61738-556-8

**Printed from e-media with permission by:**

Curran Associates, Inc.
57 Morehouse Lane
Red Hook, NY 12571

**Some format issues inherent in the e-media version may also appear in this print version.**



Printed by Curran Associates, Inc. (2010)

For permission requests, please contact the Association for Computational Linguistics at the address below.

Association for Computational Linguistics
209 N. Eighth Street
Stroudsburg, Pennsylvania 18360

Phone: 1-570-476-8006
Fax: 1-570-476-0860

acl@aclweb.org

**Additional copies of this publication are available from:**

Curran Associates, Inc.
57 Morehouse Lane
Red Hook, NY 12571 USA
Phone: 845-758-0400
Fax: 845-758-2634
Email: curran@proceedings.com
Web: www.proceedings.com

# Preface

We are pleased to present the Proceedings of the 12th European Workshop on Natural Language Generation (ENLG 2009). ENLG 2009 was held in Athens, Greece, as a workshop at the 12th Conference of the European Chapter of the Association for Computational Linguistics (EACL 2009). It was endorsed by the ACL Special Interest Group on Generation (SIGGEN).

The ENLG 2009 workshop continued a biennial series of workshops on natural language generation that has been running since 1987. Previous European workshops have been held at Royaumont, Edinburgh, Judenstein, Pisa, Leiden, Duisburg, Toulouse, Budapest, Aberdeen and Dagstuhl. The series provides a regular forum for presentation of research in this area, both for NLG specialists and for researchers from other areas, and together with INLG (the International Conference on Natural Language Generation) with which it alternates, ENLG is the main forum for NLG research.

As always, ENLG invited substantial, original, and unpublished submissions on all topics related to natural language generation. Following our call, we received 37 submissions (both long and short) of which 14 long papers and 10 short papers were accepted after a careful reviewing process. These Proceedings include the final versions of the accepted papers.

Following up on a number of earlier evaluation campaigns, the Generation Challenges 2009 were organized as one umbrella event designed to bring together different shared-task evaluation efforts involving the generation of natural language. Two of these Generation Challenges were held in conjunction with ENLG 2009. The GIVE Challenge (organized by a team consisting of Donna Byron, Justine Cassell, Robert Dale, Alexander Koller, Johanna Moore, Jon Oberlander and Kristina Striegnitz) tackled the generation of natural-language instructions to aid human task-solving in a virtual environment. The TUNA Progress Test (organized by Albert Gatt, Anja Belz and Eric Kow) offered an opportunity to improve on the 2008 Referring Expression Generation (REG 2008) challenge, producing natural language referring expressions based on the TUNA domain representations. The papers associated with the TUNA challenge are included in these proceedings, those associated with the GIVE challenge will be published on line.

We would like to thank all who submitted papers and our programme committee for their hard work. Thanks to the invited speakers, Regina Barzilay and Kees van Deemter, for their willingness to participate in ENLG 2009. We would also like to thank Lennard van de Laar (`www.dualler.nl`) for doing an excellent job designing the ENLG 2009 website. Many thanks also to Hendri Hondorp for his help in preparing the proceedings. We received financial support from The Netherlands Organization for Scientific Research (NWO), via the Vici project "Bridging the gap between computational linguistics and psycholinguistics: The case of referring expressions" (Krahmer; 277-70-007), which is gratefully acknowledged.

Emiel Krahmer and Mariët Theune

# Organizers

**Organizers:**

Emiel Krahmer, Tilburg University (The Netherlands)
Mariët Theune, University of Twente (The Netherlands)

**Program Committee:**

Regina Barzilay, MIT (USA)
John Bateman, Universität Bremen (Germany)
Anja Belz, University of Brighton (UK)
Stephan Busemann, DFKI (Germany)
Charles Callaway, University of Edinburgh (UK)
Roger Evans, University of Brighton (UK)
Leo Ferres, University of Concepcion (Chile)
Mary-Ellen Foster, University of Munich (Germany)
Claire Gardent, CNRS/LORIA (France)
Albert Gatt, University of Aberdeen (UK)
John Kelleher, Dublin Insitute of Technology (Ireland)
Geert-Jan Kruijff, DFKI GmbH (Germany)
David McDonald, BBN Technologies (USA)
Jon Oberlander, University of Edinburgh (UK)
Paul Piwek, The Open University (UK)
Ehud Reiter, University of Aberdeen (UK)
David Reitter, Carnegie Mellon University (USA)
Graeme Ritchie, University of Aberdeen (UK)
Matthew Stone, Rutgers University (USA)
Takenobu Tokunaga, Tokyo Institute of Technology (Japan)
Kees van Deemter, University of Aberdeen (UK)
Manfred Stede, Universität Potsdam (Germany)
Ielka van der Sluis, Trinity College Dublin (Ireland)
Jette Viethen, Macquarie University (Australia)
Michael White, Ohio State University (USA)

**Invited Speakers:**

Regina Barzilay, MIT (USA)
Kees van Deemter, University of Aberdeen (UK)

# Table of Contents

# Using NLG to Help Language-Impaired Users Tell Stories and Participate in Social Dialogues

**Ehud Reiter, Ross Turner**
University of Aberdeen
Aberdeen, UK
e.reiter@abdn.ac.uk
csc272@abdn.ac.uk

**Norman Alm, Rolf Black, Martin Dempster, Annalu Waller**
University of Dundee
Dundee, UK
{nalm,rolfblack,martindempster,awaller}@computing.dundee.ac.uk

**Abstract**

Augmentative and Alternative Communication (AAC) systems are communication aids for people who cannot speak because of motor or cognitive impairments. We are developing AAC systems where users select information they wish to communicate, and this is expressed using an NLG system. We believe this model will work well in contexts where AAC users wish to go beyond simply making requests or answering questions, and have more complex communicative goals such as story-telling and social interaction.

## 1 Introduction

Many people have difficulty in communicating linguistically because of cognitive or motor impairments. Such people typically use communication aids to help them interact with other people. Such communication aids range from simple tools that do not involve computers, such as picture cards, to complex software systems that attempt to "speak" for the impaired user.

From a technological perspective, even the most complex communication aids have typically been based on fixed (canned) texts or simple fill-in-the-blank templates; essentially the user selects a text or template from a set of possible utterances, and the system utters it. We believe that while this may be adequate if the user is simply making a request (e.g., *please give me a drink*) or answering a question (e.g., *I live at home*), it is not adequate if the user has a more complex communicative goal, such as engaging in social interaction, or telling a story.

We are exploring the idea of supporting such interactions by building a system which uses external data and/or knowledge sources, plus domain and conversational models, to dynamically suggest possible *messages* (event, facts, or opinions, represented as ontology instances) which are appropriate to the conversation. The user selects the specific message which he wishes the system to speak, and possibly adds simple annotations (e.g., *I like this*) or otherwise edits the message. The system then creates an appropriate linguistic utterance from the selected message, taking into consideration contextual factors.

In this paper we describe two projects on which we are working within this framework. The goal of the first project is to help non-speaking children tell stories about their day at school to their parents; the goal of the second project is to help non-speaking adults engage in social conversation.

## 2 Background

### 2.1 Augmentative and alternative communication

Augmentative and alternative communication (AAC) is a term that describes a variety of methods of communication for non-speaking people which can supplement or replace speech. The term covers techniques which require no equipment, such as sign language and cards with images; and also more technologically complex systems which use speech synthesis and a variety of strategies to create utterances.

The most flexible AAC systems allow users to specify arbitrary words, but communication rates are extremely low, averaging 2-10 words per minute. This is because many AAC users interact slowly with computers because of their impairments. For example, some of the children we work with cannot use their hands, so they use scanning interfaces with head switches. In other words, the computer displays a number of op-

*Proceedings of the 12th European Workshop on Natural Language Generation*, pages 1–8,
Athens, Greece, 30 – 31 March 2009. 

tions to them, and then scans through these, briefly highlighting each option. When the desired option is highlighted, the child selects it by pressing a switch with her head. This is adequate for communicating basic needs (such as hunger or thirst); the computer can display a menu of possible needs, and the child can select one of the items. But creating arbitrary messages with such an interface is extremely slow, even if word prediction is used; and in general such interfaces do not well support complex social interactions such as story telling (Waller, 2006).

A number of research projects in AAC have developed prototype systems which attempt to facilitate this type of human-human interaction. At their most basic, these systems provide users with a library of fixed "conversational moves" which can be selected and uttered. These moves are based on models of the usual shape and content of conversational encounters (Todman & Alm, 2003), and for example include standard conversational openings and closings, such as *Hello* and *How are you*. They also include backchannel communication such as *Uh-huh*, *Great!*, and *Sorry, can you repeat that*.

It would be very useful to go beyond standard openings, closings, and backchannel messages, and allow the user to select utterances which were relevant to the particular communicative context and goals. Dye et al (1998) developed a system based on scripts of common interactions (Schank & Abelson, 1977). For example, a user could activate the MakeAnAppointment script, and then could select utterances relevant to this script, such as *I would like to make an appointment to see the doctor*. As the interaction progressed, the system would update the selections offered to the user based on the current stage of the script; for example during time negotiation a possible utterance would be *I would like to see him next week*. This system proved effective in trials, but needed a large number of scripts to be generally effective. Users could author their own texts, which were added to the scripts, but this was time-consuming and had to be done in advance of the conversation.

Another goal of AAC is to help users narrate stories. Narrative and storytelling play a very important part in the communicative repertoire of all speakers (Schank, 1990). In particular, the ability to draw on episodes from one's life history in current conversation is vital to maintaining a full impression of one's personality in dealing with others (Polkinghorne, 1991). Story telling tools for AAC users have been developed, which include ways to introduce a story, tell it at the pace required (with diversions) and give feedback to comments from listeners (Waller, 2006); but again these tools are based on a library of fixed texts and templates.

### 2.2 NLG and AAC

Natural language generation (NLG) systems generate texts in English and other human languages from non-linguistic input (Reiter and Dale, 2000). In their review of NLP and AAC, Newell, Langer, and Hickey (1998) suggest that NLG could be used to generate complete utterances from the limited input that AAC users are able to provide. For example, the Compansion project (McCoy, Pennington, Badman 1998) used NLP and NLG techniques to expand telegraphic user input, such as *Mary go store?*, into complete utterances, such as *Did Mary go to the store*? Netzer and Elhadad (2006) allowed users to author utterances in the symbolic language BLISS, and used NLG to translate this to English and Hebrew texts.

In recent years there has been growing interest in *data-to-text* NLG systems (Reiter, 2007); these systems generate texts based on sensor and other numerical data, supplemented with ontologies that specify domain knowledge. In principle, it seems that data-to-text techniques should allow NLG systems to provide more assistance than the syntactic help provided by Compansion. For example, if the user wanted to talk about a recent football (soccer) match, a data-to-text system could get actual data about the match from the web, and generate potential utterances from this data, such as *Arsenal beat Chelsea 2-1* and *Van Persie scored two goals*; the user could then select one of these to utter.

In addition to helping users interact with other people, NLG techniques can also be used to educate and encourage children with disabilities. The STANDUP system (Manurung, Ritchie et al., 2008), for example, used NLG and computational humour techniques to allow children who use AAC devices to generate novel punning jokes. This provided the children with successful experiences of controlling language, gave them an opportunity to play with language and explore new vocabulary (Waller et al., in press). In a small study with nine children with cerebral palsy, the children used their regular AAC tools more and also performed better on a test measuring linguistic abilities after they used STANDUP for ten weeks.

## 3 Our Architecture

Our goal is help AAC users engage in complex social interaction by using NLG and data-to-text technology to create potential utterances and conversational contributions for the users. The general architecture is shown in Figure 1, and Sections 4 and 5 describe two systems based on this architecture.

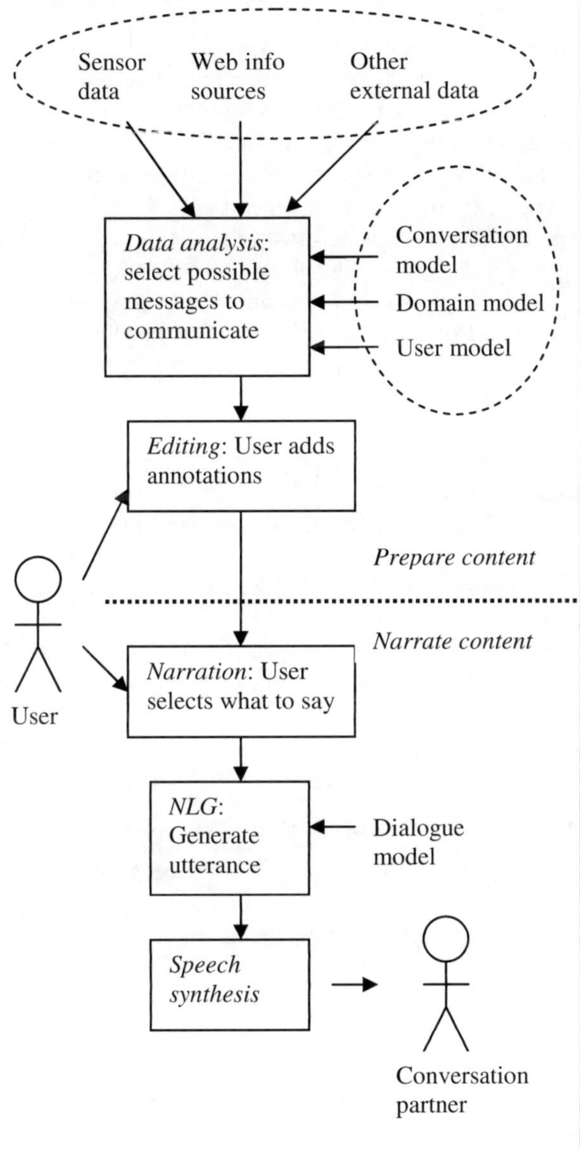


*Figure 1:* General architecture

The system has the following components:

*Data analysis*: read in data, from sensors, web information sources, databases, and so forth. This module analyses this data and identifies messages (in the sense of Reiter and Dale (2000)) that the user is likely to want to communicate; this analysis is partially based on domain, conversation, and user models, which may be represented as ontologies.

*Editing*: allow the user to edit the messages. Editing ranges from adding simple annotations to specify opinions (e.g., add BAD to *Arsenal beat Chelsea 2-1* if the user is a Chelsea fan), to using an on-screen keyboard to type free-text comments. Users can also delete messages, specify which messages they are most likely to want to utter, and create new messages. Editing is done before the actual conversation, so the user does not have to do this under time pressure. The amount of editing which can be done partially depends on the extent of the user's disabilities.

*Narration*: allows the user to select messages, and perhaps conversational moves (e.g., *Hello*), in an actual conversational context. Editing is possible, but is limited by the need to keep the conversation flowing.

*NLG and Speech Synthesis*: Generates actual utterances from the selected messages, taking into account linguistic context, especially a dialogue model.

## 4 Narrative for Children: *How was School Today*

The goal of the *How was School Today* project is to enable non-speaking children with major motor disabilities but reasonable cognitive skills to tell a story about what they did at school during the day. The particular children we are working with have cerebral palsy, and use wheelchairs. A few of them can use touch screens, but most of them use a head switch and scanning interface, as described above. By 'story', we mean something similar to Labov's (1972) conversational narrative, i.e., a series of linked real-world events which are unusual or otherwise interesting, possibly annotated with information about the child's feelings, which can be narrated orally. We are not expecting stories in the literary sense, with character development and complex plots.

The motivation of the project is to provide the children with successful narrative experience. Typically developing children develop narrative skills from an early age with adults scaffolding conversations to elicit narrative, e.g. *"What did you do at school today?"* (Bruner, 1975). As the child's vocabulary and language competence develops, scaffolding is reduced. This progression is seldom seen in children with complex communication needs – they respond to closed questions but seldom take control of conversation (von Tetzchner and Grove, 2003). Many children who use AAC have very limited narrative skills (Soto et al, 2006). Research has shown that providing children who use AAC with successful narrative experiences by providing full narrative text can help the development of written and spoken narrative skills (Waller, 2008).

The system follows the architecture described above. Input data comes from RFID sensors that track where the child went during the day; an RFID reader is mounted on the child's wheelchair, and RFID tags are placed around the school, especially in doorways so we can monitor children entering and leaving rooms. Teachers have also been given RFID swipe cards which they can swipe against a reader, to record that they are interacting with the child; this is more robust than attempting to infer interaction automatically by tracking teachers' position. Teachers can also record interactions with objects (toys, musical instruments, etc), by using special swipe cards associated with these objects. Last but not least, teachers can record spoken messages about what happened during the day. An example of how the child's wheelchair is set up is shown in Figure 2.

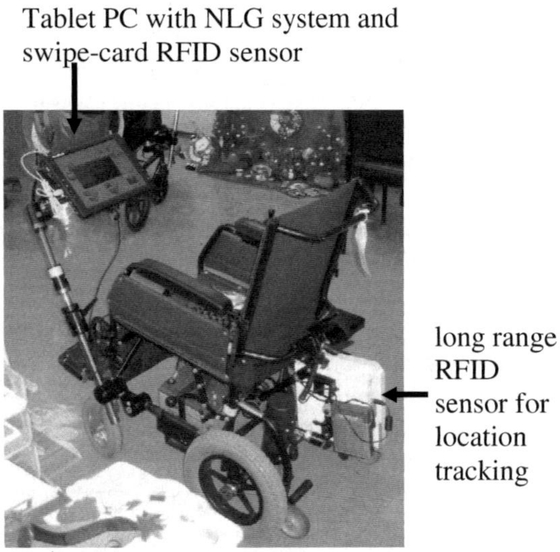


Figure 2: System configuration

The data analysis module combines sensor-derived location and interaction data with a timetable which records what the child was expected to do during the day, and a domain knowledge base which includes information about typical activities (e.g., if the child's location is SwimmingPool, the child's activity is probably Swimming). From this it creates a series of events (each of which contain a number of messages) which describe the child's lessons and activities, including divergences from what is expected in the timetable. Several messages may be associated with an event. The data analysis module also infers which events and messages it believes are most interesting to the child; this is partially based on heuristics about what children are interested in (e.g., swimming is more interesting than lunch), and partially based on the general principle that unexpected things (divergences from the timetable) are more interesting than expected things. No more than five events are flagged as interesting, and only these events are shown in the editing interface.

The editing interface allows children to remove events they do not want to talk about (perhaps for privacy reasons) from the list of interesting events. It also allows children to add messages that express simple opinions about events; i.e., *I liked it* or *I didn't like it*. The interface is designed to be used with a scanning interface, and is based on symbols that represent events, annotations, etc.

The narration interface, shown in Figure 3, is similar to the editing interface. It allows children to choose a specific event to communicate, which must be one of the ones they selected during the editing phase. Children are encouraged to tell events in temporal order (this is one of the narration skills we are trying to teach), but this is not mandated, and they can deviate from temporal order if they wish.

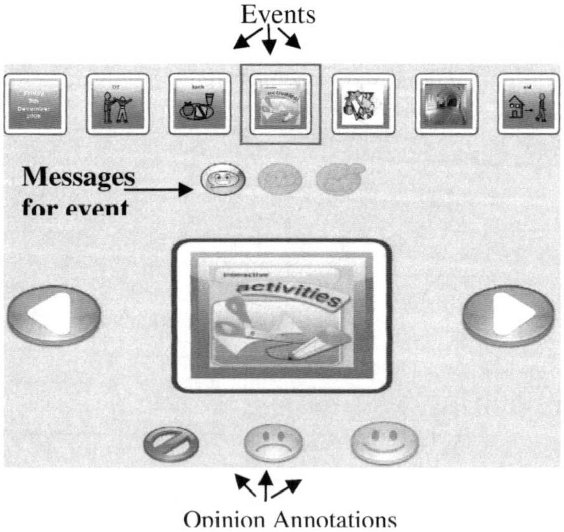


Figure 3: Narration Interface

The NLG system generates actual texts from the events selected by the children. Most of this is fairly simple, since the system deliberately uses simple "child-like" language (Section 6). However, the system does need to make some decisions based on discourse context, including choosing appropriate referring expressions (especially pronouns), and temporal expressions (especially when children deviate from pure temporal order).

### 4.1 Example

For example, assume that the timetable specifies the following information

| Time | Activity | Location | Teacher |
|---|---|---|---|
| ...... | ...... | ...... | ...... |
| 13.20 -14 | Arts and Crafts | CL_SEC2 | Mrs Smith |
| 14 -14.40 | Physiotherapy | PHYSIO1 | Mrs Jones |
| ...... | ...... | ...... | ...... |

Assume that the sensors then recorded the following information

```
Event 1
    Location: CL_SEC2
    Time: 13:23:00.0 - 14:07:00.0
    Interactions: Mrs. Smith, Rolf, Ross

Event 2
    Location: HALL
    Time: 14:10:00.0 – 14:39:00.0
    Interactions: none
```

The data analysis module associates Event 1 with the Arts and Crafts timetable entry, since the location is right, the timetabled teacher is present, and the times approximately match. From this two messages are produced: one corresponding to *I had Arts and Crafts this afternoon with Mrs. Smith* (the core activity description), and the other corresponding to *Rolf and Ross were there* (additional information about people not timetabled to be there). The child can add opinions using the editing interface; for example, if he added a positive annotation to the event, this would become an additional message corresponding to *It was great*.

For Event 2, the data analysis module notes that it does not match a timetabled event. The timetable indicates the child should be at Physiotherapy after Art and Crafts; however, the sensor information indicates they were in the hall. The system generates a single message corresponding to *Then I went to the Hall instead of Physiotherapy* to describe this event. If the child added a negative annotation to this message, this would become an additional message expressed as *I didn't like it.*

### 4.2 Evaluation

We conducted an initial evaluation of the How was School Today system in January, 2009. Two children used the system for four days: Julie, age 11, who had good cognitive skills but was non-verbal because of severe motor impairments; and Jessica, age 13, who had less severe motor impairments but who had some cognitive and memory impairments (these are not the childrens' real names). Julie used the system as a communication and interaction aid, as described above; Jessica used the system partially as a memory aid. The evaluation was primarily qualitative: we observed how Julie and Jessica used the system, and interviewed their teachers, speech therapists, care assistants, and Julie's mother (Jessica's parents were not available).

The system worked very well for Julie; she learned it quickly, and was able to use it to have real conversations about her day with adults, almost for the first time in her life. This validated our vision that our technology could help AAC users engage in real interaction, and go beyond simple question answering and communication of basic needs. The system also worked reasonably well as a memory aid for Jessica, but she had a harder time using it, perhaps because of her cognitive impairments.

Staff and Julie's mother were very supportive and pleased with the system. They had suggestions for improving the system, including a wider range of annotations; more phrases about the conversation itself, such as *Guess what happened at school today*; and allowing children to request teenager language (e.g., *really cool*).

From a technical perspective, the system worked well overall. School staff were happy to use the swipe cards, which worked well. There were some problems with the location sensors, we need better techniques for distinguishing real readings from noise. A surprising amount of effort was needed to enter up-to-date knowledge (e.g., daily lunch menus), this would need to be addressed if the system was used for a period of months as opposed to days.

## 5 Social Conversation for Adults

In our second project, we want to build a tool to help adults with cerebral palsy engage in social conversation about a football match, movie, weather, and so forth. Many people with severe disabilities have great difficulty developing new interpersonal relationships, and indeed report that forming new relationships and taking part in new activities are major priorities in their lives (Datillo et al., 2007). Supporting these goals through the development of appropriate technologies is important as it could lead to improved social outcomes.

This project builds on the TALK system (Todman and Alm, 2003), which helped AAC users engage in active social conversation. TALK partially overcame the problem of low communication rate by requiring users to pre-author their conversational material ahead of time, so that when it was needed it could simply be selected and output. TALK also used insights from Conversation Analysis (Sacks, 1995) to provide appropriate functionality in the system for social conversation. For example, it supported opening and closing statements, stepwise topic change, and the use of quick-fire utterances to provide fast, idiomatic responses to commonly encountered situations. This approach led to more dynamic AAC-facilitated interactions with higher communication rates, and had a positive impact on the perceived communicative competence of the user (Todman, Alm et al., 2007).

TALK requires the user to spend a substantial amount of time pre-authoring material; this is perhaps its greatest weakness. Our idea is to reduce the amount of pre-authoring needed, by using the architecture shown in Fig 1, where much of the material is automatically created from data sources, ontologies, etc, and the user's role is largely to edit and annotate this material, not to create it from scratch.

We developed an initial prototype system to demonstrate this concept in the domain of football results (Dempster, 2008). We are now working on another prototype, whose goal is to support social conversations about movies, music, television shows, etc (which is a much broader domain than football). We have created an ontology which can describe *events* such as watching a film, listening to a music track, or reading a book. Each 'event' has both temporal and spatial properties which allow descriptions to be produced about where and when an event took place, and other particulars relating to that particular class of event. For example, if the user listened to a radio show, we record the name of the show, the presenter and the station it was broadcast on. Ultimately we plan to obtain information about movies, music tracks, etc from web-based databases such as IMDB (movies) and last.fm (music).

Of course, databases such as IMDB do not contain information such as what the user thought of the movie, or who he saw it with. Hence we will allow users to add annotations with such information. Some of these annotations will be entered via a structured tool, such as a calendar interface that allows users to specify when they watched or listened to something. We would like to use NaturalOWL (Galanis and Androutsopoulos, 2007) as the NLG component of the system; it is well suited to describing objects, and is intended to be integrated with an ontology. As with the How Was School Today project, some of the main low-level NLG challenges are choosing appropriate referring expressions and temporal references, based on the current discourse context. Speech output is done using Cereproc (Aylett and Pidcock, 2007).

An example of our current narration interface is shown in Figure 4. In the editing interface, the user has specified that he went to a concert at 8pm on Thursday, and that he rated it 8 out of 10. The narration interface gives the user a choice of a number of messages based on this information, together with some standard messages such as *Thanks* and *Agree.*

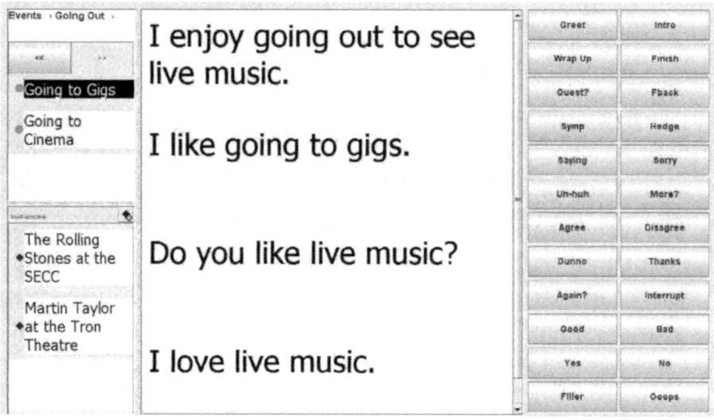


Note that unlike the How Was School Today project, in this project we do not attempt to infer event information from sensors, but we allow (and expect) the user to enter much more information at the editing stage. We could in principle use sensors to pick up some information, such as the fact that the user was in the cinema from 12 to 2PM on Tuesday, but this is not the research focus of this project.

We plan to evaluate the system using groups of both disabled and non-disabled users. This has been shown in the past to be an effective approach for the evaluation of prototype AAC systems (Higginbotham, 1995). Initially pairs of non-disabled participants will be asked to produce short conversations with one person using the prototype and the other conversing normally. Quantitative measures of the communication rate will be taken as well as more qualitative observations relating to the usability of the system. After this evaluation we will improve the system based on our findings, and then conduct a final evaluation with a small group of AAC users.

## 6 Discussion: Challenges for NLG

From an NLG perspective, generating AAC texts of the sort we describe here presents different challenges from many other NLG applications.

First of all, realization and even microplanning are probably not difficult, because in this context the AAC system should generate short simple sentences if possible. This is because the system is speaking "for" someone with limited or developing linguistic abilities, and it should try to produce something similar to what the user would say himself if he or she had the time to explicitly write a text using an on-screen keyboard.

To take a concrete example, we had originally considered using past-perfect tense (a fairly complex linguistic construct) in the How was School project, when the narrative jumped to an earlier point in time. For example *I ate lunch at 12. I had gone swimming at 11.* But it was clear from corpora of child-written texts that these children never used perfect tenses, so instead we opted for *I ate lunch at 12. I went swimming at 11.* This is less linguistically polished, but much more in line with what the children might actually produce.

Given this desire for linguistic simplicity, realisation is very simple, as is lexical choice (use simple words) and aggregation (keep sentences short). The main microplanning challenges relate to discourse coherence, in particular referring expressions and temporal descriptions.

On the other hand, there are major challenges in document planning. In particular, in the How Was School project, we want the output to be a proper narrative, in the sense of Labov (1972). That is, not just a list of facts and events, but a structure with a beginning and end, and with explanatory and other links between components (e.g., *I had math in the afternoon because we went swimming in the morning*, if the child normally has math in the morning). We also wanted the narrative to be interesting and hold the interest of the person the child is communicating with. As pointed out by Reiter et al (2008), current NLG systems do not do a good job of generating narratives.

Similarly, in the Social Conversations project we want the system to generate a social dialogue, not just a list of facts about movies and songs. Little previous research has been done on generating social (as opposed to task-oriented) dialogues. One exception is the NECA Socialite system (van Deemter et al, 2008), but this focused on techniques for expressing affect, not on high-level conversational structure.

For both stories and social conversations, it would be extremely useful to be able to monitor what the conversational partner is saying. This is something we hope to investigate in the future. As most AAC users interact with a small number of conversational partners, it may be feasible to use a speech dictation system to detect at least some of what the conversational partner says.

Last but not least, a major challenge implicit in our systems and indeed in the general architecture is letting users control the NLG system. Our systems are intended to be speaking aids, ideally they should produce the same utterances as the user would if he was able to talk. This means that users must be able to control the systems, so that it does what they want it to do, in terms of both content and expression. To the best of our knowledge, little is known about how users can best control an NLG system.

## 7 Conclusion

Many people are in the unfortunate position of not being able to speak or type, due to cognitive and/or motor impairments. Current AAC tools allow such people to engage in simple needs-based communication, but they do not provide good support for richer use of language, such as story-telling and social conversation. We are trying to develop more sophisticated AAC tools which support such interactions, by using external data and knowledge sources to produce candidate messages, which can be expressed using NLG and speech synthesis technology. Our work is still at an early stage, but we believe that it has the potential to help AAC users engage in richer interactions with other people.

## Acknowledgements

We are very grateful to Julie, Jessica, and their teachers, therapists, carers, and parents for their help in building and evaluating the system described in Section 4. Many thanks to the anonymous referees and our colleagues at Aberdeen and Dundee for their very helpful comments. This research is supported by EPSRC grants EP/F067151/1 and EP/F066880/1, and by a Northern Research Partnership studentship.

## References


Aylett, M. and C. Pidcock (2007). The CereVoice Characterful Speech Synthesiser SDK. *Proceedings of Proceedings of the 7th International Conference on Intelligent Virtual Agents*, pages 413-414.

Bruner, J. (1975). From communication to language: A psychological perspective. *Cognition* **3**: 255-289.

Datillo, J., G. Estrella, L. Estrella, J. Light, D. McNaughton and M. Seabury (2007). "I have chosen to live life abundantly": Perceptions of leisure by adults who use Augmentative and Alternative Communication. *Augmentative & Alternative Communication* **24**(1): 16-28.

van Deemter, K., B Krenn, P Piwek, M Klesen, M Schröder and S Baumann. Fully generated scripted dialogue for embodied agents. *Artificial Intelligence* **172**: 1219–1244.

Dempster, M. (2008). Using natural language generation to encourage effective communication in non-speaking people. *Proceedings of Young Researchers Consortium, ICCHP'08.*

Dye, R., N. Alm, J. Arnott, G. Harper, and A. Morrison (1998). A script-based AAC system for transactional interaction. *Natural Language Engineering*, *4*(1), 57-71.

Galanis, D. and I. Androutsopoulos (2007). Generating Multilingual Descriptions from Linguistically Annotated OWL Ontologies: the NaturalOWL System. *Proceedings of ENLG 2007.*

Higginbotham, D. J. (1995). Use of nondisabled subjects in AAC Research : Confessions of a research infidel. *Augmentative and Alternative Communication* **11**(1): 2-5.

Labov, W (1972). *Language in the Inner City*. University of Pennsylvania Press.

Manurung, R., G. Ritchie, H. Pain, A. Waller, D. O'Mara and R. Black (2008). The Construction of a Pun Generator for Language Skills Development. *Applied Artificial Intelligence* **22**(9): 841 – 869.

McCoy, K., C. Pennington and A. Badman (1998). Compansion: From research prototype to practical integration. *Natural Language Engineering* **4**:73-95.

Netzer, Y and Elhadad, M (2006). Using Semantic Authoring for Blissymbols Communication Boards. In *Proc of HLT-2006.*

Newell, A., S. Langer and M. Hickey (1998). The role of natural language processing in alternative and augmentative communication. *Natural Language Engineering* **4**:1-16.

Polkinghorne, D. (1991). Narrative and self-concept. *Journal of Narrative and Life History*, **1**(2/3), 135-153

Reiter, E (2007). An Architecture for Data-to-Text Systems. In *Proceedings of ENLG-2007, pages* 147-155.

Reiter, E. and R. Dale (2000). *Building Natural Language Generation Systems*. Cambridge University Press.

Reiter, E, A. Gatt, F Portet, and M van der Meulen (2008). The Importance of Narrative and Other Lessons from an Evaluation of an NLG System that Summarises Clinical Data (2007). In *Proceedings of INLG-2008,* pages 97-104.

Sacks, H. (1995). *Lectures on Conversation*. G. Jefferson. Cambridge, MA, Blackwell.

Schank, R. C. (1990). *Tell me a story: A new look at real and artificial intelligence*. New York, Macmillan Publishing Co.

Schank, R., and R. Abelson (1977). *Scripts, plans, goals, and understanding*. New Jersey: Lawrence Erlbaum.

Soto, G., E. Hartmann, and D. Wilkins (2006). Exploring the Elements of Narrative that Emerge in the Interactions between an 8-Year-Old Child who uses an AAC Device and her Teacher. *Augmentative and Alternative Communication* **4**:231 – 241.

Todman, J. and N. A. Alm (2003). Modelling conversational pragmatics in communication aids. *Journal of Pragmatics* **35**: 523-538.

Todman, J., N. A. Alm, D. J. Higginbotham and P. File (2007). Whole Utterance Approaches in AAC. *Augmentative and Alternative Communication* **24**(3): 235-254.

von Tetzchner, S. and N. Grove (2003). The development of alternative language forms. In S. von Tetzchner and N. Grove (eds), *Augmentative and Alternative Communication: Developmental Issues*, pages 1-27. Wiley.

Waller, A. (2006). Communication Access to Conversational Narrative. *Topics in Language Disorders* **26**(3): 221-239.

Waller, A. (2008). Narrative-based Augmentative and Alternative Communication: From transactional to interactional conversation. *Proceedings of ISAAC 2008,* pages 149-160.

Waller, A., R. Black, D. A. O'Mara, H. Pain, G. Ritchie and R. Manurung (In Press). Evaluating the STANDUP Pun Generating Software with Children with Cerebral Palsy. *ACM Transactions on Accessible Computing*.

# Towards a Generation-Based Semantic Web Authoring Tool

**Richard Power**
Department of Computing
Open University
Milton Keynes, UK
r.power@open.ac.uk

## Abstract

Widespread use of Semantic Web technologies requires interfaces through which knowledge can be viewed and edited without deep understanding of Description Logic and formalisms like OWL and RDF. Several groups are pursuing approaches based on Controlled Natural Languages (CNLs), so that editing can be performed by typing in sentences which are automatically interpreted as statements in OWL. We suggest here a variant of this approach which relies entirely on Natural Language Generation (NLG), and propose requirements for a system that can reliably generate transparent realisations of statements in Description Logic.

## 1 Introduction

We describe here a simple prototype of an editing tool that allows a user to create an ontology through an open-ended Natural Language interface. By 'open-ended' we mean that when introducing class or property names into the ontology, the user also decides how they should be expressed linguistically: thus the lexicon of the Natural Language interface is not predetermined. The purpose of such a tool is to support knowledge editing on the Semantic Web, which at present requires training in graphical user interfaces like Protégé (Rector et al., 2004), or direct coding in OWL and RDF. Linking OWL to Controlled Natural Language is currently the topic of an OWL1-1 task force, and several groups are already working in this area (Schwitter and Tilbrook, 2004; Thompson et al., 2005; Bernstein and Kaufmann, 2006; Pool, 2006; Dongilli, 2007); the novelty in our approach is that we rely entirely on Natural Language Generation (NLG), extending the WYSIWYM (or Conceptual Authoring) method (Power and Scott, 1998; Hallett et al., 2007) so that it supports knowledge editing for ontologies as well as for assertions about individuals.

The idea of linking formal and natural languages can be traced back to Frege (1879), who observed that mathematical proofs were made up of formulae *interspersed with passages in natural language*, and invented formal logic as a way of rendering these passages in a precise notation. With the arrival of Artificial Intelligence in the 1950s, formal logic became the foundation for knowledge representation and automatic reasoning — a trend leading to the recent concept of a 'semantic web' that would open up knowledge encoding and utilisation to a world-wide community (Berners-Lee et al., 2001). However, accessible knowledge management requires accessible presentation: hence the current interest in methods of 'sugaring' formal logic into natural language text (Ranta, 1994; Horacek, 1999), thus in a sense turning Frege upside-down.

### 1.1 Description Logic

The theoretical underpinning of OWL (and hence of the semantic web) is a discipline that evolved under various names in the 1980s and 1990s and is now called Description Logic (Baader et al., 2003). This refers not to a single logical language, but to a family of languages. All of these languages allow statements to be built from individuals, classes and properties, but they differ in the resources provided in order to construct classes and properties, thus allowing different balances to be drawn between the conflicting demands of expressiveness and tractability (i.e., decidability and efficiency of reasoning).

Figure 1 shows some common class constructors, using mathematical notation rather than OWL syntax (which is equivalent, but much lengthier). There are in fact three versions of OWL (Lite, DL and Full) which provide pro-

*Proceedings of the 12th European Workshop on Natural Language Generation*, pages 9–15,
Athens, Greece, 30 – 31 March 2009. 

| Description | Syntax |
|---|---|
| atomic class | $A$ (etc.) |
| universal class | $\top$ |
| negation | $\neg C$ |
| intersection | $C \sqcap D$ |
| union | $C \sqcup D$ |
| value restriction | $\forall R.C$ |
| exists restriction | $\exists R.C$ |
| enumeration | $\{a\}$ |

Table 1: Class constructors

gressively more constructors, not only for classes but also for properties and axioms. Having chosen the desired logic, the ontology builder is free to introduce new atomic classes (and also properties and individuals), which can be given any name consistent with the RDF naming conventions (i.e., names must be Unique Resource Identifiers). Thus a new class might be named `http://myontology.net/parent` and a new property `http://myontology.net/hasChild`, although for brevity we will henceforth omit namespaces (i.e., $parent$, $hasChild$). Statements about classes can then be expressed by axioms, the most important of which are $C \sqsubseteq D$ (C is subsumed by D) and $C \equiv D$ (C is equivalent to D). For instance:

(1) $parent \equiv person \sqcap \exists hasChild.\top$
(2) $person \sqsubseteq \forall hasChild.person$

The meanings are probably obvious: (1) a parent is defined as a person with one or more children; (2) every person only has persons as children. Note that expressing these axioms in clear English is not trivial — for instance, in (2) we must take care not to imply that every person has children.

A collection of such axioms is called a TBox: intuitively, a TBox expresses concept definitions and generalisations. Description Logics also contain names for individual instances (e.g., $Abraham, Isaac$) and formulas expressing facts about individuals: thus $father(Abraham)$ would express class membership ('Abraham is a father'), and $hasChild(Abraham, Isaac)$ a relationship between individuals ('Isaac is Abraham's child'). A collection of such assertions is called an ABox, and TBox and ABox together make up a Knowledge Base (KB).

### 1.2 Reasoning services

The reason for proposing Description Logic as the foundation for the Semantic Web is that it allows for efficient reasoning services. Much effort is still going into the mathematical task of proving decidability and efficiency results for increasingly expressive dialects. Informally, the standard reasoning services are as follows:

1. **Class Satisfiability**: Checking whether in a given KB it is possible for a class to have at least one member.

2. **Subsumption**: Checking whether a given KB implies a specified subsumption relationship between two classes.

3. **Consistency**: Checking whether a given KB is consistent.

4. **Instance Checking**: Checking whether a given KB implies a specified ABox assertion that an individual $a$ belongs to a class $C$.

Consider for instance the following miniature KB:

$man \sqcup woman \equiv person$
$man \sqsubseteq \neg woman$
$man(Abraham)$

In respect to this KB, a reasoning engine should be able to show (1) that the class $man \sqcap woman$ is unsatisfiable, (2) that $man$ is subsumed by $person$ ($man \sqsubseteq person$), (3) that the KB is consistent, and (4) that the assertion $person(Abraham)$ holds.

The ability to perform these reasoning tasks efficiently can be exploited not only in applications that utilize knowledge in problem-solving, but in knowledge editing and natural language generation. For instance, when an ontology builder adds a new axiom to a KB, the editor can run the subsumption and consistency checks and give feedback on whether the axiom is informative, redundant, or inconsistent. Or when producing a natural language gloss for the class $\exists hasChild.female$, the generator could choose between 'something with at least one female child' and 'someone with at least one female child' by checking the subsumption relationship $\exists hasChild.female \sqsubseteq person$.

## 2 Aligning DL to CNL

We have explained informally the technical features of description logics. Briefly, they include rules for constructing classes, axioms, and assertions about individuals; the resulting expressions are interpreted through a relatively simple model-theoretic semantics (Baader et al., 2005). They also include efficient algorithms for performing reasoning tasks. We now turn to issues in the design of Controlled Natural Languages (CNLs) which can be aligned with specific DLs, and thus serve as useful interfaces for working with complex formalisms like OWL and RDF.

As a provisional list of requirements, we would suggest the following:

1. **Completeness**: A sentence (or text) can be generated for any axiom permitted by the DL.

2. **Uniqueness**: Different sentences are generated for different axioms.

3. **Transparency**: Sentences in the CNL are accurately interpreted by human readers.

4. **Fluency**: Sentences in the CNL are interpreted easily by human readers and judged natural.

5. **Interpretability**: Sentences conforming to the CNL can be automatically interpreted to recover the corresponding DL axiom.

6. **Editability**: Interactive texts in the CNL can be manipulated by domain experts in order to extend and revise the KB.

7. **Extensibility**: Domain experts can extend the CNL by linking lexical entries to new individuals, classes or properties in the KB.

Note that these are essentially practical requirements, which concern the CNL's role as an interface for a particular DL. We see no reason to insist that the alignment between DL and CNL should conform to general theories of natural language semantics.

### 2.1 Completeness

If we propose to use generated CNL as an interface to a knowledge base, it is important that generation should be reliable. A minimal test of reliability is that the grammar and lexicon are complete, in the sense that they produce a text for any well-formed semantic input. Elsewhere, we have described a generation method that allows completeness to be checked by a computer program (Hardcastle and Power, 2008). For any non-trivial DL the set of classes is infinite (e.g., through recursion on $C \sqcap D$ or $\exists R.C$); however, completeness can be proved through an enumeration of all local contexts for which a linguistic realisation rule is needed. As well as guaranteeing reliability, completeness checking is obviously useful as an aid to grammar development.

### 2.2 Uniqueness

Although necessary, completeness is not a sufficient condition on the grammar of a CNL, since it could be trivially met by generating the same string (perhaps 'Hallo World') for any semantic input. It would also be useful to have an automatic check that the same sentence is not generated for two different semantic inputs — i.e., that every sentence in the CNL has a unique meaning. This seems a harder problem than completeness, and we have not seen any proposals on how it could be done.

To pose this problem precisely we would need to define what is meant by 'different' semantic inputs. Complex class descriptions can be manipulated by well-known logical equivalences like De Morgan's laws: for instance, $\neg(C \sqcap D)$ is equivalent to $(\neg C) \sqcup (\neg D)$. Should these be treated as different inputs or the same input? We think users would probably prefer them to be treated as different, but the issue needs to be investigated further.

### 2.3 Transparency

Transparency is obviously at the heart of the enterprise: completeness and uniqueness proofs are no help if the generated texts are unclear to human readers. Unlike the preceding requirements, transparency is a matter of degree: we cannot expect, far less prove, that every sentence in the CNL will be accurately understood by all target users on all occasions. Transparency can only be assessed, and gradually improved, through experiments and user feedback.

### 2.4 Fluency

Fluency is another aspect of readability: whereas transparency concerns *accuracy* of interpretation, fluency concerns *ease*. These requirements potentially conflict. For instance, to express the axiom $parent \sqsubseteq \exists hasChild.\top$ fluently we could say 'every parent has a child', while for transparency we might prefer the pedantic 'every parent has one or more children'. In a CNL designed for editing a KB, transparency will have priority, but one can imagine other purposes (e.g., an informal report) for which fluency would matter more.

### 2.5 Interpretability

This is an essential requirement for knowledge editors that rely on automatic parsing and interpretation of texts typed in by human authors (Schwitter and Tilbrook, 2004; Bernstein and Kaufmann, 2006). A recent innovation has been to pursue the goal of 'roundtripping' (Davis et al., 2008), so that a CNL text can be generated from an existing ontology, revised in a text editor, and then interpreted automatically to obtain an updated ontology in the original format. For our approach, which relies entirely on generation, automatic interpretability is not essential (although one can imagine contexts in which it would be useful, for instance to allow knowledge encoding outside the NLG-based editing environment).

### 2.6 Editability

The key feature of Conceptual Authoring (WYSIWYM) is that editing operations are defined on the semantic input, not the text. This means that authors cannot produce a text in the normal way by typing in words from left to right. Some kind of non-specific initial configuration has to be gradually refined through semantic distinctions made by choices from menus (an example will be given later). To validate the approach, it has to be shown that this editing process is efficient and easily learned. Usability results from ABox editing applications have been encouraging (Hallett et al., 2007), but whether similar results can be achieved for KB editing (TBox as well as ABox) remains unproven.

### 2.7 Extensibility

Ontology development requires that authors should be able to introduce new terms for individuals, classes and properties. The designer of a CNL-based editor cannot foresee what these terms will be, and therefore cannot provide a mapping to suitable lexical entries. This must be done by the ontology developer, and take-up accordingly depends on making this task not only feasible but easy (Hielkema et al., 2007). We will explore two ideas on how this might be done: (a) providing a wide-coverage lexicon from which users can select words to extend the CNL, and (b) using conventions for controlling the naming of classes and properties, so that the two decisions (term name, CNL lexical entry) become essentially a single decision.

## 3 Editing process

As a first experiment we have written a Prolog program which allows a KB to be built up from scratch for a very simple DL with only one kind of statement ($C \sqsubseteq D$), four class constructors ($A$, $\top$, $\exists R.C$, $\{a\}$), and one property constructor (property inversion, which will be explained shortly). Using just these resources we can formulate ABox assertions as well as TBox axioms by the trick of representing individuals through enumerated classes. For instance, $man(Abraham)$ can be asserted through the axiom $\{Abraham\} \sqsubseteq man$ (the class containing only Abraham is a subclass of the class of men).

A generic grammar is provided for realising axioms and complex class descriptions (a handful of rules suffices); the grammar assumes that the words for realising individuals, atomic classes and properties will conform to the following (very strict) regulations:

1. Individuals are realised by proper names
2. Atomic classes are realised by count nouns
3. Properties are realised either by transitive verbs or by count nouns

We also simplify by assuming that the name of every atomic term in the DL is identical to the root form of the word realising the term — for instance, the count noun realising the class $person$ will be 'person'.

When the editor is launched there are no individuals, atomic classes or properties, and the only word in the lexicon is 'thing', which denotes the class $\top$ (i.e., the class containing all individuals). The KB is construed as a sequence of axioms, and to start the ball rolling it is seeded with a single vacuous axiom $\top \sqsubseteq \top$. The program generates a sentence expressing this axiom and adds a list of editing options as follows:

```
1: Every thing/1 is a thing/2.

t   Add a new term
a   Add a new axiom
A/C Edit class C in axiom A
A/d Delete axiom A
```

Note that in every sentence expressing an axiom, the head word of every span denoting a class is given a numerical label; in a simple Prolog interface this allows the class to be selected for editing. There is no point in attempting any editing yet, since no terms have been introduced.

| Word | Syntax | Type |
|---|---|---|
| Mary | name | individual |
| pet | noun | class |
| animal | noun | class |
| own | verb | property |

Table 2: Lexical entries for terms

The user should therefore choose option `t` to add a new term. This is done by specifying three things: a word (any string), a syntactic category (either `name`, `noun`, or `verb`), and a logical type (`individual`, `class`, or `property`). In this way the user might define the set of terms in figure 2 from the people+pets domain, which will be familiar to students of Description Logic.

Editing of the axiom $\top \sqsubseteq \top$ can now begin. Assuming that the target is $pet \sqsubseteq animal$, the user first selects the first class in the first axiom by typing `1/1` (in a GUI this would be done simply by clicking on the word). The program returns a menu of substitutions computed from the current ontology and expressed in English phrases adapted to the context of the selected class:

```
1 Mary
2 Every pet
3 Every animal
4 Everything that owns one or more things
5 Everything owned by one or more things
```

These phrases express respectively the classes $\{Mary\}$, $pet$, $animal$, $\exists own.\top$ and $\exists own^{-1}.\top$ which can be formed from the terms in figure 2. Note that the last class results from the inversion of the property $own$: if $own(a, b)$ means that $a$ owns $b$, the inverse $own^{-1}(a, b)$ means that $b$ owns $a$ — a relationship that can conveniently be expressed by passivisation ($a$ is owned by $b$).

When the user chooses option 2 (in a GUI this would of course be done by clicking on the menu item), the program updates the knowledge base and regenerates:

```
1: Every pet/1 is a thing/2
```

Selecting the second class by typing `1/2` now yields the same menu of options, differently phrased to suit the different context of the class in the axiom:

```
1 Mary
2 a pet
3 an animal
4 owns one or more things
5 is owned by one or more things
```

Choosing option 3 completes the first axiom, after which the user can use the option `a` (see above) to obtain a second default axiom for editing:

```
1: Every pet/1 is an animal/2
2: Every thing/1 is a thing/2
```

A similar series of operations on the second axiom (starting by selecting `2/1`) might then yield the following:

```
1: Every pet/1 is an animal/2
2: Mary/1 owns/2 one or more pets/3
```

Even in such a simple example, we can see how editing could be supported by the reasoning services. For instance, if the user added a third axiom 'Mary owns one or more animals', the program could point out that this is redundant, since $\{Mary\} \sqsubseteq \exists own.animal$ can be deduced from $pet \sqsubseteq animal$ and $\{Mary\} \sqsubseteq \exists own.pet$.

## 4 Discussion

We have shown through a small prototype how a KB could be built up from scratch using an NLG-based authoring tool, with the lexicon almost entirely specified by the ontology developer. Although modest in scope, the prototype extends previous work on Conceptual Authoring (WYSIWYM) in several ways:

- It allows editing of the TBox as well as the ABox, by defining editing operations on classes rather than individuals (with individuals treated as singleton enumerated classes).
- It allows users to extend the CNL through the constrained choice of words/phrases to express new individuals, classes and properties.
- It allows feedback based on reasoning services (e.g, on whether a new axiom is inconsistent, informative or redundant).

An obvious objection to our approach is that we are increasing the load on users by requiring them to build not only a KB but also a CNL lexicon. Much will therefore depend on the tools that support users in the latter task. Ideally, the construction of a lexical entry would depend on making a single selection from a wide-coverage lexicon that has already been built by computational linguists. However, although this ideal is feasible for classes and properties like $pet$ and $own$ which can be mapped to single words, any encounter with real ontologies is likely to reveal terms like $hasDietaryPreference$ that would have to be expressed by a phrase. Probably there are solutions to this problem — one could imagine for instance an algorithm that builds new entries in a phrasal lexicon from examples — but they remain to be demonstrated and tested.

More generally, an important question is whether such a method will scale up. It seems to work reasonably well in the above example with a handful of class constructors, terms and axioms, but what happens when we tackle an expressive DL like OWL Full, and support the editing of a KB with thousands of terms and axioms?

As regards more expressive DLs, we have already cited promising work on developing CNLs for OWL. As one might expect, the Boolean class constructors ($C \sqcap D$, $C \sqcup D$, $\neg C$) can lead to problems of structural ambiguity, e.g. in a description like $old \sqcap (man \sqcup woman)$. Here an NLG-based editor should have the advantage over one that requires human authoring of texts, since it can apply the best available aids of punctuation and formatting (Hallett et al., 2007), a task that would require great care and skill from human authors.

Increasing the number of terms would mean that during editing, classes had to be selected from thousands of alternatives; some kind of search mechanism would therefore be needed. A simple solution already used in WYSIWYM applications (Bouayad-Agha et al., 2002; Hallett et al., 2007; Evans et al., 2008) is a menu equipped with a text field allowing users to narrow the focus by typing in some characters from the desired word or phrase. In an ontology editor this search mechanism could be enhanced by using the ontology itself in order to pick options that are conceptual rather than orthographic neighbours — for instance on typing in 'dog' the user would obtain a focussed list containing 'poodle' and 'pekingese' as well as 'doggerel'.

Increasing the number of axioms has no effect on the editing process, since we are assuming that axioms will be realised by separate sentences, each generated without regard to context. However, a text comprising a long list of unorganised axioms hardly makes for easy reading or navigation. There is therefore potential here for a more interesting application of NLG technology that would draw on topics like generation of referring expressions, pronominalisation, aggregation, discourse planning, and summarisation. Presenting a KB through a fluent and well-organised report would give users a valuable return on their efforts in linking terms to lexical entries, and would address a pressing problem in ontology building — how to maintain trasparency in an ontology as it expands, possibly through contributions from multiple users.

In a word, the advantage of applying NLG in this area is *flexibility*. Once we have a mapping from logical terms to lexical entries in English or another natural language, we can tailor generated texts to different tasks in knowledge management, using fluent organised reports for purposes of overview and navigation, and short pedantically precise sentences for editing — backed up if necessary with footnotes explaining unintuitive logical implications in detail, or painstakingly formatted Boolean constructions that avoid potential structural ambiguities.

## References


Franz Baader, Diego Calvanese, Deborah L. McGuinness, Daniele Nardi, and Peter F. Patel-Schneider, editors. 2003. *The Description Logic Handbook: Theory, Implementation, and Applications*. Cambridge University Press.

F. Baader, I. R. Horrocks, and U. Sattler. 2005. Description logics as ontology languages for the semantic web. *Lecture Notes in Artificial Intelligence*, 2605:228–248.

T. Berners-Lee, J. Hendler, and O. Lassila. 2001. The semantic web. *Scientific American*, 284(5):34–43.

A. Bernstein and E. Kaufmann. 2006. GINO – a guided input natural language ontology editor. In *Proceedings of the 5th International Semantic Web Conference*, Athens, Georgia.

Nadjet Bouayad-Agha, Richard Power, Donia Scott, and Anja Belz. 2002. PILLS: Multilingual generation of medical information documents with overlapping content. In *Proceedings of the Third International Conference on Language Resoures and Evaluation (LREC 2002)*, pages 2111–2114, Las Palmas.

Brian Davis, Ahmad Ali Iqbal, Adam Funk, Valentin Tablan, Kalina Bontcheva, Hamish Cunningham, and Siegfried Handschuh. 2008. Roundtrip ontology authoring. In *International Semantic Web Conference*, volume 5318 of *Lecture Notes in Computer Science*, pages 50–65. Springer.

Paolo Dongilli. 2007. Discourse Planning Strategies for Complex Concept Descriptions. In *Proceedings of the 7th International Symposium on Natural Language Processing*, Pattaya, Chonburi, Thailand.

R. Evans, P. Piwek, L. Cahill, and N. Tipper. 2008. Natural Language Processing in CLIME, a Multilingual Legal Advisory System. *Journal of Natural Language Engineering*, 14(1):101–132.

Gottlob Frege. 1879. *Begriffsschrift*. Halle.

Catalina Hallett, Donia Scott, and Richard Power. 2007. Composing queries through conceptual authoring. *Computational Linguistics*, 33(1):105–133.

D. Hardcastle and R. Power. 2008. Fast, Scalable and Reliable Generation of Controlled Natural Language. In *Proceedings of SETQA-NLP Workshop at the 46th Annual Meeting of the Association for Computational Linguistics*, Ohio, US.

F. Hielkema, C. Mellish, and P. Edwards. 2007. Using WYSIWYM to create an open-ended interface for the semantic grid. In *Proceedings of the 11th European Workshop on Natural Language Generation*, Schloss Dagstuhl.

Helmut Horacek. 1999. Presenting Proofs in a Human-Oriented Way. In *Proceedings of the 16th International Conference on Automated Deduction*, pages 142–156, London, UK. Springer-Verlag.

J. Pool. 2006. Can controlled languages scale to the web? In *5th International Workshop on Controlled Language Applications (CLAW'06)*, Boston, USA.

R. Power and D. Scott. 1998. Multilingual authoring using feedback texts. In *Proceedings of the 17th International Conference on Computational Linguistics and 36th Annual Meeting of the Association for Computational Linguistics*, pages 1053–1059, Montreal, Canada.

Aarne Ranta. 1994. Type theory and the informal language of mathematics. In *Proceedings of the 1993 Types Worshop, Nijmegen, LNCS 806*, pages 352–365. Spinger Verlag.

Alan Rector, Nick Drummond, Matthew Horridge, Jeremy Rogers, Holger Knublauch, Robert Stevens, Hai Wang, and Chris Wroe. 2004. OWL Pizzas: Practical Experience of Teaching OWL-DL: Common Errors and Common Patterns. In *14th International Conference on Knowledge Engineering and Knowledge Management*, pages 63–81.

R. Schwitter and M. Tilbrook. 2004. Controlled natural language meets the semantic web. In *Proceedings of the Australasian Language Technology Workshop*, pages 55–62, Macquarie University.

C. Thompson, P. Pazandak, and H. Tennant. 2005. Talk to your semantic web. *IEEE Internet Computing*, 9(6):75–78.

# System Building Cost vs. Output Quality in Data-To-Text Generation

**Anja Belz** **Eric Kow**
Natural Language Technology Group
University of Brighton
Brighton BN2 4GJ, UK
{asb,eykk10}@bton.ac.uk

## Abstract

Data-to-text generation systems tend to be knowledge-based and manually built, which limits their reusability and makes them time and cost-intensive to create and maintain. Methods for automating (part of) the system building process exist, but do such methods risk a loss in output quality? In this paper, we investigate the cost/quality trade-off in generation system building. We compare four new data-to-text systems which were created by predominantly automatic techniques against six existing systems for the same domain which were created by predominantly manual techniques. We evaluate the ten systems using intrinsic automatic metrics and human quality ratings. We find that increasing the degree to which system building is automated does not necessarily result in a reduction in output quality. We find furthermore that standard automatic evaluation metrics underestimate the quality of handcrafted systems and over-estimate the quality of automatically created systems.

## 1 Introduction

Traditional Natural Language Generation (NLG) systems tend to be handcrafted knowledge-based systems. Such systems tend to be brittle, expensive to create and hard to adapt to new domains or applications. Over the last decade or so, in particular following Knight and Langkilde's work on n-gram-based generate-and-select surface realisation (Knight and Langkilde, 1998; Langkilde, 2000), NLG researchers have become increasingly interested in systems that are automatically trainable from data. Systems that have a trainable component tend to be easier to adapt to new domains and applications, and increased automation is often taken as self-evidently a good thing. The question is, however, whether reduced system building cost and increased adaptability are achieved at the price of a reduction in output quality, and if so, how great the price is. This in turn raises the question of how to evaluate output quality so that a potential decrease can be detected and quantified.

In this paper we set about trying to find answers to these questions. We start, in the following section, we briefly describing the SUMTIME corpus of weather forecasts which we used in our experiments. In the next section (Section 2), we outline four different approaches to building data-to-text generation systems which involve different combinations of manual and automatic techniques. Next (Section 4) we describe ten systems in the four categories that generate weather forecast texts in the SUMTIME domain. In Section 5 we describe the human-assessed and automatically computed evaluation methods we used to comparatively evaluate the quality of the outputs of the ten systems. We then present the evaluation results and discuss implications of discrepancies we found between the results of the human and automatic evaluations (Section 6).

## 2 Data

The SUMTIME-METEO corpus was created by the SUMTIME project team in collaboration with WNI Oceanroutes (Sripada et al., 2002). The corpus was collected by WNI Oceanroutes from the commercial output of five different (human) forecasters, and each instance in the corpus consists of numerical data files paired with a weather forecast. The experiments in this paper focussed on the part of the forecasts that predicts wind characteristics for the next 15 hours.

Figure 1 shows an example data file and Figure 2 shows the corresponding wind forecast written by one of the meteorologists. In Figure 1, the

*Proceedings of the 12th European Workshop on Natural Language Generation*, pages 16–24,
Athens, Greece, 30 – 31 March 2009. 

```
Oil1/Oil2/Oil3_FIELDS
05-10-00

05/06  SSW  18  22  27   3.0  4.8  SSW  2.59
05/09  S    16  20  25   2.7  4.3  SSW  2.39
05/12  S    14  17  21   2.5  4.0  SSW  2.29
05/15  S    14  17  21   2.3  3.7  SSW  2.28
05/18  SSE  12  15  18   2.4  3.8  SSW  2.38
05/21  SSE  10  12  15   2.4  3.8  SSW  2.48
06/00  VAR  6   7   8    2.4  3.8  SSW  2.48
...
```

Figure 1: Meteorological data file for 05-10-2000, a.m. (names of oil fields anonymised).

```
FORECAST FOR:-
Oil1/Oil2/Oil3 FIELDS
...
2. FORECAST 06-24 GMT, THURSDAY, 05-Oct 2000
=====WARNINGS: RISK THUNDERSTORM.     =======
WIND(KTS)   CONFIDENCE: HIGH
 10M:   SSW 16-20 GRADUALLY BACKING SSE THEN
        FALLING VARIABLE 04-08 BY LATE EVENING
 50M:   SSW 20-26 GRADUALLY BACKING SSE THEN
        FALLING VARIABLE 08-12 BY LATE EVENING
...
```

Figure 2: Wind forecast for 05-10-2000, a.m. (names of oil fields anonymised).

first column is the day/hour time stamp, the second the wind direction predicted for the corresponding time period; the third the wind speed at 10m above the ground; the fourth the gust speed at 10m; and the fifth the gust speed at 50m. The remaining columns contain wave data.

We used a version of the corpus reported previously (Belz, 2008) which contains pairs of wind statements and the wind data that is actually included in the statement, e.g.:

Data: `1 SSW 16 20 - - 0600 2 SSE - - - - NOTIME 3 VAR 04 08 - - 2400`

Text: `SSW 16-20 GRADUALLY BACKING SSE THEN FALLING VARIABLE 4-8 BY LATE EVENING`

The input vector represents a sequence of 7-tuples $\langle i, d, s_{min}, s_{max}, g_{min}, g_{max}, t\rangle$ where $i$ is the tuple's ID, $d$ is the wind direction, $s_{min}$ and $s_{max}$ are the minimum and maximum wind speeds, $g_{min}$ and $g_{max}$ are the minimum and maximum gust speeds, and $t$ is a time stamp (indicating for what time of the day the data is valid). The corpus consists of 2,123 instances, corresponding to a total of 22,985 words.

## 3 Four Ways to Build an NLG Systems

In this section, we describe four approaches to building language generators involving different combinations of automatic and manual techniques: traditional handcrafted systems (Section 3.1); handcrafted but trainable probabilistic context-free grammar (PCFG) generators (Section 3.2); partly automatically constructed and trainable probabilistic synchronous context-free grammar (PSCFG) generators; and generators automatically built with phrase-based statistical machine translation (PBSMT) methods (Section 3.4). In Section 4 we explain how we used these techniques to build the ten systems in our evaluation.

### 3.1 Rule-based NLG

Traditional NLG systems are handcrafted as rule-based deterministic decision-makers that make decisions locally, at each step in the generation process. Decisions are encoded as generation rules with conditions for rule application (often in the form of if-then rules or rules with parameters to be matched), usually on the basis of corpus analysis and expert consultation. Reiter and Dale's influential paper (1997) recommended that NLG systems be built largely "by careful analysis of the target text corpus, and by talking to domain experts" (p. 74, and reiterated on pp. 58, 61, 72 and 73).

Handcrafted generation tools have always formed the mainstay of NLG research, a situation virtually unchanged by the statistical revolution that swept through other NLP fields in the 1990s. Well-known examples include the surface realisers Penman, FUF/SURGE and RealPro, the referring expression generation components created by Dale, Reiter, Horacek and van Deemter, and content-to-text generators built in the PLANDoc and M-PIRO projects, to name but a very few.

### 3.2 PCFG generation

Context-free grammars are non-directional, and can be used for generation as well as for analysis (parsing). One approach that uses CFGs for generation is Probabilistic Context-free Representationally Underspecified (*p*CRU) language generation (Belz, 2008). As mentioned above, traditional NLG systems tend to be composed of generation rules that apply transformations to representations. The basic idea in *p*CRU is that as long as the generation rules are all of the form $relation(arg_1, ...arg_n) \rightarrow relation_1(arg_1, ...arg_p) ... relation_m(arg_1, ...arg_q)$, $m \geq 1, n, p, q \geq 0$, then the set of all generation rules can be seen as defining a context-free language and a single probabilistic model can be estimated from raw or annotated text to guide generation processes.

In this approach, a CFG is created by hand that encodes the space of all possible generation pro-

| | |
|---|---|
| Input | [[1,SSW,16,20,-,-,0600],[2,SSE,-,-,-,-,NOTIME],[3,VAR,04,08,-,-,2400]] |
| Corpus | SSW 16-20 GRADUALLY BACKING SSE THEN FALLING VARIABLE 4-8 BY LATE EVENING |
| SUMTIME-Hybrid | SSW 16-20 GRADUALLY BACKING SSE THEN BECOMING VARIABLE 10 OR LESS BY MIDNIGHT |
| PCFG-greedy | SSW 16-20 BACKING SSE FOR A TIME THEN FALLING VARIABLE 4-8 BY LATE EVENING |
| PCFG-roulette | SSW 16-20 GRADUALLY BACKING SSE AND VARIABLE 4-8 |
| PCFG-viterbi | SSW 16-20 BACKING SSE VARIABLE 4-8 LATER |
| PCFG-2gram | SSW 16-20 BACKING SSE VARIABLE 4-8 LATER |
| PCFG-random | SSW 16-20 AT FIRST FROM MIDDAY BECOMING SSE DURING THE AFTERNOON THEN VARIABLE 4-8 |
| PSCFG-semantic | SSW 16-20 BACKING SSE THEN FALLING VARIABLE 04-08 BY LATE EVENING |
| PSCFG-unstructured | SSW 16-20 GRADUALLY BACKING SSE THEN FALLING VARIABLE 04-08 BY LATE EVENING |
| PBSMT-unstructured | LESS SSW 16-20 SOON BACKING SSE BY END OF THEN FALLING VARIABLE 04-08 BY LATE EVENING |
| PBSMT-structured | GUSTS SSW 16-20 BY EVENING STEADILY LESS GUSTS GRADUALLY BACKING SSE BY LATE EVENING MINONE BY MIDDAY THEN AND FALLING UNKNOWN VARIABLE 04-08 LATER GUSTS |

Table 1: Example input with corresponding outputs by all systems and from the corpus (for 5 Oct 2000).

cesses from inputs to outputs, and has no decision-making ability. A probability distribution over this base CFG is estimated from a corpus, and this is what enables decisions between alternative generation rules to be made. The *p*CRU package permits this distribution to be used in one of the following three modes to drive generation processes: (i) greedy – apply only the most likely rule at each choice point; (ii) Viterbi – apply all expansion rules to each nonterminal to create the generation forest for the input, then do a Viterbi search of the generation forest; (iii) greedy roulette-wheel – select a rule to expand a nonterminal according to a non-uniform random distribution proportional to the likelihoods of expansion rules.

In addition there are two baseline modes: (i) random – where generation rules are randomly selected at each choice point; and (ii) n-gram – where all alternatives are generated and the most likely is selected according to an *n*-gram language model (as in HALOGEN).

For the simple SUMTIME domain, *p*CRU generators trained on raw corpora have been shown to perform well (Belz, 2008), but for more complex domains it is likely that manually annotated corpora will be needed for training the CFG base generator. As this is in addition to the manually constructed CFG base generator, the manual component in PCFG generator building is potentially substantial.

### 3.3 PSCFG generation

Synchronous context-free grammars (SCFGs) are used in machine translation (Chiang, 2006), but have also been used for simple concept-to-text generation (Wong and Mooney, 2007). The simplest form of SCFG can be viewed as a pair of CFGs $G_1, G_2$ with paired production rules such that for each rule in $G_1$ there is a rule in $G_2$ with the same left-hand side, and the same non-terminals in the right-hand side. The order of non-terminals on the RHSs may differ, and each RHS may additionally contain any terminals in any order. SCFGs can be trained from aligned corpora to produce probabilistic (or 'weighted') SCFGs.

An SCFG can equivalently be seen as a single grammar $G$ encoding a set of pairs of strings. A probabilistic SCFG is defined by the 6-tuple $G = \langle \mathcal{N}, \mathcal{T}_e, \mathcal{T}_f, L, S, \lambda \rangle$, where $\mathcal{N}$ is a finite set of non-terminals, $\mathcal{T}_e$, $\mathcal{T}_f$ are finite sets of terminal symbols, $L$ is a set of paired production rules, $S$ is a start symbol $\in \mathcal{N}$, and $\lambda$ is a set of parameters that define a probability distribution of derivations under $G$. Each rule in $L$ has the form $A \rightarrow \langle \alpha; \beta \rangle$, where $A \in \mathcal{N}$, $\alpha \in N \cup \mathcal{T}_e{}^+$, $\beta \in N \cup \mathcal{T}_f{}^+$, and $N \subseteq \mathcal{N}$.

In MT the two CFGs that make up an SCFG are used to encode (the structure of) the two languages which the MT system translates between. Translation with an SCFG then consists of (i) parsing the input string with the source language CFG to produce a derivation tree, and then (ii) generating along the same derivation tree, but using the target language CFG to produce the output string.

When using SCFGs for content-to-text generation one of the paired CFGs encodes the meaning representation language, and the other the (natural) language in which text is supposed to be generated. A generation process then consists in (i) 'parsing' the meaning representation (MR) into its constituent structure, and, in the opposite direction, (ii) assembling strings of words corresponding to constituent parts of the input MR into a sentence or text that realises the entire MR.

We used the WASP$^{-1}$ method (Wong and Mooney, 2006; Wong and Mooney, 2007) which provides a way in which a probabilistic SCFG can be constructed for the most part automatically. The training process requires two resources as input: a CFG of MRs and a set of sentences paired with their MRs. As output, it produces a probabilistic SCFG. The training process works in two phases, producing a (non-probabilistic) SCFG in the 'lexical acquisition phase', and associating the rules with probabilities in the 'parameter estimation phase'.

The lexical acquisition phase uses the GIZA++ word-alignment tool, an implementation (Och and Ney, 2003) of IBM Model 5 (Brown et al., 1993) to construct an alignment of MRs with NL strings. An SCFG is then constructed by using the MR CFG as a skeleton and inferring the NL grammar from the alignment.

For the parameter estimation phase, WASP$^{-1}$ uses a log-linear model from Koehn et al. (2003) which defines a conditional probability distribution over derivations $d$ given an input MR $f$ as

$$\Pr_{\lambda}(\mathbf{d}|\mathbf{f}) \propto \Pr(e(d))^{\lambda_1} \prod_{d \in \mathbf{d}} w\lambda(r(d))$$

where $w_\lambda(r(d))$ is the weight an individual rule used in a derivation, defined as

$$w_\lambda(A \rightarrow \langle e, f \rangle) =$$

$$P(f|e)^{\lambda_2} P(e|f)^{\lambda_3} P_w(f|e)^{\lambda_4} P_w(e|f)^{\lambda_5} \exp(-|\alpha|)^{\lambda_6}$$

where $P(\beta|\alpha)$ and $P(\alpha|\beta)$ are the relative frequencies of $\beta$ and $\alpha$, $P_w(\beta|\alpha)$ and $P_w(\alpha|\beta)$ are lexical weights, and $\exp(-|\alpha|)$ is a word penalty to control output sentence length. The model parameters $\lambda_i$ are trained using minimum error rate training.

Compared to probabilistic CFGs, WASP$^{-1}$-trained probabilistic SCFGs have a much reduced manual component in system building. In the latter, the NL grammar for the output language, the mapping from MRs to word strings and the rule probabilities are all created automatically, moreover from raw corpora, whereas in PCFGs, only the rule probabilities are created automatically.

### 3.4 SMT methods

A Statistical Machine Translation (SMT) system is essentially composed of a translation model and a language model, where the former translates source language substrings into target language substrings, and the language model determines the most likely linearisation of the translated substrings. The currently most popular phrase-based SMT (PBSMT) approach translates phrases (an arbitrary sequence of words, rather than the linguistic sense), whereas the original 'IBM models' translated words. Different PBSMT methods differ in how they construct the phrase translation table.

We used the phrase-based translation model proposed by Koehn et al. (2003) and implemented in the MOSES toolkit (Koehn et al., 2007) which is based on the noisy channel model, where Bayes's rule is used to reformulate the task of translating a source language string $f$ into a target language string $e$ as finding the sentence $\mathbf{e}^*$ such that $\mathbf{e}^* = \text{argmax}_{\mathbf{e}} \Pr(\mathbf{e}) \Pr(\mathbf{f}|\mathbf{e})$.

The translation model (which gives $\Pr(\mathbf{f}|\mathbf{e})$) is obtained from a parallel corpus of source and target language texts, where the first step is automatic alignment using the GIZA++ word-level aligner. Word-level alignments are used to obtain phrase translation pairs using a set of heuristics.

A 3-gram language model (which gives $\Pr(\mathbf{e})$) for the target language is trained either on the same or a different corpus. For full details refer to Koehn et al. (2003; 2007).

PBSMT offers a completely automatic method for constructing generators, where all that is required as input to the system building process is a corpus of paired MRs and realisations, on the basis of which the PBSMT approach constructs a mapping from MSRs to realisations.

## 4 Ten Weather Forecast Text Generators

### 4.1 SUMTIME-Hybrid

We included the original SUMTIME system (Reiter et al., 2005) in our evaluations. This rule-based system has two modules: a content-determination module and a microplanning and realisation module. It can be run without the content-determination module, taking content representations (tuple sequence as described in Section 2) as inputs, and is then called SUMTIME-Hybrid. SUMTIME-Hybrid is a traditional deterministic rule-based generation system, and took about one year to build.[1] Table 1 shows an example forecast from the SUMTIME system (and corresponding outputs from the other systems, described below).

[1]Belz (2008), estimated on the basis of personal communication with E. Reiter and S. Sripada.

### 4.2 PCFG generators

We also included five *p*CRU generators for the SUMTIME domain created previously (Belz, 2008). The *p*CRU base generator for SUMTIME is a set of generation rules with atomic arguments that convert an input into a set of NL forecasts. To create inputs to the *p*CRU generators, the input vectors as they appear in the corpus (see Section 2) are augmented and converted into sequence of nonterminals: First, information is added to each of the 7-tuples in an automatic preprocessing phase encoding whether the change in wind direction compared to the preceding 7-tuple was clockwise or anti-clockwise; whether change in wind speed was an increase or a decrease; and whether a 7-tuple was the last in the vector. Then, the augmented tuples are converted into a representation of nonterminals with 7 arguments.

A probability distribution over the base generator was obtained by the multi-treebanking method (Belz, 2008) from the un-annotated SUMTIME corpus. This method first parses the corpus with the base CFG and then obtains rule-application frequency counts from the parsed corpus which are used to obtain a probability distribution by straighforward maximum likelihood estimation. If there is more than one parse for a sentence then the frequency count increment is equally split over rules in alternative parses.

### 4.3 PSCFG generators

We created two probabilistic synchronous CFG (PSCFG) generators for the SUMTIME domain using WASP$^{-1}$. The main task here was to create a CFG for wind data representations. We used two different grammars (resulting in two different generators). The 'unstructured' grammar encodes raw corpus input vectors augmented as described in Section 4.2, whereas the 'semantic' grammar encodes representations with recursive predicate-argument structure that more resemble semantic forms. These were produced automatically from the raw input vectors.

Both the PSCFG-unstructured and the PSCFG-semantic generators were built in the same way, by feeding the CFG for wind data representations and the corpus of paired wind data representations and forecasts to WASP$^{-1}$, which then created probabilistic SCFGs from it.

| System | BLEU | Homogeneous subsets | | | | | | | |
|---|---|---|---|---|---|---|---|---|---|
| corpus | 1.00 | A | | | | | | | |
| PCFG-greedy | .65 | | B | | | | | | |
| PSCFG-sem | .637 | | B | | | | | | |
| PSCFG-unstr | .617 | | B | C | | | | | |
| PCFG-viterbi | .57 | | | C | D | | | | |
| PCFG-2gram | .561 | | | | D | | | | |
| PCFG-roule | .516 | | | | D | E | | | |
| PBSMT-unstr | .500 | | | | | E | | | |
| SUMTIME | .437 | | | | | | F | | |
| PBSMT-struc | .338 | | | | | | | G | |
| PCFG-rand | .269 | | | | | | | | H |

Table 2: Mean forecast-level BLEU scores and homogeneous subsets (Tukey HSD, alpha = .05) for SUMTIME test sets.

### 4.4 PBSMT generators

We also created two SUMTIME generators with the MOSES toolkit. The main question here was how to represent the 'source language' inputs. While SMT methods are often applied with no linguistic knowledge at all (and are therefore blind as to whether paired inputs and outputs are NL strings or something else), it was not clear how well they would cope with the task of mapping from number/symbol vectors to NL strings. We tested two different input representations, one of which was simply the augmented corpus input vectors as described above (PBSMT-unstructured), and another in which the individual 7-tuples of which the vectors are composed are explicitly marked by predicate-argument structure (PBSMT-structured). For comparability with Wong & Mooney (2007) the structure markers were treated as tokens.

We built two different generators by feeding the two different versions of the paired corpus to MOSES. We did not use a factored translation model (the words used in weather forecasts did not vary sufficiently), or tuning.

## 5 Evaluation Methods

### 5.1 Automatic evaluation methods

The two automatic metrics used in the evaluations, NIST[2] and BLEU[3], have been shown to correlate well with expert judgments (Pearson's $r = 0.82$ and $0.79$ respectively) in the SUMTIME domain (Belz and Reiter, 2006).

[2] http://cio.nist.gov/esd/emaildir/lists/mt_list/bin00000.bin

[3] ftp://jaguar.ncsl.nist.gov/mt/resources/mteval-v11b.pl

BLEU-$x$ is an n-gram based string comparison measure, originally proposed by Papineni et al. (2001) for evaluation of MT systems. It computes the proportion of word n-grams of length $x$ and less that a system output shares with several reference outputs. Setting $x = 4$ (i.e. considering all n-grams of length $\leq 4$) is standard. NIST (Doddington, 2002) is a version of BLEU, but where BLEU gives equal weight to all n-grams, NIST gives more importance to less frequent (hence more informative) n-grams, and the range of NIST scores depends on the size of the test set. Some research has shown NIST to correlate with human judgments more highly than BLEU (Doddington, 2002; Riezler and Maxwell, 2005; Belz and Reiter, 2006).

### 5.2 Human evaluation

We designed an experiment in which participants were asked to rate forecast texts for Clarity and Readability on scales of 1–7. Clarity was explained as indicating how understandable a forecast was, and Readability as indicating how fluent and readable it was. After an introduction and detailed explanations, participants carried out the evaluations over the web. They were able to interrupt and resume the evaluation at any time.

We randomly selected 22 forecast dates and used outputs from all 10 systems for those dates (as well as the corresponding forecasts in the corpus) in the evaluation, i.e. a total of 242 forecast texts. We used a repeated Latin squares design where each combination of forecast date and system is assigned two trials. As there were 2 evaluation criteria, there were 968 individual ratings in this experiment. An evaluation session started with three training examples; the real trials were then presented in random order.

We recruited 22 participants from among our university colleagues whose first language was English and who had no experience of NLP. We did not try to recruit master mariners as in earlier experiments reported by Reiter and Belz (2006), because these experiments also demonstrated that the correlation between the ratings by such expert evaluators and lay-people is very strong in the SUMTIME domain (Pearson's $r = 0.845$).

## 6 Results

For each evaluation method, we carried out a one-way ANOVA with 'System' as the fixed factor, and the evaluation measure as the dependent variable.

| System | NIST | Homogeneous subsets | | | | | | |
|---|---|---|---|---|---|---|---|---|
| corpus | 4.062 | A | | | | | | |
| PCFG-greedy | 3.361 | | B | | | | | |
| PSCFG-sem | 3.303 | | B | | | | | |
| PSCFG-unstr | 3.191 | | B | C | | | | |
| PCFG-roule | 3.033 | | | C | D | | | |
| PBSMT-unstr | 2.924 | | | | D | | | |
| PCFG-viterbi | 2.854 | | | | D | E | | |
| PCFG-2gram | 2.854 | | | | D | E | | |
| SUMTIME | 2.707 | | | | | E | F | |
| PCFG-rand | 2.540 | | | | | | F | |
| PBSMT-struc | 2.331 | | | | | | | G |

Table 3: Mean forecast-level NIST scores and homogeneous subsets (Tukey HSD, alpha = .05) for SUMTIME test sets.

In each case we report the main effect of System on the measure and (if it is significant) we also report significant differences between pairs of systems in the form of homogeneous subsets obtained with a post-hoc Tukey HSD analysis.

Tables 2 and 3 display the results for the BLEU and NIST evaluations, where scores were calculated on test data sets, using a 5-fold cross-validation set-up. System names (in abbreviated form) are shown in the first column, mean forecast-level scores in the second, and the remaining columns indicate significant differences between systems. The way to read the homogeneous subsets is that two systems which do not have a letter in common are significantly different with $p < .05$.

For the BLEU evaluation, the main effect of System on BLEU score was $F = 248.274$, at $p < .001$. PCFG-greedy, PSCFG-semantic and PSCFG-unstructured come out top, although only the first two are significantly better than all other systems. SUMTIME-Hybrid, PBSMT-structured and PCFG-random bring up the rear, with the remaining systems distributed over the middle ground. A striking result is that the handcrafted SUMTIME system comes out near the bottom, being significantly worse than all other systems except PCFG-structured and PBSMT-random.

For the NIST evaluation, the main effect of System on BLEU score was $F = 108.086$, at $p < .001$. The systems were ranked in the same way as in the BLEU evaluation except for the systems in the D subset. The correlation between the NIST and BLEU scores is Pearson's $r = .739, p < .001$, Spearman's $\rho = .748, p < .001$.

| | Scores on data from human evaluation | | | |
|---|---|---|---|---|
| | Clarity | Readability | NIST | BLEU |
| SUMTIME | 6.06 | 6.18 | 5.71 | 0.52 |
| PSCFG-semantic | 5.79 | 5.70 | 6.76 | 0.65 |
| corpus | 5.79 | 5.93 | 8.45 | 1 |
| PCFG-greedy | 5.79 | 5.63 | 6.73 | 0.67 |
| PSCFG-unstruc | 5.72 | 5.84 | 6.61 | 0.64 |
| PCFG-roulette | 5.29 | 5.56 | 6.07 | 0.52 |
| PCFG-2gram | 5.29 | 5.29 | 5.23 | 0.52 |
| PCFG-viterbi | 4.90 | 5.34 | 5.15 | 0.51 |
| PCFG-random | 4.43 | 4.52 | 4.52 | 0.25 |
| PBSMT-unstruc | 3.70 | 3.93 | 5.38 | 0.49 |
| PBSMT-struc | 2.79 | 2.77 | 4.21 | 0.33 |

Table 4: Mean Clarity and Readability ratings from human evaluation; NIST and BLEU scores on same 22 forecasts as used in human evaluation.

The main results from the automatic evaluations are that the two PSCFG systems and the PCFG system with the greedy generation algorithm are best overall. However, the human evaluations produced rather different results.

Figure 3 is a series of bar charts representing the results of the human evaluation for Clarity. For each system (indicated by the labels on the x-axis), there are 7 bars, showing how many ratings of 1, 2, 3, 4, 5, 6 and 7 (7 being the best) a system was given. So the left-most bar for a system shows how many ratings of 1 a system was given, the second bar how many ratings of 2, etc. Systems are shown in descending order of mode (the value of the most frequently assigned rating, e.g. 7 for PSCFG-unstructured on the left, and 1 for PBSMT-structured on the right). The PSCFG-unstructured and SUMTIME systems come out top in this evaluation, with PSCFG-semantic, PCFG-roulette and PCFG-greedy close behind. Conversely, PBSMT-structured clearly came out worst, with no ratings of 7 and a mode of 1 (=completely unclear).

Figure 4 consists of the same kind of bar charts, for the Readability ratings. Here the SUMTIME system is the clear winner, with no ratings of 1 and 2 and 22 ratings of 7 (=excellent, all parts read well). It is closely followed by PSCFG-unstructured, the corpus forecasts and PSCFG-semantic. Again, PBSMT-structured is clearly worst with no ratings of 7, although this time the mode is 3 (=fairly bad).

We also looked at the means of the ratings, and these are shown in the second and third columns of Table 4. The means have to be treated with some caution, because ratings are ordinal data and it is not clear how meaningful it is to compute means. However, it is a simple way of obtaining a system ranking for comparison with the two automatic scores (shown in the remaining two columns of Table 4, for the 22 dates in the human evaluation only). In terms of means, SUMTIME comes out top for both Clarity and Readability. In Clarity, it is followed by the two PSCFG systems, the corpus files (the only forecasts actually written by humans), and PCFG-greedy which have virtually the same means. For Readability, corpus and PSCFG-unstructured are ahead of PSCFG-semantic and PCFG-greedy (in this order). Bringing up the rear for both Clarity and Readability, as in the NIST evaluations, is PBSMT-structured, with PCFG-random and and PBSMT-unstructured faring somewhat better.

There are some striking differences between the automatic and human evaluations. For one, the human evaluators rank the SUMTIME system very high, whereas both automatic metrics rank it very low, just above PCFG-random and PBSMT-structured. Furthermore, the metrics rank PBSMT-unstructured more highly than the human evaluators, placing it above the SUMTIME system and in the case of NIST, also above two of the PCFG systems (Table 3). The human and the automatic evaluations agree only that the PSCFG systems and PCFG-greedy are equally good.

## 7 Conclusions

Reports of research on automating (part of) system building often take it as read that such automation is a good thing. The resulting systems are not often compared to handcrafted alternatives in terms of output quality or other quality criteria, and little is therefore known about the loss of system quality that results from automation. The existence of several independently developed systems for the SUMTIME domain of weather forecasts, to which we have added four new systems in the research reported in this paper, provides a unique opportunity to examine the system building cost vs. system quality trade-off in data-to-text generation.

We investigated 10 systems which fall into four categories in terms of the manual work involved in creating them, ranging from completely manual to completely automatic system building. We found that increasing the automatic component in system building from a handcrafted system to an automat-

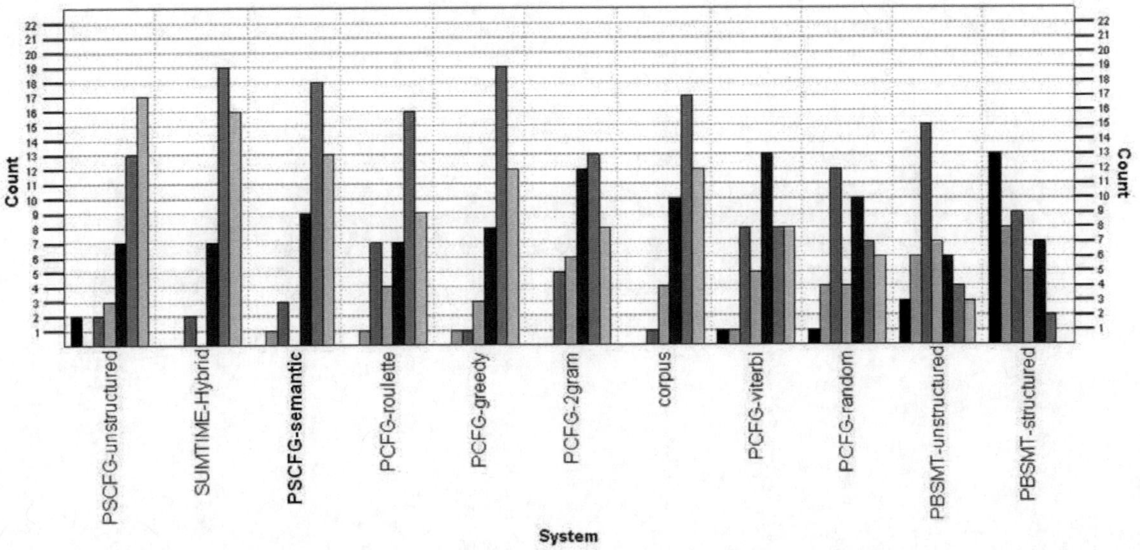


Figure 3: Clarity ratings: Number of times each system was rated 1, 2, 3, 4, 5, 6, and 7 on Clarity. Systems in descending order of mode (most frequent rating).

ically trained but manually crafted generator led to a loss of acceptability to human readers, but an improvement in terms of n-gram similarity to corpus texts. Further increasing the automatic component to the point where only a CFG for meaning representations is created manually did not result in a further reduction in quality in either acceptability to humans or corpus similarity. However, completely removing the manual component resulted in a reduction in quality in both human acceptability and corpus similarity (although this is more apparent in the former).

We found striking differences between the results from tests of human acceptability and measurements of corpus similarity. Compared to the human ratings, the automatic metrics severely underestimated the quality of the handcrafted SUMTIME system, but overestimated the quality of the automatically constructed SMT systems. This will not come as a surprise to those familiar with the machine translation evaluation literature where this is a major complaint about BLEU (Callison-Burch et al., 2006). From our results it seems clear that when the quality of diverse types of systems is compared, automatic metrics such as BLEU do not give a complete and reliable picture, and carrying out additional evaluations is crucial.

Increased reusability and adaptability of systems and components have cost and time benefits, and methods for automatically training systems from data offer advantages in both these respects. However, careful evaluation is needed to ensure that these advantages are not achieved at the price of a reduction in system quality that renders systems unacceptable to human users.

## Acknowledgments

The research reported in this paper was supported under EPSRC grant EP/E029116/1 (the Prodigy Project). We thank the anonymous reviewers for their helpful comments.

## References

A. Belz and E. Reiter. 2006. Comparing automatic and human evaluation of NLG systems. In *Proceedings of the 11th Conference of the European Chapter of the Association for Computational Linguistics (EACL'06)*, pages 313–320.

A. Belz. 2008. Automatic generation of weather forecast texts using comprehensive probabilistic generation-space models. *Natural Language Engineering*, 14(4):431–455.

P. F. Brown, V. J. Della Pietra, S. A. Della Pietra, and R. L. Mercer. 1993. The mathematics of statistical machine translation: parameter estimation. *Computational Linguistics*, 19(2):263–311.

D. Chiang. 2006. An introduction to synchronous grammars (part of the course materials for the ACL'06 tutorial on synchronous grammars).

G. Doddington. 2002. Automatic evaluation of machine translation quality using n-gram co-

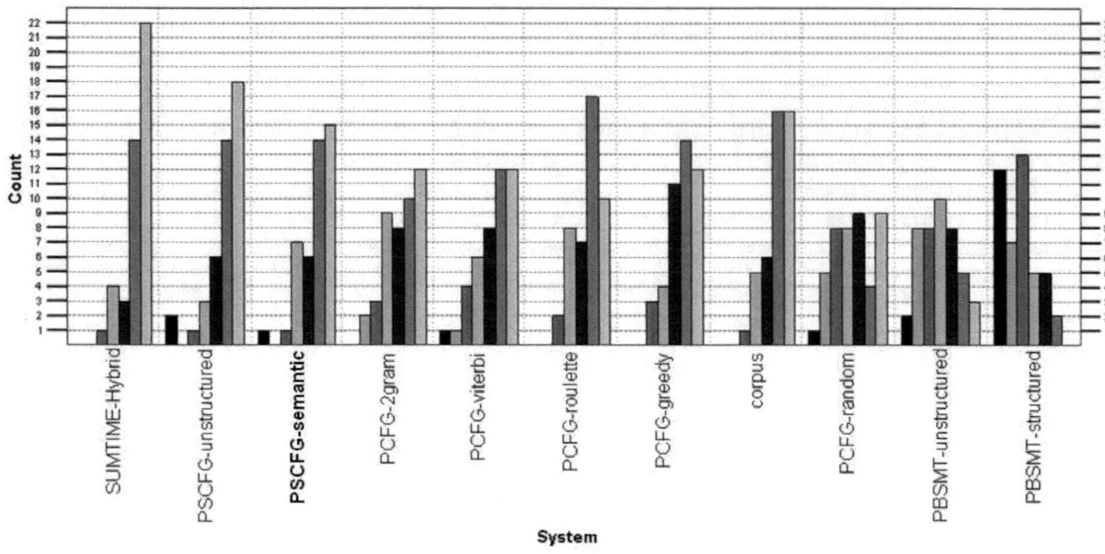


Figure 4: Readability ratings: Number of times each system was rated 1, 2, 3, 4, 5, 6, and 7 on Readability. Systems in descending order of mode (most frequent rating).

occurrence statistics. In *Proceedings of the ARPA Workshop on Human Language Technology*.

K. Knight and I. Langkilde. 1998. Generation that exploits corpus-based statistical knowledge. In *Proceedings of the 36th Annual Meeting of the Association for Computational Linguistics and 17th International Conference on Computational Linguistics (COLING-ACL'98)*, pages 704–710.

P. Koehn, F. J. Och, and D. Marcu. 2003. Statistical phrase-based translation. In *Proceedings of Human Language Technologies: The Annual Conference of the North American Chapter of the Association for Computational Linguistics on Human Language Technology (HLT-NAACL'03)*, pages 48–54.

P. Koehn, H. Hoang, A. Birch, C. Callison-Burch, M. Federico, N. Bertoldi, B. Cowan, W. Shen, C. Moran, R. Zens, C. Dyer, O. Bojar, A. Constantin, and E. Herbst. 2007. Moses: Open source toolkit for statistical machine translation. In *Proceedings of the 45th Annual Meeting of the Association for Computational Linguistics (ACL'07)*, pages 177–180.

I. Langkilde. 2000. Forest-based statistical sentence generation. In *Proceedings of the 6th Applied Natural Language Processing Conference and the 1st Meeting of the North American Chapter of the Association of Computational Linguistics (ANLP-NAACL '00)*, pages 170–177.

F. J. Och and H. Ney. 2003. A Systematic Comparison of Various Statistical Alignment Models. *Computational Linguistics*, 29(1):19–51.

K. Papineni, S. Roukos, T. Ward, and W.-J. Zhu. 2001. BLEU: A method for automatic evaluation of machine translation. IBM research report, IBM Research Division.

E. Reiter and R. Dale. 1997. Building applied natural language generation systems. *Natural Langauge Engineering*, 3(1):57–87.

E. Reiter, S. Sripada, J. Hunter, and J. Yu. 2005. Choosing words in computer-generated weather forecasts. *Artificial Intelligence*, 167:137–169.

S. Riezler and J. T. Maxwell. 2005. On some pitfalls in automatic evaluation and significance testing for MT. In *Proceedings of the ACL'05 Workshop on Intrinsic and Extrinsic Evaluation Measures for MT and/or Summarization*, pages 57–64.

S. Sripada, E. Reiter, J. Hunter, and J. Yu. 2002. SUMTIME-METEO: A parallel corpus of naturally occurring forecast texts and weather data. Technical Report AUCS/TR0201, Computing Science Department, University of Aberdeen.

Y. W. Wong and R. Mooney. 2006. Learning for semantic parsing with statistical machine translation. In *Proceedings of Human Language Technologies: The Annual Conference of the North American Chapter of the Association for Computational Linguistics on Human Language Technology (HLT-NAACL'06)*, pages 439–446.

Y. W. Wong and R.J. Mooney. 2007. Generation by inverting a semantic parser that uses statistical machine translation. In *Proceedings of Human Language Technologies: The Annual Conference of the North American Chapter of the Association for Computational Linguistics on Human Language Technology (HLT-NAACL'07)*, pages 172–179.

# Is sentence compression an NLG task?

**Erwin Marsi, Emiel Krahmer**
Tilburg University
Tilburg, The Netherlands
e.j.krahmer@uvt.nl
e.c.marsi@uvt.nl

**Iris Hendrickx, Walter Daelemans**
Antwerp University
Antwerpen, Belgium
iris.hendrickx@ua.ac.be
walter.daelemans@ua.ac.be

## Abstract

Data-driven approaches to sentence compression define the task as dropping any subset of words from the input sentence while retaining important information and grammaticality. We show that only 16% of the observed compressed sentences in the domain of subtitling can be accounted for in this way. We argue that part of this is due to evaluation issues and estimate that a deletion model is in fact compatible with approximately 55% of the observed data. We analyse the remaining problems and conclude that in those cases word order changes and paraphrasing are crucial, and argue for more elaborate sentence compression models which build on NLG work.

## 1 Introduction

The task of *sentence compression* (or *sentence reduction*) can be defined as summarizing a single sentence by removing information from it (Jing and McKeown, 2000). The compressed sentence should retain the most important information and remain grammatical. One of the applications is in automatic summarization in order to compress sentences extracted for the summary (Lin, 2003; Jing and McKeown, 2000). Other applications include automatic subtitling (Vandeghinste and Tsjong Kim Sang, 2004; Vandeghinste and Pan, 2004; Daelemans et al., 2004) and displaying text on devices with very small screens (Corston-Oliver, 2001).

A more restricted version defines sentence compression as dropping any subset of words from the input sentence while retaining important information and grammaticality (Knight and Marcu, 2002). This formulation of the task provided the basis for the noisy-channel en decision-tree based algorithms presented in (Knight and Marcu, 2002), and for virtually all follow-up work on data-driven sentence compression (Le and Horiguchi, 2003; Vandeghinste and Pan, 2004; Turner and Charniak, 2005; Clarke and Lapata, 2006; Zajic et al., 2007; Clarke and Lapata, 2008) It makes two important assumptions: (1) only word deletions are allowed – no substitutions or insertions – and therefore no paraphrases; (2) the word order is fixed. In other words, the compressed sentence must be a *subsequence* of the source sentence. We will call this *the subsequence constraint*, and refer to the corresponding compression models as *word deletion models*. Another implicit assumption in most work is that the scope of sentence compression is limited to isolated sentences and that the textual context is irrelevant.

Under this definition, sentence compression is reduced to a word deletion task. Although one may argue that even this counts as a form of text-to-text generation, and consequently an NLG task, the generation component is virtually non-existent. One can thus seriously doubt whether it really is an NLG task.

Things would become more interesting from an NLG perspective if we could show that sentence compression necessarily involves transformations beyond mere deletion of words, and that this requires linguistic knowledge and resources typical to NLG. The aim of this paper is therefore to challenge the deletion model and the underlying subsequence constraint. To use an analogy, our aim is to show that sentence compression is less like carving something out of wood - where material can only be removed - and more like molding something out of clay - where the material can be thor-

*Proceedings of the 12th European Workshop on Natural Language Generation*, pages 25–32,
Athens, Greece, 30 – 31 March 2009. 

oughly reshaped. In support of this claim we provide evidence that the coverage of deletion models is in fact rather limited and that word reordering and paraphrasing play an important role.

The remainder of this paper is structured as follows. In Section 2, we introduce our text material which comes from the domain of subtitling. We explain why not all material is equally well suited for studying sentence compression and motivate why we disregard certain parts of the data. We also describe the manual alignment procedure and the derivation of edit operations from it. In Section 3, an analysis of the number of deletions, insertions, substitutions, and reorderings in our data is presented. We determine how many of the compressed sentences actually satisfy the subsequence constraint, and how many of them could in principle be accounted for. That is, we consider alternatives with the same compression ratio which do not violate the subsequence constraint. Next is an analysis of the remaining problematic cases in which violation of the subsequence constraint is crucial to accomplish the observed compression ratio. We single out (1) reordering after deletion and (2) paraphrasing as important factors. Given the importance of paraphrases, Section 3.4 discusses the perspectives for automatic extraction of paraphrase pairs from large text corpora, and tries to estimate how much text is required to obtain a reasonable coverage. We finish with a summary and discussion in Section 4.

## 2 Material

We study sentence compression in the context of subtitling. The basic problem of subtitling is that on average reading takes more time than listening, so subtitles can not be a verbatim transcription of the speech without increasingly lagging behind. Subtitles can be presented at a rate of 690 to 780 characters per minute, while the average speech rate is considerably higher (Vandeghinste and Tsjong Kim Sang, 2004). Subtitles are therefore often a compressed representation of the original spoken text.

Our text material stems from the *NOS Journaal*, the daily news broadcast of the Dutch public television. It is parallel text with on one side the *autocue* sentences (aut), i.e. the text the news reader is reading, and on the other side the corresponding *subtitle* sentences (sub). It was originally collected and processed in two earlier research projects – Atranos and Musa – on automatic subtitling (Vandeghinste and Tsjong Kim Sang, 2004; Vandeghinste and Pan, 2004; Daelemans et al., 2004). All text was automatically tokenized and aligned at the sentence level, after which alignments were manually checked.

The same material was further annotated in an ongoing project called DAESO[1], in which the general goal is automatic detection of semantic overlap. All aligned sentences were first syntactically parsed after which their parse trees were manually aligned in more detail. Pairs of similar syntactic nodes – either words or phrases – were aligned and labeled according to a set of five semantic similarity relations (Marsi and Krahmer, 2007). For current purposes, only the alignment at the word level is used, ignoring phrasal alignments and relation labels.

Not all material in this corpus is equally well suited for studying sentence compression as defined in the introduction. As we will discuss in more detail below, this prompted us to disregard certain parts of the data.

**Sentence deletion, splitting and merging** For a start, autocue and subtitle sentences are often not in a one-to-one alignment relation. Table 1 specifies the alignment degree (i.e. the number of other sentences that a sentence is aligned to) for autocue and subtitle sentences. The first thing to notice is that there is a large number of unaligned subtitles. These correspond to non-anchor text from, e.g., interviews or reporters abroad. More interesting is that about one in five autocue sentences is completely dropped. A small number of about 4 to 8 percent of the sentence pairs are not one-to-one aligned. A long autocue sentence may be split into several simpler subtitle sentences, each containing only a part of the semantic content of the autocue sentence. Conversely, one or more - usually short - autocue sentences may be merged into a single subtitle sentence.

These decisions of sentence deletion, splitting and merging are worthy research topics in the context of automatic subtitling, but they should not be confused with sentence compression, the scope of which is by definition limited to single sentence. Accordingly we disregarded all sentence pairs where autocue and subtitle are not in a one-to-one relation with each other. This reduced the data set from 15289 to 11034 sentence pairs.

[1]`http://daeso.uvt.nl`

| Degree: | Autocue: | (%) | Subtitle: | (%) |
|---|---|---|---|---|
| 0 | 3607 | (20.74) | 12542 | (46.75) |
| 1 | 12382 | (71.19) | 13340 | (49.72) |
| 2 | 1313 | (7.55) | 901 | (3.36) |
| 3 | 83 | (0.48) | 41 | (0.15) |
| 4 | 8 | (0.05) | 6 | (0.02) |

Table 1: Degree of sentence alignment

**Word compression** A significant part of the reduction in subtitle characters is actually not obtained by deleting words but by lexical substitution of a shorter token. Examples of this include substitution by digits ("7" for "seven"), abbreviations or acronyms ("US" for "United States"), symbols (euro symbol for "Euro"), or reductions of compound words ("elections" for "state-elections"). We will call this *word compression.* Although an important part of subtitling, we prefer to abstract from word compression and focus here on sentence compression proper. Removing all sentence pairs containing a word compression has the disadvantage of further reducing the data set. Instead we choose to measure *compression ratio* (CR) in terms of tokens[2] rather than characters.

$$CR = \frac{\#tok_{sub}}{\#tok_{aut}} \quad (1)$$

This means that the majority of the word compressions do not affect the sentence CR.

**Variability in compression ratio** The CR of subtitles is not constant, but varies depending (mainly) on the amount of provided autocue material in a given time frame. The histogram in Figure 1 shows the distribution of the CR (measured in words) for one-to-one aligned sentences. In fact, autocue sentences are most likely not to be compressed at all (thus belonging to the largest bin, from 1.00 to 1.09 in the histogram).[3] In order to obtain a proper set of compression examples, we retained only those sentence pairs where the compression ratio is less than one.

**Parsing failures** As mentioned earlier detailed alignment of autocue and subtitle sentences was carried out on their syntactic trees. However, for various reasons a small number of sentences (0.2%) failed to pass the parser and received no parse tree. As a consequence, their trees could not be aligned and there is no alignment at the word level available either. Variability in CR and parsing failures are together responsible for a further reduction down to 5233 sentence pairs, the final size of our data set, with an overall CR of 0.69. Other properties of this data set are summarized in Table 2.[4]

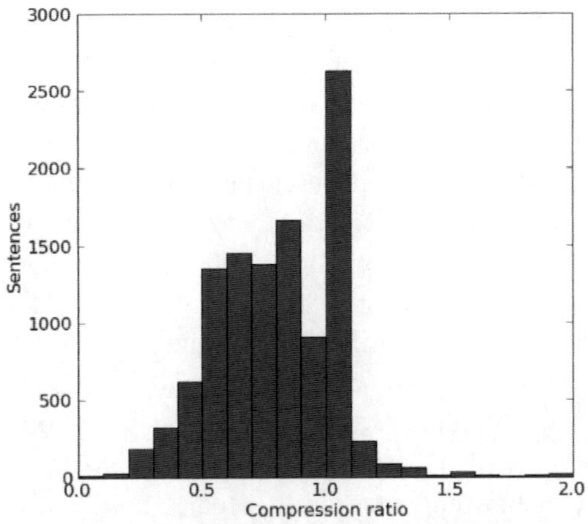


Figure 1: Histogram of compression ratio

| | Min: | Max: | Sum: | Mean: | SD: |
|---|---|---|---|---|---|
| aut-tokens | 2 | 43 | 80651 | 15.41 | 5.48 |
| sub-tokens | 1 | 29 | 53691 | 10.26 | 3.72 |
| CR | 0.07 | 0.96 | nan | 0.69 | 0.17 |

Table 2: Properties of the final data set of 5233 pairs of autocue-subtitle sentences: minimum value, maximal value, total sum, mean and standard deviation for number of tokens per autocue/subtitle sentence and Compression Ratio

**Word deletions, insertions and substitutions** Having a manual alignment of similar words in both sentences allows us to simply deduce word deletions, substitutions and insertions, as well as word order changes, in the following way:

- if an autocue word is not aligned to a subtitle word, then it is was deleted
- if a subtitle word is not aligned to an autocue word, then it was inserted
- if different autocue and subtitle words are aligned, then the former was substituted by the latter
- if alignments cross each other, then the word order was changed

The remaining option is where the aligned words are identical (ignoring differences in case).

[2]Throughout this study we ignore punctuation and letter case.

[3]Some instances even show a CR larger than one, because occasionally there is sufficient time/space to provide a clarification, disambiguation, update, or stylistic enhancement.

[4]We use the acronym *nan* ("not a number") for undefined/meaningless values.

Without the word alignment, we would have to resort to automatically calculating the edit distance, i.e. the sum of the minimal number of insertions, deletions and substitutions required to transform one sentence in to the other. However, this would result in different and often counter-intuitive sequences of edit operations. Our approach clearly distinguishes word order changes from the edit operations; the conventional edit distance, by contrast, can only account for changes in word order by sequences of the edit operations. Another difference is that substitution can also be accomplished as deletion followed by insertion, which means edit operations need to have an associated weight. Global tuning of these weights turns out to be hard.

## 3 Analysis

### 3.1 Edit operations

The observed deletions, insertions, substitutions, edit distances, and word order changes are shown in Table 3. As expected, deletion is the most frequent operation, with on average seven deletions per sentence. Insertion and substitutions are far less frequent. Note also that – even though the task is compression – insertions are somewhat more frequent than substitutions. Word order changes occur in 1688 cases (32.26%). Here, reordering is a binary variable – i.e. the word order is changed or not – hence Min, Max and SD are undefined.

Another point of view is to look at the number of sentence pairs containing a certain edit operation. Here we find 5233 pairs (100.00%) with deletion, 2738 (52.32%) with substitution, 3263 (62.35%) with insertion, and 1688 (32.26%) with reordering.

The average CR for subsequences is 0.68 ($SD = 0.20$) versus 0.69 ($SD = 0.17$) for non-subsequences. A detailed inspection of the relation between the $subsequence/non-subsequence$ ratio and CR revealed no clear correlation, so we did not find indications that non-subsequences occur more frequently at higher compression ratios.

### 3.2 Percentage of subsequences

The subtitle is a subsequence of the autocue if there are no insertions, no substitutions, and no word order changes. In contrast, if any of these do occur, the subtitle is not a subsequence. It turns out that only 843 (16.11%) subtitles are a subsequence, which is rather low.

| | Min: | Max: | Sum: | Mean: | SD: |
|---|---|---|---|---|---|
| del | 1 | 34 | 34728 | 6.64 | 4.57 |
| sub | 0 | 6 | 4116 | 0.79 | 0.94 |
| ins | 0 | 17 | 7768 | 1.48 | 1.78 |
| dist | 1 | 46 | 46612 | 8.91 | 5.78 |
| reorder | nan | nan | 1688 | 0.32 | nan |

Table 3: Observed word deletions, insertions, substitutions, and edit distances

At first sight, this appears to be bad news for any deletion model, as it seems to imply that the model cannot account for close to 84% the observed data. However, the important thing to keep in mind is that compression of a given sentence is a problem for which there are usually multiple solutions (Belz and Reiter, 2006). This is exactly what makes it so hard to perform automatic evaluation of NLG systems. There may very well exist semantically equivalent alternatives with the same CR which do satisfy the subsequence constraint. For this reason, a substantial part of the observed non-subsequences may have subsequence counterparts which can be accounted for by a deletion model. The question is: how many?

In order to address this question, we took a random sample of 200 non-subsequence sentence pairs. In each case we tried to come up with an alternative subsequence subtitle with the same meaning and the same CR (or when opportune, even a lower CR). Table 4 shows the distribution of the difference in tokens between the original non-subsequence subtitle and the manually-constructed equivalent subsequence subtitle. Apparently 95 out of 200 (47%) subsequence subtitles have the same (or even fewer) tokens, and thus the same (or an even lower) compression ratio. This suggests that the subsequence constraint is not as problematic as it seemed and that the coverage of a deletion model is in fact far better than it appeared to be. Recall that 16% of the original subtitles were already subsequences, so our analysis suggests that a deletion model is compatible with 55% (16% plus 47% of 84%).

### 3.3 Problematic non-subsequences

Another result of this exercise in rewriting subtitles is that it allows us to identify those cases where the attempt to create a proper subsequence fails. In (1), we show one representative example of a problematic subtitle, for which

(1) **Aut** de bron was een geriatrische patient die zonder het zelf te merken uitzonderlijk veel larven bij zich
the source was a geriatric patient who without it self to notice exceptionally many larvae with him
bleek te dragen en een grote verspreiding veroorzaakte
appeared to carry and a large spreading caused
"the source was a geriatric patient who unknowingly carried exceptionally many larvae and caused a wide spreading"

**Sub** een geriatrische patient met larven heeft de verspreiding veroorzaakt
a geriatric patient with larvae has the spreading caused
**Seq** de bron was een geriatrische patient die veel larven bij zich bleek te dragen en een verspreiding veroorzaakte

(2) **Aut** in verband met de lawineramp in galür hebben de politieke partijen in tirol gezamenlijk besloten de
in relation to the avalanche-disaster in Galtür have the political parties in Tirol together decided the
verkiezingscampagne voor het regionale parlement op te schorten
election-campaign for the regional parliament up to postpone
**Sub** de politieke partijen in tirol hebben besloten de verkiezingen op te schorten
the political parties in Tirol have decided the elections up to postpone
"Political parties in Tirol have decided to postpone the elections"

(3) **Aut** velen van hen worden door de serviërs in volgeladen treinen gedeporteerd
many of them are by the Serbs in crammed trains deported
**Sub** vluchtelingen worden per trein gedeporteerd
refugees are by train deported

| token-diff: | count: | (%:) |
|---|---|---|
| -2 | 4 | 2.00 |
| -1 | 18 | 9.00 |
| 0 | 73 | 36.50 |
| 1 | 42 | 21.00 |
| 2 | 32 | 16.00 |
| 3 | 11 | 5.50 |
| 4 | 9 | 4.50 |
| 5 | 5 | 2.50 |
| 7 | 2 | 1.00 |
| 8 | 2 | 1.00 |
| 9 | 1 | 0.50 |
| 11 | 1 | 0.50 |

Table 4: Distribution of difference in tokens between original non-subsequence subtitle and equivalent subsequence subtitle

the best equivalent subsequence we could obtain still has nine more tokens than the original non-subsequence. These problematic non-subsequences reveal where insertion, substitution and/or word reordering are essential to obtain a subtitle with a sufficient CR (i.e. the CR observed in the real subtitles). At least three different types of phenomena were observed.

**Word order** In some cases deletion of a constituent necessitates a change in word order to obtain a grammatical sentence. In example (2), the autocue sentence has the PP modifier *in verband met de lawineramp in galür* in its topic position (first sentence position). Deleting this modifier, as is done in the subtitle, results in a sentence that starts with the verb *hebben*, which is interpreted as a yes-no question. For a declarative interpretation, we have to move the subject *de politieke partijen* to the first position, as in the subtitle. Incidentally, this indicates that it is instructive to apply sentence compression models to multiple languages, as a word order problem like this never arises in English.

Similar problems arise whenever an embedded clause is promoted to a main clause, which requires a change in the position of the finite verb in Dutch. In total, a word order problem occurred in 24 out 200 sentences.

**Referring expressions** Referring expressions are on many occasions replaced by a shorter one – usually a little less precise. For example, *de belgische overheid* 'the Belgian authorities' is replaced by *belgie* 'Belgium'. Extreme cases of this occur where a long NP like *deze tweede impeachment-procedure in de amerikaanse geschiedenis* 'this second impeachment-procedure in the American history' is replaced by an anaphor like *het* 'it'.

Since a referring expression or anaphor must be appropriate in the given context, substitutions like these transcend the domain of a single sentence and require taking the preceding textual context into account. This is especially clear in examples like (3) in which 'many of them' is replaced the 'refugees'. It is questionable whether these types of substitutions belong to the task of sentence compression. We prefer to regard it as one of the additional tasks in automatic subtitling, apart from compression. Incidentally, it is interesting that the challenge of generating referring expressions is also relevant for automatic subtitling.

**Paraphrasing** Apart from the reduced referring expressions, there are nominal paraphrases reducing a noun phrases like *medewerkers van banken* 'employees of banks' to a compound word like *bankmedewerkers* 'bank-employees'. Likewise, there are adverbial paraphrases such as *sinds een paar jaar* 'since a few years' to *tegenwoordig* 'nowadays', and *van de afgelopen tijd* 'of the past time' to *recent* 'recent'. However, the majority of the paraphrasing concerns verbs as in the two examples below.

(4) **Aut** X neemt het initiatief tot oprichting van Y
X takes the initiative to raising of Y
**Sub** X zet Y op
X sets Y up

(5) **Aut** X om zijn uitlevering vroeg maar Y die weigerde
X for his extradition asked but Y that refused
**Sub** Y hem niet wilde uitleveren aan X
Y him not wanted extradite to Y
"Y refused to extradite him to Y"

Even though not all paraphrases are actually shorter, it seems that at least some of them boost compression beyond what can be accomplished with only word deletion. In the next Section, we look at the possibilities of automatic extraction of such paraphrases.

### 3.4 Perspectives for automatic paraphrase extraction

There is a growing amount of work on automatic extraction of paraphrases from text corpora (Lin and Pantel, 2001; Barzilay and Lee, 2003; Ibrahim et al., 2003; Dolan et al., 2004). One general prerequisite for learning a particular paraphrase pattern is that it must occur in the text corpus with a sufficiently high frequency, otherwise the chances of learning the pattern are proportionally small. In this section, we investigate to what extent the paraphrases encountered in our random sample of 200 pairs can be retrieved from a reasonably large text corpus.

In a first step, we manually extracted 106 paraphrase patterns. We filtered these patterns and excluded anaphoric expressions, general verb alternation patterns like active/passive and continuous/non-continuous, as well as verbal patterns involving more than two slots. After this filtering step, 59 pairs of paraphrases remained, including the examples shown in the preceding Section.

The aim was to estimate how big our corpus has to be to cover the majority of these paraphrase pairs. We started with counting for each of the paraphrase pairs in our sample how often they occur in a corpus of Dutch news texts, the Twente News Corpus[5], which contains approximately 325M tokens and 20M sentences. We employed regular expressions to count the number of paraphrase pattern matches. The corpus turned out to contain 70% percent of all paraphrase pairs (i.e. both patterns in the pair occur at least once). We also counted how many pairs have a frequencies of at least 10 and 100. To study the effect of corpus size on the percentage of covered paraphrases, we performed these counts on 1, 2, 5, 10, 25, 50 and 100% of the corpus. Figure 2 shows the percentage of covered paraphrases dependent on the corpus size. The most strict threshold that only counts pairs that occur at least 100 times in our corpus, does not retrieve any counts on 1% of the corpus (3M words). At 10% of the corpus size only 4% of the paraphases is found, and on the full data set 25% of the pairs is found.

For 51% percent of the patterns (with a frequency of at least 10) we find substantial evidence in our corpus of 325M tokens. We fitted a curve through our data points, and found a logarithmic line fit with adjusted $R^2$ value of .943. This suggests that in order to get 75% of the patterns, we would need a corpus that is 18 times bigger than our current one, which amounts to roughly 6 billion words. Although this seems like a lot of text, using the WWW as our corpus would easily give us these numbers. Today's estimate of the Index Dutch World Wide Web is 688 million pages[6]. If we assume that each page contains at least 100 tokens on average, this implies a corpus size of 68 billion tokens.

The patterns used here are word-based and in many cases they express a particular verb tense or verb form (e.g. 3rd person singular), and word order. This implies that our estimations are the minimum number of matches one can find. For more abstract matching, we would need syntactically parsed data (Lin and Pantel, 2001). We expect that this would also positively affect the coverage.

[5]http://www.vf.utwente.nl/~druid/TwNC/TwNC-main.html

[6]http://www.worldwidewebsize.com/index.php?lang=NL, as measured in December 2008

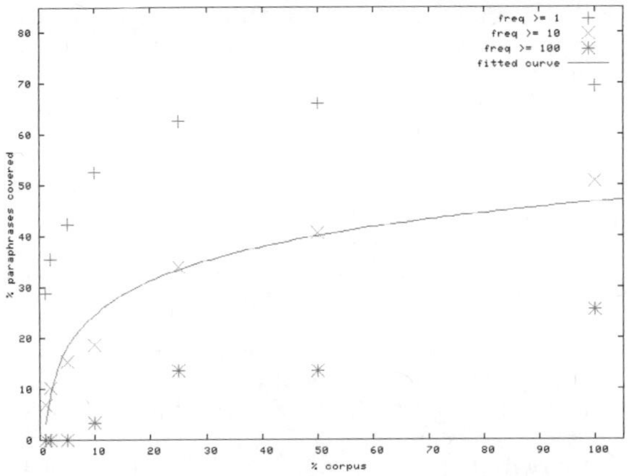


Figure 2: Percentage of covered paraphrases as a function of the corpus size

## 4 Discussion

We found that only 16.11% of 5233 subtitle sentences were proper subsequences of the corresponding autocue sentence, and therefore 84% can not be accounted for by a deletion model. One consequence appears to be that the subsequence constraint greatly reduces the amount of available training material for any word deletion model. However, an attempt to rewrite non-subsequences to semantically equivalent sequences with the same CR suggests that a deletion model could in principle be adequate for 55% of the data. Moreover, in those cases where an application can tolerate a little slack in the CR, a deletion model might be sufficient. For instance, if we are willing to tolerate up to two more tokens, we can account for as much as 169 (84%) of the 200 non-subsequences in our sample, which amounts to 87% (16% plus 84% of 84%) of the total data.

It should be noted that we have been very strict regarding what counts as a semantically equivalent subtitle: every piece of information occurring in the non-subsequence subtitle must reoccur in the sequence subtitle. However, looking at our original data, it is clear that considerable liberty is taken as far as conserving semantic content is concerned: subtitles often drop substantial pieces of information. If we relax the notion of semantic equivalence a little, an even larger part of the non-subsequences can be rewritten as proper sequences.

The remaining problematic non-subsequences are those where insertion, substitution and/or word reordering are essential to obtain a sufficient CR. One of the issues we identified is that deletion of certain constituents must be accompanied by a change in word order to prevent an ungrammatical sentence. Since changes in word order appear to require grammatical modeling or knowledge, this brings sentence compression closer to being an NLG task.

Nguyen and Horiguchi (2003) describe an extension of the decision tree-based compression model (Knight and Marcu, 2002) which allows for word order changes. The key to their approach is that dropped constituents are temporarily stored on a *deletion stack*, from which they can later be re-inserted in the tree where required. Although this provides an unlimited freedom for rearranging constituents, it also complicates the task of learning the parsing steps, which might explain why their evaluation results show marginal improvements at best.

In our data, most of the word order changes appear to be minor though, often only moving the verb to second position after deleting a constituent in the topic position. We believe that unrestricted word order changes are perhaps not necessary and that the vast majority of the word order problems can be solved by a fairly restricted way of reordering. In particular, we plan to implement a parser-based model with an additional swap operation that swaps the two topmost items on the stack. We expect that this is more feasible as a learning task than a model with a deletion stack.

Apart from reordering, other problems for word deletion models are the insertions and substitutions as a result of paraphrasing. Within a decision tree-based model, paraphrasing of words or continuous phrases may be modeled by a combination of a paraphrase lexicon and an extra operation which replaces the $n$ topmost elements on the stack by the corresponding paraphrase. However, paraphrases involving variable arguments, as typical for verbal paraphrases, cannot be accounted for in this way. More powerful compression models may draw on existing NLG methods for text revision (Inui et al., 1992) to accommodate full paraphrasing.

We also looked at the perspectives for automatic paraphrase extraction from large text corpora. About a quarter of the required paraphrase patterns was found at least a hundred times in our corpus of 325M tokens. Extrapolation suggests that using the web at its current size would give us a coverage of approximately ten counts for three quarters of the paraphrases.

Incidentally, we identified two other tasks in automatic subtitling which are closely related to NLG. First, splitting and merging of sentences (Jing and McKeown, 2000), which seems related to content planning and aggregation. Second, generation of a shorter referring expression or an anaphoric expression, which is currently one of the main themes in data-driven NLG.

In conclusion, we have presented evidence that deletion models for sentence compression are not sufficient, and that more elaborate models involving reordering and paraphrasing are required, which puts sentence compression in the field of NLG.

## Acknowledgments

We would like to thank Nienke Eckhardt, Paul van Pelt, Hanneke Schoormans and Jurry de Vos for the corpus annotation work, and Erik Tsjong Kim Sang and colleagues for the autocue-subtitle material from the ATRANOS project, and Martijn Goudbeek for help with curve fitting. This work was conducted within the DAESO project funded by the Stevin program (De Nederlandse Taalunie).

## References

Regina Barzilay and Lillian Lee. 2003. Learning to paraphrase: an unsupervised approach using multiple-sequence alignment. In *Proceedings of the 2003 Conference of the North American Chapter of the Association for Computational Linguistics on Human Language Technology*, pages 16–23, Morristown, NJ, USA.

Anja Belz and Ehud Reiter. 2006. Comparing automatic and human evaluation of NLG systems. In *Proceedings of the 11th Conference of the European Chapter of the Association for Computational Linguistics*, pages 313–320.

James Clarke and Mirella Lapata. 2006. Models for sentence compression: a comparison across domains, training requirements and evaluation measures. In *Proceedings of the 21st International Conference on Computational Linguistics and the 44th annual meeting of the Association for Computational Linguistics*, pages 377–384, Morristown, NJ, USA.

James Clarke and Mirella Lapata. 2008. Global inference for sentence compression an integer linear programming approach. *Journal of Artificial Intelligence Research*, 31:399–429.

Simon Corston-Oliver. 2001. Text compaction for display on very small screens. In *Proceedings of the Workshop on Automatic Summarization (WAS 2001)*, pages 89–98, Pittsburgh, PA, USA.

Walter Daelemans, Anita Höthker, and Erik Tjong Kim Sang. 2004. Automatic sentence simplification for subtitling in Dutch and English. In *Proceedings of the 4th International Conference on Language Resources and Evaluation*, pages 1045–1048.

Bill Dolan, Chris Quirk, and Chris Brockett. 2004. Unsupervised construction of large paraphrase corpora: Exploiting massively parallel news sources. In *Proceedings of the 20th International Conference on Computational Linguistics*, pages 350–356, Morristown, NJ, USA.

Ali Ibrahim, Boris Katz, and Jimmy Lin. 2003. Extracting structural paraphrases from aligned monolingual corpora. In *Proceedings of the 2nd International Workshop on Paraphrasing*, volume 16, pages 57–64, Sapporo, Japan.

Kentaro Inui, Takenobu Tokunaga, and Hozumi Tanaka. 1992. Text Revision: A Model and Its Implementation. In *Proceedings of the 6th International Workshop on Natural Language Generation: Aspects of Automated Natural Language Generation*, pages 215–230. Springer-Verlag London, UK.

Hongyan Jing and Kathleen McKeown. 2000. Cut and paste based text summarization. In *Proceedings of the 1st Conference of the North American Chapter of the Association for Computational Linguistics*, pages 178–185, San Francisco, CA, USA.

Kevin Knight and Daniel Marcu. 2002. Summarization beyond sentence extraction: A probabilistic approach to sentence compression. *Artificial Intelligence*, 139(1):91–107.

Nguyen Minh Le and Susumu Horiguchi. 2003. A New Sentence Reduction based on Decision Tree Model. In *Proceedings of the 17th Pacific Asia Conference on Language, Information and Computation*, pages 290–297.

Dekang Lin and Patrick Pantel. 2001. Discovery of inference rules for question answering. *Natural Language Engineering*, 7(4):343–360.

Chin-Yew Lin. 2003. Improving summarization performance by sentence compression - A pilot study. In *Proceedings of the Sixth International Workshop on Information Retrieval with Asian Languages*, volume 2003, pages 1–9.

Erwin Marsi and Emiel Krahmer. 2007. Annotating a parallel monolingual treebank with semantic similarity relations. In *Proceedings of the 6th International Workshop on Treebanks and Linguistic Theories*, pages 85–96, Bergen, Norway.

Jenine Turner and Eugene Charniak. 2005. Supervised and unsupervised learning for sentence compression. In *Proceedings of the 43rd Annual Meeting of the Association for Computational Linguistics*, pages 290–297, Ann Arbor, Michigan, June.

Vincent Vandeghinste and Yi Pan. 2004. Sentence compression for automated subtitling: A hybrid approach. In *Proceedings of the ACL Workshop on Text Summarization*, pages 89–95.

Vincent Vandeghinste and Erik Tsjong Kim Sang. 2004. Using a Parallel Transcript/Subtitle Corpus for Sentence Compression. In *Proceedings of LREC 2004*.

David Zajic, Bonnie J. Dorr, Jimmy Lin, and Richard Schwartz. 2007. Multi-candidate reduction: Sentence compression as a tool for document summarization tasks. *Information Processing Management*, 43(6):1549–1570.

# Probabilistic Approaches for Modeling Text Structure and their application to Text-to-Text Generation

**Regina Barzilay**
Computer Science and Artificial Intelligence Laboratory
Massachusetts Institute of Technology
regina@csail.mit.edu

Text-to-text generation aims to produce a coherent text by extracting, combining and rewriting information given in input texts. Examples of its applications include summarization, answer fusion in question-answering and text simplification. At first glance, text-to-text generation seems a much easier task than the traditional generation set-up where the input consists of a non-linguistic representation. Research in summarization over the last decade proved that the opposite is true — texts generated by these methods rarely match the quality of those written by humans. One of the key reasons is the lack of coherence in the generated text.

In contrast to the traditional set-up in concept-to-text generation, these applications do not have access to semantic representations and domain-specific communication knowledge. Therefore, traditional approaches for content selection cannot be employed in text-to-text applications. These considerations motivate the development of novel approaches for document organization that can exclusively rely on information available in textual input.

In this talk, I will present models of document structure that can be effectively used to guide content selection in text-to-text generation. First, I will focus on unsupervised learning of domain-specific content models. These models capture the topics addressed in a text, and the order in which these topics appear; they are close in their functionality to the content planners traditionally used in concept-to-text generation. I will present an effective method for learning content models from unannotated domain-specific documents, utilizing hierarchical Bayesian methods. Incorporation of these models into information ordering and summarization applications yields substantial improvement over previously proposed methods.

Next, I will present a method for assessing the coherence of a generated text. The key premise of our work is that the distribution of entities in coherent texts exhibits certain regularities. The models I will be presenting operate over an automatically-computed representation that reflects distributional, syntactic, and referential information about discourse entities. This representation allows us to induce the properties of coherent texts from a given corpus, without recourse to manual annotation or a predefined knowledge base. I will show how these models can be effectively integrated in text-to-text applications such as summarization and answer fusion.

This is joint work with Branavan, Harr Chen, Mirella Lapata and Lillian Lee.

*Proceedings of the 12th European Workshop on Natural Language Generation*, page 33,
Athens, Greece, 30 – 31 March 2009. ©2009 Association for Computational Linguistics

# Distinguishable Entities: Definition and Properties

**Monique Rolbert**
Laboratoire d'Informatique
Fondamentale de Marseille,
LIF, CNRS UMR 6166,
Aix-Marseille Université,
Marseille, France
monique.rolbert@lif.univ-mrs.fr

**Pascal Préa**
Laboratoire d'Informatique
Fondamentale de Marseille,
LIF, CNRS UMR 6166,
École Centrale Marseille,
Marseille, France
pprea@ec-marseille.fr

**Abstract**

Many studies in natural language processing are concerned with how to generate definite descriptions that evoke a discourse entity already introduced in the context. A solution to this problem has been initially proposed by Dale (1989) in terms of distinguishing descriptions and distinguishable entities. In this paper, we give a formal definition of the terms "distinguishable entity" in non trivial cases and we show that its properties lead us to the definition of a distance between entities. Then, we give a polynomial algorithm to compute distinguishing descriptions.

## 1 Introduction

Many studies in natural language processing are concerned with how to generate definite descriptions that evoke a discourse entity already introduced in the context (Dale, 1989; Dale and Haddock, 1991; Dale and Reiter, 1995; van Deemter, 2002; Krahmer et al., 2002; Gardent, 2002; Horacek, 2003), and more recently (Viethen and Dale, 2006; Gatt and van Deemter, 2006; Croitoru and van Deemter, 2007). Following Dale (1989), these definite descriptions are named "distinguishing descriptions". Informally, a distinguishing description is a definite description which designates one and only one entity among others in a context set. Conversely, this entity is named "distinguishable entity".

Things are simple if all the properties of the entities are unary relations. Let's give a set of entities $E = \{e_1, e_2\}$ with the following properties:
$e_1$: red, bird ; $e_2$: red, bird, eat ;

$e_1$ is not a distinguishable entity because there exists no distinguishing description that could designate $e_1$ and not $e_2$[1]. $e_2$ is a distinguishable entity and could be designated by the distinguishing description "the red bird that is eating".

Many of the works cited above are concerned with how to generate the best distinguishing description with the best algorithm, essentially in the unary case, that is if entities properties are unary ones. They focus on the length or the relevance of the generated expressions, or on the efficiency of the algorithm. But none of them give a formal definition of these "distinguishable entities". They all use an intuitive definition, more or less issued from the unary case and that could be resumed as follow: *an entity e is a distinguishable entity in E if and only if there exists a set of properties of e that are true of e and of no other entity in E.*

Unfortunately, this intuitive definition does not apply as it is in non-unary cases. The main problem comes with the notion of "set of properties of $e$": what is the set of properties of an entity if non-unary relations occur? Let us see this problem on an example. Suppose that we have an entity $b_1$ that is a bowl and that is on an entity $t_1$ which is a table. The set of entities is $E = \{b_1, t_1\}$ with:
$b_1$: bowl ; $t_1$: table ; on($b_1, t_1$)

What is the set of properties of $b_1$? Dale and Haddock (1991) and, more or less, Gardent (2002), suggest that the property set for an entity includes all the relations in which it is involved (even non unary ones), and no others. Following this definition, the set of properties of $b_1$ should be {bowl($b_1$), on($b_1, t_1$)}.

Now, what if there is another bowl ($b_2$), which is on a table ($t_2$)? The set of properties of $b_2$ is {bowl($b_2$), on($b_2, t_2$)}, which is different from that

[1] One could object that "the red bird that is not eating" is a distinguishing description for $e_1$. But we do not make the Closed World Assumption ("every thing that is not said is false"). So, negative properties have to appear explicitly, like positive one, in entities description; their treatment causes no particular problem in our model

*Proceedings of the 12th European Workshop on Natural Language Generation*, pages 34–41,
Athens, Greece, 30 – 31 March 2009. ©2009 Association for Computational Linguistics

of $b_1$. But does it follow that $b_1$ is distinguishable from $b_2$? If the "intuitive definition" is used, the answer is *yes*: the set of properties of $b_1$ (and the formula $(\lambda x\, bowl(x) \wedge on(x, t_1))$) is true for $b_1$ and for no other entity in $E = \{b_1, b_2, t_1, t_2\}$. But, one can immediately see that the "right" answer should depend on what we know about $t_1$ and $t_2$. If the only thing we know is that $t_1$ and $t_2$ are tables, then there is no definite description that designates $b_1$ and not $b_2$, and thus $b_1$ is not distinguishable from $b_2$. So, even if the formula on(-, $t_1$) is formally different from the formula on(-, $t_2$) and $b_1$ satisfies the first one and not the second one, that does not imply that $b_1$ is distinguishable from $b_2$.

So, the fact is that to determine if $b_1$ is distinguishable from $b_2$, knowing that the set of properties of $b_1$ is true for $b_1$ and not for $b_2$ is not sufficient: we have to determine if $t_1$ is distinguishable from $t_2$. That clearly leads to a non-trivial recursive definition and non-trivial recursive processes.

Two recent works describe algorithms that deal with this problem (Krahmer et al., 2003; Croitoru and van Deemter, 2007). Their works are both based on graph theory and their algorithms deal well with the non-unary case, but their computations need exponential time.

In this paper, our main goal is to give a definition of a distinguishable entity which corresponds to the intuitive sense and which works well even in non-trivial cases. Then we study its properties, which leads us to an interesting notion of distance between entities. Finally, we give a polynomial algorithm able to produce a distinguishing description whenever it is possible and which is based on this definition.

## 2 A definition of "distinguishable entity"

Intuitively, an entity $e_1$ is distinguishable from an entity $e_2$ in two cases:

- $e_1$ involves properties that are not involved by $e_2$ (we will say that $e_1$ is *0-distinguishable* from $e_2$)
- otherwise, $e_1$ and $e_2$ are in relations (we will precisely see how below) with at least two distinguishable entities $e'_1$ and $e'_2$. In this case, we will say that $e_1$ is *$(k+1)$-distinguishable* from $e_2$ if $e'_1$ is *k-distinguishable* from $e'_2$.

Basically, a *property* is an n-ary relation, together with a rank (the argument's position). For instance, with the fact $e_1$ *eats* $e_2$, $e_1$ has the property eat with rank 1 (noted $\mathsf{eat}_1$) and $e_2$ has the property $\mathsf{eat}_2$. So, $e_1$ and $e_2$ do not have the same set of properties. Conversely, if $e_1$ eats $X$ and $e_2$ eats $Y$, $e_1$ and $e_2$ involve the same property ($\mathsf{eat}_1$).

For an entity $e$, we denote $\mathcal{P}(e)$ the set of its properties. We will say that a tuple $t = (x_1, \ldots, x_p)$ *matches* a property $p_q$ with $e$ if $p(x_1, \ldots, x_{q-1}, e, x_q, \ldots, x_p)$ is true.

**Definition 1** *(k-distinguishability $D_k$):*
*An entity $e_1$ is **0-distinguishable** from an entity $e_2$ (we denote it $e_1\, D_0\, e_2$) if $\mathcal{P}(e_1)$ is not included in $\mathcal{P}(e_2)$.*
*An entity $e_1$ is **k-distinguishable** ($k > 0$) from an entity $e_2$ (we denote it $e_1\, D_k\, e_2$) if there exists a relation $R_q$ in $\mathcal{P}(e_1)$ and a tuple $(x_1, \ldots, x_p)$ such that:*

- *$(x_1, \ldots, x_p)$ matches $R_q$ with $e_1$.*
- *For every $(y_1, \ldots, y_p)$ that matches $R_q$ with $e_2$, there exists some $x_i$ and some $k' < k$ such that $x_i$ is k'-distinguishable from $y_i$.*

We remark that if $e_1\ D_k\ e_2$, then $e_1\ D_j\ e_2$, for every $j > k$. So, we can define the more general notion of distinguishability (without a rank).

**Definition 2** *(distinguishability D):*
*We say that an entity $e_1$ is **distinguishable from** an entity $e_2$ (we denote it $e_1\, D\, e_2$) if it is k-distinguishable from $e_2$, for some $k \geq 0$.*
*We say that e is **distinguishable** in a set of entities E if for every entity $e' \neq e$, e is distinguishable from $e'$.*

Distinguishable entities are the only one that can be designated by a definite description.

Definition 1 seems rather complicated (due to the universal quantifier in the second part) and thus needs some justification. Let us see some examples:

An entity $e$ which is a cat is 0-distinguishable from an entity $e$' which is a dog because $\mathcal{P}(e)$={$\mathsf{cat}_1$} is not included in $\mathcal{P}(e')$={$\mathsf{dog}_1$}.

An entity $e$ which is a cat and which eats $b$ (a bird) is 1-distinguishable from an entity $e'$ which is a cat and which eats $m$ (a mouse). Actually, $\mathcal{P}(e) = \{\mathsf{cat}_1, \mathsf{eat}_1\}$ is included in $\mathcal{P}(e') =$

$\{\mathsf{cat}_1, \mathsf{eat}_1\}$, but there exists an entity ($b$) with which $e$ is in relation (via $\mathsf{eat}_1$) and which is distinguishable from $m$, which is the only entity with which $e'$ is in relation via $\mathsf{eat}_1$. So, the situation can be resumed as in figure 1:

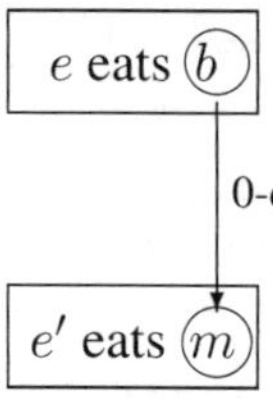


figure 1: $e$ is 1-distinguishable from $e'$

If we add the information that $e'$ also eats $f$ (a fish), the conclusion remains true, as we can see on figure 2.

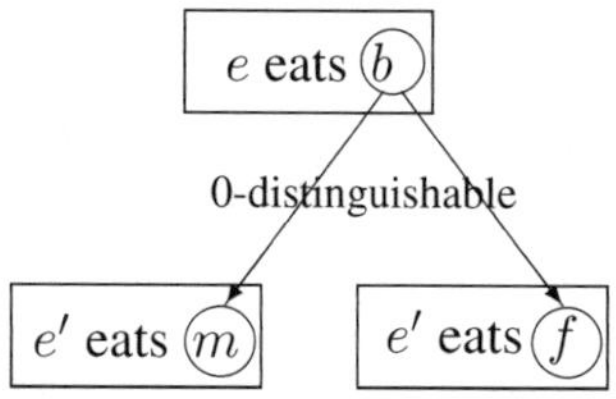


figure 2: $e$ is 1-distinguishable from $e'$

But if we add the information that $e'$ also eats $b'$, a bird not distinguishable from $b$, then the conclusion is no longer true (see fig. 3).

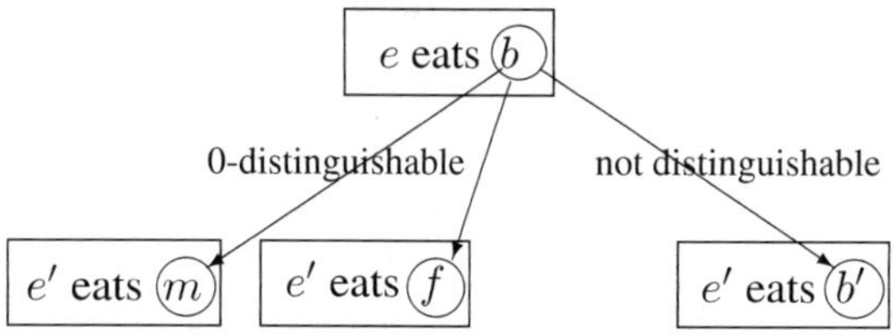


figure 3: $e$ is not distinguishable from $e'$

$e$ is not distinguishable from $e'$, no definite description can designate $e$ and not $e'$. So, we see that, in order for $e$ to be distinguishable from $e'$, $b$ has to be distinguishable from all the entities which are in relation with $e'$ via $\mathsf{eat}_1$. That illustrates the necessity of the universal quantifier in definition 1.

Let us see a more complicated example, where tuples are involved.

$E = \{e, e', x_1, y_1, z_1, x_2, y_2, z_2\}$
$e$, $e'$: man
$x_1$, $z_1$: ball – $y_1$ : cake
$x_2$, $y_2$: blond, child – $z_2$: child
$e$ gives $x_1$ to $x_2$ ($e$ gives a ball to a blond child)
$e'$ gives $y_1$ to $y_2$ ($e'$ gives a cake to a blond child)
$e'$ gives $z_1$ to $z_2$ ($e'$ gives a ball to a child)

The question is: Is $e$ distinguishable from $e'$? The answer is clearly yes, "the man who gives a ball to a blond child" is a definite description that designates $e$ and not $e'$.

First, $e$ is not 0-distinguishable from $e'$ ($\mathcal{P}(e) = \{\mathsf{man}_1, \mathsf{give}_1\}$ is included in $\mathcal{P}(e') = \{\mathsf{man}_1, \mathsf{give}_1\}$).

So, $e$ is 1-distinguishable from $e'$ if we find a relation $R$ in $\mathcal{P}(e)$ and a tuple $T$ that matches $R$ with $e$ and such that for each tuple $T'$ that matches $R$ with $e'$, $T'$ contains an entity $e'_i$ from which the entity $e_i$ in $T$ is 0-distinguishable.

Let us check if this is true for $\mathsf{give}_1$ and $(x_1, x_2)$. $T_1 = (x_1, x_2)$ matches $\mathsf{give}_1$ with $e$ ($\mathsf{give}(e, y_1, z_1)$ is true). There are two tuples $T_2 = (y_1, y_2)$ and $T_3 = (z_1, z_2)$ that match $\mathsf{give}_1$ with $e'$.
$x_1$ is 0-distinguishable from $y_1$. So it is right for $T_2$.
$x_2$ is 0-distinguishable from $z_2$. So it is right for $T_3$.

The situation can be resumed by the schema in figure 4:

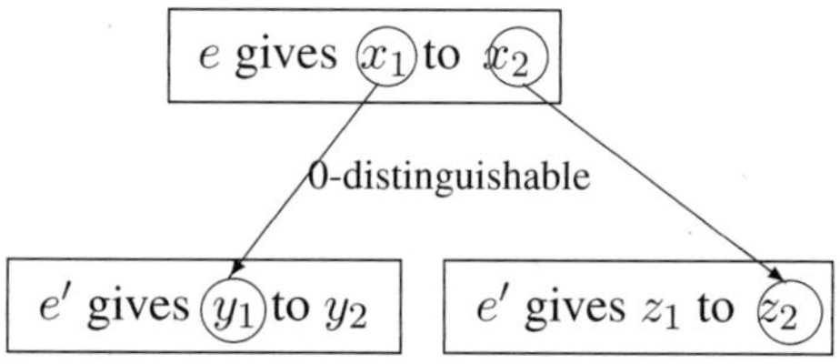


figure 4: $e$ is 1-distinguishable from $e'$

Let us add "$e'$ gives $z_1$ to $y_2$" to the above example:
$T_4 = (z_1, y_2)$ matches $\mathsf{give}_1$ with $e'$. But $x_1$ is not distinguishable from $z_1$ and $x_2$ is not distinguishable from $y_2$. This new information prevents $e$ being distinguishable from $e'$.
This case is represented on figure 5:

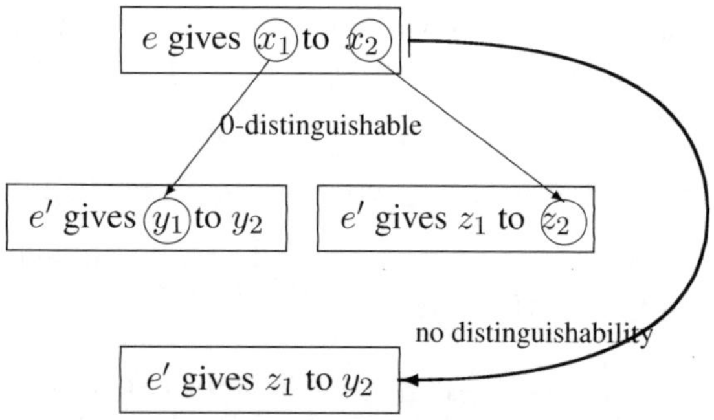


figure 5: $e$ is not distinguishable from $e'$

Again, we see that it is not sufficient to check the existence of a tuple and a relation in $\mathcal{P}(e')$ that introduce the distinguishability to $e$ via $\mathsf{give}_1$. We have to check this for each tuple that matches $\mathsf{give}_1$ with $e'$.

Moreover, one can also notice in the above example that the entity which "leads to" the k'-distinguishability is not unique. It may be different upon each tuple ($x_1$ for $T_2$ and $x_2$ for $T_3$). This is quiet different from the often used shortcut: $e_1$ is k-distinguishable from $e_2$ if it is in relation with *one* entity $e'_1$ which is k'-distinguishable from an entity $e'_2$ which is related to $e_2$.

So, although our definition may seem complicated, it cannot be simplified if we want it to seize the notion of distinguishability. We will now study some of its properties.

## 3 Some properties

This definition of the k-distinguishability of an entity leads to two interesting ideas:

- A set of entities can be organised in subsets or classes via a related notion, confusability. Confusability is a transitive relation and thus it defines a partial order on subsets of $E$.
- A notion of distance can be defined from k-distinguishability. Actually, the greatest $k$ is, the less distinguishable the related entities are. The inverse of this $k$ defines a distance between entities.

### 3.1 A partial order on the set of entities

**Definition 3** *(Confusability $C$):*
*We say that $e_1$ is* ***k-confusable*** *with $e_2$ (we denote it $e_1\, C_k\, e_2$) when not $e_1\, D_k\, e_2$.*
*We say that an entity $e_1$ is* ***confusable*** *with another entity $e_2$ if $e_1\, C_k\, e_2$ for every $k$ (we denote it $e_1\, C\, e_2$). It is equivalent to say that an entity $e_1$ is confusable with an entity $e_2$ if $e_1$ is not distinguishable from $e_2$.*

For example, $e_1$ is 1-confusable with $e_2$ if $e_1$ is not 1-distinguishable (nor 0-distinguishable) from $e_2$. But, in the same time, $e_1$ can be 2-distinguishable from $e_2$ and thus, not confusable with $e_2$.
We remark that if $e_1\, C_k\, e_2$, then $e_1\, C_j\, e_2$, for every $j < k$.

Intuitively, one would like $C$ to be transitive (if an entity $e_1$ is confusable with an entity $e_2$ which is confusable with an entity $e_3$, then $e_1$ should be confusable with $e_3$).

**Theorem 1** *$C$ is transitive.*

**Proof**: We shall prove by induction on $k$ that if $e_1\, C\, e_2$ and $e_2\, C\, e_3$, then $e_1\, C_k\, e_3$, for every $k \geq 0$.

If $e_1\, C\, e_2$ and $e_2\, C\, e_3$, then $\mathcal{P}(e_1) \subset \mathcal{P}(e_2) \subset \mathcal{P}(e_3)$, and so, $e_1\, C_0\, e_3$.

Let us suppose that, for every $e_1$, $e_2$ and $e_3$, if $e_1\, C\, e_2$ and $e_2\, C\, e_3$, then $e_1\, C_k\, e_3$, and that there exist three entities $f$, $g$, and $h$ such that:
$f\, C\, g$, $g\, C\, h$ and $f\, D_{k+1}\, h$.
By the induction hypothesis, $f\, C_k\, h$, and so $\mathcal{P}(f) \subset \mathcal{P}(h)$. Thus, as $f\, D_{k+1}\, h$, there exist $(x_1, \ldots, x_n)$ and a relation $R$ such that:
$R(f, x_1, \ldots x_n)$
$\forall(z_1, \ldots z_n)$ such that $R(h, z_1, \ldots, z_n)$, $\exists i \leq n, k' < k$ such that $x_i\, D_{k'}\, z_i$. (a)
(We have supposed, with no loss of generality, that $f$ has rank 1 in $R$)
As $f\, C\, g$, $\exists(y_1, \ldots, y_n)$ such that:
$R(g, y_1, \ldots, y_n)$
$\forall i \leq n, x_i\, C\, y_i$
As $g\, C\, h$, $\exists(z'_1, \ldots, z'_n)$ such that:
$R(h, z'_1, \ldots, z'_n)$
$\forall i \leq n, y_i\, C\, z'_i$
Thus, for every $i \leq n$ :
$x_i\, C\, y_i$ and $y_i\, C\, z'_i$
By the induction hypothesis, for every $i \leq n$, $x_i\, C_k\, z'_i$, which is in contradiction with (a).
□

We remark that $C$ is reflexive and not symmetric. But, since $C$ is a transitive relation, the relation $\mathcal{E}$ defined by $e_1\, \mathcal{E}\, e_2$ if $e_1\, C\, e_2$ and $e_2\, C\, e_1$ is an equivalence relation (with this relation, we put in the same class entities which are confusable) and $C$, when restricted to the quotient set (the set of the equivalence classes) $E/\mathcal{E}$, is a partial order that we denote $<_C$.

Since $<_C$ is an (partial) order relation on $E/\mathcal{E}$, which is a finite set, it has maximal and minimal elements. The maximal elements can be seen as *very well defined entities* (they are confusable with no other entity in other subsets) and the minimal elements as the *conceptual entities* (no entities in other subsets are confusable with them, but they are confusable with many other entities). We remark that two minimal entities (as two maximal ones) are not confusable, since the set of the minimal elements of an ordered set is an antichain (as the set of the maximal elements).

Thus, for example, a set of entities can be organised as in figure 6:

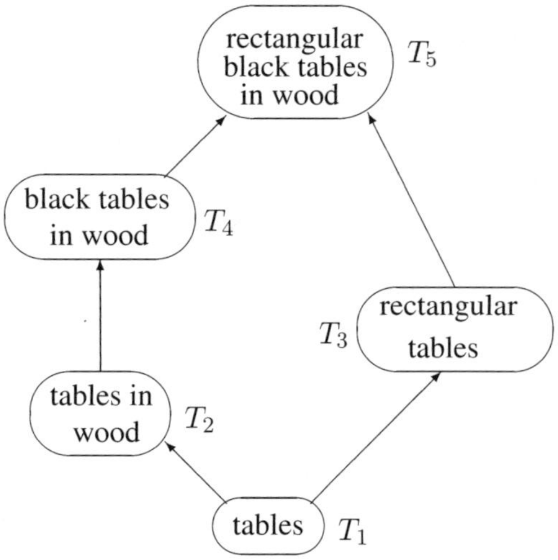


Figure 6: sets of entities ordered by $<_C$

$T_1 <_C T_2 <_C T_4 <_C T_5$
$T_1 <_C T_3 <_C T_5$

### 3.2 A distance between entities

Now, let us see that the notion of k-distinguishability leads to a notion of distance between entities. By now, if we take the smallest $k$ such that $e_1$ is k-distinguishable from $e_2$ (we note it $\kappa(e_1, e_2)$ (if $e_1\, C\, e_2$, $\kappa(e_1, e_2) = \infty$)) the smaller $\kappa(e_1, e_2)$ is, the further $e_1$ is from $e_2$.

For example, if $e_1$ is 0-distinguishable from $e_2$, $e_1$ is very different from $e_2$ (a cat and a dog, for instance). But if $e_1$ is not 0-distinguishable from $e_2$ but is 1-distinguishable from it, then $e_1$ is nearer from $e_2$ (two cats, one that eats a bird and the other that eats a mouse, for instance).

So, one could expect that $\kappa$ is like the inverse of a distance. Let us see that point.

**Definition 4** *Let $E$ be a set of entities. We define on $E/\mathcal{E}$:*

$\Theta(e, e) = 0$

$\Theta(e_1, e_2) = \max\{(\kappa(e_1, e_2) + 1)^{-1}, (\kappa(e_2, e_1) + 1)^{-1}\}$ *if* $e_1 \neq e_2$[2].

**Theorem 2** *$\Theta$ is a distance on $E/\mathcal{E}$.*

We recall that a *distance* on a set $X$ is an application $d : X \times X \rightarrow \mathbb{R}^+$ such that:

$\forall x, y, d(x, y) = 0 \iff x = y$
$\forall x, y, d(x, y) = d(y, x)$
$\forall x, y, z, d(x, y) \leq d(x, z) + d(z, y)$.

Theorem 2 follows immediately from the following:

**Lemma 1** *If $e_1\, D_k\, e_2$, then, for every $e_3$:*
*$e_1\, D_k\, e_3$ or $e_3\, D_k\, e_2$.*

[2]We take $1/\infty = 0$

**Proof of Lemma 1**: The proof is by induction on $k$.
If $k = 0$, then $\mathcal{P}(e_1) \not\subset \mathcal{P}(e_2)$. Thus, if $\mathcal{P}(e_1) \subset \mathcal{P}(e_3)$ (i.e. $e_1\, C_0\, e_3$), then $\mathcal{P}(e_3) \not\subset \mathcal{P}(e_2)$, and so $e_3\, D_0\, e_2$.
Let us suppose that the property is true for $k - 1$ and that $\kappa(e_1, e_2) = k > 0$. There exists a relation $R$ and $(x_1, \dots x_n)$ with $R(e_1, x_1, \dots, x_n)$ such that for every $(y_1, \dots, y_n)$ with $R(e_2, y_1, \dots, y_n)$ (such a $(y_1, \dots y_n)$ exists, otherwise $\kappa(e_1, e_2) = 0$), there exists $i$ with $x_i\, D_{k-1}\, y_i$.
(We have supposed, with no loss of generality, that $e_1$ has rank 1 in $R$)
Let $(z_1, \dots, z_n)$ be such that $R(e_3, z_1, \dots, z_n)$. If such a $(z_1, \dots, z_n)$ does not exist, we would have $e_1\, D_0\, e_3$, and the property would hold for $k$. By the induction hypothesis, we have:

(a) $x_i\, D_{k-1}\, z_i$ or (b) $z_i\, D_{k-1}\, y_i$.

If there exists a $(z_1, \dots, z_n)$ such that, for every $(y_1, \dots, y_n)$, we are in case (b), then $e_3\, D_k\, e_2$.
Otherwise, for every $(z_1, \dots, z_n)$ such that $R(e_3, z_1, \dots, z_n)$, there exists a $(y_1, \dots, y_n)$ for which we are in case (a). In fact, $(y_1, \dots, y_n)$ does not matter for this case, and so, that is to say that $e_1\, D_k\, e_3$.
□

Actually, this lemma shows much more than theorem 2. It says that the entity set is structured by distinguishability in such a way that whatever the couple of entities we take, there is no other entity between them. This lemma induces a stronger property for $\Theta$:
Let $d$ be a distance on a set $X$. If we have:

$\forall x, y, z, \max\{d(x, y), d(x, z)\} \geq d(z, y)$

(which is equivalent to say that for any triple, the two greatest distances are equal[3]), then the distance is *ultrametric*.

**Theorem 3** *$\Theta$ is an ultrametric distance on $E/\mathcal{E}$.*

Ultrametric distances have a lot of properties (See (Barthélémy and Guénoche, 1991)). In particular, they are equivalent to a hierarchical classification of the underlying set[4] (like the phylogenetic classification of natural species).

More precisely, given a set $X$ with an ultrametric distance $d$, the sets $C_{x,y} = \{z/d(x, z) \leq$

[3]Suppose that for a triple $(x, y, z)$, we have, for instance, $d(x, y) \geq d(x, z) \geq d(y, z)$. Since $\max\{d(y, z), d(x, z)\} \geq d(x, y)$, we also have $d(x, z) \geq d(x, y)$, and thus $d(x, z) = d(x, y)$.

[4]The set is partioned into non-overlapping subsets, each subset being (eventually) divided into non overlapping subsets,...

$d(x, y)\}$ form a hierarchical classification of $X$. Conversely, given a finite set $X$ with a hierarchical classification, if, for $x \neq y$, we define $d(x, y)$ as the cardinality of the smallest class containing $x$ and $y$, and $d(x, x) = 0$ for all $x$ in $X$, then $d$ is an ultrametric distance.

In addition, given a set $X$ with an ultrametric distance $d$, there exists a tree (called *ultrametric tree*) with labels on its internal nodes, its leaves indexed by the elements of $X$ and such that:

- for any two leaves $x$ and $y$, the label of their lowest common ancestor is $d(x, y)$.
- for any leaf $x$, the labels on the path from the root to $x$ form a decreasing sequence.

For instance, with the example shown on figure 5, we obtain the tree on $E/\mathcal{E}$ which is shown on figure 7 (for this example, since there is no pairwise confusable entities, $E/\mathcal{E} = E$):

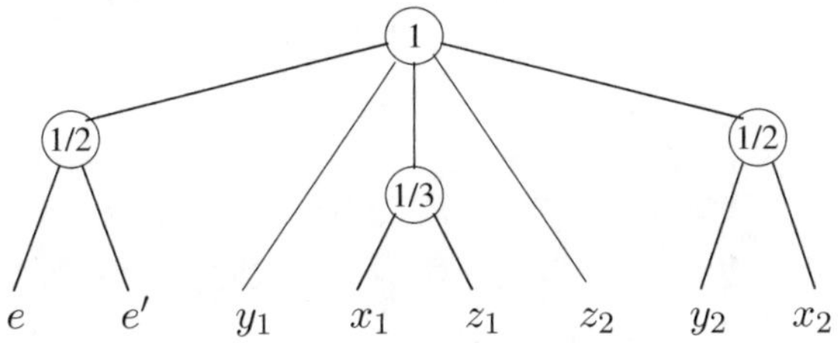


Figure 7: a tree on $E/\mathcal{E}$

On this tree, given a couple of entities, one can see the difficulty to distinguish them. This information has been construct in a global way (by using all the relations between entities) and it is rather different (and more accurate) from what one would say at a first glance. For instance, we can see that $x_1$ and $y_1$ are more difficult to distinguish than $x_2$ and $z_2$ or than $e$ and $e'$ (the label of their lowest common ancestor is 1/3 instead of 1/2).

## 4 An algorithm for searching distinguishable entities

The algorithm is based on dynamic programming (Aho et al., 1974). This is a standard technique which is used, for instance, to calculate distances in graphs. We work on a set $E = \{e_1, \ldots e_n\}$ of entities. The main structure is a $n \times n$ matrix $\mathcal{M}$. At each step $k$, the algorithm determines the couples $(e_i, e_j)$ of entities such that $\kappa(e_i, e_j) = k$ and loads $k$ into $\mathcal{M}[i, j]$.

- At step 0, we check for each couple $(e_i, e_j)$ whether $\mathcal{P}(e_i) \subset \mathcal{P}(e_j)$ or not. If $\mathcal{P}(e_i) \not\subset \mathcal{P}(e_j)$, we load 0 into $\mathcal{M}[i, j]$.
- At step $k > 0$, for every couple $(e_i, e_j)$ such that $\mathcal{M}[i, j]$ is not yet calculated, we determine if $\kappa(e_i, e_j) = k$ or not, using already calculated values in $\mathcal{M}$ to check conditions of definition 1. If it is the case, we load $k$ into $\mathcal{M}[i, j]$.
  If no value of $\mathcal{M}$ is updated, then the algorithm stops (if there are no $e, e'$ in $E$ such that $e \, D_k \, e'$, then there exist no $f, f'$ in $E$ such that $f \, D_{k+1} \, f'$)

At the end of the algorithm, if $e_i \, D \, e_j$, $\mathcal{M}[i, j]$ contains $\kappa(e_i, e_j)$. We also compute an auxiliary matrix $\mathcal{A}$ in which we put the relations that have been used to calculate $\kappa(e_i, e_j)$. The matrix $\mathcal{A}$ will be used to build referring expressions.

The algorithm runs in $O(n^2 \cdot K \cdot N \cdot T^2)$, where $K = \max\{\kappa(e, e'), e \, D \, e'\}$, $N$ is the greatest property arity, and $T$ is the cardinality of the greatest set $\mathcal{T}(e_i)$ of all couples $(p, t)$, where $p$ is a property and $t$ a tuple that matches $p$ with $e_i$.

$N$, $T$ and $K$ are rather small and can be assimilated to constants[5]; so, if we are only concerned with the number of entities, our algorithm is in $O(n^2)$.

Let us see how it works on an example from (Croitoru and van Deemter, 2007):

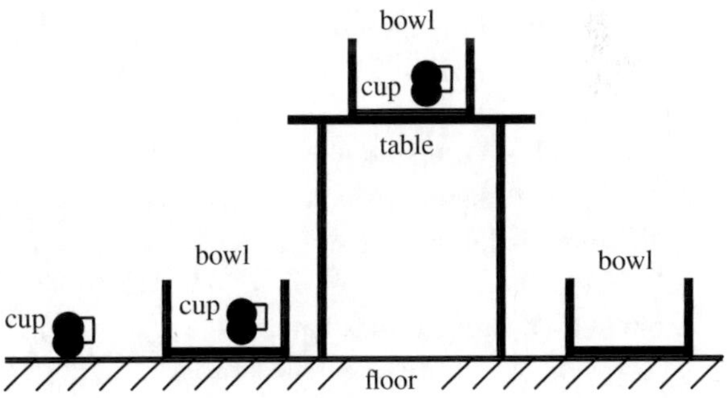


Figure 8: a scene

Croitoru and van Deemter (2007) represent the scene of figure 8 by an entity set $E = \{v_0, \ldots v_7\}$ with the following properties:

$v_0, v_3, v_7$: cup
$v_1, v_5, v_6$: bowl
$v_2$: table

[5]Actually, from a theoretical point of vue, we only have $K \leq n$, and no limit on $T$ and $N$. But, from a practical point of vue, one can have a scene with (for instance) 10000 entities, but there is no property of arity 10, no entity with 100 properties and no distinguishing expression of length 50 (even if such an expression would exist, it would be impossible to use it); so $N$, $T$ and $K$ are small

$v_4$: floor
$v_0$ is in $v_1$
$v_1$ is on $v_2$
$v_3$ is on $v_4$
$v_2$ is on $v_4$
$v_5$ is on $v_4$
$v_6$ is on $v_4$
$v_7$ is in $v_6$

Our algorithm produces the following matrix $\mathcal{M}$ (due to lack of space, we do not show the matrix $\mathcal{A}$: its breadth would exceed the sheet):

$$\mathcal{M} = \begin{array}{c} \\ v_0 \\ v_1 \\ v_2 \\ v_3 \\ v_4 \\ v_5 \\ v_6 \\ v_7 \end{array} \begin{array}{c} \begin{array}{cccccccc} v_0 & v_1 & v_2 & v_3 & v_4 & v_5 & v_6 & v_7 \end{array} \\ \left( \begin{array}{cccccccc} / & 0 & 0 & 0 & 0 & 0 & 0 & 2 \\ 0 & / & 0 & 0 & 0 & 1 & 1 & 0 \\ 0 & 0 & / & 0 & 0 & 0 & 0 & 0 \\ 0 & 0 & 0 & / & 0 & 0 & 0 & 0 \\ 0 & 0 & 0 & 0 & / & 0 & 0 & 0 \\ 0 & 1 & 0 & 0 & 0 & / & \infty & 0 \\ 0 & 1 & 0 & 0 & 0 & 0 & / & 0 \\ 2 & 0 & 0 & 0 & 0 & 0 & 0 & / \end{array} \right) \end{array}$$

With this matrix $\mathcal{M}$, one can easily determine which entities are distinguishable: they are the one with no $+\infty$ on their line. Here, we can see that $v_5$ is not distinguishable: it is distinghishable from all entities but $v_6$

It is also easy to construct sets of distinguishing properties, using matrix $\mathcal{A}$. For instance, if we want to distinguish $v_0$ from $v_7$, we use the following elements of $\mathcal{A}$:

$\mathcal{A}[v_0, v_7] = \{(isin_1, 2, v_1, v_6)\}$
$\mathcal{A}[v_1, v_6] = \{(ison_1, 2, v_2, v_4)\}$
$\mathcal{A}[v_2, v_4] = \{table_1, ison_1\}$.

Since $v_2$ is 0-distinguishable from $v_4$, we get the following distinguishing formula:

$\lambda x\, \lambda y\, \lambda z\ isin(x, y) \wedge ison(y, z) \wedge table(z)$[6]

from which one can easily obtain the following expression which distinguishes $v_0$ from $v_7$: "*the entity which is in an entity which is on an entity which is a table*".

Using this method, we obtain minimal expressions to distinguish one entity $e$ from another entity $e'$. A referring expression (which distinguishes one entity $e$ from all the others) can be obtained by computing the conjunction of all these minimal expressions. This conjunction contains many redundancies, and it can be reduced in $O(n \log n)$. Actually, by this way, one generally obtains an expression which is very close to the expression which distinguishishes $e$ from the nearest other entity (i.e. the entity $e'$ for which $\kappa(e, e')$ is maximal). For instance, in the example above, the expression which distinguishes $v_0$ from $v_7$ is a referring one for $v_0$: there is no other entity "*in something on a table*".

So, we get sets of distinguishing properties for all the distinguishable entities of a scene in polynomial time (and more precisely in $O(n^2 \log n)$). This is much better than the methods of Kramer and al. (2003) and of Croitoru and van Deemter (2007), which both rely on subgraph isomorphisms (which is a NP-complete problem).

[6] We can obtain another distinguishing expression by taking $ison_1$ instead of $table_1$ in $\mathcal{A}[v_2, v_4]$. We choose $table_1$ because its arity is smaller, so we get a simpler formula.

## 5 Conclusion

The two main results of this paper are:

- An efficient algorithm to compute distinguishing descriptions. Our algorithm is efficient enough to be applied on complex scenes.
- An ultrametric distance which captures the difficulty to distinguish two entities and provides a phylogenic classification of the entities.

These two results follow from our definition of k-distinguishability. More precisely, they are due to the incremental nature of the k-distinguishability, which thus reveals to be a pivot for the Generation of Referring Expressions (GRE).

## Acknowledgments

P. Préa is supported in part by ANR grant BLAN06-1-138894 (projet OPTICOMB)

## References

Alfred V. Aho, John E. Hopcroft, and Jeffrey D. Ullman. 1974. *The Design and Analysis of Computer Algorithms*. Addison-Wesley, Reading, MA.

Jean-Pierre Barthélémy and Alain Guénoche. 1991. *Trees and Proximity Representations*. J. Wiley & sons, New York, NY.

Madalina Croitoru and Kees van Deemter. 2007. A conceptual graph approach to the generation of referring expressions. *International Joint Conference on Artificial Intelligence*, Hyderabad.

Robert Dale. 1989. Cooking up referring expressions. *Proceedings of the Twenty-Seventh Annual Meeting of the Association for Computational Linguistics*, Vancouver.

Robert Dale and Nicholas Haddock. 1991. Generating Referring Expression Involving Relations. *Proceedings of the fifth conference of the European ACL*, Berlin.

Robert Dale and Ehud Reiter. 1995. Computational Interpretations of the Gricean Maxims in the Generation of Referring Expressions. *Cognitive Science*, 19(2):233-263.

Kees van Deemter. 2002. Generating Referring Expressions: Boolean Extensions of the Incremental Algorithm. *Computational Linguistics*, 28(1):37-52.

Claire Gardent. 2002. Generating Minimal Definite Descriptions. *Proceedings of the 40th Annual Meeting of the Association for Computational Linguistics*, Philadelphia.

Albert Gatt and Kees van Deemter. 2006. Conceptual Coherence in the Generation of Referring Expressions. *Proceedings of ACL*, Sydney.

Helmut Horacek. 2003. A Best-First Search Algorithm for Generating Referring Expressions. *Proceedings of the 11th Conference of the European Chapter of the Association for Computational Linguistics*, Budapest.

Emiel Krahmer, Sebastian van Erk and André Verleg. 2003. Graph-based Generation of Referring Expressions. *Computational Linguistics*, 29(1):53-72.

Jette Viethen and Robert Dale. 2006. Algorithms for Generating Referring Expressions: Do They Do What People Do? *Proceedings of the International Conference on Natural Language Generation*, Sydney.

# Generating Approximate Geographic Descriptions

**Ross Turner, Yaji Sripada and Ehud Reiter**
Dept of Computing Science,
University of Aberdeen, UK
{r.turner,yaji.sripada,e.reiter}@abdn.ac.uk

## Abstract

Georeferenced data sets are often large and complex. Natural Language Generation (NLG) systems are beginning to emerge that generate texts from such data. One of the challenges these systems face is the generation of geographic descriptions referring to the location of events or patterns in the data. Based on our studies in the domain of meteorology we present a two staged approach to generating geographic descriptions. The first stage involves using domain knowledge based on the task context to select a frame of reference, and the second involves using constraints imposed by the end user to select values within a frame of reference. Because geographic concepts are inherently vague our approach does not guarantee a distinguishing description. Our evaluation studies show that NLG systems, because they can analyse input data exhaustively, can produce more fine-grained geographic descriptions that are more useful to end users than those generated by human experts.

## 1 Introduction

Disciplines such as environmental studies, geography, geology, planning and business marketing make extensive use of Geographical Information Systems (GIS); however, despite an explosion of available mapping software, GIS remains a specialist tool with specialist skills required to analyse and understand the information presented using map displays. Complementing such displays with textual summaries therefore provides an immediate niche for NLG systems.

Recently, research into NLG systems that generate text from georeferenced data has begun to emerge (Dale et al., 2005; Turner et al., 2006; Turner et al., 2008b; Thomas and Sripada, 2008). These systems are required to textually describe the geographic distribution of domain variables such as road surface temperature and unemployment rates. For example, descriptions such as 'road surface temperatures will fall below zero in some places in the southwest' and 'unemployment is highest in the rural areas' need to be generated by these systems. One of the main challenges such systems face is the generation of geographic descriptions such as 'in some places in the southwest' and 'in the rural areas'. Such a task is challenging for a number of reasons:

- many geographic concepts are inherently vague (see for example (Varzi, 2001) for a discussion on this topic);
- often the underlying data sets contain little explicit geographic information for a generation system to make use of (Turner et al., 2008b);
- as input to a generation system, georeferenced data is often complex, constraints imposed on the output text (such as length) may make the traditional approach to the Referring Expression Generation (REG) problem in NLG of finding a distinguishing description implausible (Turner et al., 2008b).

This paper looks at the problem in the context of work the authors have carried out on summarising georeferenced data sets in the meteorology domain. The main feature of our approach is that geographic descriptions perform the dual function of referring to a specific geographic locations unambiguously (traditional function of REG) and also communicate the relationship between the domain information and the geography of the region (novel function of geographic descriptions).

We present a two staged approach to generating geographic descriptions that involve regions. The first stage involves using domain knowledge (meteorological knowledge in our case) to select a frame of reference and the second involves using constraints imposed by the end user to select values within a frame of reference. While generating geographic descriptions it is not always possible to produce a distinguishing description because of the inherent vagueness in geographic concepts. Therefore, in our case we aim to produce a distinguishing description wherever possible, but more often allow non-distinguishing descriptions in the output text, which approximate the location of the event being described as accurately as possible.

After a short overview of the background in §2, some empirical observations on geographic descrip-

*Proceedings of the 12th European Workshop on Natural Language Generation*, pages 42–49,
Athens, Greece, 30 – 31 March 2009. 

tions from knowledge acquisition (KA) studies we have carried out are discussed in §3. Taking these observations into account, in §4 we describe how this problem is approached using examples from RoadSafe (Turner et al., 2008b), which generates spatial references to events in georeferenced data in terms of regions that approximate their location. It pays particular attention to the use of different perspectives to describe the same situation and how factors that affect what makes a good reference in this domain are taken into account by the system. In §5 we present a qualitative discussion of aspects of geographic description from the evaluations of RoadSafe that were carried out, and how this relates to future possible work on this topic.

## 2 Background

Much work on generation of spatial descriptions has concentrated on smaller scale spaces that are immediately perceivable. For example, spatial descriptions have been studied from the perspective of robot communication (Kelleher and Kruijff, 2006), 3D animation (Towns et al., 1998) and basic visual scenes (Viethen and Dale, 2008; Ebert et al., 1996). In a more geographical context route description generation systems such as (Dale et al., 2005) and (Moulin and Kettani, 1999) have had wide appeal to NLG researchers. (Varges, 2005) also generate landmark based spatial descriptions using maps from the map task dialogue corpus.

RoadSafe is an NLG system that has been operationally deployed at Aerospace and Marine International (AMI) to produce weather forecast texts for winter road maintenance. It generates forecast texts describing various weather conditions on a road network as shown in Figure 1.

**Overview:** Road surface temperatures will fall below zero on all routes during the late evening until around midnight.

**Wind (mph):** NE 15-25 gusts 50-55 this afternoon in most places, backing NNW and easing 10-20 tomorrow morning, gusts 30-35 during this evening until tomorrow morning in areas above 200M.

**Weather:** Snow will affect all routes at first, clearing at times then turning moderate during tonight and the early morning in all areas, and persisting until end of period. Ice will affect all routes from the late evening until early morning. Hoar frost will affect some southwestern and central routes by early morning. Road surface temperatures will fall slowly during the evening and tonight, **reaching zero in some far southern and southwestern places** by 21:00. Fog will affect some northeastern and southwestern routes during tonight and the early morning, turning freezing in some places above 400M.

Figure 1: RoadSafe forecast text showing geographic descriptions underlined

The input to the system is a data set consisting of numerical weather predictions (NWP) calculated over a large set of point locations across a road network. An example static snapshot of the input to RoadSafe for one parameter is shown in Figure 2. The complete input is a series of such snapshots for a number of parameters (see (Turner et al., 2008b) for details).

In applications such as RoadSafe, the same geographical situation can be expressed in a variety of different ways dependent upon the perspective employed, henceforth termed as a frame of reference. Space (geographic or otherwise) is inherently tied to a frame of reference that provides a framework for assigning different values to different locations in space. For example, locations on Earth's surface can be specified by latitude and longitude which provide an absolute frame of reference for geographic space. Cardinal directions such as {North, East, West and South} provide an alternative frame of reference for geographic space. As was noted in (Turner et al., 2008b), characterising the data in terms of frames of reference is important because often the only geographic information input data contains are coordinates (latitude and longitude), while the output texts are required to employ a wider choice of frames of reference such as altitude, direction, coastal proximity and population. In RoadSafe the frames of reference employed are always absolute according to Levinson's terminology (Levinson, 2003).

Because the geographic descriptions in RoadSafe do not fit the traditional formulation of the REG problem as finding the most distinguishing description, the most pressing question to address is what makes an adequate reference strategy in this case? This is of course a difficult question and is reliant to a large extent on the communication goal of the system. This paper looks into this problem in the context of the RoadSafe application, that uses a simple spatial sublanguage to generate the types of descriptions required in this application domain.

## 3 Observations on geographic descriptions from the weather domain

In this section we summarise some empirical observations on how meteorologists use geographic descriptions in weather forecasts. It describes work carried out over the course of the RoadSafe project involving knowledge acquisition (KA) studies with experts on summarising georeferenced weather data, observations from data-text corpora (one aimed at the general public and one aimed at experts) and a small study with people from the general public. During RoadSafe we built two prototype georeferenced data-to-text systems that summarised georeferenced weather data: one that produces pollen forecasts based on very simple data (Turner et al., 2006), and the RoadSafe system, which

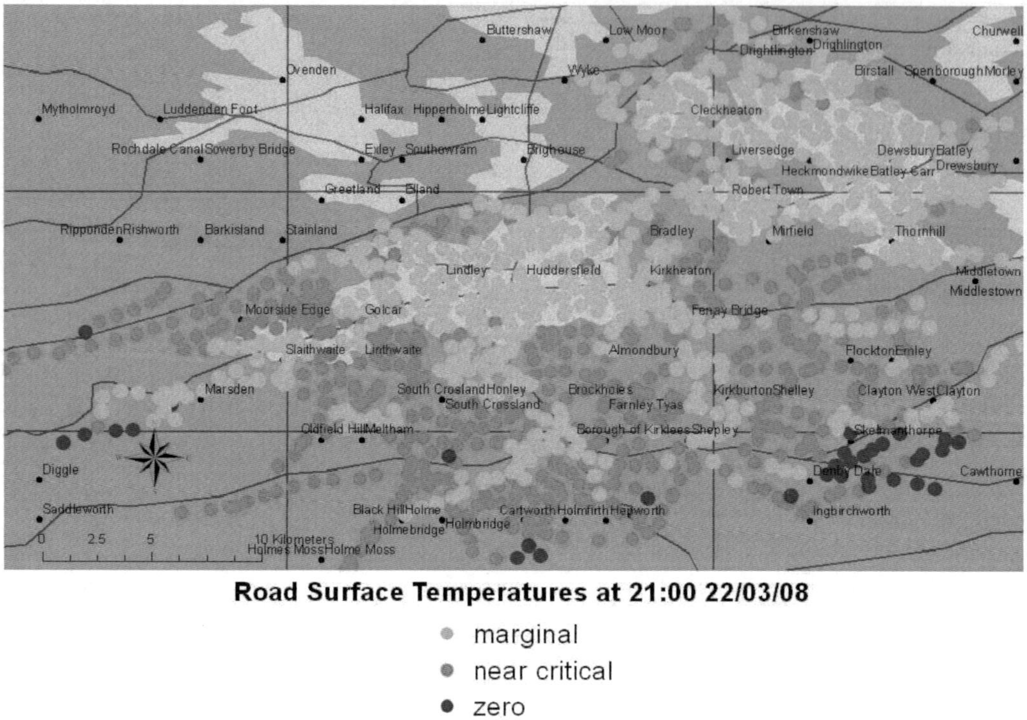


Figure 2: Input data for 'reaching zero in some far southern and southwestern places' in Figure 1

generates road ice forecasts based on complex data. Small corpora consisting of forecast texts and their underlying NWP data were collected in both application domains. Using techniques described in (Reiter et al., 2005) these corpora have been analysed to understand the experts' strategies to describe georeferenced data.

The major finding from our studies is the fact that experts tailor their geographic descriptions to the task context. Not only does the geographic knowledge of the end user have to be taken into account in their descriptions, but also how the geography of the region causes events and patterns in the data. The latter consideration has a large affect on the frame of reference experts employ to describe particular geographic situations. §3.1 looks at these observations from the point of view of end users of weather forecasts, while §3.2 looks at the descriptive strategies of experts.

### 3.1 End users' geographic knowledge

It is a well known and accepted fact that geographic knowledge varies greatly between individuals. To illustrate this point 24 students of a further education college in Scotland were asked a geography question, without reference to a map. Which of four major place names in Scotland (Ayr, Glasgow, Isle of Arran and Stirling) did they consider to be in the south west of the country? The responses showed a great variation in the subjects' geographic knowledge. Half of all subjects considered Glasgow and Ayr to be in the south west, one third considered Stirling to be in the south west and most surprisingly only four considered this to be true of the Isle of Arran. The results of this study are surprising because Stirling is the least south westerly place in the list while Isle of Arran is the most south westerly. This study actually agrees well with the studies in psychology on variation in individuals' mental representation of their geographic environment (Tversky, 1993).

Contrast this with the detailed knowledge of a road engineer who the RoadSafe texts are intended for. Road engineers rely upon a large amount of local geographic knowledge and experience when treating roads. Indeed, their spatial mental models are specified at a much finer detail. For example, they get to know where frost hollows tend to form and also come to learn of particular unexpected black spots, such as where garages allow hose water to cover part of a road during winter. This is an important point to be taken into account when communicating georeferenced data as geographic descriptions should be sensitive to that knowledge because it dictates how accurately they will be interpreted by the end user.

Both task context and structural features of data (e.g. number of observations, granularity of measurement), as well as functional features of data (how the entities being described function in space) influence how it is described geographically. Analysis of a small pollen forecast corpus (Turner et al., 2006) revealed that forecast texts, contain a rich variety of spatial descriptions for a location despite the data containing only six data points for the whole of Scotland. In general, the same region could be referred to by its proper name e.g. Sutherland and Caithness, by its relation to a well known geographical landmark e.g. North of the Great Glen, or simply by its geographical location on the map e.g. the far North and Northwest. In other words, experts characterise the limited geographic information contained within the data according to the task context. As the consumers of such forecasts are the general public, there is a greater onus on the expert to make the texts more interesting, unlike more restricted domains such as marine (see (Reiter et al., 2005)) or road ice forecasts that require consistent terminology.

### 3.2 Experts' descriptive strategy

Work in psychology has suggested that meteorologists use a dynamic mental model to arrive at an inference to predict and explain weather conditions (Trafton, 2007). Vital to this process is also their ability to take into account how the geography of a region influences the general weather conditions. Understanding the weathers interaction with the terrain enables them to make reliable meteorological inferences particularly when a certain pattern in the data may appear random. It is often unfeasible for a human forecaster to spend large amounts of time inspecting every data point in a detailed visual display. Using experience and expertise a forecaster can use her mental model to 'play out different hypothetical situations' (Trafton, 2007, p.2) and thus arrive at a plausible explanation for an apparently random weather pattern. Consider the following example description of a weather event by an expert taken from our road ice corpus:

- 'exposed locations may have gales at times.'

This is a good example of a forecaster using her meteorological expertise to make an inference about a random weather pattern. Clearly there is no way from inspection of a map one can ascertain with certainty where the exposed locations are in a region. However, an expert's knowledge of how the referent entity (the wind parameter) is affected by geographical features allow her to make such an inference. These pragmatic factors play a large part in determining an experts descriptive strategy, where certain frames of reference may be considered more appropriate to describe certain weather events (Turner et al., 2008a). This comes from weather forecasters' explicit knowledge of spatial dependence (the fact that observations points in georeferenced data at nearby locations are related, and the values of their non-spatial attributes will be influenced by certain geographical features). This is one of the most important and widely understood fact about spatial data from an analysis point of view, and one of the main reasons that it requires special treatment in comparison to other types of non-spatial data. This fact is most clearly outlined by an observation made in (Tobler, 1970, p.3) that *'everything is related to everything else, but near things are more related than distant things'*. This is commonly known as the first law of geography and still resonates strongly today amongst geographers (Miller, 2004). The implication of Tobler's first law (TFL) is that samples in spatial data are not independent, and observations located at nearby locations are more likely to be similar. Recasting this into meteorological terms, exposed locations are more likely to be windier and elevated areas colder for example.

In fact, an analogy can be drawn between how meteorologists consider perspectives in their descriptive strategy and the preferred attribute list in the seminal work on REG by (Dale and Reiter, 1995). In their specification of an algorithm for generating referring expressions content selection is performed through the iteration over a pre-determined and task specific list of attributes. In our context, preferred attributes are replaced by preferred frames of reference. This means describing georeferenced data requires situational knowledge of when to apply a particular frame of reference given a particular geographic distribution to describe.

The most striking observation about the expert strategy is that the geographic descriptions in the corpora are approximations of the input (Turner et al., 2008a). The input is highly overspecified with 1000s of points for a small forecast region, sampled at sub hourly intervals during a forecast period. Meteorologists use vague descriptions in the texts to refer to weather events such as:

- 'in some places in the south, temperatures will drop to around zero or just above zero.'

There are a number of reasons they use this descriptive strategy: the forecasts are highly compressed summaries, as a few sentences describes megabytes of data; very specific descriptions are avoided unless the pattern in the data is very clear cut; experts try to avoid misinterpretation, road engineers often have detailed local geographic knowledge and experts may not be aware the more provincial terminology they use to refer to specific areas. The following section demonstrates how the problem of generating such descriptions is addressed in RoadSafe.

## 4 Generating Approximate Geographic Descriptions

In its current form, where summaries are meant to give a brief synopsis of conditions to the user, RoadSafe follows the approach taken by forecasters as discussed previously. This is unconventional in comparison to traditional REG approaches that aim to rule out all distractors in the domain (properties that are not true of the referent). In a description such as 'reaching zero in some places above 100M by 16:00' above, distractors can be defined as the set of points above 100M that do not satisfy the premise that temperatures will drop below zero. More succinctly, these can be defined as false positives. In fact, the problem can be formulated as a trade off between false positives and false negatives, where false negatives constitute points that are wrongly omitted from the description. For road gritting purposes, costs can be assigned to each type of error: road accidents in the case of false negatives and wasted salt in the case of false positives. As the task dictates, with the higher associated cost it is imperative that a referring expression eliminates all false negatives. Ideally a truly optimal description should then seek to minimise false positives as far as possible, thus reducing the overall cost for the reader. While reducing errors descriptions should also be meteorologically correct, as discussed in the previous section. Using certain frames of reference in certain contexts may result in a poor inference about a particular weather situation (Turner et al., 2008b).

Given this domain knowledge, we can formulate constraints for what makes a good approximate geographic description in this task context:

1. Meteorological correctness (inferencing about causal relationships).
2. Minimise false positives.
3. Complete coverage of the event being described (no false negatives).

These constraints have been realized in a two staged approach to generating geographic descriptions. The first stage involves using domain knowledge (meteorological knowledge in our case) to select a frame of reference, while the second accounts for end-user constraints to select values within that frame of reference. Before we describe the individual stages, two necessary pre-processing stages for generation are described.

### 4.1 Geographic characterisation

As noted in §2, observations in georeferenced data often contain little explicit geographic information apart from their coordinates. Geographic characterisation is responsible for assigning a set of qualitative descriptors to each observation based upon a set of reference frames, such that observations can be collectively distinguished from each other. This provides both a criterion for partitioning the data, and a set of properties to generate geographic descriptions. A frame of reference in this context consists of a set of descriptions based upon a common theme such as coastal proximity e.g. {inland,coastal} or population e.g. {urban,rural}. In RoadSafe four frames of reference have been implemented: altitude, coastal proximity, population and direction. Those that make use of human (population) and physical geographical features (altitude, coastal Proximity) can be represented by existing GIS data sets; therefore, in these cases geographic characterisation is simply responsible for mapping observation coordinates to areas of these data sets. In contrast, directions are abstract and require definition. In RoadSafe, geographic characterisation maps each observation to a set of directional areas with crisp boundaries, described in the following section.

### 4.2 Pattern formation

To generate descriptions, the geographic distribution of the event to be communicated has to be approximated using data analysis techniques such as clustering. While not new to data-to-text systems, the novel aspect here is that the data is partitioned based upon the frames of reference that make up the spatial sublanguage of the system. This process summarises the location of the event by measuring its density within each frame of reference's set of descriptions. An example of such a distribution is shown in Figure 3.

| Reference Frame | Description | Proportion |
|---|---|---|
| Altitude | | |
| | 100M | 0.033 |
| | 200M: | 0.017 |
| | 300M | 0.095 |
| | 400M | 0.042 |
| Direction | | |
| | SSE | 0.037 |
| | SSW | 0.014 |
| | WSW: | 0.048 |
| | TSE | 0.489 |
| | TSW | 0.444 |
| Population | | |
| | Rural: | 0.039 |

Figure 3: Density of zero temperatures in Figure 2

While the descriptions within each frame of reference with human and geographical features are dictated by the granularity of available GIS data sets (altitude resolution for example), the boundaries of directional areas require definition. In RoadSafe, because some flexibility in the generated geographic descriptions is desirable, the system uses a four by four grid to split the domain into sixteen equally sized directional areas defined by their their latitude longitude extents. This configuration is shown below where T stands for true and C for central in this case:

| | | | |
|---|---|---|---|
| TNW | NNW | NNE | TNE |
| WNW | CNW | CNE | ENE |
| WSW | CSW | CSE | ESE |
| TSW | SSW | SSE | TSE |

Using a simple set of adjacency matrices based on this grid, RoadSafe represents a set of descriptions depicting the traditional eight main points of the compass plus a further five that we term gradable (central, far south, far north, far east and far west). Alternative configurations using a greater number of gradable descriptions are possible. These matrices are used by the microplanner to choose attributes to refer to events using the direction frame of reference. One example matrix for each category of directional description are listed below. In each matrix a value of 1 indicates that the event has a non-zero density in that area.

**Gradable**

- Far South:

$$\{TSW, SSW, SSE, TSE\} = \begin{bmatrix} 0 & 0 & 0 & 0 \\ 0 & 0 & 0 & 0 \\ 0 & 0 & 0 & 0 \\ 1 & 1 & 1 & 1 \end{bmatrix}$$

**Intercardinal**

- South West:

$$\{TSW, WSW, SSW, CSW\} = \begin{bmatrix} 0 & 0 & 0 & 0 \\ 0 & 0 & 0 & 0 \\ 1 & 1 & 0 & 0 \\ 1 & 1 & 0 & 0 \end{bmatrix}$$

**Cardinal**

- South:

$$SouthEast \cup SouthWest = \begin{bmatrix} 0 & 0 & 0 & 0 \\ 0 & 0 & 0 & 0 \\ 1 & 1 & 1 & 1 \\ 1 & 1 & 1 & 1 \end{bmatrix}$$

In what follows we describe how our two stage strategy is implemented in our system.

### 4.3 Frame of reference selection

The main content selection decision made by the document planner is the choice of which frame of reference to describe a specific weather event such as wind gusts increasing or road surface temperature falling below zero. This decision is based upon both the location of the event as discussed previously, and situational knowledge stored in the knowledge base of the system. Frames of reference where all descriptions have non-zero densities are not considered. Situational knowledge consists of the probability of using each frame of reference given the context (the weather parameter to describe), and is based on corpus frequencies. Rather than simply choosing the frame of reference with the highest density, weighting each frame of reference in this way ensures meteorological correctness as far as possible.

### 4.4 Attribute selection

Once a frame of reference has been selected the microplanner maps the descriptions to abstract syntax templates. As this is fairly trivial for most frames of reference in RoadSafe, because they contain a limited number of descriptions, we will provide an example how this is accomplished for directional descriptions. The input to the microplanner is a structure comprised of the density of the event within the containing area plus its associated adjacency matrix as shown in Figure 4.

$$\begin{array}{lll} Location & \{Pointratio: & 0.21 \\ & \quad Relation: & in \\ & \quad Container: & \begin{bmatrix} 0 & 0 & 0 & 0 \\ 0 & 0 & 0 & 0 \\ 1 & 0 & 0 & 0 \\ 1 & 1 & 1 & 1 \end{bmatrix} \\ & \} & \end{array}$$

Figure 4: REG input to describe Figure 2

The attribute selection algorithm is based upon four constraints incorporating the first two principles of the descriptive strategy outlined at the beginning of this section. They are:

1. Minimise false positives - The description describing the distribution should introduce the least number of distractors. For the above example distribution the set {South} ensures coverage but introduces three distractors: CSW, CSE and ESE. While the set of directions {Far South, South West} only introduces one: CSW. In general, a measure of how distinguishing a description $x$ is of a distribution $y$ is given by:

$$distinguishing(x, y) = \frac{|x \cap y|}{|x|}$$

Thus, for a distribution $z$ and descriptions $x$ and $y$, $x$ is a more distinguishing description of $z$ than $y$ iff distinguishing($x$,$z$) > distinguishing($y$,$z$).

2. Coverage (no false negatives) - The description should completely describe the distribution. The set of directions {Far South,South West} completely describes the above example distribution while {Far South} does not. For the set of directions $x$ and distribution $y$, the predicate $covers(x, y)$ is true iff

$$\frac{|x \cap y|}{|y|} = 1$$

3. Brevity - The set of directions should yield the shortest description of the distribution. For the above example distribution there is only one set of directions that ensures complete coverage. But when faced with a choice for example {South} and {South West, South East} brevity constraint favours {South}. In general,the set $x$ should be chosen over $y$ because it is a shorter description. For the distribution $z$ and sets of directions $x$, $y$ with equal coverage of $z$, $x$ is a shorter description of $z$ than $y$ iff $|x| < |y|$.

4. Ordering: If two descriptions have equal coverage, cardinality and are equally distinguishing for a

given distribution, a description is chosen based upon a predefined preference ordering. Each type of property is assigned a score: Cardinal = 3, Intercardinal = 2 and Gradeable = 1. Therefore, the set of directions {Far South, South West} would be assigned a value of 3.

In classification terms, the first constraint can be considered as precision and the second as recall. The algorithm firstly ranks each individual description in the set described in §4.2 according to the constraints outlined above. If a single directional term cannot be used to describe the distribution it then incrementally tries to find the highest ranking combination of directions that satisfy the coverage constraint and do not cover the whole region; otherwise, the algorithm terminates by returning the empty set. So, for the example input provided at the beginning of this section it would return the abstract syntax template shown in Figure 4. Quantifiers are selected by applying a simple threshold to the point ratio (which is recalculated should distractors be introduced): some $=> 0$, many $=> 0.5$, most $=> 0.7$. This would be realised as 'in some far southern and southwestern places'.

```
[Type: LocationSyntax
 Head: | in |
 Object: [Head: | place |
          Features: [definite:false
                     plural:true]
          Quantifier: | some |
          Modifier: [Head: | and |
                     Coord1 [Head: | southern |
                             Modifier: | far | ]
                     Coord2 [Head | southwestern | ]]]]
```

Figure 5: Phrase syntax for input in Figure 4

## 5 Evaluation and Discussion

RoadSafe has been evaluated in post-edit evaluations with meteorologists at AMI and by asking potential users to compare the quality of the summaries to corpus texts based on the same data. While evaluations have been intended to test the overall quality of the texts we have received much feedback on the geographic descriptions the system generates. We have also carried out some comparison of the direction descriptions to those in the corpus, by annotating the corpus descriptions with our adjacency matrices and running them through the system. Descriptions were compared by calculating the Jaccard coefficient between the two matrices. Overall the mean score was 0.53, with a fairly low perfect recall percentage of 30%. The low precision score is perhaps not surprising as the descriptions generated by RoadSafe are crisp and the corpus descriptions are not solely based on the input data we have available. However, the majority (67%) of partial alignments were the result of RoadSafe producing a subset of the human desciprition, e.g. northwest versus north, which indicates the system descriptions are more fine grained. In terms of the human descriptions, what was most apparent from this evaluation is the fact that they almost exclusively used the eight major points of the compass.

In terms of feedback experts have commented that generally the location descriptions generated by the system are accurate but should be more general. Of 97 post edited texts generated by the system 20% of the geographic descriptions were edited.

Most notable was feedback from twenty one road maintenance personnel, who participated in an experiment asking them to compare expert written texts to RoadSafe generated texts based on the same five data sets. The details of this experiment are to be published elsewhere; however, one of the main reasons they gave for liking the style of the generated texts was because they contained more geographic descriptions than the corresponding human ones. The fact that a data-to-text system can analyse every data point is an advantage. In contrast experts have a huge amount of knowledge and experience to draw upon and this reflects in their more general and conservative approach in their geographic descriptions. Perhaps one of their biggest criticisms of the system as a whole is that it doesn't do a good job of generating geographic descriptions that involve motion, such as 'a band of rain works east across the area'. Indeed, this was the most edited type of generated phrase during the post-edit evaluation. There has been little work to our knowledge on describing motion in the NLG literature.

There are many aspects of the generation of geographic that haven't been addressed in this paper and warrant further exploration. Particularly at the content level, there is a need to consider how to account for semantic composition effects caused by overlaying frames of reference. Another question that arises is when is it best to use an intensional rather than extensional description. There is also the question of when to use descriptions that involve relations or gradable properties. These are all choices that a data-to-text system can make that will affect how the summary is interpreted.

## 6 Conclusions

This paper has described an approach for generating approximate geographic descriptions involving regions in the RoadSafe system, which is based on empirical work carried out in the weather domain. Our strategy takes into account constraints on what constitutes a good reference in the application domain described, by taking into account pragmatic factors imposed by both the task context and the end user. What is most apparent from our empirical studies is that geographic descriptions describing georeferenced data are influenced by not only by location but also task context. An important observation based on our evaluation studies is that NLG systems by virtue of their ability to analyse input data exhaustively can generate descriptions that are more useful to end users than those generated by human experts.

## References


R. Dale and E. Reiter. 1995. Computational interpretations of the gricean maxims in the generation of referring expressions. *Cognitive Science*, 19:233–263.

R Dale, S Geldof, and J-P Prost. 2005. Using natural language generation in automatic route description. *Journal of Research and Practice in Information Technology*, 37(1):89–105.

C. Ebert, D. Glatz, M. Jansche, R. Meyer-Klabunde, and R. Porzel. 1996. From conceptualization to formulation in generating spatial descriptions. In U. Schmid, J. Krems, and F. Wysotzki, editors, *Proceedings of the First European Workshop on Cognitive Modeling*, pages 235–241.

John D. Kelleher and Geert-Jan M. Kruijff. 2006. Incremental generation of spatial referring expressions in situated dialog. In *Proceedings of ACL06*, pages 1041–1048.

S. Levinson. 2003. Spatial language. In Nadel L., editor, *Encyclopedia of Cognitive Science*, volume 4, pages 131–137. Nature Publishing Group.

Harvey J. Miller. 2004. Tobler's first law and spatial analysis. *Annals of the Association of American Geographers*, 93(3),:574–594.

B. Moulin and D. Kettani. 1999. Route generation and description using the notions of objects influence area and spatial conceptual map. *Spatial Cognition and Computation*, 1:227–259.

E. Reiter, S. Sripada, J. Hunter, J. Yu, and I. Davy. 2005. Choosing words in computer-generated weather forecasts. In *Artificial Intelligence*, volume 67, pages 137–169.

Kavita E Thomas and Somayajulu Sripada. 2008. What's in a message? interpreting geo-referenced data for the visually-impaired. In *Proceedings of INLG08*.

Waldo Tobler. 1970. A computer movie simulating urban growth in the detroit region. *Economic Geography*, 46(2):234–240.

Stuart Towns, Charles Callaway, and James Lester. 1998. Generating coordinated natural language and 3D animations for complex spatial explanations. In *Proceedings of the Fifteenth National Conference on Artificial Intelligence*, pages 112–119, Madison, WI.

J. Gregory Trafton. 2007. Dynamic mental models in weather forecasting. In *Proceedings of the Human Factors and Ergonomics Society 51st Annual Meeting*, pages 311–314.

R. Turner, S. Sripada, E. Reiter, and I. Davy. 2006. Generating spatio-temporal descriptions in pollen forecasts. *EACL06 Companion Volume*, pages 163–166.

R. Turner, S. Sripada, E. Reiter, and I. Davy. 2008a. Building a parallel spatio-temporal data-text corpus for summary generation. In *Proceedings of the LREC2008 Workshop on Methodologies and Resources for Processing Spatial Language*, Marrakech, Morocco.

R. Turner, S. Sripada, E. Reiter, and I Davy. 2008b. Using spatial reference frames to generate grounded textual summaries of georeferenced data. In *Proceedings of INLG08*.

B. Tversky. 1993. Cognitive maps, cognitive collages, and spatial mental models. In A.U. Frank and I. Campari, editors, *Spatial Information Theory*, pages 14–24. Springer-Verlag, Berlin.

Sebastian Varges. 2005. Spatial descriptions as referring expressions in the maptask domain. In *ENLG-05*, Aberdeen, UK.

Achille C. Varzi. 2001. Vagueness in geography. *Philosophy & Geography*, 4:1:4965.

Jette Viethen and Robert Dale. 2008. The use of spatial relations in referring expressions. In *Proceedings of INLG08*, Salt Fork, Ohio, USA.

# Class-Based Ordering of Prenominal Modifiers

**Margaret Mitchell**
Center for Spoken Language Understanding
Portland, Oregon, U.S.A
itallow@cslu.ogi.edu

### Abstract

This paper introduces a class-based approach to ordering prenominal modifiers. Modifiers are grouped into broad classes based on where they tend to occur prenominally, and a framework is developed to order sets of modifiers based on their classes. This system is developed to generate several orderings for modifiers with more flexible positional constraints, and lends itself to bootstrapping for the classification of previously unseen modifiers.

## 1 Introduction

Ordering prenominal modifiers is a necessary task in the generation of natural language. For a system to effectively generate fluent utterances, the system must determine the proper order for any given set of modifiers. The order of modifiers before a noun affects the meaning and fluency of generated utterances. Determining ways to order modifiers prenominally has been an area of considerable research (cf. Shaw and Hatzivassiloglou, 1999; Malouf, 2000).

In this paper, we establish and evaluate a classification system that can be used to order prenominal modifiers automatically. This may be implemented in a surface realization component of a natural language generation system, or may be used to help specify the ordering of properties that feed into a referring expression generation algorithm. Predictions of prenominal modifier ordering based on these classes are shown to be robust and accurate.

The work here diverges from the approaches commonly employed in modifier classification by assuming no underlying relationship between semantics and prenominal order or morphology and prenominal order. The approach instead relies on generalizing empirical evidence from a corpus. This allows the system to be robust and portable to a variety of applications, without precluding any underlying linguistic constraints.

In the next section, we discuss prior work on this topic, and address the differences in our approach. Section 3 discusses the relationship between modifier ordering and referring expression generation, a principal component of natural language generation. Section 4 describes the ideas behind the modifier classification system. Sections 5 and 6 present the materials and methodology of the current study, with a discussion of the corpus involved and the basic modules used in the process. In Section 7 we discuss the results of our study. Finally, in Section 8, we outline areas for improvement and possible future work.

## 2 Related Work

Discerning the rules governing the ordering of adjectives has been an area of research for quite some time (see, for example, Panini's work on Sanskrit grammar ca. 350 BCE). Most approaches assume an underlying relationship between semantics and prenominal position (cf. Whorf, 1945; Ziff, 1960; Bever, 1970; Danks and Glucksberg, 1971). These approaches can be characterized as predicting modifier order based on degrees of semantic closeness to the noun. This follows what is known as **Behaghel's First Law** (Behaghel, 1930):

> *Word groups:* What belongs together mentally is placed close together syntactically.
> (Clark and Clark, 1977: 545)

However, there is disagreement on the exact qualities that affect position. These theories are also difficult to implement in a generation system, as they require determining the semantic properties of each modifier used, relative to the context in which it occurs. If a modifier classification

*Proceedings of the 12th European Workshop on Natural Language Generation*, pages 50–57,
Athens, Greece, 30 – 31 March 2009. ©2009 Association for Computational Linguistics

scheme is to be implemented, it should be able to create a variety of natural, unmarked orders; be robust enough to handle a wide variety of modifiers; and be flexible enough to allow different natural orderings.

Shaw and Hatzivassiloglou (1999) examine this problem, and develop ways to order all prenominal modifier types. This includes adjectives as well as nouns, such as "baseball" in "baseball field"; gerunds, such as "running" in "running man"; and past participles, such as "heated" in "heated debate". The authors devise three different methods that may be implemented in a generation system to order these kinds of prenominal modifiers. These are the *direct evidence* method, the *transitivity* method, and the *clustering* method.

Briefly, given prenominal modifiers $a$ and $b$ in a training corpus, the direct evidence method utilizes probabilistic reasoning to determine whether the frequency count of the ordered sequence $<a,b>$ or $<b,a>$ is stronger. The transitivity method makes inferences about unseen orderings among prenominal modifiers; given a third prenominal modifier $c$, where $a$ precedes $b$ and $b$ precedes $c$, the authors can conclude that $a$ precedes $c$. In the clustering method, an order similarity metric is used to group modifiers together that share a similar relative order to other modifiers.

Shaw and Hatzivassiloglou achieve their highest prediction accuracy of 90.67% using their transitivity technique on prenominal modifiers from a medical corpus. However, with their system trained on the medical corpus and then tested on the Wall Street Journal corpus (Marcus et al., 1993), they achieve an overall prediction accuracy of only 54%. The authors conclude that prenominal modifier ordering is domain-specific.

Malouf (2000) continues this work, determining the order for sequences of prenominal adjectives by examining several different statistical and machine learning techniques. These achieve good results, ranging from 78.28% to 89.73% accuracy. Malouf achieves the best results by combining memory-based learning and positional probability, which reaches 91.85% accuracy at predicting the prenominal adjective orderings in the first 100 million tokens of the BNC. However, this analysis does not extend to other kinds of prenominal modifiers. The model is also not tested on a different domain.

The approach to modifier classification taken here is similar to the clustering method discussed by Shaw and Hatzivassiloglou. Modifiers are grouped into classes based on where they occur prenominally. This approach differs, however, in how classes are assigned. In our approach, modifiers are grouped into classes based on the frequencies with which they occur in different prenominal positions. Classes are built based not on where modifiers are positioned in respect to other modifiers, but on where modifiers are positioned in general. Grouping modifiers into classes based on prenominal positions mitigates the problems noted by Shaw and Hatzivassiloglou that ordering predictions cannot be made (1) when both $a$ and $b$ belong to the same class, (2) when either $a$ or $b$ are not associated to a class that can be ordered with respect to the other, and (3) when the evidence for one class preceding the other is equally strong for both classes.

This approach allows modifiers with strong positional preferences to be in a class separate from modifiers with weaker positional preferences. This also ensures that any prenominal modifiers $a$ and $b$ seen in the training corpus can be ordered, regardless of which particular modifiers they appear with and whether they occur together in the training data at all. This approach also has the added benefit of developing modifier classes that are usable across many different domains. Further, this method is conceptually simple and easy to implement. Although this approach is less context-sensitive than earlier work, we find that it is highly accurate, with comparable token precision. We discuss this in greater detail in Sections 6 and 7.

## 3 The Problem of Ordering Prenominal Modifiers

Generating referring expressions in part requires generating the adjectives, verbs, and nouns that modify head nouns. In order for these expressions to clearly convey the intended referent, the modifiers must appear in an order that sounds natural and mimics human language use.

For example, consider the alternation given in Figure 1. Some combinations of modifiers before a noun are more marked than others, although all are strictly speaking grammatical. This speaks to the need for a broad modifier classes to order prenominal modifiers, where individual modifiers

(1) big beautiful white wooden house

(2) ?white wooden beautiful big house

(3) comfortable red chair

(4) ?red comfortable chair

(5) big rectangular green Chinese silk carpet

(6) ?Chinese big silk green rectangular carpet

Figure 1: Grammatical Modifier Alternations (Vendler, 1968: 122)

may be ordered separately as required by particular contexts.

Along these lines, almost all referring expression generation algorithms rely on the availability of a predefined ordering or weighting of properties (Dale and Reiter, 1995; van Deemter, 2002; Krahmer et al., 2003). This requires that for every referent, an ordered or weighted listing of all the properties that can apply to it must be created before referring expression generation begins. In these models, the order or weights of the input properties map to the order of the output modifiers.

However, the method used to determine the ordering or weighting of properties is an open issue. The difficulty with capturing the ordering of properties and their corresponding modifiers stems from the problem of data sparsity. In the example in Figure 1, the modifier *silk* may be rare enough in any corpus that finding it in combination with another modifier, in order to create a generalization about its ordering constraints, is nearly impossible. Malouf (2000) examined the first million sentences of the British National Corpus and found only one sequence of adjectives for every twenty sentences. With sequences of adjectives occurring so rarely, the chances of finding information on any particular sequence is small. The data is just too sparse.

## 4 Towards a Solution

To create a flexible system capable of predicting a wide variety of orderings, we used several corpora to build broad modifier classes. Modifiers are classified by where they tend to appear prenominally, and ordering constraints between the classes determine the order for any set of modifiers. This system incorporates three main ideas:

1. Not all modifiers have equally stringent ordering preferences.
2. Modifier ordering preferences can be learned empirically.
3. Modifiers can be grouped into classes indicative of their ordering preferences.

The classification scheme therefore allows rigid as well as more loose orders (compare *big red ball* and *?red big ball* with *white floppy hat* and *floppy white hat*). It is not based on any mapping between position and semantics, morphology, or phonology, but does not exclude any such relationship in the classification: This classification scheme builds on what there is direct evidence for, independent of why each modifier appears where it does.

To create our model, all simplex noun phrases (NPs) are extracted from parsed corpora. A *simplex NP* is defined as a maximal noun phrase that includes premodifiers such as determiners and possessives but no post-nominal constituents such as prepositional phrases or relative clauses (Shaw and Hatzivassiloglou, 1999: 137). From these simplex NPs, we extract all those headed by a noun and preceded by only prenominal modifiers. This includes modifiers tagged as adjectives (JJ), nouns (NN), gerunds (VBG), and past participles (VBN). The counts and relative positions of each modifier are stored, and these are converted into position probabilities in vector file format. Modifiers are classified based on the positions in which they have the highest probabilities of occurring.

Examples of the intermediary files in this process are given in Tables 1 and 2. Table 1 lists modifiers followed by their frequency counts in each prenominal position. Table 2 lists these modifiers associated to their classes, with the proportions that determine the class.

| | | | | |
|---|---|---|---|---|
| wealthy | four 2 | three 2 | two 3 | one 1 |
| red | four 13 | three 35 | two 35 | one 21 |
| golden | four 1 | three 5 | two 5 | one 3 |
| strongest | four 5 | three 5 | two 5 | one 5 |

Table 1: Example Modifier Classification Intermediate File: Step 3

## 5 Materials

To create the training and test data, we utilize the Penn Treebank-3 (Marcus et al., 1999) releases of

| | | | | | | | |
|---|---|---|---|---|---|---|---|
| wealthy | two | two | 0.38 | | | | |
| red | two_three | three | 0.34 | two | 0.34 | | |
| golden | one_two_three | three | 0.33 | two | 0.33 | one | 0.29 |
| strongest | two_three_four | four | 0.33 | three | 0.33 | two | 0.33 |

Table 2: Example Modifier Classification Intermediate File: Step 4

the parsed Wall Street Journal corpus, the parsed Brown corpus, and the parsed Switchboard corpus. The Wall Street Journal corpus is a selection of over one million words collected from the Wall Street Journal over a three-year period. The Brown corpus is over one million words of prose written in various genres, including mystery, humor, and popular lore, collected from newspapers and periodicals in 1961. The Switchboard corpus is over one million words of spontaneous speech collected from thousands of five-minute telephone conversations. Several programs were constructed to analyze the information provided by these data. The details of each module are outlined below.

### 5.1 Code Modules

The following five components were developed (in Python) for this project.

**Modifier Extractor** – This program takes as input a parsed corpus, and outputs a list of all occurrences of all noun phrases in that corpus.
**input:** Parsed Corpus
**output:** List of simplex NPs

**Modifier Organizer** – This program takes as input a list of simplex NPs and filters out words that appear prenominally and are occasionally mistagged as modifiers. A list of these filtered words is available in Table 3. This returns a vector with frequency counts for all positions in which each observed modifier occurs.
**input:** Modifier-rich noun phrases and their frequencies
**output:** Vector file with distributional information for each modifier position

**Modifier Classifier** – This program takes as input a vector file with distributional information for each modifier's position, and from this builds our model by determining the classification for each modifier.

| | | |
|---|---|---|
| about | behind | on |
| above | in | under |
| after | inside | out |
| outside | up | over |
| down | like | past |
| near | through | off |
| the | a | |

Table 3: Filtered Mistagged Words

**input:** Vector file with distributional information for each modifier position
**output:** Ordering model: File with each modifier associated to a class

**Prenominal Modifier Ordering Predictor** – This program takes as input two files: an ordering model and a list of simplex NPs (for testing). The program then uses the model to assign a class to each modifier seen in the testing data, and predicts the ordering for all the modifiers that appear prenominally. A discussion of the ordering decisions is given below. This program then compares its predicted ordering of modifiers prenominally to the observed ordering of modifiers prenominally. It returns precision and recall values for its predictions.
**input:** Vector file with each modifier associated to a class, list of simplex NPs
**output:** Precision and recall for modifier ordering predictions

## 6 Method

### 6.1 Classification Scheme

To develop modifier classes and create our model, we assume four primary modifier positions. This assumption is based on the idea that people rarely produce more than four modifiers before a noun. This assumption covers 99.70% of our data (see Table 5). The longest noun phrases for this experiment are therefore those with five words: Four modifiers followed by a noun.

| small | smiling | white | fuzzy | bunny |
|---|---|---|---|---|
| four | three | two | one | |

Figure 2: Example Simplex NP with Prenominal Positions

Each modifier's class is determined by counting the frequency of each modifier in each position.

| | |
|---|---|
| **Class 1:** one | **Class 6:** two-three |
| **Class 2:** two | **Class 7:** three-four |
| **Class 3:** three | **Class 8:** one-two-three |
| **Class 4:** four | **Class 9:** two-three-four |
| **Class 5:** one-two | |

Table 4: Modifier Classes

This is turned into a probability over all four positions. All position probabilities $\leq 0.25$ (baseline) are discarded. Those positions that remain determine the modifier class.

To calculate modifier position for each phrase, counts were incremented for all feasible positions. This is a way of sharing evidence among several positions. For example, in the phrase *clean wooden spoon*, the adjective *clean* was counted as occurring in positions two, three, and four, while the adjective *wooden* was counted as occurring in positions one, two, and three.

The classification that emerges after applying this technique to a large body of data gives rise to the broad positional preferences of each modifier. In this way, a modifier with a strict positional preference can emerge as occurring in just one position; a modifier with a less strict preference can emerge as occurring in three.

The final class for each modifier is dependent on the positions the modifier appears in more than 25% of the time. Since there are four possible positions, 25% is the baseline: A single modifier preceding a noun has equal probability of being in each of the four positions. There are nine derivable modifier classes in this approach, listed in Table 4.

A diagram of how a modifier is associated to a class is shown in Figure 3. In this example, *red* appears in several simplex NPs. In each sequence, we associate *red* to its possible positions within the four prenominal slots. We see that *red* occurs in positions one, two and three; two, three, and four; and three and four. With only this data, *red* has a 12.5% probability of being in position one; a 25% probability of being in position two; a 37.5% probability of being in position three; and a 25% probability of being in position four. It can therefore be classified as belonging to Class 3, the class for modifiers that tend to occur in position three.

This kind of classification allows the system to be flexible to the idea that some modifiers exhibit stringent ordering constraints, while others have more loose constraints. Some modifiers may always appear immediately before the noun, while

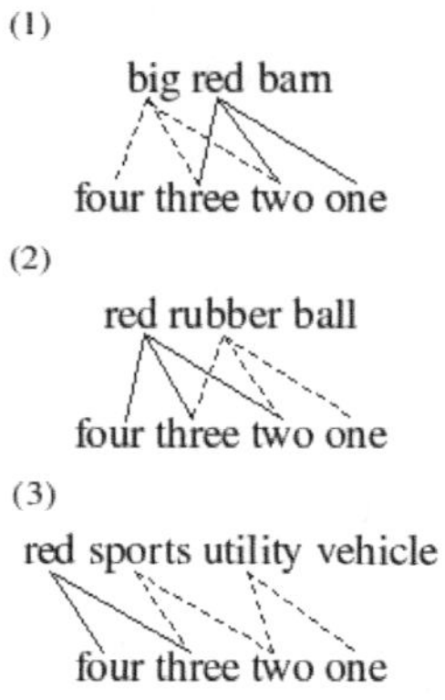


Figure 3: Constructing the Class of the Modifier *red*

others may generally appear close to or far from the noun. By counting the occurrences of each modifier in each position, classes for all observed modifiers may be derived.

The frequencies of all extracted groupings of prenominal modifiers used to build our model are shown in Table 5. The frequencies of the extracted classes are shown in Table 6.

| Mods | Count | Percentage |
|---|---|---|
| 2 | 15856 | 88.90% |
| 3 | 1770 | 9.92% |
| 4 | 155 | 0.87% |
| 5 | 21 | 0.12% |
| 6 | 1 | .03% |

Table 5: Frequency of Prenominal Modifier Amounts

| Class | Position | Count | Percentage |
|---|---|---|---|
| 1 | one | 18 | 0.23% |
| 2 | two | 46 | 0.68% |
| 3 | three | 62 | 0.92% |
| 4 | four | 21 | 0.31% |
| 5 | one-two | 329 | 4.88% |
| 6 | two-three | 1136 | 16.86% |
| 7 | three-four | 261 | 3.87% |
| 8 | one-two-three | 2671 | 39.65% |
| 9 | two-three-four | 2193 | 32.55% |

Table 6: Modifier Class Distribution

Modifiers of Class 8, the class for modifiers that show a general preference to be closer to the head noun but do not have a strict positional preference, make up the largest portion of the data. An example of a modifier from Class 8 is *golden*. The next

| Class | Position | Generated Before Class | | | | | | | |
|---|---|---|---|---|---|---|---|---|---|
| 1 | one | 2 | 3 | 4 | 5 | 6 | 7 | 8 | 9 |
| 2 | two | 3 | 4 | 6 | 7 | 9 | | | |
| 3 | three | 4 | 7 | | | | | | |
| 4 | four | | | | | | | | |
| 5 | one-two | 2 | 3 | 4 | 6 | 7 | 8 | 9 | |
| 6 | two-three | 3 | 4 | 7 | 9 | | | | |
| 7 | three-four | 4 | | | | | | | |
| 8 | one-two-three | 4 | 6 | 7 | 9 | | | | |
| 9 | two-three-four | 4 | 7 | | | | | | |

Table 7: Proposed Modifier Ordering

largest portion of the data are modifiers of Class 9, the class for modifiers that show a general preference to be farther from the head noun. An example of a modifier from Class 9 is *strongest*. With these defined, *strongest golden arch* is predicted to sound grammatical and unmarked, but *?golden strongest arch* is not.

Some expected patterns also emerge in these groupings. For example, *green*, *yellow*, *red* and other colors are determined to be Class 6. *Explained* and *unexplained* are both determined to be Class 5, and *big* and *small* are both determined to be Class 9.

Once classified, modifiers may be ordered according to their classes. The proposed ordering constraints for these classes are listed in Table 7. Note that using this classification scheme, the ordering of modifiers that belong to the same class is not predicted. This seems to be reflective of natural language use. For example, both *wealthy* and *performing* are predicted to be Class 2. This seems reasonable; whether *wealthy performing man* or *performing wealthy man* is a more natural ordering of prenominal modifiers is at least debatable. The freedom of intra-class positioning allows for some randomization in the generation of prenominal modifiers, where other factors may be used to determine the final ordering.

### 6.2 Evaluation

In order to test how well the proposed system works, 10-fold cross-validation was used on the extracted corpora. The held-out data was selected as random lines from the corpus, with a list storing the index of each selected line to ensure no line was selected more than once. In each trial, modifier classification was learned from 90% of the data and the resulting model was used to predict the prenominal ordering of modifiers in the remaining 10%.

The modifiers preceding each noun were stored in unordered groups, and the ordering for each unordered prenominal modifier pair $\{a,b\}$ was predicted based on the classes of the modifiers in our model. The ordering predictions followed the constraints listed in Table 7. When the class was known for one modifier but not for the other, the two modifiers were ordered based on the class of the known modifier: Modifiers in Classes 1, 2, 5, and 8 were placed closer to the head noun than the unknown modifier, while modifiers in Classes 3, 4, 7, and 9 were placed farther from the head noun than the unknown modifier. If the known modifier was of Class 6 (occurring in position two-three), a random guess decided the ordering. This reflects the idea that Classes 1, 2, 5, and 8 are all classes for modifiers that broadly prefer to be closer to the head noun, while Classes 3, 4, 7, and 9 are all classes for modifiers that broadly prefer to be farther from the head noun.

In the context of classification tasks, precision and recall measurements provide useful information of system accuracy. Precision, as defined in (7), is the number of true positives divided by the number of true positives plus false positives. This is calculated here as tp/(tp + fp), where tp is the number of orderings that were correctly predicted, and fp is the number of orderings not correctly predicted. This measure provides information about how accurate the modifier classification is. Recall, as defined in (8), is the number of true positives divided by the number of true positives plus false negatives. This is calculated here as tp/(tp + fn), where tp is the number of orderings that were correctly predicted, and fn is the total number of orderings that could not be predicted by our system. This measure provides information about the proportion of modifiers in the training data that can be correctly ordered.

(7) **Precision** = tp/(tp + fp)
tp = number of orderings correctly predicted
fp = number of orderings not correctly predicted

(8) **Recall** = tp/(tp + fn)
tp = number of orderings correctly predicted
fn = number of orderings that could not be predicted

| | Precision | Recall |
|---|---|---|
| **Token** | 89.63% (0.02) | 74.14% (0.03) |
| **Type** | 90.26% (0.02) | 67.17% (0.03) |

Table 8: Precision and Recall for Prenominal Modifier Ordering

## 7 Results

Results are shown in Table 8. Our model predicts the correct order for 89.63% of unordered modifiers $\{a,b\}$ for which an ordering decision can be made, making correct predictions for 74.14% of all unordered modifiers in the test data. The system also correctly predicts 90.26% of the unordered modifier $\{a,b\}$ types in the test data for which an ordering decision can be made. This covers 67.17% of the modifier pair types in the test data. This lower value appears to be due to the large amount of modifier pairs that are in the data only once.

The values given are averages over each trial. The standard deviation for each average is given in parentheses. On average, 191 modifier pairs were ordered in each trial, based on the assigned orders of 273 individual modifiers, with an average of 23.01% of the modifiers outside of the vocabulary in each trial.

The system precision and recall here are comparable to previously reported results (see Section 2). Extending our analysis over entire simplex NPs, where we generate all possible orderings based on our system constraints, we are able to predict an average of 94.44% of the sequences for which a determination can be made. This is a correct prediction for 78.59% of all the simplex NPs in the data.

Previous attempts have achieved very poor results when testing their models on a new domain. We conclude our analysis by testing the accuracy of our models on different domains. To do this, we combine two corpora to build our model and then test this model on the third.

Combining the WSJ corpus and the Brown corpus to build our modifier classes and then testing on the Switchboard (Swbd) corpus, we achieve quite promising results. Our token precision is 89.57% and our type precision is 94.17%. However, our recall values are much lower than those reported above (63.47% and 58.18%). Other training and testing combinations follow this pattern: A model built from the Switchboard corpus and the WSJ corpus achieves 82.75% token precision and 87% type precision when tested on the Brown corpus (57.14% token recall, 51.18% type recall), while a model built from the Switchboard corpus and the Brown corpus achieves 79.82% token precision and 82.43% type precision when tested on the WSJ corpus (39.55% token recall and 27.16% type recall).

| **Training Corpus** | **Testing Corpus** | **Token Precision** | **Token Recall** |
|---|---|---|---|
| Brown+WSJ | Swbd | 89.57% | 63.47% |
| Swbd+WSJ | Brown | 82.75% | 57.14% |
| Swbd+Brown | WSJ | 79.82% | 39.55% |
| **Training Corpus** | **Testing Corpus** | **Type Precision** | **Type Recall** |
| Brown+WSJ | Swbd | 94.17% | 58.18% |
| Swbd+WSJ | Brown | 87.00% | 51.18% |
| Swbd+Brown | WSJ | 82.43% | 27.16% |

Table 9: Precision and Recall for Prenominal Modifier Ordering of a New Domain

## 8 Discussion

The system precision is comparable to previously reported results. The results show that ordering modifiers based on this classification system can aid in generating simplex noun phrases with prenominal modifiers ordered in a way that sounds natural. We now turn to a discussion of areas for future work.

It seems reasonable that the classes for previously unseen modifiers could be developed based on the known classes of surrounding modifiers. This system lends itself to bootstrapping, where a lexical acquisition task that constructed class probabilities based on the surrounding context could classify previously unseen modifiers:

| grey | shining | metallic | chain |
|---|---|---|---|
| three-four | unknown | one-two | head-noun |

Given its position and the classes of the surrounding modifiers, unknown could be two-three.

Grouping modifiers into classes that determine their order also lends itself to incorporation into generative grammars. For example, Head-driven Phrase Structure Grammar (Sag et al., 2003), a constraint-based grammatical framework that groups lexical items into broader classes, could utilize the classes proposed here to determine modifier positions prenominally. Advancing research in this area could help grow the generative capabilities of class-based grammars.

It bears mentioning that this same system was attempted on the Google Web 1T 5-Gram corpus (Brants and Franz, 2006), where we used WordNet (Miller et al., 2006) to extract sequences of nouns preceded by modifiers. The precision and recall were similar to the values reported here, however, the proportions of prenominal modifiers belied a problem in using such a corpus for this approach: 82.56% of our data had two prenominal modifiers, 16.79% had four, but only 0.65% had three. This pattern was due to the many extracted sequences of modifiers preceding a noun that were not actually simplex NPs. That is, the 5-Grams include many sequences of words in which the final one has a use as a noun and the earlier ones have uses as adjectives, but the 5-Gram itself may not be a noun phrase. We found that many of our extracted 5-Grams were actually lists of words (for example, *Chinese Polish Portuguese Romanian Russian* was observed 115 times). In the future, we would like to examine ways to use the 5-Gram corpus to supplement our system.

The results reported here are encouraging, and we hope to continue this work on a parsed version of the Gutenberg corpus (Hart, 2009). This corpus is a collection of text versions of novels and other written works, and is available online. Using a corpus of modifier-rich text such as this would aid the system in classifying a greater number of modifiers. Further work should also test how robust the acquisition of unseen modifiers is using these classes, and examine implementing this ordering system into a language generation system.

## References


Otto Behaghel. 1930. *Von Deutscher Wortstellung*, volume 44. Zeitschrift Für Deutschen, Unterricht.

Thomas G. Bever. 1970. The cognitive basis for linguistic structures. In J. R. Hayes, editor, *Cognition and the Development of Language*. Wiley, New York.

Gemma Boleda and Laura Alonso. 2003. Clustering adjectives for class acquisition. In *Proceedings of the EACL'03 Student Session*, pages 9–16, Budapest.

Thorsten Brants and Alex Franz. 2006. Web 1T 5-gram version 1. http://www.ldc.upenn.edu. Linguistic Data Consortium.

H. H. Clark and E. V. Clark. 1976. *Psychology and language: An introduction to psycholinguistics*. Harcourt Brace Jovanovich, New York.

Robert Dale and Ehud Reiter. 1995. Computational interpretations of the gricean maxims in the generation of referring expressions. *Cognitive Science*, 18:233–263.

M.A.K. Halliday and Christian Matthiessen. 1999. *Construing experience as meaning: a language-based approach to cognition*. Cassell, London.

Michael Hart. 2009. Project Gutenberg collection. http://www.gutenberg.org. Project Gutenberg.

Emiel Krahmer, Sebastiaan van Erk, and André Verleg. 2003. Graph-based generation of referring expressions. *Computational Linguistics*, 29(1):53–72.

Robert Malouf. 2000. The order of prenominal adjectives in natural language generation. In *Proceedings of the 38th Annual Meeting of the Association for Computational Linguistics*, pages 85–92, Hong Kong.

Christopher D. Manning. 1993. Automatic acquisition of a large subcategorization dictionary from corpora. In *Meeting of the Association for Computational Linguistics*, pages 235–242.

Mitchell P. Marcus, Beatrice Santorini, and Mary Ann Marcinkiewicz. 1993. Building a Large Annotated Corpus of English: The Penn Treebank. *Computational Linguistics*, 19:313–330.

Mitchell P. Marcus, Beatrice Santorini, Mary Ann Marcinkiewicz, and Ann Taylor. 1999. Treebank-3. Linguistic Data Consortium.

George A. Miller, Christiane Fellbaum, Randee Tengi, Pamela Wakefield, Helen Langone, and Benjamin R. Haskell. 2006. *WordNet: A lexical database for the english language*.

Ivan Sag, Tom Wasow, and Emily Bender. 2003. *Syntactic Theory: A Formal Introduction*. CSLI Publications, Stanford University.

James Shaw and Vasileios Hatzivassiloglou. 1999. Ordering among premodifiers. In *Proceedings of the 37th Annual Meeting of the Association for Computational Linguistics on Computational Linguistics*, pages 135–143, Morristown, NJ, USA. Association for Computational Linguistics.

Kees van Deemter. 2002. Generating referring expressions: Boolean extensions of the incremental algorithm. *Computational Linguistics*, 28(1):37–52.

Zeno Vendler. 1968. *Adjectives and Nominalizations*. Mouton.

Benjamin Lee Whorf. 1945. Grammatical categories. *Language*, 21(1):1–11.

Paul Ziff. 1960. *Semantic Analysis*. Cornell University Press, Ithaca, New York.

# Referring Expression Generation through Attribute-Based Heuristics

**Robert Dale and Jette Viethen**
Centre for Language Technology
Macquarie University
Sydney, Australia
rdale@ics.mq.edu.au | jviethen@ics.mq.edu.au

## Abstract

In this paper, we explore a corpus of human-produced referring expressions to see to what extent we can learn the referential behaviour the corpus represents. Despite a wide variation in the way subjects refer across a set of ten stimuli, we demonstrate that component elements of the referring expression generation process appear to generalise across participants to a significant degree. This leads us to propose an alternative way of thinking of referring expression generation, where each attribute in a description is provided by a separate heuristic.

## 1 Introduction

The last few years have witnessed a considerable move towards empiricism in referring expression generation; this is evidenced both by the growing body of work that analyses and tries to replicate the content of corpora of human-produced referring expressions, and particularly by the significant participation in the TUNA and GREC challenge tasks built around such activities (see, for example, (Belz and Gatt, 2007; Belz et al., 2008; Gatt et al., 2008)). One increasingly widespread observation—obvious in hindsight, but surprisingly absent from much earlier work on referring expression generation—is that one person's referential behaviour differs from that of another: given the same referential task, different subjects will choose different referring expressions to identify a target referent. Faced with this apparent lack of cross-speaker consistency in how to refer to entities, we might question the validity of any exercise that tries to develop an algorithm on the basis of data from multiple speakers.

In this paper we revisit the corpus of data that was introduced and discussed in (Viethen and Dale, 2008a; Viethen and Dale, 2008b) with the objective of determining what referential behaviour, if any, might be learned automatically from the data. We find that, despite the apparent diversity of the data when we consider the production of referring expressions across subjects, a closer examination reveals that individual attributes within referring expressions do appear to be selected on the basis of contextual factors with a high degree of consistency. This suggests that referring behaviour might be best thought of as consisting of a combination of lower-level heuristics, with each individual's overall referring behaviour being constructed from a potentially distinct combination of these common heuristics.

In Section 2 we describe the corpus we use for the experiments in this paper. In Section 3 we explore to what extent we can use this corpus to learn an algorithm for referring expression generation; in Section 4 we look more closely at the nature of individual variation within the corpus. Section 5 briefly discusses related work on the use of machine learning in referring expression generation, and Section 6 draws some conclusions and points to future work.

## 2 The Corpus

### 2.1 General Overview

The corpus we use was collected via a data gathering experiment described in (Viethen and Dale, 2008a; Viethen and Dale, 2008b). The purpose of the data gathering was to gain some insight into how human subjects use relational referring expressions, a relatively unexplored aspect of referring expression generation. Participants visited a website, where they first saw an introductory page with a set of simple instructions and a sample stimulus scene consisting of three objects. Each participant was then assigned one of two trial sets of ten scenes each; the two trial sets are superficially

*Proceedings of the 12th European Workshop on Natural Language Generation*, pages 58–65,
Athens, Greece, 30 – 31 March 2009. ©2009 Association for Computational Linguistics

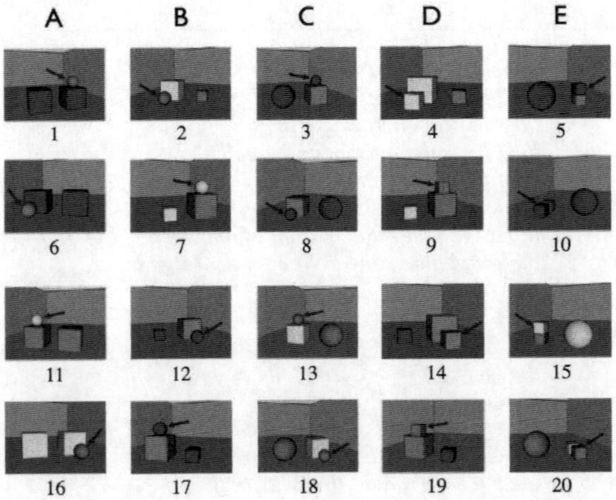


Figure 1: The stimulus scenes. The letters indicate which schema from Figure 2 each column of scenes is based on.

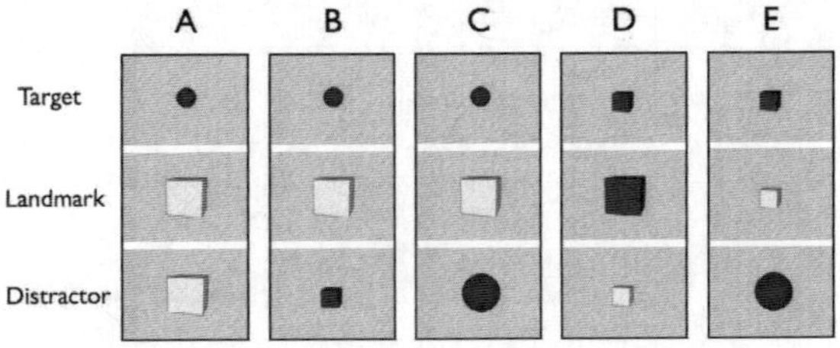


Figure 2: The *schemata* which form the basis for the stimulus scenes.

different, but the elements of the sets are pairwise identical in terms of the factors explored in the research. The complete set of 20 scenes is shown in Figure 1, where Trial Set 1 consists of Scenes 1 through 10, and Trial Set 2 consists of Scenes 11 through 20.[1]

The scenes were presented successively in a preset order, which was the same for each participant. Below each scene, the participant had to complete the sentence *Please pick up the ...* in a text box before clicking on a button to see the next scene. The task was to describe the target referent in the scene (marked by a grey arrow) in a way that would enable a friend looking at the same scene to pick it out from the other objects.

The experiment was completed by 74 participants from a variety of different backgrounds and ages; most were university-educated and in their early or mid twenties. For reasons discussed in (Viethen and Dale, 2008b), the data of 11 participants was discarded. Of the remaining 63 participants, 29 were female, while 34 were male.

## 2.2 Stimulus Design

The design of the stimuli used in the experiment is described in detail in (Viethen and Dale, 2008a). We provide a summary of the key points here.

In order to explore even the most basic hypotheses with respect to the use of relational expressions, which was the aim of the original study, scenes containing at least three objects were required. One of these objects is the intended referent, which is referred to here as the *target*. The subject has to describe the target in such a way as to distinguish it from the other two objects in the scene. Although the scenes presented to the subjects are such that spatial relations are never *necessary* to distinguish the target, they are set up so that one of the two non-target objects was clearly closer to the target. This object is referred to as the (potential) *landmark*; and we call the third object in the scene the *distractor*.

To minimise the number of variables in the experiments, scenes are restricted to only two kinds of objects, cubes and balls. The objects also vary in two dimensions: colour (either green, blue, yellow, or red); and size (either large or small).

To further reduce the number of factors in the scene design, the landmark and distractor are always placed clearly side by side, and the target is located on_top_of or directly in_front_of the landmark.

Finally, to reduce the set of possible stimuli to a manageable number, five *schemata* (see Figure 2) were created as a basis for the final stimulus set. The design of these schemata was informed by a number of research questions with regard to the use of relations; see (Viethen and Dale, 2008b). A schema determines the type and size of each object in the scenes that are based on it, and determines which objects share colour. So, for example, in scenes based on Schema C, the target is a small ball; the landmark is a large cube with different colour from the target; and the distractor is a large ball sharing its colour with the target.

[1]Scene 1 is paired with Scene 11, Scene 2 with Scene 12, and so on; in each pair, the only differences are the colour scheme used and the left–right orientation, with these variations being introduced to make the experiment less monotonous for subjects; (Viethen and Dale, 2008a) report that these characteristics of the scenes appear to have no significant effect on the forms of reference used.

| Label | Pattern | Example |
|---|---|---|
| A | ⟨tg_col, tg_type⟩ | *the blue cube* |
| B | ⟨tg_col, tg_type, rel, lm_col, lm_type⟩ | *the blue cube in front of the red ball* |
| C | ⟨tg_col, tg_type, rel, lm_size, lm_col, lm_type⟩ | *the blue cube in front of the large red ball* |
| D | ⟨tg_col, tg_type, rel, lm_size, lm_type⟩ | *the blue cube in front of the large ball* |
| E | ⟨tg_col, tg_type, rel, lm_type⟩ | *the blue cube in front of the ball* |
| F | ⟨tg_size, tg_col, tg_type⟩ | *the large blue cube* |
| G | ⟨tg_size, tg_col, tg_type, rel, lm_col, lm_type⟩ | *the large blue cube in front of the red ball* |
| H | ⟨tg_size, tg_col, tg_type, rel, lm_size, lm_col, lm_type⟩ | *the large blue cube in front of the large red ball* |
| I | ⟨tg_size, tg_col, tg_type, rel, lm_size, lm_type⟩ | *the large blue cube in front of the large ball* |
| J | ⟨tg_size, tg_col, tg_type, rel, lm_type⟩ | *the large blue cube in front of the ball* |
| K | ⟨tg_size, tg_type⟩ | *the large cube* |
| L | ⟨tg_size, tg_type, rel, lm_size, lm_type⟩ | *the large cube in front of the large ball* |
| M | ⟨tg_size, tg_type, rel, lm_type⟩ | *the large cube in front of the ball* |
| N | ⟨tg_type⟩ | *the cube* |
| O | ⟨tg_type, rel, lm_col, lm_type⟩ | *the cube in front of the red ball* |
| P | ⟨tg_type, rel, lm_size, lm_col, lm_type⟩ | *the cube in front of the large red ball* |
| Q | ⟨tg_type, rel, lm_size, lm_type⟩ | *the cube in front of the large ball* |
| R | ⟨tg_type, rel, lm_type⟩ | *the cube in front of the ball* |

Table 1: The 18 different patterns corresponding to the different forms of description that occur in the GRE3D3 corpus.

From each schema, four distinct scenes were generated, resulting in the 20 stimulus scenes shown in Figure 1. As noted above, there are really only 10 distinct 'underlying' scene types here, so in the remainder of this paper we will talk in terms of Scenes 1 through 10, where the data from the pairwise matched scenes are conflated.

### 2.3 The GRE3D3 Corpus[2]

Before conducting any quantitative data analysis, some syntactic and lexical normalisation was carried out on the data provided by the participants. In particular, spelling mistakes were corrected; normalised names were used for colour values and head nouns (for example, *box* was replaced by *cube*); and complex syntactic structures such as relative clauses were replaced with semantically equivalent simpler ones such as adjectives. These normalisation steps should be of no consequence to the analysis presented here, since we are solely interested in exploring the *semantic* content of referring expressions, not their lexical and syntactic surface structure.

For the purposes of the machine learning experiments described in this paper, we made a few further changes to the data set in order to keep the number of properties and their possible values low. We removed locative expressions that made reference to a part of the scene (58 instances) and references to size as *the same* (4 instances); so, for example, *the blue cube on top of the green cube in the right* and *the blue cube on top of the green cube of the same size* both became *the blue cube on top of the green cube*. We also removed the mention of a third object from ten descriptions in order to keep the number of possible objects per description to a maximum of two. These changes resulted in seven descriptions no longer satisfying the criterion of being fully distinguishing, so we removed these descriptions from the corpus.

[2]The data set resulting from the experiment described above is known as the GRE3D3 Corpus; the name stands for '**G**eneration of **R**eferring **E**xpressions in **3D** scenes with **3** Objects'.

## 3 Learning Description Patterns

The resulting corpus consists of 623 descriptions. Every one of these is an instance of one of the 18 patterns shown in Table 1; for ease of reference, we label these patterns A through R. Each pattern indicates the sequence of attributes used in the description, where each attribute is identified by the object it describes (tg for target, lm for landmark) and the attribute used (col, size and type for colour, size and type respectively).

Most work on referring expression generation attempts to determine what attributes should be used in a description by taking account of aspects of the context of reference. An obvious question is then whether we can learn the description patterns in this data from the contexts in which they were produced. To explore this, we chose to capture the relevant aspects of context by means of the notion of *characteristics of scenes*. The char-

| Label | Attribute | Values |
|---|---|---|
| tg_type = lm_type | Target and Landmark share Type | TRUE, FALSE |
| tg_type = dr_type | Target and Distractor share Type | TRUE, FALSE |
| lm_type = dr_type | Landmark and Distractor share Type | TRUE, FALSE |
| tg_col = lm_col | Target and Landmark share Colour | TRUE, FALSE |
| tg_col = dr_col | Target and Distractor share Colour | TRUE, FALSE |
| lm_col = dr_col | Landmark and Distractor share Colour | TRUE, FALSE |
| tg_size = lm_size | Target and Landmark share Size | TRUE, FALSE |
| tg_size = dr_size | Target and Distractor share Size | TRUE, FALSE |
| lm_size = dr_size | Landmark and Distractor share Size | TRUE, FALSE |
| rel | Relation between Target and Landmark | on top of, in front of |

Table 2: The 10 characteristics of scenes

acteristics of scenes which we hypothesize might have an impact on the choice of referential form are those summarised in Table 2; these are precisely the characteristics that were manipulated in the design of the schemata in Figure 2.

Of course, there is no one correct answer for how to refer to the target in any given scene. Figure 3 shows the distribution of different patterns across the different scenes; so, for example, some scenes (Scenes 4, 5, 9 and 10) result in only five semantically distinct referring expression forms, whereas Scene 7 results in 12 distinct referring expression forms. All of these are distinguishing descriptions, so all are acceptable forms of reference, although some contain more redundancy than others. Most obvious from the chart is that, for many scenes, there is a predominant form of reference used; so, for example, pattern F ($\langle$tg_size, tg_col, tg_type$\rangle$) accounts for 43 (68%) of the descriptions used in Scene 4, and pattern A ($\langle$tg_col, tg_type$\rangle$) is very frequently used in a number of scenes.[3]

We used Weka (Witten and Eibe, 2005) with the J48 decision tree classifer to see what correspondences might be learned between the characterisics of the scenes listed in Table 2 and the forms of referring expression used for the target referents, as shown in Table 1. The pruned decision tree learned by this method predicted the actual form of reference used in only 48% of cases under 10-fold cross-validation, but given that there are many 'gold standard' descriptions for each scene, this low score is hardly surprising; a mechanism which learns only one answer will inevitably be 'wrong' in many cases. More revealing, however, is the rule learned from the data:

**if** tg_type = dr_type
**then** use F ($\langle$tg_size, tg_col, tg_type$\rangle$)
**else** use A ($\langle$tg_col, tg_type$\rangle$)
**endif**

Patterns A and F are the two most prevalent patterns in the data, and indeed one or other appears at least once in the human data for each scene; consequently, the learned rule is able to produce a 'correct' answer for every scene.[4]

## 4 Individual Variation

One of the most striking things about the data in this corpus is the extent to which different subjects appear to do different things when they construct referring expressions, as demonstrated by the distribution of patterns in Figure 3. Another way of looking at this variation is to characterise the behaviour of each subject in terms of the sequence of descriptions they provide in response to the set of 10 stimuli.

Across the 63 subjects, there are 47 different sequences; of these, only four occur more than once (in other words, 43 subjects did not produce the same sequence of descriptions for the ten scenes as anyone else). The recurrent sequences, i.e. those used by at least two people, are shown in Table 3. Note that the most frequently recurring sequence,

[3]The chart as presented here is obviously too small to enable detailed examination, and our use of colour coding will be of no value in a monchrome rendering of the paper; however, the overall shape of the data is sufficient to demonstrate the points we make here.

[4]The fact that the rule is conditioned on a property of the distractor object may be an artefact of the stimulus set construction; this would require a more diverse set of scenes to determine.

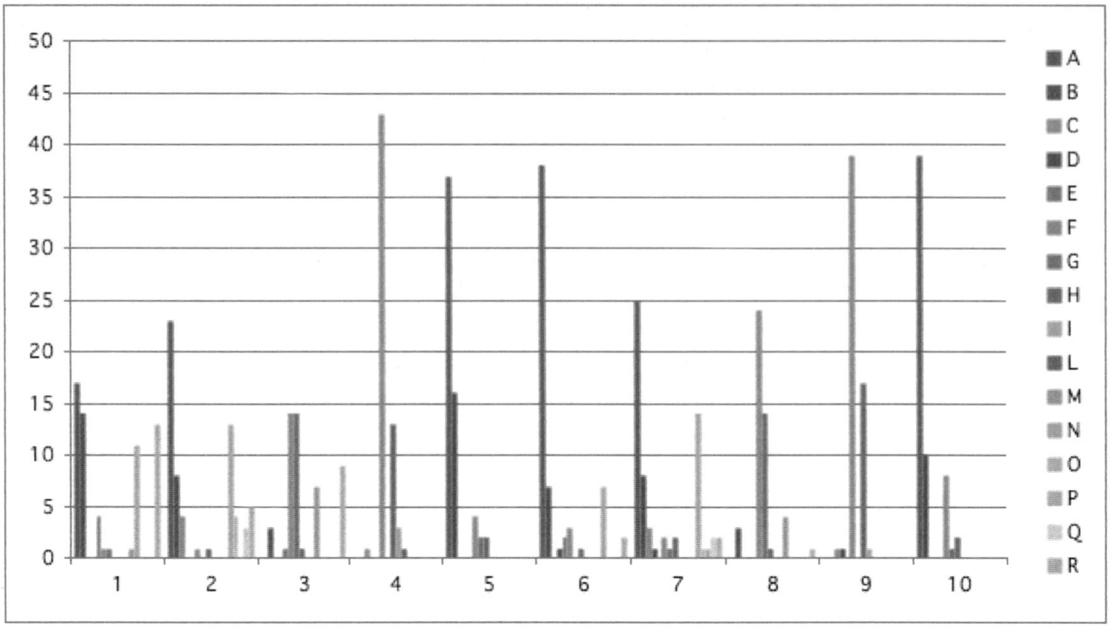


Figure 3: The profile of different description patterns (A through R) for each of the 10 scenes. The length of the bar indicates how often each of the 18 patterns is used.

which matches the behaviour of nine separate subjects, consists only of uses of patterns A and F. It remains to be seen to what extent a larger data set would demonstrate more convergence; however, the point to be made at present is that any attempt to predict the behaviour of a given speaker by means of a model of referring behaviour is going to have to take account of a great deal of indiviual variation.

Nonetheless, we re-ran the J48 classifier described in the previous section, this time using the participant ID as well as the scene characteristics in Table 2 as features. This improved pattern prediction to 57.62%. This suggests that individual differences may indeed be capturable from the data, although we would need more data than the mere 10 examples we have from each subject to learn a good predictive model.

In the face of this lack of data, another approach is to look for commonalities in the data in terms of the *constituent elements* of the different reference patterns used for each scene. This way of thinking about the data was foreshadowed by (Viethen and Dale, 2008b), who observed that the subjects could be separated into those who always used relations, those who never used relations, and those who sometimes used relations. This leads us to consider whether there are characteristics of scenes or speakers which are highly likely to result in *specific attributes* being used in descriptions. If this is the case, a decision tree learner should be able to learn for each individual attribute whether it should be included in a given situation.

An appropriate baseline for any experiments here is the success rate of simply including or not including each attribute (basically a 0-R majority class classifier), irrespective of the characteristics of the scene. Table 4 compares the results for this 'context-free' approach with one model that is trained on the characteristics of scenes, and another that takes both the characteristics of scenes and the participant ID into account.[5]

Interestingly, the 'context-free' strategies work suprisingly well for predicting the inclusion of some attributes in the human data. As has been noted in other work (see for example (Viethen et al., 2008)), colour is often included in referring expressions irrespective of its discriminatory power, and this is borne out by the data here. Perhaps more suprising is the large degree to which the inclusion of landmark size is captured by a context-free strategy.

[5]As before, the results reported are for the accuracy of a pruned J48 decision tree, under 10-fold cross-validation.

Improvement on all attribues other than target colour improves when we take into account the characteristics of the scenes, consistent with our assumptions that context does matter. When we add participant ID to the features used in the learner, performance improves further still, indicating that there are speaker-specific consistencies in the data.

It is instructive to look at the rules learned on the basis of the scene characteristics. Not surprisingly, the rule derived for target colour inclusion is simply to always include the colour (i.e., the same context-free colour inclusion rule that proves most effective in modelling the data without reference to scene characteristics). The rules for including the other attributes on the basis of scene characteristics (but not participant ID) are shown in Figure 4.

The rules learned when we include participant ID are more conplex, but can be summarised in a way that demonstrates how this approach can reveal something about the variety of ways in which speakers appear to approach the task of referring expression generation. Focussing, as an example, just on the question of whether or not to use the target object's colour in a referring expression, we find the following:

- 48 participants always used colour, irrespective of the context (this corresponds to the baseline rule learned above).

- The other participants always use colour if the target and the landmark are of the same type (which again is intuitively quite appropriate).

- When the landmark and the target are not of the same type, we see more variation in behaviour; 19 participants simply don't use colour, and the behaviour of seven can be captured via a more complex analysis: four use colour if the target and the distractor are the same size, two use colour if the target and distractor are of the same size and the target is on top of the landmark, and one uses colour if the target and distractor share colour.

Again, the specific details of the rules learned here are probably not particularly significant, based as they are on a limited data set and a set of stimuli that may give elevated status to incidental properties. However, the general point remains that we

**Target Size:**
**if** tg_type = dr_type **then** include tg_size

**Relation:**
**if** rel = on_top_of and lm_size = dr_size
**then** include rel

**Landmark Colour:**
**if** we have used a relation **then** include lm_col

**Landmark Size:**
**if** we have used a relation and tg_col = lm_col
**then** include lm_size

Figure 4: Rules learned on the basis of scene characteristics

can use this kind of analysis to identify possible rules for the inclusion of individual attributes in referring expressions.

What this suggests is that we might be able to capture the behaviour of individual speakers not in terms of an overall strategy, but as a composite of heuristics, where each heuristic accounts for the inclusion of a specific attribute. The rules, or heuristics, shown in Figure 4 are just those which are most successful in predicting the data; but there can be many other rules that might be used for the inclusion of particular attributes. So, for example, I might be the kind of speaker who just automatically includes the colour of an intended referent without any analysis of the scene; and I might be the kind of speaker who always uses a relation to a nearby landmark in describing the intended referent. Or I might be the kind of speaker who surveys the scene and takes note of whether the landmark's colour is distinctive; and so on.

Thought of in this way, each speaker's approach to reference is like a set of 'parallel gestalts' that contribute information to the description being constructed. The particular rules for inclusion that any speaker uses might vary depending on their personal past history, and perhaps even on the basis of situation-specific factors that on a given occasion might lean the speaker towards either being 'risky' or 'cautious' (Carletta, 1992).

As alluded to earlier, the specific content of the rules shown in Figure 4 may appear idiosyncratic; they are just what the limited data in the corpus

| Pattern Sequence ($\langle$Scene#, DescriptionPattern$\rangle$) | Number of subjects |
|---|---|
| $\langle$1, A$\rangle$, $\langle$2, A$\rangle$, $\langle$3, G$\rangle$, $\langle$4, F$\rangle$, $\langle$5, A$\rangle$, $\langle$6, A$\rangle$, $\langle$7, A$\rangle$, $\langle$8, G$\rangle$, $\langle$9, F$\rangle$, $\langle$10, A$\rangle$ | 2 |
| $\langle$1, B$\rangle$, $\langle$2, B$\rangle$, $\langle$3, G$\rangle$, $\langle$4, H$\rangle$, $\langle$5, B$\rangle$, $\langle$6, B$\rangle$, $\langle$7, B$\rangle$, $\langle$8, G$\rangle$, $\langle$9, H$\rangle$, $\langle$10, B$\rangle$ | 2 |
| $\langle$1, N$\rangle$, $\langle$2, N$\rangle$, $\langle$3, K$\rangle$, $\langle$4, F$\rangle$, $\langle$5, A$\rangle$, $\langle$6, N$\rangle$, $\langle$7, N$\rangle$, $\langle$8, K$\rangle$, $\langle$9, F$\rangle$, $\langle$10, A$\rangle$ | 6 |
| $\langle$1, A$\rangle$, $\langle$2, A$\rangle$, $\langle$3, F$\rangle$, $\langle$4, F$\rangle$, $\langle$5, A$\rangle$, $\langle$6, A$\rangle$, $\langle$7, A$\rangle$, $\langle$8, F$\rangle$, $\langle$9, F$\rangle$, $\langle$10, A$\rangle$ | 9 |

Table 3: Sequences of description patterns found more than once

| Attribute to Include | Baseline (0-R) | Using Scene Characteristics | Using Scene Characteristics and Participant |
|---|---|---|---|
| Target Colour | 78.33% | 78.33% | **89.57%** |
| Target Size | 57.46% | **90.85%** | 90.85% |
| Relation | 64.04% | 65.00% | **81.22%** |
| Landmark Colour | 74.80% | **87.31%** | **93.74%** |
| Landmark Size | 88.92% | **95.02%** | 95.02% |

Table 4: Accuracy of Learning Attribute Inclusion; statistically significant increases (p<.01) in bold.

supports, and some elements of the rules may be due to artefacts of the specific stimuli used in the data gathering. We would require a more diverse set of stimuli to determine whether this is the case, but the basic point stands: we can find correlations between characteristics of the scenes and the presence or absence of particular attributes in referring expressions, even if we cannot predict so well the particular combinations of these correlations that a given speaker will use in a given situation.

## 5 Related Work

There is a significant body of work on the use of machine learning in referring expression generation, although typically focussed on aspects of the problem that are distinct from those considered here.

In the context of museum item descriptions, Poesio et al. (1999) explore the decision of what *type* of referring expression NP to use to refer to a given discourse entity, using a statistical model to choose between using a proper name, a definite description, or a pronoun. More recently, Stoia et al. (2006) attempt a similar task, but this time in an interactive navigational domain; as well as determining what type of referring expression to use, they also try to learn whether a modifier should be included. Cheng et al. (2001) try to learn rules for the incorporation of non-referring modifiers into noun phrases.

A number of the contributions to the 2008 GREC and TUNA evaluation tasks (Gatt et al., 2008) have made use of machine learning techniques. The GREC task is primarily concerned with the choice of form of reference (i.e. whether a proper name, a descriptive NP or a pronoun should be used), and so is less relevant to the focus of the present paper. Much of the work on the TUNA Task is relevant, however, since this also is concerned with determining the content of referring expressions in terms of the attributes used to build a distinguishing description. In particular, Fabbrizio et al. (2008) explore the impact of individual style and priming on attribute selection for referring expression generation, and Bohnet (2008) uses a nearest-neighbour learning technique to acquire an individual referring expression generation model for each person.

Other related approaches to attribute selection in the context of the TUNA task are explored in (Gervás et al., 2008; de Lucena and Paraboni, 2008; Kelleher and Mac Namee, 2008; King, 2008).

## 6 Conclusions

We know that people's referential behaviour varies significantly. Despite this apparent variation, we have demonstrated above that there does appear to be a reasonable correlation between characteristics of the scene and the incorporation of particular attributes in a referring expression. One way to conceptualise this is that the decision as to whether or not to incorporate a given feature such as colour or size may vary from speaker to speaker; this is evidenced by the data. We might think of these as individual *reference strategies*; a good example of such a strategy, widely attested across many experiments, is the decision to include colour in a referring expression independent of its discriminatory power, perhaps because it is an easily perceivable and often-useful attribute. The overall approach to reference that is demonstrated by a given speaker then consists of the gathering together of a number of strategies; the particular combinations may vary from speaker to speaker, but as is demonstrated by the analysis in this paper, some of the strategies are widely used.

In current work, we are gathering a much larger data set using more complex stimuli. This will allow the further development and testing of the basic ideas proposed in this paper as well as their integration into a full referring expression generation algorithm.

## References


Anja Belz and Albert Gatt. 2007. The attribute selection for GRE challenge: Overview and evaluation results. In *Proceedings of UCNLG+MT: Language Generation and Machine Translation*, pages 75–83, Copenhagen, Denmark.

Anja Belz, Eric Kow, Jette Viethen, and Albert Gatt. 2008. The GREC challenge 2008: Overview and evaluation results. In *Proceedings of the Fifth International Natural Language Generation Conference*, pages 183–191, Salt Fork OH, USA.

Bernd Bohnet. 2008. The fingerprint of human referring expressions and their surface realization with graph transducers. In *Proceedings of the 5th International Conference on Natural Language Generation*, pages 207–210, Salt Fork OH, USA.

Jean C. Carletta. 1992. *Risk-taking and Recovery in Task-Oriented Dialogue*. Ph.D. thesis, University of Edinburgh.

Hua Cheng, Massimo Poesio, Renate Henschel, and Chris Mellish. 2001. Corpus-based NP modifier generation. In *Proceedings of the Second Meeting of the North American Chapter of the Association for Computational Linguistics*, Pittsburgh PA, USA.

Diego Jesus de Lucena and Ivandré Paraboni. 2008. USP-EACH: Frequency-based greedy attribute selection for referring expressions generation. In *Proceedings of the Fifth International Natural Language Generation Conference*, pages 219–220, Salt Fork OH, USA.

Giuseppe Di Fabbrizio, Amanda J. Stent, and Srinivas Bangalore. 2008. Referring expression generation using speaker-based attribute selection and trainable realization (ATTR). In *Proceedings of the Fifth International Natural Language Generation Conference*, Salt Fork OH, USA.

Albert Gatt, Anja Belz, and Eric Kow. 2008. The TUNA challenge 2008: Overview and evaluation results. In *Proceedings of the Fifth International Natural Language Generation Conference*, pages 198–206, Salt Fork OH, USA.

Pablo Gervás, Raquel Hervás, and Carlos León. 2008. NIL-UCM: Most-frequent-value-first attribute selection and best-scoring-choice realization. In *Proceedings of the Fifth International Natural Language Generation Conference*, pages 215–218, Salt Fork OH, USA.

John D. Kelleher and Brian Mac Namee. 2008. Referring expression generation challenge 2008: DIT system descriptions. In *Proceedings of the Fifth International Natural Language Generation Conference*, pages 221–223, Salt Fork OH, USA.

Josh King. 2008. OSU-GP: Attribute selection using genetic programming. In *Proceedings of the Fifth International Natural Language Generation Conference*, pages 225–226, Salt Fork OH, USA.

Massimo Poesio, Renate Henschel, Janet Hitzeman, and Rodger Kibble. 1999. Statistical NP generation: A first report. In *Proceedings of the ESSLLI Workshop on NP Generation*, Utrecht, The Netherlands.

Laura Stoia, Darla Magdalene Shockley, Donna K. Byron, and Eric Fosler-Lussier. 2006. Noun phrase generation for situated dialogs. In *Proceedings of the 4th International Conference on Natural Language Generation*, pages 81–88, Sydney, Australia.

Jette Viethen and Robert Dale. 2008a. Generating referring expressions: What makes a difference? In *Australasian Language Technology Association Workshop 2008*, pages 160–168, Hobart, Australia.

Jette Viethen and Robert Dale. 2008b. The use of spatial relations in referring expression generation. In *Proceedings of the 5th International Conference on Natural Language Generation*, pages 59–67, Salt Fork OH, USA.

Jette Viethen, Robert Dale, Emiel Krahmer, Mariët Theune, and Pascal Touset. 2008. Controlling redundancy in referring expressions. In *Proceedings of the 6th Language Resources and Evaluation Conference*, Marrakech, Morocco.

Ian H. Witten and Frank Eibe. 2005. *Data Mining: Practical Machine Learning Tools and Techniques*. Morgan Kaufmann, San Francisco, 2nd edition.

# A Model for Human Readable Instruction Generation Using Level-Based Discourse Planning and Dynamic Inference of Attributes Disambiguation

**Daniel Dionne, Salvador de la Puente, Carlos León, Raquel Hervás, Pablo Gervás**
Universidad Complutense de Madrid
Madrid, Spain
{dionnegonzalez,neo.salvador}@gmail.com,
{cleon,raquelhb}@fdi.ucm.es,pgervas@sip.ucm.es

## Abstract

This paper shows a model of automatic instruction giving for guiding human users in virtual 3D environments. A multilevel model for choosing what instruction to give in every state is presented, and so are the different modules that compose the whole generation system. How 3D information in the virtual world is used is explained, and the final order generation is detailed. This model has been implemented as a solution for the *GIVE Challenge*, an instruction generation challenge.

## 1 Introduction

Recent technology advances have made it possible to use handheld devices, like mobile phones or PDAs, to guide the user by issuing commands or descriptions about the world the user is perceiving in some sense (Muller, 2002). This possibility opens interesting avenues of research in the shape of Natural Language Generation (NLG) Systems that adapt to the user in order to provide him with the most accurate expression. However, fully operational systems applicable in real life situations are difficult and expensive to implement. Under these circumstances, virtual environments may be seen as an intermediate solution, suitable for fast prototyping of experimental solutions. Virtual environments permit experimenting in a reduced, closed world, where everything that is relevant for the purpose at hand is explicitly represented in a graphical model and under the direct control of the researcher. This allows fast set up of experimental situations where the topography, the position of landscape features, colour, light conditions and visibility factors can be modified and adapted to suit the best conditions for testing particular approaches (Blue et al., 2002) or challenges (such as guidance for disabled users with different disabilities, for instance). In view of these observations, our research is focused on developing an interactive *virtual guide (VG)*, based on NLG, to give to a human user the required set of instructions to complete a specific task.

Such a set of instructions is called a *plan*. Formally, a plan is a sorted-in-time list of instructions that the user must fulfill in order to reach some goal. There are many planning algorithms that, with the proper world representation and a list of goals, can return a list like this (LaValle, 2006). The VG can take this basic plan as the actual set of instructions to convert into natural language to explain what the user must do to complete the task. However, these instructions are usually exhaustive (step by step) and very simple because they are based on basic world representations (and interpretations) and are simple enough to perform computational operations on them. A VG that generates this kind of simple instructions, from the point of view of a human user, can be tedious, boring and a time wasting. Consider the discourse *"Turn right. Turn right. Go ahead. Turn left. Press button-1. Turn around. Go ahead. Go ahead. Take item-1...* " as an example. Instead, the VG should take advantage of the environmental knowledge of the user inferring higher level instructions (less detailed and more human-like) from the basic plan (something more along the lines of *"Go press the buton in the far wall, come back and take item-1"*). The difference is shown graphically for a simple example in Figure 1.

There are several aspects to be considered in achieving this goal. First, a human guide would phrase his or her instructions at different levels of abstraction, to optimise the communicative effect of his/her utterances in terms of striking balance between sufficient informative content and economy of expression. Second, a human guide may operate in a reactive manner, providing additional feedback whenever the user requests help. But

*Proceedings of the 12th European Workshop on Natural Language Generation*, pages 66–73,
Athens, Greece, 30 – 31 March 2009. ©2009 Association for Computational Linguistics

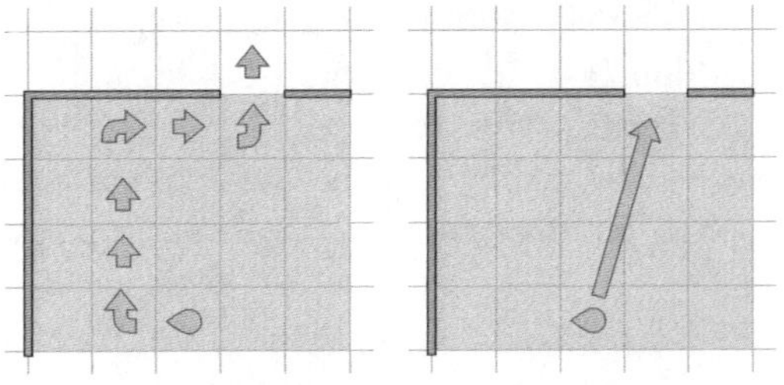


Figure 1: A comparison of a step by step plan versus a human readable plan like *"Walk out the door"*. Note the difference in the number of instructions given.

human guides are also likely to observe the person that is being guided, and be ready to intervene proactively if they notice the user seems lost or at risk. These two points are elaborated below.

In order to build *more human* levels, a VG must consider the virtual environment in a manner as close as possible to the way a human being senses the real world. To model the different levels of abstraction employed by human guides, a good solution may be to model *the world as a hierarchy of spatial levels*. People tend to limit the area where they do certain activities by some kind of logical borders. Sometimes, these borders match physical borders such as the walls that define a room or a corridor, the outside perimeter of a building, the limits of a park, or a city boundary. In other cases, such as outdoor settings, borders can be more abstract, such as the line of horizon in all directions from the observer's current position. The areas defined by these borders may be contained inside one other, resulting in a tree-like structure from the smallest spaces to greater areas, i.e. from the room where the user is standing to the city he lives in. Of course, the areas are connected in a multigraph way where each edge is a connection like a door or a natural transition. To build a usable model of this type of cognitive representation of the world is far from trivial. We will describe how we faced this point in Section 3.1 (Constructing the World). Considering such a hierarchical view of the environment when generating instructions, results in more natural and human-friendly results. Instructing someone to *"exit the room"* works better than asking them to *"advance until passing through the door"*; *"leave the building using the main entrance"* is better than a set of instructions refering to more specific spaces like *"exit this room, now go down the stairs, now go to the elevator"* and so on. We return to this matter in Section 3.2 (Planning the Discourse).

The issue of abstractions in world modelling also affects a different language generation task: referring expression generation. In providing instructions, human guides often refer to abstract concepts such as corners or "the middle of the room". These are not usually represented explicitly in your run of the mill world representation, which usually prevents NLG systems from employing them as means of optimising references. In Section 3.4 (Hidden Reference Discovery), we will see how, besides visible information, a natural approach based on the inference of other "hidden" elements or references that can be extracted from the environment helps to reduce the length of the explanation needed, and to build better references. These elements are hidden because they are not visible or trivial, and they require a specific study and calculation.

The second point to consider is reactive versus proactive guidance. A reactive guidance system may rely on feedback from the user to decide when to intervene. Consider the following two representative examples: the user can say *"I did not undertand last instruction"* and the VG system can answer by repeating the instruction or building a new one phrased in a different way but with the same meaning; or the user can say *"I am lost"* and the VG will ask the planning software to recalculate the plan considering the new user's situation. However, there are situations where the user may not realize that he is lost or that he is about to perform a dangerous action (like walking on a slippery surface, pressing an incorrect button, going in the wrong direction or crossing a street when the traffic light is red). A good guide will warn the user before he does something wrong but it should not oppress the user each time he decides to explore another route to reach the goal. In other words, the VG must watch the user actions and take part when he is on the verge of commiting a serious mistake. We will discuss about how to warn the user in Section 3.3 (Warning the User).

## 2 Previous Work

Many NLG systems have considered generation of instructions in the past. A good review is provided in (Bourne, 1999). However, most existing instruction generating system focused on performing different types of static actions (actions that do not involve changes of location of the user). The present work is focused on the task of guiding the user through virtual environments.

The GIVE (**G**enerating **I**nstructions in **V**irtual **E**nvironments) Challenge (Byron et al., 2007) operates on a scenario where a user has to solve a particular task in a simulated 3D space. A generation module has to guide the human user using natural language instructions. A software architecture is provided that allows the generation module to abstract away from the rest of the system, while having access to world information from the 3D environment, user feedback from the client module, and plans generated by an off-the-shelf planner. The work presented in this paper arose from the author's participation in the GIVE Challenge, and relies on the software architecture provided for the challenge to implement all details of the system other than the NLG module.

A fundamental task to be solved for correct instruction generation is the construction of appropriate referring expressions. This task has been the object of many research efforts in the recent past. To construct a reference to a particular entity, the algorithm takes as input a symbol corresponding to the intended referent and a list of symbols corresponding to other entities in focus based the intended referent, known as the *contrast set*. The algorithm returns a list of attribute-value pairs that correspond to the semantic content of the referring expression to be realized. The algorithm operates by iterating over the list of available attributes, looking for one that is known to the user and rules out the largest number of elements of the contrast set that have not already been ruled out.

Referring Expression Generation in physically situated environments has been studied in (Kelleher and Kruijff, 2005). The goal of this work is to develop embodied conversational robots that are capable of natural, fluent visually situated dialog with one or more interlocutors. In this kind of situation a very important aspect to take into account is how to refer to objects located in the physical environment. The authors present in the paper a computational framework for the generation of spatial locative expressions in such contexts, relying on the Reiter and Dale (Reiter and Dale, 1992) algorithm.

Another interesting work related to referring expression generation in spatial environments can be found in (Varges, 2005). The author uses the maps of the Map Task dialogue corpus as domain models, and treats spatial descriptions as referring expressions that distinguish particular points on the map from all other points (considered as distractors).

Related research can be found in (Stoia et al., 2006), where a study of how humans give orders in navigation environmnets and an algorithm implementing the observed behaviour is shown. There are many other approaches to instruction giving. Directly related with this work, it is worth mentioning `CORAL` (Dale and Geldof, 2003), which shows a full architecture for instruction giving, and `REAL` (Muller, 2002), which shows a multimodal system (graphics and text) for communicating with the user, adapting them to user behaviour.

## 3 A Functional Model of a Virtual Guide

The model of a virtual guide presented here addresses four specific issues: how to construct a representation of the world with higher levels of representation, how to generate higher instructions referring to the more abstract levels of representation, how the construction of references is implemented in terms of reference agents. A brief overview of the complete architecture of the module is also included.

### 3.1 Constructing the World

In GIVE, the world is discretized as a set of tiles. These tiles are the minimum portions of space and the user can move around from tile to tile. Orientations are discretized: the user can only face North, East, South or West. By default, the world consists of an infinite area of adjacent and accesible tiles. World representation assertations may state there is a wall between two adjacent tiles, blocking access from one to other. A 3D representation of this basic world gives the user an illusion of rooms but, from the point of view of the VG there is no data structure that reflects a hierarchy of rooms. This representation does not fit very well with the human sense of space, so a more abstract one had to be built to provide the abstract referents (rooms, corners, intersections, doors...) which we wanted our guide to use.

The first problem we had was defining a room. In architecture, a definition of room is *"any distinguishable space within a structure"*, but *distinguishable* is too vague to be of use. Figure 2 illus-

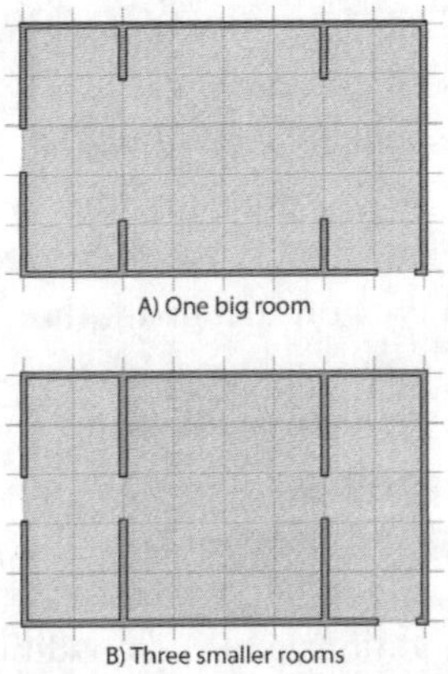


Figure 2: Defining a *distinguishable* space.

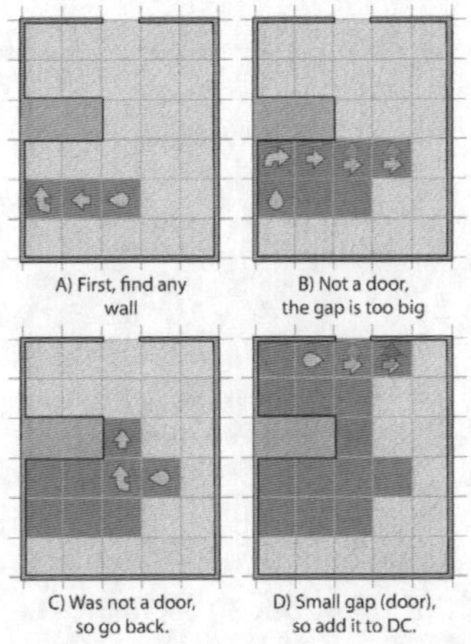


Figure 3: Looking for rooms.

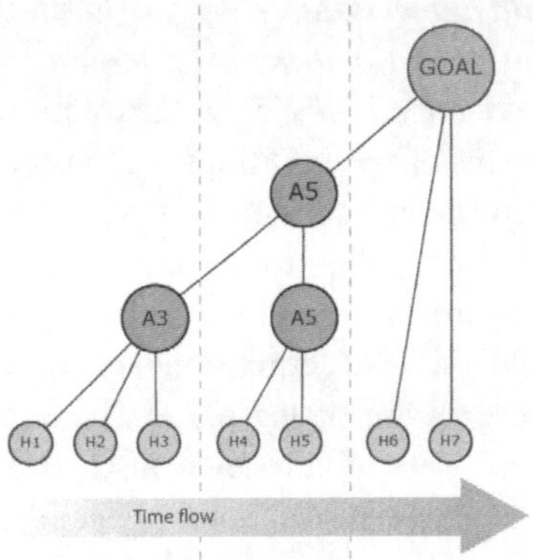


Figure 4: Tree representation of the plan at several levels.

trates the problem of defining when two spaces are distiguishable. Notice the only difference betwen A and B is the width of the gaps in relation to the size of the rooms. This problem has been extensively studied in robotics. An interesting example (Galindo et al., 2005) consists on identifying interconected "open spaces" in order to obtain an adjacency graph. From that graph, another graph can be calculated, grouping spaces to form rooms, corridors, etc.

For practical purposes, we have decided to consider that two spaces are distinguishable when the user has to go through a door to get from one to the other, with a door being a one-tile gap in a wall.

Based on this definition, we have developed an algorithm to group adjacent tiles into rooms. The idea is to follow a wall around the room until the starting point is reached, thereby establishing the perimeter of the room, then establish the set of tiles corresponding to the room using a floodfill algorithm. Breaks in walls are handled by checking whether they are small enough to be considered doors into other rooms or not. If they are doors, they are noted as entrances to other rooms (which are stored in a *room list* for subsequent processing). If they are not, the wall beyond the gap is followed as part of the boundary of the current room. A small practical example of the algorithm in operation is shown in Figure 3.

Adjoining rooms stored in the `room list` are recursively processed. Each new room discovered is connected to its adjacent rooms to obtain a high level map of the available space. An analyzer is applied to each room to establish its type (room, hall, corridor, etc) and additional properties such as size or shape. This new world representation allows the VG to refer to doors and rooms.

### 3.2 Planning the Discourse

Discourse planning must take place at two different levels of detail. The VG must plan the discourse corresponding to the whole set of instructions to be imparted until the final goal is reached. But it also needs to plan how much of that is to be communicated to the user in the next turn of the dialogue. We solve the first issue by building a multi-level representation of the expected discourse for the whole of the plan to be carried out by the user. This representation is structured like a tree, with the set of low-level instructions as leafs, and subsequent nodes of the tree representing higher level instructions that group together the lower level instructions represented by their subtrees. The solution to the second issue is described below.

We define **action** as *anything the user can do*

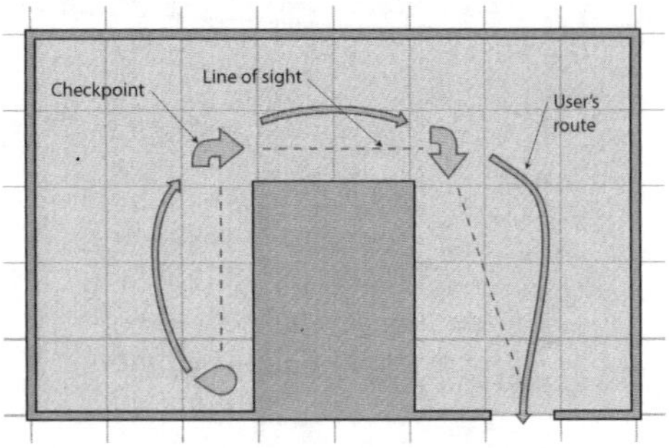


Figure 5: An n-shaped room does not let the user see the exit of the room so VG can guide the user from checkpoint to checkpoint.

*that modifies the state of the world* and **instruction** as *an action that the user should perform in order to advance in the plan.* Instructions are defined in terms of preconditions and postconditions. **Preconditions** are conditions that must be satisfied for the instruction to be performed, and **postconditions** are the conditions that must be satisfied to consider the instruction done. The *instruction tree* representation of the plan is built by grouping together sets of low-level instructions into a single high-level instruction. For instance, we group all tile-by-tile steps inside the same room to build a new instruction such as *"go from room1 to room2"*. We do not discard any low-level instruction, we just group them under the new high-level instruction, building a tree that represents the plan at different levels of abstraction (see Figure 4). This allows the user to fall back on low-level instructions at need (if, for instance, the light goes out and the VG has to guide him step by step).

An additional abstraction has been introduced to account for the tendency of humans to break the description of a complex path (where not all of the path is visible at the start) into segments made of the portions of the path that are visible at each particular point (see Figure 5). The concept of *checkpoint* is introduced for the end of each of these segments.

We have defined five types of high-level instructions: **MovementInstruction** (guides the user from tile to tile), **CheckPointInstruction** (guides the user from a his current position to a checkpoint), **Room2RoomInstruction** (guides the user from room to room), **ActionInstruction** (tells the user to interact with some element) and **GoalInstruction** (subtype of ActionInstruction concerned with achieving the final goal). Each of these high-level instructions has its own preconditions and postconditions.

The issue of how much of the instruction tree representation of the plan is addressed in terms of two conditions: how far in the original plan the user has advanced, and what level of abstraction is required for the next instruction. The first condition is easily checked over the state of the world, to establish what the current situation is. The second condition is determined by checking for satisfaction of preconditions and postconditions of the instructions at all possible levels that start from the current situation. The check starts at the highest possible level.

Instructions whose postconditions are already satisfied are pruned from the tree, as there is no longer any need to provide that instruction to the user. If preconditions are met but postconditions are not, the VG uses this instruction in the next turn, and then waits for a user action. If neither postconditions nor preconditions are satisfied for this instruction, the next (lower) level of instructions in the instruction tree is considered instead of this one. These decisions are handled by modules known as *Guide Agents.*

### 3.3 Warning the User

If the user is going to cross a street when the traffic light is red, the VG will have to warn him about it. If the warning information is more important than the guiding, the VG will have to delay instruction giving, and warn the user first. To decide about the importance of the warning part of the discourse, we defined *agents* as entities in charge of watching for special situations. Each agent takes care of a specific kind of situation that may imply some sort of hazardous or bad result. They are all independent, and may differ depending on the kind of environment, goals or even the kind of user.

Each agent has a weight that reflects its priority when being considered. An agent always evaluates its situation and returns a value in the $[0, 1]$ interval. A near zero value means there are low probabilities for the situation to happen and a near to one value means the situation is on the verge to happening. All agents that exceed a threshold value will be considered as contributors to the discourse. We sort them in descending order based on the result of multiplying each return value by the weight of the agent. If an agent is considered as a contributor, its warning is introduced in the discourse.

We defined three types of agents: **information agents** watch for interesting hotspots in an area, **status agents** watch over the user's status, and **area agents** watch over special areas, including dangerous areas.

In our entry for the GIVE challenge there was a status agent that checked how much time had passed since the last user action to identify when the user might be lost. There was one agent that checked for booby traps the user might step on (some of them resulted in loosing the game inmediately). Another one ensured the user remained within a *security area* that abstracted all possible common routes to reach the intended destination. If a user leaves the security area, he is going in the wrong direction.This security area is dynamicaly updated attending to the current user's position. Finally, **alarm agents** watch for wrong actions, controlling if user is on the verge of pressing the wrong button or leaving the room using a wrong exit. We implemented no information agents, but they would be interesting in real situations.

### 3.4 Hidden Reference Discovery

The center spot in a room is not a visible or tangible object, and finding it requires a non-trivial calculation of the room's shape. Adding it to the references container can help creating simpler and richer sentences. A reference like "the table across the room" can be generated when the listener and the target are in line with the center spot of the room, on opposite sides, independently of where the user is facing. In an indoor environment, architectural elements usually make many inferences possible. Two hallways that intersect make an intersection, two walls make a corner, etc. and though these elements might not be referenced as they are in the given environment, they should be taken into account. In a similar way, hidden relations discovery can be accomplished. Object alignments or arrangements can be revealed and used for the same purpose. Sentences like "the car in line with these pillars" can be generated. All of these additional high-level concepts and relations between them and low-level world entities are obtained by abstraction over the available representation. We create a family of *reference agents*, each one specialized in identifying candidate disambiguating properties of a different kind. Some of these properties are already explicit in the world representation (colour) and some require a process of abstraction (relations to corners, for instance). Once obtained, they become available as additional properties that may be used to disambiguate references.

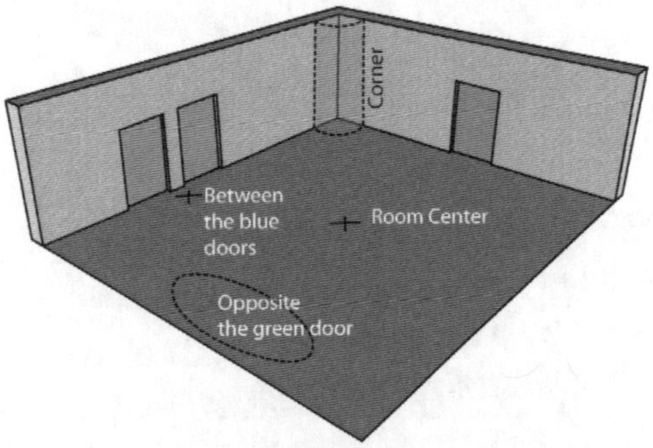


Figure 6: Hidden references in a room.

The goal of our design is to leverage the system's ability to express itself using different combinations of the complete set of disambiguating properties made available in this manner. This gives system designers a choice between having many simple agents or fewer more expressive, complex agents. This choice should be considered in terms of particular implementation details.

Reference agents rely on the Reiter and Dale algorithm (Reiter and Dale, 1992). Considering a list of distractors and the reference object, the goal is to filter the distractors list, building a reference that takes out all the distractors, so that the reference is good, not ambiguous. Each reference agent has the ability of taking out a different set of distractors, using different properties that are trivial or hidden, as explained above. Combining these agents in different ways generates different reference sentences, some of them longer but more specific, others shorter but ambiguous. What we tried to achieve is to find the right combination of reference agents that create the shortest non-ambiguous sentence. This is not a natural approach, as someone could prefer to have an ambiguous (but more human) spatial relation (Viethen and Dale, 2008) in a reference sentence. Or for example, someone could prefer having a longer reference like "the big red box that's on the third shelf from the bottom" than a perfectly specific (but not natural) reference like "the 3 kg box".

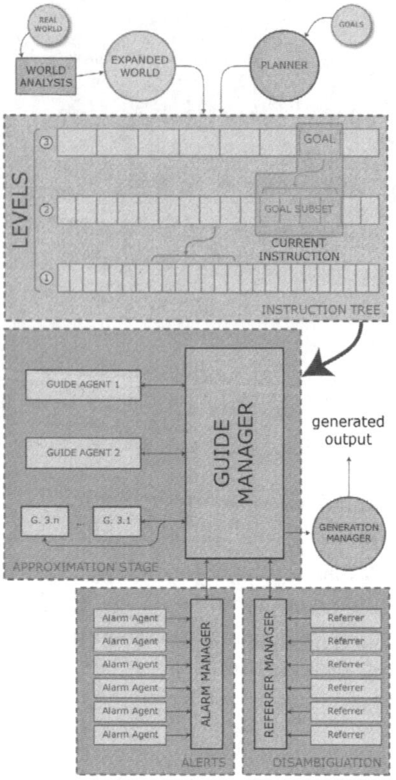


Figure 7: General design.

### 3.5 Guide architecture

The architecture design can be divided into two main parts. The *instruction tree*, shown as three interconnected lists in Figure 7, that contains all the generated levels of instructions as explained in section 3.2, and a set of components that perform the different guiding tasks. One input for the system is the "Real World", as opposed to the *Expanded World* that is generated after the analysis, as explained in sections 3.1 and 3.4. The second input is the set of goals to be achieved. After the basic instruction set is generated by the planner from the given set of goals, the *instruction tree* is generated, level by level.

Figure 7 represents a state of the guiding process where the user is trying to achieve some intermediate GOAL. The *current instruction* marker represents the location of the instruction that is to be given to the user to achieve the current GOAL (the one on the upper level). Since at this point the system has determined that *level 2* instructions should be used, the level 2 subset of instructions are represented here as part of the *current instruction*. As explained in section 3.2, the algorithm chooses what level should be used at each moment.

The *Guide Manager* makes use of the *Alarm Manager* and *Referrer Manager* to create the proper output. As explained in 3.3, the Alarm Agents examine the environment, and tell the *Guide Manager* if the user should be warned about any hazardous situation. The *Referrers* help building the proper reference sentences, as explained in sections 3.2 and 3.4, finally the different *Guide* help building the proper guiding sentences. The *Guide Manager* sends the output to the *Generation Manager*, which is in charge of generating the final output.

## 4 Discussion

The layered, multilevel hierarchy tries to imitate the way humans think about local plans, and the agent based view attemps to make instruction giving proactive rather than reactive. The algorithm first gives generalistic, global orders to get the user near the particular objective. Then, once the irrelevant information has been removed from the user point of view and it can not confuse the user, more specific orders are given. In this way, the algorithm decides what to say the "human way". Although the "human" generation of instructions could have been obtained with different algorithms, doing it the same way creates a more maintainable, natural form of expressing the operation. It would be interesting to input real human data, as done in (Stoia et al., 2006), in order to guarantee this objective.

Traditionally, planning systems have certain world representation based on discrete states which are more or less useful for finding a good solution (Chih-Wei Hsu and Chen, 2006). However, this representation is not necessarily useful for creating a natural language representation of each planning operator. For a good instruction to be generated, plain operators like "turn right" usually do not contain much information. Instruction generation systems have to find a compromise between planning efficiency and natural language content. Creating the instruction tree depends directly on figuring out what elements to include in the discourse.

The architecture shown in Section 3 has been designed with adaptability in mind, following the architecture presented in (Dale and Geldof, 2003). This shows a module layout where the text planner and the surface realizer are independently connected in the generation pipeline.

## 5 Conclusions and Future Work

The decisions to consider higher level of abstraction for both the representation of the world and the granularity of instructions, and the introduction of alarms have shown very satisfactory results over informal tests with users. Further evaluation is in process as part of the GIVE Challenge (Koller et al., 2007)[1]. The decisions presented in this paper should be revised in view of these results. The definition of a security area enables the system to provide suitable warning when the user really goes out of the way, but makes the system robust with respect to minor variations with respect to the literal plan provided by the planner.

The GIVE challenge set up was a good starting point to begin our experiments, but we are considering more complex environments to test advanced features. Extensions that promise interesting challenges are: the consideration of a continuous world representation (rather than discretised in terms of tiles and four cardinal points), more realistic test maps to extend the level of hierarchy to buildings and urban areas, and new environments designed to experiment with distorted representations of the scenary in order to simulate physical impediments like blindness.

## Acknowledgments

This research is funded by the Ministerio de Investigación, Ciencia e Innovación (GALANTE: TIN2006-14433-C02-01), and Universidad Complutense de Madrid and Comunidad de Madrid (MILU: CCG07-UCM/TIC 2803).

## References

Russell S. Blue, Jeff Wampler, G. Bowden Wise, Louis J. Hoebel, Boris Yamrom, Christopher R. Volpe, Bruce Wilde, Pascale Rondot, Ann E. Kelly, Anne Gilman, Wesley Turner, Steve Linthicum, and George Ryon. 2002. An automated approach and virtual environment for generating maintenance instructions. In *CHI '02: CHI '02 extended abstracts on Human factors in computing systems*, pages 494–495, New York, NY, USA. ACM.

Juliet C. Bourne. 1999. *Generating Effective Natural Language Instructions based on Agent Expertise*. Ph.D. thesis, University of Pennsylvania.

[1]The results of this challenge will be made available as part of the ENLG 2009 Workshop.

Donna Byron, Alexander Koller, Jon Oberlander, Laura Stoia, and Kristina Striegnitz. 2007. Generating instructions in virtual environments (GIVE): A challenge and evaluation testbed for NLG. In *Proceedings of the Workshop on Shared Tasks and Comparative Evaluation in Natural Language Generation*, Arlington.

Ruoyun Huang Chih-Wei Hsu, Benjamin W. Wah and Yixin Chen. 2006. Handling soft constraints and goals preferences in SGPlan. In *ICAPS Workshop on Preferences and Soft Constraints in Planning*.

Robert Dale and Sabine Geldof. 2003. Coral: Using natural language generation for navigational assistance. In *Proceedings of the 26th Australasian Computer Science Conference*.

C. Galindo, A. Saffiotti, S. Coradeschi, P. Buschka, J.A. Fernandez-Madrigal, and J. Gonzalez. 2005. Multi-hierarchical semantic maps for mobile robotics. *Intelligent Robots and Systems, 2005. (IROS 2005). 2005 IEEE/RSJ International Conference on*, pages 2278–2283, Aug.

John D. Kelleher and Geert-Jan M. Kruijff. 2005. A context-dependent algorithm for generating locative expressions in physically situated environments. In *Proceedings of ENLG-05*, Aberdeen, Scotland.

Alexander Koller, Johanna Moore, Barbara di Eugenio, James Lester, Laura Stoia, Donna Byron, Jon Oberlander, and Kristina Striegnitz. 2007. Shared task proposal: Instruction giving in virtual worlds. In Michael White and Robert Dale, editors, *Working group reports of the Workshop on Shared Tasks and Comparative Evaluation in Natural Language Generation*.

S. M. LaValle. 2006. *Planning Algorithms*. Cambridge University Press, Cambridge, U.K. Available at http://planning.cs.uiuc.edu/.

Christian Muller. 2002. Multimodal dialog in a mobile pedestrian navigation system. *IDS-2002*.

E. Reiter and R. Dale. 1992. A fast algorithm for the generation of referring expressions. In *Proceedings of the 14th conference on Computational linguistics*, Nantes, France.

Laura Stoia, Donna Byron, Darla Shockley, and Eric Fosler-Lussier. 2006. Sentence planning for realtime navigational instructions. In *Proceedings of the Human Language Technology Conference of the North American Chapter of the ACL*.

Sebastian Varges. 2005. Spatial descriptions as referring expressions in the maptask domain. In *Proc. of the 10th European Workshop on Natural Language Generation*.

Jett Viethen and Robert Dale. 2008. The use of spatial relations in referring expression generation. In *Fifth International Natural Language Generation Conference*.

# Learning Lexical Alignment Policies for Generating Referring Expressions in Spoken Dialogue Systems

**Srinivasan Janarthanam**
School of Informatics
University of Edinburgh
Edinburgh EH8 9AB
s.janarthanam@ed.ac.uk

**Oliver Lemon**
School of Informatics
University of Edinburgh
Edinburgh EH8 9AB
olemon@inf.ed.ac.uk

## Abstract

We address the problem that different users have different lexical knowledge about problem domains, so that automated dialogue systems need to adapt their generation choices online to the users' domain knowledge as it encounters them. We approach this problem using policy learning in Markov Decision Processes (MDP). In contrast to related work we propose a new statistical user model which incorporates the lexical knowledge of different users. We evaluate this user model by showing that it allows us to learn dialogue policies that automatically adapt their choice of referring expressions online to different users, and that these policies are significantly better than adaptive hand-coded policies for this problem. The learned policies are consistently between 2 and 8 turns shorter than a range of different hand-coded but adaptive baseline lexical alignment policies.

## 1 Introduction

In current "troubleshooting" spoken dialogue systems (SDS)(Williams, 2007), the major part of the conversation is directed by the system, while the user follows the system's instructions. Once the system decides what instruction to give the user (at the dialogue management level), it faces several decisions to be made at the natural language generation (NLG) level. These include, deciding which concepts to include in the utterance, deciding the referring expressions (RE) to use in the utterance and so on. A little-studied problem is to what extent a system could automatically align to the user's lexical knowledge by adapting its RE choices, in particular based on his domain expertise, and how this can be modelled and optimised computationally.

(Issacs and Clark, 1987) show how two interlocutors adapt their language in a conversation by assessing each other's domain expertise during dialogue, by observing how they react to each other's RE choices. This is called alignment through *Audience Design* (Clark, 1996; Bell, 1984). Using inappropriate REs in instructions has been identified as a serious problem affecting a system's usability (Molich and Nielsen, 1990).

In this paper, we treat NLG within a computational learning paradigm (Lemon, 2008; Rieser and Lemon, 2009; Janarthanam and Lemon, 2008). We examine whether a SDS can automatically learn a lexical alignment policy for audience design, which enables it to choose appropriate REs by predicting the user's lexical knowledge dynamically during the course of the dialogue. This can avoid clarification requests from the users and keep the dialogues short. The example given below describes the kind of lexical alignment behaviour that we want the system to learn. The system chooses "small white box" instead of "ADSL filter" and "monitor symbol" instead of "network icon", because it learnt that the user is a novice based on their clarification requests. However, it switches to using technical terms like "browser", when it learns that the user is not a complete novice (as he verifies the description for the network icon in Usr 4).

```
Example 1.
Sys 1>> Is your router connected
to the computer?
Usr 1>> Uh.  What's a router?
Sys 2>> It's the big black box.
Usr 2>> Ok..  yes.
Sys 3>> Do you see a small white
box connected to the router?
Usr 3>> Yes.
Sys 4>> Ok.  Is there a flashing
monitor symbol at the bottom
```

*Proceedings of the 12th European Workshop on Natural Language Generation*, pages 74–81,
Athens, Greece, 30 – 31 March 2009. ©2009 Association for Computational Linguistics

```
right of the screen?
Usr 4>> the network icon?
Sys 5>> Yes.  Is it flashing?
Usr 5>> Yes.  It is flashing.
Sys 6>> Ok.  Please open your
browser.
```

We study lexical alignment in the context of troubleshooting dialogues – where users wish to mend their broken internet connection. This task demands a new type of User Simulation.

In this paper, after a review of related work (section 2), we first present (section 3) a statistical User Simulation which supports different domain knowledge profiles and reacts accordingly to questions or instructions from an SDS. We then present a reinforcement learning model of lexical alignment due to audience design (in sections 4 & 5). We then evaluate the User Simulation (section 6), testing whether a simulation that is sensitive to a system's RE choices can be used to learn good lexical alignment policies. Finally, we compare policies learned in interaction with the User Simulation with hand-coded policies, and present the results in section 7.

## 2 Related work

Several statistical user simulation models that model a user's behaviour in a conversation have been proposed (Georgila et al., 2005; Schatzmann et al., 2006; Schatzmann et al., 2007). These models issue task specific dialogue acts like informing their search constraints, confirming values, rejecting misrecognised values, etc. However, they do not model a user population with varying domain expertise. Also, none of these models seek clarification at conceptual or lexical levels that occur naturally in conversations between real users. (Komatani et al., 2003) proposed using user models with features like skills, domain knowledge and hastiness as a part of the dialogue manager to produce adaptive responses. (Janarthanam and Lemon, 2008) presented a user simulation model that simulates a variety of users with different domain knowledge profiles. Although this model incorporated clarification acts at the conceptual level, these users ignore the issues concerning the user's understanding of the REs used by the system. In this work, in contrast to the above, we present a User Simulation model which explicitly encodes the user's lexical knowledge of the domain, understands descriptive expressions, and issues clarification requests at the lexical level.

## 3 User Simulation

Our User Simulation module simulates dialogue behaviour of different users, and interacts with the dialogue system by exchanging both dialogue acts and REs. It produces users with different knowledge profiles. The user population produced by the simulation comprises a spectrum from complete novices to experts in the domain. Simulated users behave differently from one another because of differences in their knowledge profiles. Simulated users are also able to learn new REs during interaction with the SDS. These new expressions are held in the user simulation's short term memory for later use in the conversation. Simulated users interact with the environment using an interactive mechanism that allows them to observe and manipulate the states of various domain objects. The interaction between the user and the other components is given in figure 1 (notations explained in later sections).

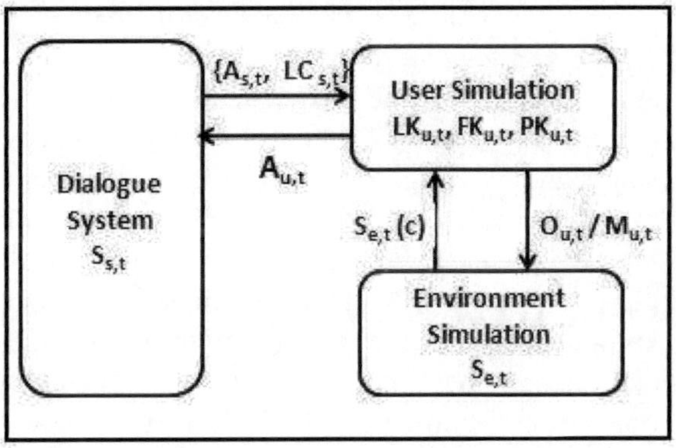


Figure 1: Experimental setup

### 3.1 Domain knowledge model

Domain experts know most of the technical terms that are used to refer to domain objects whereas novice users can only reliably identify them when descriptive expressions are used. While in the model of (Janarthanam and Lemon, 2008) knowledge profiles were presented only at conceptual levels (e.g. does the user know what a modem is?), we present them in a more granular fashion. In this model, the user's domain knowledge profile is factored into lexical ($LK_{u,t}$), factual ($FK_{u,t}$) and procedural knowledge ($PK_{u,t}$) components.

| Lexical knowledge $LK_{u,t}$ |
|---|
| vocab([modem, router], dobj1)<br>vocab([wireless, WiFi], dobj3)<br>vocab([modem power light], dobj7) |
| **Factual knowledge** $FK_{u,t}$ |
| location(dobj1)<br>location(dobj7) |
| **Procedural knowledge** $PK_{u,t}$ |
| procedure(replace_filter)<br>procedure(refresh_page) |

Table 1: Knowledge profile - Intermediate user.

A user's lexical knowledge is encoded in the format:

*vocab(referring_expressions, domain_object)*

where *referring_expressions* can be a list of expressions that the user knows can be used to talk about each $domain\_object$.

Whether the user knows facts like the location of the domain objects *(location(domain_object))* is encoded in the factual component. Similarly, the procedural component encodes the user's knowledge of how to find or manipulate domain objects (*procedure(domain_action)*). Table 1 shows an example user knowledge profile.

In order to create a knowledge spectrum, a Bayesian knowledge model is used. The current model incorporates patterns of only the lexical knowledge among the users. For instance, people who know the word "router" most likely also know "DSL light" and "modem" and so on. These dependencies between REs are encoded as conditional probabilities in the Bayesian model. Figure 2 shows the dependencies between knowledge of REs.

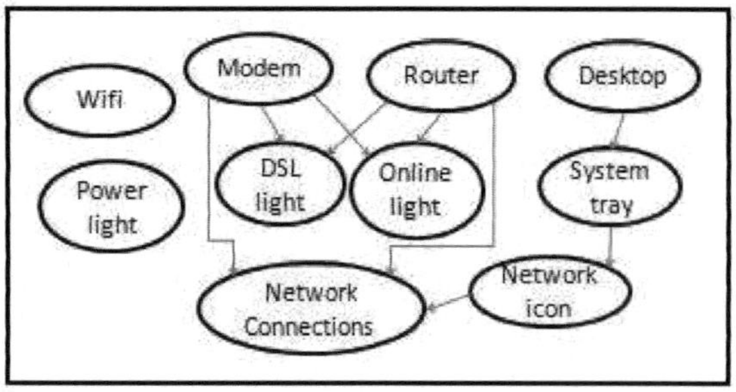


Figure 2: Bayes Net for User Lexical Knowledge

Using this Bayesian model, we instantiate different knowledge profiles for different users. The current conditional probabilities were set by hand based on intuition. In future work, these values will be populated based on simple knowledge surveys performed on real users (Janarthanam and Lemon, 2009). This method creates a spectrum of users from ones who have no knowledge of technical terms to ones who know all the technical jargon, though every profile will have a different frequency of occurrence. This difference in frequency reflects that expert users are less common than novice users.

The user's domain knowledge can be dynamically updated. The new REs, both technical and descriptive, presented by the system through clarification moves are stored in the user's short term memory. Exactly how long (in terms of dialogue turns) to retain the newly acquired knowledge is given by a retention index $RI_u$. At the end of $RI_u$ turns, the lexical item is removed from user's short term memory.

### 3.2 User Dialogue Action set

Apart from environment-directed acts, simulated users issue a number of dialogue acts. The list of dialogue actions that the user can perform in this model is given in Table 2. It consists of default moves like *provide_info* and *acknowledge* as well as some clarification moves. *Request_description* is issued when the SDS uses technical terms that the simulated user does not know, e.g. "What is a router?". *Request_verification* is issued when the SDS uses descriptive lexical items for domain objects that the user knows more technical terms for, e.g. System: "Is the black box plugged in?" User: "Do you mean the router?". *Request_disambiguation* is issued when the user faces an underspecified and ambiguous descriptive expression, e.g."User: I have two black boxes here - one with lights and one without. Which one is it?". These clarification strategies have been modeled based on (Schlangen, 2004). The user simulation also issues *request_location* and *request_procedure* dialogue acts, when it does not know the location of domain objects or how to manipulate them, respectively.

### 3.3 Environment simulation

The environment simulation includes both physical objects, such as the computer, modem, ADSL filter, etc and virtual objects, such as the browser, control panel, etc in the user's environment. Physical and virtual connections between these objects

| |
|---|
| report_problem |
| provide_info(dobj, info) |
| acknowledge |
| request_verification(x, y) |
| request_description(x) |
| request_disambiguation(x, [y1,y2]) |
| request_location(dobj) |
| request_procedure(daction) |
| thank_system |

Table 2: User Dialogue Acts.

are also simulated. At the start of every dialogue, the environment is initiated to a faulty condition. Following a system instruction or question, the user issues two kinds of environment acts. It issues an observation act $O_{u,t}$ to observe the status of a domain object and a manipulation act $M_{u,t}$ to change the state of the environment ($S_{e,t}$). The simulation also includes task irrelevant objects in order to confuse the users with underspecified descriptive expressions. For instance, we simulate two domain objects that are black in colour - an external hard disk and a router. So, the users may get confused when the system uses the expression, "black box".

### 3.4 User Action Selection

User Action selection has several steps. The user's dialogue behaviour is described in the action selection algorithm (Table 3). Firstly, the user must identify all the RE choices ($REC_{s,t}$) that are used to refer to different domain objects ($dobj$) and domain actions ($daction$) in the system instruction (step 1). Secondly, the user's knowledge of the prerequisite factual ($FK_{prereq}$) and procedural ($PK_{prereq}$) knowledge components connected to the observation or manipulation action is checked. If the user does not satisfy the knowledge requirements, the user simulation issues an appropriate clarification request (steps 2 & 3). After the knowledge requirements are satisfied, the user issues environment directed actions and responds to system instruction $A_{s,t}$ (steps 4 & 5). When the system provides the user specific information, they are added to the user's short term memory (steps 6-8). Although, the action selection process is deterministic at this level, it is dependent on the users' diverse knowledge profiles, which ensures stochastic dialogue behaviour amongst different users created by the module.

| |
|---|
| greet_the_user |
| request_status(x) |
| request_action(x) |
| give_description(x) |
| accept_verification(x,y) |
| give_location(dobj) |
| give_procedure(daction) |
| close_dialogue |

Table 4: System Dialogue acts.

## 4 Dialogue System Model

The dialogue system is modeled as a reinforcement learning agent in a Markov Decision Process framework (Levin et al., 1997). At every turn, it interacts with the Simulated User by issuing a System Dialogue Act ($A_{s,t}$) along with a set of REs, called the System RE Choices ($REC_{s,t}$). $REC_{s,t}$ contains the REs that refer to various domain objects in the dialogue act $A_{s,t}$. First, the system decides the dialogue act to issue using a hand-coded dialogue strategy. Troubleshooting instructions are coded in the troubleshooting decision tree[1]. Dialogue repair moves include selecting clarification moves in response to user's request. The list of system dialogue acts is given Table 4.

The system issues various repair moves when the users are unable to carry out the system's instructions due to ignorance, non-understanding or the ambiguous nature of the instructions. The *give_description* act is used to give the user a description of the domain object previously referred to using a technical term. It is also used when the user requests disambiguation. Similarly, *accept_verification* is given when the user wants to verify whether the system is referring to a certain domain object *y* using the expression *x*.

After selecting the dialogue act $A_{s,t}$, a set of REs must be chosen to refer to each of the domain objects/actions used in the dialogue act. For instance, the dialogue act *request_status(router_dsl_light)* requires references to be made to domain objects "router" and "DSL light". For each of these references, the system chooses a RE, creating the System RE Choice $REC_{s,t}$. In this study, we have 7 domain objects and they can either be referred to using technical

[1] The Troubleshooting decision tree was hand-built using guidelines from www.orange.co.uk and is similar to the one used by their Customer Support personnel

| | |
|---|---|
| Input: | System Dialogue Act $A_{s,t}$, System Referring Expressions Choice $REC_{s,t}$ and User State $S_{u,t}$: $LK_{u,t}$, $FK_{u,t}$, $PK_{u,t}$ |
| Step 1. | $\forall$ x $\in REC_{s,t}$ |
| Step 1a. | if (vocab(x, dobj)$\in LK_{u,t}$) then next x. |
| Step 1b. | else if (description(x, dobj) & $\exists$ j ((is_jargon(j) & vocab(j, dobj) $\notin LK_{u,t}$))) then next x. |
| Step 1c. | else if (is_jargon(x) & (vocab(x, dobj) $\notin LK_{u,t}$)) then return request_description(x). |
| Step 1d. | else if (is_ambiguous(x)) then return request_disambiguation(x). |
| Step 1e. | else if (description(x, dobj) & $\exists$ j ((is_jargon(j) & vocab(j, dobj) $\in LK_{u,t}$))) then return request_verification(x, j). |
| Step 2. | if ($\exists$dobj location(dobj) $\in FK_{prereq}$ & location(dobj) $\notin FK_{u,t}$) then return request_location(dobj). |
| Step 3. | else if ($\exists$daction procedure(daction) $\in PK_{prereq}$ & procedure(daction) $\notin PK_{u,t}$) then return request_procedure(daction). |
| Step 4. | else if ($A_{s,t}$ = request_status(dobj)) then observe_env(dobj, status), return provide_info(dobj, status) |
| Step 5. | else if ($A_{s,t}$ = request_action(daction)) then manipulate_env(daction), return acknowledge. |
| Step 6. | else if ($A_{s,t}$ = give_description(j, d) & description(d, dobj)) then add_to_short_term_memory(vocab(j, dobj)), return acknowledge. |
| Step 7. | else if ($A_{s,t}$ = give_location(dobj)) then add_to_short_term_memory(location(dobj)), return acknowledge. |
| Step 8. | else if ($A_{s,t}$ = give_procedure(daction)) then add_to_short_term_memory(procedure(daction)), return acknowledge. |

Table 3: Algorithm: Simulated User Action Selection

terms or descriptive expressions. For instance, the DSL light on the router can be descriptively referred to as the "second light on the panel" or using the technical term, "DSL light". Sometimes the system has to choose between a lesser known technical term and a well-known one. Some descriptive expressions may be underspecified and therefore can be ambiguous to the user (for example, "the black box"). Choosing inappropriate expressions can make the conversation longer with lots of clarification and repair episodes. This can lead to long frustrating dialogues, affecting the task success rate. Therefore, the dialogue system must learn to use appropriate REs in its utterances. The RE choices available to the system are given in Table 5.

| |
|---|
| 1. router / black box / black box with lights |
| 2. power light / first light on the panel |
| 3. DSL light / second light on the panel |
| 4. online light / third light on the panel |
| 5. network icon / flashing computer symbol |
| 6. network connections / earth with plug |
| 7. WiFi / wireless |

Table 5: System RE choices.

The system's RE choices are based on a part of the dialogue state that records which of the technical terms the user knows. These variables are initially set to *unknown* $(u)$. During the dialogue, they are updated to *user_knows* $(y)$ or *user_doesnot_know* $(n)$ states. We therefore record the user's lexical knowledge during the course of the dialogue and let the system learn the statistical usage patterns by itself. Part of the dialogue state relevant to system's RE choices is given in Table 6.

The state can be extended to include other relevant information like the usage of various REs by the user as well to enable alignment with the user through priming (Pickering and Garrod, 2004) and personal experience (Clark, 1996). However they are not yet implemented in the present work.

## 5 Reward function

The reward function calculates the reward awarded to the reinforcement learning agent at the end of each dialogue session. Successful task completion is rewarded with 1000 points. Dialogues running beyond 50 turns are deemed

| Feature | Values |
|---|---|
| user_knows_router | y/n/u |
| user_knows_power_light | y/n/u |
| user_knows_dsl_light | y/n/u |
| user_knows_online_light | y/n/u |
| user_knows_network_icon | y/n/u |
| user_knows_network_connections | y/n/u |
| user_knows_wifi | y/n/u |

Table 6: (Part of) Dialogue state for Lexical Alignment.

unsuccessful and are awarded 0 points. The number of turns in each dialogue varies according to the system's RE choices and the simulated user's response moves. Each turn costs 10 points. The final reward is calculated as follows:

$$TaskCompletionReward(TCR) = 1000$$
$$TurnCost(TC) = 10$$
$$TotalTurnCost(TTC) = \#(Turns) * TC$$
$$FinalReward = TCR - TTC$$

The reward function therefore gives high rewards when the system produces shorter dialogues, which is possible by adaptively using appropriate REs for each user.

## 6 Training

The system was trained to produce an adaptive lexical alignment policy, which can adapt to users with different lexical knowledge profiles. Ideally, the system must interact with a number of different users in order to learn to align with them. However, with a large number of distinct Bayesian user profiles (there are 90 possible user profiles), the time taken for learning to converge is exorbitantly high. Hence the system was trained with selected profiles from the distribution. It was initially trained using two user profiles from the very extremes of the knowledge spectrum produced by the Bayesian model - complete experts and complete novices. In this study, we calibrated all users to know all the factual and procedural knowledge components, because the learning exercise was targeted only at the lexical level. With respect to the lexical knowledge, complete experts knew all the technical terms in the domain. Complete novices, on the other hand, knew only one: $power\_light$. We set the $RI_u$ to 10, so that the users do not forget newly learned lexical items for 10 subsequent turns. Ideally, we expected the system to learn to use technical terms with experts and to use descriptive expressions with novices and a mixture for intermediates. The system was trained using SARSA reinforcement learning algorithm (Sutton and Barto, 1998), with linear function approximation, for 50000 cycles. It produced around 1500 dialogues and produced an alignment policy (RL1) that adapted to users after the first turn which provides evidence about the kind of user the system is dealing with.

The system learns to get high reward by producing shorter dialogues. By learning to choose REs by adapting to the lexical knowledge of the user, it avoids unnecessary clarification and repair episodes. It learns to choose descriptive expressions for novice users and jargon for expert users. It also learns to use technical terms when all users know them (for instance, "power_light"). Due to the user's high retention (10 turns), the system learned to use newly learned items later in the dialogue.

We also trained another alignment policy (RL2) with two other intermediate high frequency user lexical profiles. These profiles (Int1 and Int2) were chosen from either ends of the knowledge spectrum close to the extremes. Int1 is a knowledge profile that is close to the novice end. It only knows two technical terms: "power_light" and "WiFi". On the other hand, Int2 is profile that is close to the expert end and knows all technical terms except: "dsl_light" and "online_light" (which are the least well-known technical terms in the user population). With respect to the other knowledge components - factual and procedural, both users know every component equally. We trained the system for 50000 cycles following the same procedure as above. This produced an alignment policy (RL2) that learned to optimize the moves, similar to RL1, but with respect to the given distinct intermediate users.

Figure 3 shows the overall dialogue reward for the 2 policies during training.

Both policies RL1 and RL2, apart from learning to adapt to the users, also learned not to use ambiguous expressions. Ambiguous expressions lead to confusion and the system has to spend extra turns for clarification. Therefore both policies learnt to avoid using ambiguous expressions.

Figure 4 shows the dialogue length variation for the 2 policies during training.

## 7 Evaluation and baselines

We evaluated both the learned policies using a testing simulation and compared the results to other baseline hand-coded policies. Unlike the training simulation, the testing simulation used the Bayesian knowledge model to produce all different kinds of user knowledge profiles. It produced around 90 different profiles in varying distribution, resembling a realistic user population. The tests were run over 250 simulated dialogues each.

Several rule-based baseline policies were manually created for the sake of comparison:

1. Random - Choose REs at random.
2. Descriptive only - Only choose descriptive expressions. If there is more than one descriptive expression it picks one randomly.
3. Jargon only - Chooses the technical terms.
4. Adaptive 1 - It starts with a descriptive expression. If the user asks for verification, it switches to technical terms for the rest of the dialogue.
5. Adaptive 2 - It starts with a technical term and switches to descriptive expressions if the user does not understand in the first turn.
6. Adaptive 3 - This rule-based policy adapts continuously based on the previous expression. For instance, if the user did not understand the technical reference to the current object, it uses a descriptive expression for the next object in the dialogue.

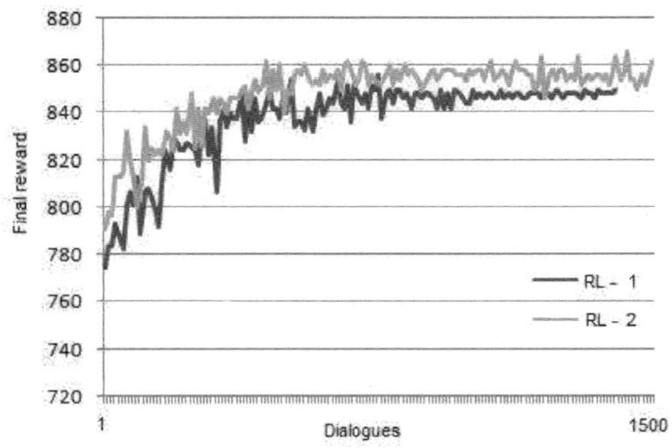


Figure 3: Final reward for RL1 & RL2.

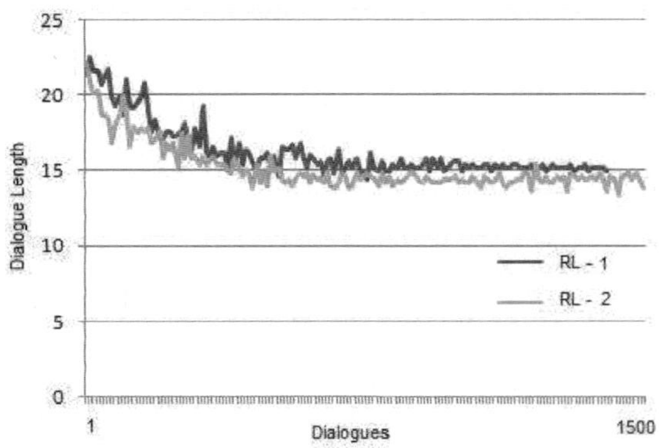


Figure 4: Dialogue length for RL1 & RL2.

| Policy | Avg. Reward | Avg. Length |
|---|---|---|
| RL2 | 830.4 | 16.98 |
| RL1 | 812.3 | 18.77 |
| Adaptive 1 | 809.6 | 19.04 |
| Adaptive 2 | 792.1 | 20.79 |
| Adaptive 3 | 780.2 | 21.98 |
| Random | 749.8 | 25.02 |
| Desc only | 796.6 | 20.34 |
| Jargon only | 762.0 | 23.8 |

Table 7: Rewards and Dialogue Length.

The first three policies (random, descriptive only and jargon only) are equivalent to policies learned using user simulations that are not sensitive to system's RE choices. In such cases, the learned policies will not have a well-defined strategy to choose REs based on user's lexical knowledge. Table 7 shows the comparative results for the different policies. RL (1 & 2) are significantly better than all the hand-coded policies. Also, RL2 is significantly better than RL1 ($p < 0.05$).

Ideally the system with complete knowledge of the user would be able to finish the dialogue in 13 turns. Similarly, if it got it wrong every time it would take 28 turns. From table 7 we see that RL2 performs better than other policies, with an average dialogue length of around 17 turns. The learned policies were able to discover the hidden dependencies between lexical items that were encoded in the Bayesian knowledge model. Although trained only on two knowledge profiles, the learned policies adapt well to unseen users, due to the generalisation properties of the linear function approximation method. Many unseen states arise when interacting with users with new profiles and both the learned policies generalise very well in such situations, whereas the baseline policies do not.

## 8 Conclusion

In this paper, we have shown that by using a statistical User Simulation that is sensitive to RE choices we are able to learn NLG policies that adaptively decide which REs to use based on audience design. We have shown that the lexical alignment policies learned with this type of simulation are better than a range of hand-coded policies.

Although lexical alignment policies could be hand-coded, the designers would need to invest significant resources every time the list of referring expressions is revised or the conditions of the dialogue change. Using reinforcement learning, near-optimal lexical alignment policies can be learned quickly and automatically. This model can be used in any task where interactions need to be tailored to different users' lexical knowledge of the domain.

### 8.1 Future work

Lexical alignment in dialogue also happens due to priming (Pickering and Garrod, 2004) and personal experience (Clark, 1996). We will examine trade-offs in various conditions, like 'instruct' versus 'teach' and low versus high retention users. Using Wizard-of-Oz studies and knowledge surveys, we plan to make the model more data-driven and realistic (Janarthanam and Lemon, 2009). We will also evaluate the learned policies with real users.

## Acknowledgements

The research leading to these results has received funding from the European Community's Seventh Framework (FP7) under grant agreement no. 216594 (CLASSiC Project www.classic-project.org), EPSRC project no. EP/E019501/1, and the British Council (UKIERI PhD Scholarships 2007-08).

## References

A. Bell. 1984. Language style as audience design. *Language in Society*, 13(2):145–204.

H. H. Clark. 1996. *Using Language*. Cambridge University Press, Cambridge.

K. Georgila, J. Henderson, and O. Lemon. 2005. Learning User Simulations for Information State Update Dialogue Systems. In *Proceedings of Eurospeech/Interspeech*.

E. A. Issacs and H. H. Clark. 1987. References in conversations between experts and novices. *Journal of Experimental Psychology: General*, 116:26–37.

S. Janarthanam and O. Lemon. 2008. User simulations for online adaptation and knowledge-alignment in Troubleshooting dialogue systems. In *Proc. SEMdial'08*.

S. Janarthanam and O. Lemon. 2009. A Wizard-of-Oz environment to study Referring Expression Generation in a Situated Spoken Dialogue Task. In *Proc. ENLG'09*.

K. Komatani, S. Ueno, T. Kawahara, and H. G. Okuno. 2003. Flexible Guidance Generation using User Model in Spoken Dialogue Systems. In *Proc. ACL'03*.

O. Lemon. 2008. Adaptive Natural Language Generation in Dialogue using Reinforcement Learning. In *Proc. SEMdial'08*.

E. Levin, R. Pieraccini, and W. Eckert. 1997. Learning Dialogue Strategies within the Markov Decision Process Framework. In *Proceedings of ASRU97*.

R. Molich and J. Nielsen. 1990. Improving a Human-Computer Dialogue. *Communications of the ACM*, 33-3:338–348.

M. J. Pickering and S. Garrod. 2004. Toward a mechanistic psychology of dialogue. *Behavioral and Brain Sciences*, 27:169–225.

V. Rieser and O. Lemon. 2009. Natural Language Generation as Planning Under Uncertainty for Spoken Dialogue Systems. In *Proc. EACL'09*.

J. Schatzmann, K. WeilHammer, M. N. Stuttle, and S. J. Young. 2006. A Survey of Statistical User Simulation Techniques for Reinforcement Learning of Dialogue Management Strategies. *Knowledge Engineering Review*, pages 97–126.

J. Schatzmann, B. Thomson, K. Weilhammer, H. Ye, and S. J. Young. 2007. Agenda-based User Simulation for Bootstrapping a POMDP Dialogue System. In *Proceedings of HLT/NAACL 2007*.

D. Schlangen. 2004. Causes and strategies for requesting clarification in dialogue. *Proceedings of the 5th SIGdial Workshop on Discourse and Dialogue (SIGDIAL 04), Boston*.

R. Sutton and A. Barto. 1998. *Reinforcement Learning*. MIT Press.

J. Williams. 2007. Applying POMDPs to Dialog Systems in the Troubleshooting Domain. In *Proc HLT/NAACL Workshop on Bridging the Gap: Academic and Industrial Research in Dialog Technology*.

# An Alignment-capable Microplanner for Natural Language Generation

**Hendrik Buschmeier**, **Kirsten Bergmann** and **Stefan Kopp**
Sociable Agents Group, CITEC, Bielefeld University
PO-Box 10 01 31, 33501 Bielefeld, Germany
{hbuschme, kbergman, skopp}@TechFak.Uni-Bielefeld.DE

## Abstract

Alignment of interlocutors is a well known psycholinguistic phenomenon of great relevance for dialogue systems in general and natural language generation in particular. In this paper, we present the alignment-capable microplanner SPUD *prime*. Using a priming-based model of interactive alignment, it is flexible enough to model the alignment behaviour of human speakers to a high degree. This will allow for further investigation of which parameters are important to model alignment and how the human–computer interaction changes when the computer aligns to its users.

## 1 Introduction

A well known phenomenon in dialogue situations is *alignment* of the interlocutors. An illustrative example is given by Levelt and Kelter (1982), who telephoned shops and either asked the question "What time does your shop close?" or the question "*At* what time does your shop close?". The answers were likely to mirror the form of the question. When asked "At what ... ?", answers tended to begin with the preposition 'at' (e.g., "At five o'clock."). Conversely, when asked "What ... ?", answers tended to begin without the preposition (e.g., "Five o'clock."). Similar alignment phenomena can be observed in many aspects of speech production *inter alia* in syntactic and lexical choice.

Pickering and Garrod (2004) present the *interactive alignment model* bringing together all alignment phenomena of speech processing in dialogue. According to this model, human language comprehension and production are greatly facilitated by alignment of the interlocutors during conversation. The process of alignment is explained through mutual priming of the interlocutors' linguistic representations. Thus, it is automatic, efficient, and non-conscious. A stronger claim of the authors is that alignment — in combination with routines and a dialogue lexicon — is a prerequisite for fluent speech production in humans.

Alignment effects also occur in human–computer interaction. Brennan (1991) and Branigan et al. (in press) present evidence that syntactic structures and lexical items used by a computer are subsequently adopted by users. For this reason, alignment is an important concept for natural language human–computer interaction in general, and for dialogue systems with natural language generation in particular. Integrating ideas from the interactive alignment model into the microplanning component of natural language generation systems should be beneficial for several reasons. First, microplanning may become more efficient since the subsets of rules or lexical items in the dialogue lexicon that have been used before can be preferentially searched. Second, due to *self*-alignment, the output of the system can become more consistent and therefore easier to understand for the user. Finally, mutual alignment of user and dialogue system might make the conversation itself more natural and, presumably, cognitively more lightweight for the user.

In this paper we present a computational model for parts of the interactive alignment model that are particularly important in the context of natural language generation. We describe how this model has been incorporated into the existing SPUD *lite* system (Stone et al., 2003; Stone, 2002) to yield the *alignment-capable* microplanner SPUD *prime*. In Section 2 we describe previous approaches to integrate alignment into natural language generation. In Sections 3 and 4, we present our priming-based model of alignment and its implementation in SPUD *prime*. In Section 5, we describe results of an evaluation on a corpus of task-oriented dialogue, and in Section 6 we conclude our work and describe possible future directions.

*Proceedings of the 12th European Workshop on Natural Language Generation*, pages 82–89,
Athens, Greece, 30 – 31 March 2009. 

## 2 Related Work

Computational modelling is an important methodology for evaluating and testing psycholinguistic theories. Thus, it is certainly not a new idea to implement the interactive alignment model computationally. Indeed, a call for "explicit computational models" is made as early as in the open peer commentary on Pickering and Garrod's (2004) paper.

Brockmann et al. (2005) and Isard et al. (2006) present a 'massive over-generation' approach to modelling alignment and individuality in natural language generation. Their system generates a huge number of alternative sentences — up to 3000 — and evaluates each of these sentences with a trigram model consisting of two parts: a default language model computed from a large corpus and a cache model which is calculated from the user's last utterance. The default language model is linearly interpolated with the cache model, whose influence on the resulting combined language model is determined by a weighting factor $\lambda \in [0, 1]$ that controls the amount of alignment the system exhibits.

Purver et al. (2006) take a more formal approach. They use an implementation of the Dynamic Syntax formalism, which uses the same representations and mechanisms for parsing as well as for generation of natural language, and extend it with a model of context. In their model, context consists of two distinct representations: a record of the semantic trees generated and parsed so far and a record of the transformation actions used for the construction of these semantic trees. *Re-use* of semantic trees and actions is used to model many dialogue phenomena in Dynamic Syntax and can also explain alignment. Thus, the authors declare alignment to be a corollary of context re-use. In particular, re-use of actions is assumed to have a considerable influence on alignment in natural language generation. Instead of looking through the complete lexicon each time a lexical item is chosen, this kind of lexical search is only necessary if no action — which constructed the same meaning in the given context before — exists in the record. If such an action exists, it can simply be re-used, which obviously leads to alignment.

A completely different approach to alignment in natural language generation is presented by de Jong et al. (2008), whose goal is to make a virtual museum guide more believable by aligning to the user's level of politeness and formality. In order to achieve this, the virtual guide analyses several features of the user's utterance and generates a reply with the same level of politeness and formality. According to the authors, lexical and syntactic alignment occur automatically because the lexical items and syntactic constructions to choose from are constrained by the linguistic style adopted.

Finally, Bateman (2006) advocates another proposal according to which alignment in dialogue is predictable for it is an inherently social activity. Following the social-semiotic view of language, Bateman suggests to model alignment as arising from register and microregister. More specifically, in his opinion priming of a linguistic representation is comparable with pre-selecting a microregister that must be considered when generating an utterance in a particular social context.

The approaches presented above primarily focus on the linguistic aspects of alignment in natural language generation. The work of Brockmann et al. (2005) and Isard et al. (2006) concentrates on the surface form of language, Bateman (2006) sees alignment arising from social-semiotic aspects, and Purver et al. (2006) are primarily interested in fitting alignment into a formal linguistic framework. In this paper we adopt a more psycholinguistic and cognitive stance on alignment. Pickering and Garrod (2004) propose that low-level priming is the basic mechanism underlying interactive alignment. Here, we propose that computational modelling of these priming mechanisms also opens up an interesting and new perspective for alignment in natural language generation.

## 3 A Priming-based Model of Alignment

We are interested here in those parts of the interactive alignment model that are most relevant for microplanning in natural language generation and it is out of our scope to model all the facets and details of direct/repetition priming in the alignment of linguistic representations. For instance, exact timing effects are likely to be not even relevant as, in an actual system, it does not matter how many milliseconds faster the retrieval of a primed lexical item is in contrast to the retrieval of an item that is not primed. For this reason we adopt an idealised view, in which priming of linguistic structures results from two basic activation mechanisms:

**Temporary activation** This kind of activation should increase abruptly and then decrease slowly over time until it reaches zero again.

**Permanent activation** This kind of activation should increase by a certain quantity and then maintain the new level.

These two mechanisms of priming are in accordance with empirical findings. Branigan et al. (1999) present evidence for rapid decay of activation of primed syntactic structures, whereas Bock and Griffin (2000) report evidence for their long(er) term activation. In any case, Reitter (2008) found both types of priming in his analysis of several corpora, with temporary activation being the more important one. The assumption that both mechanisms play a role in dialogue is also supported by Brennan and Clark (1996) whose terminology will be followed in this paper: temporary priming will be called 'recency of use effects' and permanent priming will be called 'frequency of use effects'.

Reitter (2008) assumes the repetition probability of primed syntactic structures to depend logarithmically on the distance between priming and usage. Here, recency of use effects are modelled by a more general *exponential decay* function, modified to meet the needs for modelling activation decay of primed structures:

$$ta(\Delta r) = \exp\left(-\frac{\Delta r - 1}{\alpha}\right), \qquad (1)$$

$$\Delta r \in \mathbb{N}^+; \ \alpha > 0; \quad ta \in [0,1]$$

$ta(\Delta r)$ is the temporary activation value of a linguistic structure depending on the distance $\Delta r$ between the current time $T$ and the time $r$ at which the structure was primed. The slope of the function is determined by the parameter $\alpha$. Additionally, the function is shifted right in order to yield an activation value of 1 for $\Delta r = 1$. This shift is due to the assumption of discrete time steps with a minimal distance of 1. A plot of $ta(\Delta r)$ with different values for $\alpha$ is given in Figure 1a.

Using exponential decay to model temporary activation appears to be a sensible choice that is often used to model natural processes. The advantage of this model of temporary activation lies in its flexibility. By changing the slope parameter $\alpha$, different empirical findings as well as variation among humans can be modelled easily.

Next, a mathematical model for frequency of use effects is needed. To prevent that frequency effects lead to an ever increasing activation value, a maximum activation level exists. This is also found in Reitter's (2008) corpus studies, which indicate that the frequency effect is inversely connected to the recency effect. Here, we model recency effects with a general *exponential saturation* function, modified to meet the requirements for modelling permanent activation of linguistic structures:

$$pa(f) = 1 - \exp\left(-\frac{f - 1}{\beta}\right), \qquad (2)$$

$$f \in \mathbb{N}^+; \ \beta > 0; \quad pa \in [0,1]$$

The most important point to note here is that the permanent activation value $pa(f)$ is not a function of time but a function of the frequency-counter $f$ attached to each linguistic structure. Whenever a structure is primed, its counter is increased by the value of 1. Again, the slope of the function is determined by the parameter $\beta$ and the function is

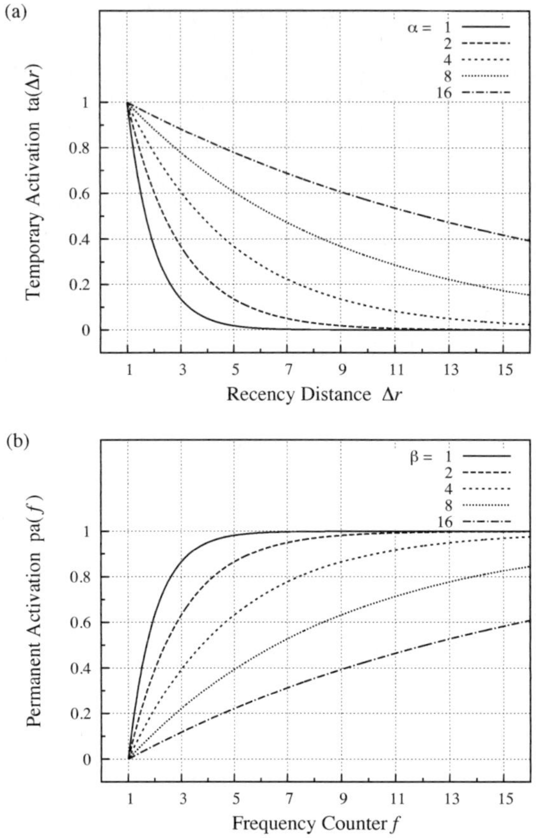


Figure 1: Plots of the mathematical functions that model recency and frequency effects. Plot (a) displays temporary activation depending on the recency of priming. Plot (b) shows permanent activation depending on the frequency count. Both are shown for different values of the slope parameter $\alpha$ respectively $\beta$.

shifted right in order to get an activation value of 0 for $f = 1$. A plot of equation (2) with different slope parameters is given in Figure 1b. Similar to the advantages of the model of temporary activation, this model for frequency effects is very flexible so that different empirical findings and human individuality can be expressed easily.

Now, both priming models need to be combined for a model of alignment. We opted for a weighted linear combination of temporary and permanent activation:

$$ca(\Delta r, f) = \nu \cdot ta(\Delta r) + (1 - \nu) \cdot pa(f), \quad (3)$$

$$0 \leq \nu \leq 1; \quad ca \in [0, 1]$$

Different values of $\nu$ allow different forms of alignment. With a value of $\nu = 0.5$ recency and frequency effects are equally important, with a value of $\nu = 1$ alignment depends on recency only, and with a value of $\nu = 0$ alignment is governed solely by frequency. Being able to adjust the influence of the different sorts of priming on alignment is crucial as it has not yet been empirically determined to what extent recency and frequency of use affect alignment (in Section 5.2 we will exploit this flexibility for matching empircial data).

In contrast to the models of alignment presented in Section 2, the computational alignment model presented here will not only consider alignment between the interlocutors (interpersonal- or *other-alignment),* but also alignment to oneself (intrapersonal- or *self-alignment*). Pickering et al. (2003) present results from three experiments which suggest self-alignment to be even more important than other-alignment. In our model, self-alignment is accounted for with the same priming-based mechanisms. To this end, four counters are attached to each linguistic structure:

- $\Delta r_s$: recency of use by the system itself
- $\Delta r_o$: recency of use by the interlocutor
- $f_s$: frequency of use by the system itself
- $f_o$: frequency of use by the interlocutor

The overall activation value of the structure is a linear combination of the combined activation value $ca(\Delta r_s, f_s)$ and the combined activation value $ca(\Delta r_o, f_o)$ from equation (3):

$$act(\Delta r_s, f_s, \Delta r_o, f_o) = \lambda \cdot (\mu \cdot ca(\Delta r_s, f_s) + (1 - \mu) \cdot ca(\Delta r_o, f_o)), \quad (4)$$

$$0 \leq \lambda, \mu \leq 1; \quad act \in [0, 1]$$

Again, by changing the factor $\mu$, smooth interpolation between pure self-alignment ($\mu = 1$) and pure other-alignment ($\mu = 0$) is possible, which can account for different empirical findings or human individual differences. Furthermore, the strength of alignment is modelled with a scaling factor $\lambda$, which determines whether alignment is considered during generation ($\lambda > 0$) or not ($\lambda = 0$).

## 4 The Alignment-capable Microplanner SPUD *prime*

The previously described priming-based model of alignment has been implemented by extending the integrated microplanning system SPUD *lite* (Stone, 2002). SPUD *lite* is a lightweight Prolog re-implementation of the SPUD microplanning system (Stone et al., 2003) based on the context-free tree rewriting grammar formalism TAGLET. Not only the microplanner itself, but also the linguistic structures (the initial TAGLET trees) are represented as Prolog clauses.

SPUD *lite* carries out the different microplanning tasks (lexical choice, syntactic choice, referring expression generation and aggregation) at once by treating microplanning as a search problem. During generation it tries to find an utterance which is in accordance with the constraints set by its input (a grammar, a knowledge base and a query). This is done by searching the search space spanned by the linguistic grammar rules and the knowledge base until a goal state is found. Non-goal search states are preliminary utterances that are extended by one linguistic structure in each step until a syntactically complete utterance is found which conveys all the specified communicative goals. Since this search space is large even for relatively small grammars, a heuristic greedy search strategy is utilised.

Our alignment-capable microplanner SPUD *prime* extends SPUD *lite* in several ways. First, we altered the predicate for the initial TAGLET trees by adding a unique identifier ID as well as counters for self/other-recency/frequency values ($r_s$, $f_s$, $r_o$ and $f_o$; see Section 3). The activation value of an initial tree is then calculated with equation (4).

Furthermore, we have created a mechanism that enables SPUD *lite* to change the recency and frequency information attached to the initial trees online during generation. This is done in three steps with the help of Prolog's meta-programming capabilities: Firstly, the clause of a tree is retrieved from the knowledge base. Secondly, it is retracted from the knowledge base. Finally, the clause is (re-)asserted in the knowledge base with updated recency and frequency information. As a welcome side effect of this procedure, primed initial trees are moved to the top of the knowledge base and — since Prolog evaluates clauses and facts in the order of their appearance in the knowledge base — they can be accessed earlier than unprimed initial trees or initial trees that were primed longer ago. Thus, in SPUD *prime* recency of priming directly influences the access of linguistic structures.

Most importantly, the activation values of the initial trees are considered during generation. Thus, in addition to the evaluation measures used by SPUD *lite*'s heuristic state evaluation function, the mean activation value

$$\overline{act}(S) = \frac{\sum_{i=1}^{N} act_{t_i}(\Delta r_{s_{t_i}}, f_{s_{t_i}}, \Delta r_{o_{t_i}}, f_{o_{t_i}})}{N}$$

of the $N$ initial trees $\{t_1, \ldots, t_N\}$ of a given search state $S$ is taken into account as a further evaluation measure. Hence, when SPUD *prime* evaluates (otherwise equal) successor search states, the one with the highest mean activation value is chosen as the next current state.

## 5 Evaluation

In order to find out whether our priming-based alignment model and its implementation work as intended, we evaluated SPUD *prime* on a corpus that was collected in an experiment designed to investigate the alignment behaviour of humans in a controlled fashion (Weiß et al., 2008). The part of the corpus that we used consists of eight recorded and transcribed dialogues between two interlocutors that play the 'Jigsaw Map Game', a task in which different objects have to be placed correctly on a table. Speakers take turns in explaining each other where to place the next object in relation to the objects that are already on the table. Each speaker has to learn a set of name–object relations before the game, such that both use the same names for all but three objects. Due to this precondition, both speakers use the same lexical referring expressions for most objects and the speaker's lexical alignment behaviour for the differently named objects can be observed easily.

In our evaluation, we concentrate on the generation of nouns by simulating the uses of the three differently learned nouns in the eight dialogues from the perspective of all sixteen interlocutors. In each test, SPUD *prime* plays the role of one of the speakers talking to a simulated interlocutor who behaves exactly as in the real experiment. With this test setup we examined, first, how well SPUD *prime* can model the alignment behaviour of a real speaker in a real dialogue context and, second, whether our model is flexible enough to consistently emulate different speakers with different alignment behaviour.

In order to find the best model (i.e., the best parameter set $\{\alpha, \beta, \mu, \nu\}$) for each speaker, we simulated all tests with all parameter combinations and counted the number of mismatches between our model's choice and the real speaker's choice. To make this exhaustive search possible, we limit the set of values for the parameters $\alpha$ and $\beta$ to $\{1, 2, 4, 6, 8, 10, 14, 18, 24, 30\}$ and the set of values for the parameters $\mu$ and $\nu$ to $\{0, 0.1, 0.2, ..., 1\}$, resulting in a total of $11^2 \times 10^2 = 12100$ different parameter sets. Since we want to investigate alignment, $\lambda$ is constantly set to 1.

### 5.1 An Illustrative Example

To illustrate our evaluation method, we first present and discuss the simulation of one particular dialogue (from the Jigsaw Map Game corpus) from the perspective of participant (A). Before the experiment started, both interlocutors learned the name–object relations 'Raute' (rhombus), 'Ring' (ring), 'Schraube' (bolt) and 'Würfel' (cube), additionally participant (A) learned 'Spielfigur' (token), 'Ball' (sphere) and 'Block' (cuboid) and participant (B) learned 'Männchen' (token), 'Kugel' (sphere) and 'Klotz' (cuboid). In our simulation, we focus on the use of the differently learned names (the targets) and not on the other names (non-targets). Table 1 shows the sequence of target nouns as they occurred in the real dialogue (non-targets omitted).

For each parameter set $\{\alpha, \beta, \mu, \nu\}$ the dialogue is simulated in the following way:

- When participant (A) used a referring *non-target* noun in the dialogue, self-priming of the corresponding rule(s) in SPUD *prime*'s knowledge base is simulated (i.e., the recency and frequency counters are increased).

- When participant (A) used a referring *target* noun in the dialogue, SPUD *prime* is queried to generate a noun for the target object. Then it is noted whether the noun actually generated

| | | | | | |
|---|---|---|---|---|---|
| | B: | der Klotz | 14 | A: | der Klotz |
| 1 | A: | die Spielfigur | **15** | **A:** | **die Kugel** |
| 2 | A: | der Klotz | 16 | A: | der Klotz |
| | B: | das Männchen | | B: | der Klotz |
| | B: | der Klotz | | B: | die Kugel |
| 3 | A: | die Spielfigur | | B: | der Klotz |
| | B: | das Männchen | 17 | A: | der Klotz |
| 4 | A: | das Männchen | | B: | das Männchen |
| 5 | A: | das Männchen | | B: | der Klotz |
| 6 | A: | das Männchen | 18 | A: | das Männchen |
| 7 | A: | das Männchen | 19 | A: | der Klotz |
| 8 | A: | das Männchen | | B: | das Männchen |
| | B: | das Männchen | 20 | A: | der Ball |
| 9 | A: | das Männchen | 21 | A: | das Männchen |
| 10 | A: | der Ball | | B: | der Ball |
| | B: | der Ball | | B: | das Männchen |
| 11 | A: | der Ball | **22** | **A:** | **die Kugel** |
| 12 | A: | der Ball | 23 | A: | der Ball |
| | B: | die Kugel | | B: | der Klotz |
| | B: | das Männchen | 24 | A: | der Ball |
| 13 | A: | der Ball | | B: | der Klotz |
| | B: | die Kugel | 25 | A: | der Klotz |

Table 1: Sequence of referring target nouns used by participants (A) and (B) in our example dialogue.

is the noun used in the actual dialogue (match) or not (mismatch).

- When participant (B) used a referring noun (target or non-target), priming of the corresponding rule(s) in SPUD *prime*'s knowledge base is simulated.

The evaluation measure for a specific parameter set is the number of mismatches it produces when simulating a dialogue. Thus the parameter set (or rather sets) which produce the least number of mismatches are the ones that best model the particular speaker under consideration. For participant (A) of our example dialogue the distribution of parameter sets $p$ producing $m$ mismatches is shown in Table 2. Four parameter sets produce only two mismatches (in phrase 15 and 22; cf. Table 1) and thus our priming-based alignment model can account for 92% of the target nouns produced by speaker (A). However, it must be noted that these two mismatches occur at points in the dialogue where the alignment behaviour of (A) is not straightforward. At target noun 15, both interlocutors have already used the name 'Ball' and then both switch to 'Kugel'. The mismatch at target 22 is a special case: (A) used 'Kugel' and immediately corrected himself to 'Ball', the name he learned prior to the experiment. It seems as if the task instruction, to use the learned nouns, suddenly became prevalent.

| $m$ | 0 | 1 | 2 | 3 | 4 | 5 |
|---|---|---|---|---|---|---|
| # $p$ | 0 | 0 | 4 | 833 | 3777 | 2248 |

| $m$ | 6 | 7 | 8 | 9 | 10 | ... |
|---|---|---|---|---|---|---|
| # $p$ | 3204 | 1105 | 478 | 148 | 294 | 0 |

Table 2: Number of parameter sets $p$ leading to $m$ mismatches for participant (A) in dialogue 7.

### 5.2 Simulation Results

To evaluate our alignment-capable microplanner, we simulated the noun production for each of the interlocutors from the experiment. One dialogue has been excluded from the data analysis as the dialogue partners used nouns that none of them had learned in the priming phase. For each of the remaining 14 interlocutors we varied the parameters $\alpha$, $\beta$, $\mu$ and $\nu$ as described above to identify those parameter set(s) which result in the least number of mismatches.

Each interlocutor produced between 18 and 32 target nouns (N=14, M=23.071, SD=3.936). Our simulation runs contain between 0 and 19 mismatches overall (N=169400, M=6.35, SD=3.398). The minimal number of mismatches for each speaker simulation ranges between 0 and 6 (N=14, M=2.286, SD=1.684). That is, our model can simulate a mean of 89.9% of all target nouns (N=14, M=.899, Min=.667, Max=1.000, SD=.082), which is an improvement of 24.6% on the baseline condition (alignment switched off), where 65.3% of the target nouns are generated correctly (N=14, M=.653, Min=.360, Max=1.000, SD=.071). As already illustrated in Section 5.1, mismatches typically occur at points in the dialogue where the alignment behaviour of the interlocutor is not straightforward.

As displayed in Table 3 the parameter assignments resulting in least mismatches differ considerably from speaker to speaker. However, there are some remarkable trends to be observed in the data. As concerns the parameter $\mu$, which determines the combination of self- and other-alignment, the majority of values are in the upper range of the interval [0,1]. For 8 of 14 speakers the mean is above 0.7 with relatively low standard deviations. Only for one speaker (P13) the mean $\mu$ is below 0.3. Thus, the parameter values indicate a considerable tendency toward self-alignment in contrast to other-alignment.

For the parameter $\nu$ that interpolates between recency and frequency effects of priming, the res-

| | | | $\alpha$ | | $\beta$ | | $\mu$ | | $\nu$ | |
|---|---|---|---|---|---|---|---|---|---|---|
| | **m** | **# p** | M | SD | M | SD | M | SD | M | SD |
| P13 | 2 | 4 | 3.0 | 1.155 | 19.5 | 9.14 | .1 | .0 | .3 | .0 |
| P14 | 1 | 72 | 5.53 | 1.52 | 14.32 | 9.61 | .819 | .040 | .901 | .108 |
| P17 | 1 | 200 | 1.66 | .823 | 12.94 | 9.529 | .353 | .169 | .955 | .069 |
| P18 | 3 | 2445 | 15.37 | 8.758 | 10.98 | 9.76 | .597 | .211 | .706 | .236 |
| P19 | 0 | 4321 | 11.81 | 9.492 | 11.01 | 8.929 | .824 | .148 | .387 | .291 |
| P20 | 2 | 8 | 1.0 | .0 | 15.75 | 9.285 | .737 | .052 | .388 | .146 |
| P23 | 6 | 987 | 6.85 | 6.681 | 12.08 | 9.354 | .331 | .374 | .4 | .33 |
| P24 | 3 | 256 | 12.95 | 9.703 | 13.63 | 8.937 | .537 | .201 | .468 | .298 |
| P39 | 5 | 1 | 1.0 | .0 | 2.0 | .0 | .9 | .0 | .8 | .0 |
| P40 | 0 | 3504 | 12.08 | 9.33 | 10.30 | 8.753 | .843 | .147 | .343 | .282 |
| P41 | 2 | 609 | 11.37 | 8.475 | 15.34 | 8.921 | .770 | .106 | .655 | .213 |
| P42 | 3 | 30 | 6.0 | 1.486 | 17.53 | 9.016 | .783 | .059 | .760 | .122 |
| P47 | 2 | 326 | 13.75 | 7.794 | 13.53 | 9.508 | .772 | .095 | .816 | .166 |
| P48 | 2 | 2478 | 12.87 | 9.545 | 10.74 | 8.538 | .764 | .175 | .166 | .148 |

Table 3: Mean parameter values for those simulation runs which result in a minimal number of mismatches for each speaker.

ults are less revealing. For two speaker simulations (P13 and P48) the mean $\nu$ is 0.3 or lower, for another four speaker simulations the mean $\nu$ is above 0.7. That is, our model produces good matching behaviour in adopting different alignment strategies, depending either primarily on frequency or recency, respectively. All other simulations, however, are characterised by a mean $\nu$ in the medium range along with a relatively high standard deviation.

## 6 Conclusion

In this paper, we introduced a priming-based model of alignment which focusses more on the psycholinguistic aspects of interactive alignment and models recency and frequency of use effects — as proposed by Reitter (2008) and Brennan and Clark (1996) — as well as the difference between intrapersonal and interpersonal alignment (Pickering et al., 2003; Pickering and Garrod, 2004). The presented model is fully parameterisable and can account for different empirical findings and 'personalities'. It has been implemented in the SPUD *prime* microplanner which activates linguistic rules by changing its knowledge base on-line and considers the activation values of those rules used in constructing the current utterance by using their mean activation value as an additional feature in its state evaluation function.

We evaluated our alignment model and its implementation in SPUD *prime* on a corpus of task-oriented dialogue collected in an experimental setup especially designed for alignment research. The results of this evaluation show that our priming-based model of alignment is flexible enough to simulate the alignment behaviour of different human speakers (generating target nouns) in the experimental setting. It should be noted, however, that our model tries to give a purely mechanistic explanation of lexical and syntactic choice and that it, therefore, cannot explain alignment phenomena that are due to social factors (e.g., politeness, relationship, etc.), audience design or cases, in which a speaker consciously decides whether to align or not (e.g., whether to use a word or its synonym). While the evaluation has shown that our model can reproduce human alignment behaviour to a high degree, it remains to be investigated which influence each parameter exerts and how exactly the parameters vary across individual speakers.

Nevertheless, the development of the alignment-capable microplanner is only one step in the direction of an intuitive natural language human–computer interaction system. In order to reach this goal, the next step is to combine SPUD*prime* with a natural language understanding system, which should ideally work with the same linguistic representations so that the linguistic structures used by the interlocutor could be primed automatically. This work is underway.

Furthermore, user studies should be carried out in order to evaluate SPUD*prime* in a more sophisticated way. Branigan et al. (in press) found that human–computer alignment was even stronger than human–human alignment. But how would the alignment behaviour of human interlocutors change if the computer they are speaking to also aligns to them? Further, would integration of an alignment-capable dialogue system into a computer interface make the interaction more natural? And would an embodied conversational agent appear more resonant and more sociable (Kopp, 2008) if it aligned to users during conversation? The work presented here provides a starting point for the investigation of these questions.

**Acknowledgements** – This research is supported by the Deutsche Forschungsgemeinschaft (DFG) in the Center of Excellence in 'Cognitive Interaction Technology' (CITEC) as well as in the Collaborative Research Center 673 'Alignment in Communication'. We also thank Petra Weiß for making the 'Jigsaw Map Game' corpus available and three anonymous reviewers for their helpful comments.

## References

John A. Bateman. 2006. A social-semiotic view of interactive alignment and its computational instantiation: A brief position statement and proposal. In Kerstin Fischer, editor, *How People Talk to Computers, Robots and Other Artificial Communication Partners*, SFB/TR 8 Report No. 010-09/2006, pages 157–170, Bremen, Germany.

J. Kathryn Bock and Zenzi M. Griffin. 2000. The persistence of structural priming: Transient activation or implicit learning? *Journal of Experimental Psychology: General*, 129(2):177–192.

Holly P. Branigan, Martin J. Pickering, and Alexandra A. Cleland. 1999. Syntactic priming in written production: Evidence for rapid decay. *Psychonomic Bulletin & Review*, 6(4):635–640.

Holly P. Branigan, Martin J. Pickering, Jamie Pearson, and Janet F. McLean. in press. Linguistic alignment between people and computers. *Journal of Pragmatics*.

Susan E. Brennan and Herbert H. Clark. 1996. Conceptual pacts and lexical choice in conversation. *Journal of Experimental Psychology: Learning, Memory, and Cognition*, 22(6):1482–1493.

Susan E. Brennan. 1991. Conversation with and through computers. *User Modeling and User-Adapted Interaction*, 1(1):67–86.

Carsten Brockmann, Amy Isard, Jon Oberlander, and Michael White. 2005. Modelling alignment for affective dialogue. In *Proc. of the Workshop on Adapting the Interaction Style to Affective Factors at the 10th Int. Conf. on User Modeling*.

Markus A. de Jong, Mariët Theune, and Dennis Hofs. 2008. Politeness and alignment in dialogues with a virtual guide. In *Proc. of the 7th Int. Conf. on Autonomous Agents and Multiagent Systems*, pages 207–214.

Amy Isard, Carsten Brockmann, and Jon Oberlander. 2006. Individuality and alignment in generated dialogues. In *Proc. of the 4th Int. Natural Language Generation Conf.*, pages 25–32.

Stefan Kopp. 2008. From communicators to resonators – Making embodied conversational agents sociable. In *Proc. of the Speech and Face to Face Communication Workshop in Memory of Christian Benoît*, pages 34–36.

Willem J. M. Levelt and Stephanie Kelter. 1982. Surface form and memory in question answering. *Cognitive Psychology*, 14(1):78–106.

Martin J. Pickering and Simon Garrod. 2004. Toward a mechanistic psychology of dialogue. *Behavioral and Brain Sciences*, 27(2):169–226.

Martin J. Pickering, Holly P. Branigan, and Janet F. McLean. 2003. Dialogue structure and the activation of syntactic information. In *Proc. of the 9th Annual Conf. on Architectures and Mechanisms for Language Processing*, page 126.

Matthew Purver, Ronnie Cann, and Ruth Kempson. 2006. Grammars as parsers: Meeting the dialogue challenge. *Research on Language and Computation*, 4(2–3):289–326.

David Reitter. 2008. *Context Effects in Language Production: Models of Syntactic Priming in Dialogue Corpora*. Ph.D. thesis, University of Edinburgh.

Matthew Stone, Christine Doran, Bonnie Webber, Tonia Bleam, and Martha Palmer. 2003. Microplanning with communicative intentions: The SPUD system. *Computational Intelligence*, 19(4):311–381.

Matthew Stone. 2002. Lexicalized grammar 101. In *Proc. of the ACL-02 Workshop on Effective Tools and Methodologies for Teaching Natural Language Processing and Computational Linguistics*, pages 77–84.

Petra Weiß, Thies Pfeiffer, Gesche Schaffranietz, and Gert Rickheit. 2008. Coordination in dialog: Alignment of object naming in the Jigsaw Map Game. In *Proc. of the 8th Annual Conf. of the Cognitive Science Society of Germany*, pages 4–20.

# SimpleNLG: A realisation engine for practical applications

**Albert Gatt and Ehud Reiter**
Department of Computing Science
University of Aberdeen
Aberdeen AB24 3UE, UK
{a.gatt,e.reiter}@abdn.ac.uk

**Abstract**

This paper describes SimpleNLG, a realisation engine for English which aims to provide simple and robust interfaces to generate syntactic structures and linearise them. The library is also flexible in allowing the use of mixed (canned and non-canned) representations.

## 1 Introduction

Over the past several years, a significant consensus has emerged over the definition of the realisation task, through the development of realisers such as REALPRO (Lavoie and Rambow, 1997), ALETHGEN (Coch, 1996), KPML (Bateman, 1997), FUF/SURGE (Elhadad and Robin, 1996), HALOGEN (Langkilde, 2000), YAG (McRoy et al., 2000), and OPENCCG (White, 2006).

Realisation involves two logically distinguishable tasks. *Tactical generation* involves making appropriate linguistic choices given the semantic input. However, once tactical decisions have been taken, building a syntactic representation, applying the right morphological operations, and linearising the sentence as a string are comparatively mechanical tasks. With the possible exception of template-based realisers, such as YAG, existing wide-coverage realisers usually carry out both tasks. By contrast, a *realisation engine* focuses on the second of the two tasks, making no commitments as to how semantic inputs are mapped to syntactic outputs. This leaves the (tactical) problem of defining mappings from semantic inputs to morphosyntactic structures entirely up to the developer, something which may be attractive in those applications where full control of the output of generation is required. Such control is not always easily available in wide-coverage tactical generators, for a number of reasons:

1. Many such realisers define an input formalism, which effectively circumscribes the (semantic) space of possibilities that the realiser handles. The developer needs to ensure that the input to realisation is mapped to the requisite formalism.

2. Since the tactical problem involves search through a space of linguistic choices, the broader the coverage, the more efficiency may be compromised. Where real-time deployment is a goal, this may be an obstacle.

3. Many application domains have *sublanguage* requirements. For example, the language used in summaries of weather data (Reiter et al., 2005) or patient information (Portet et al., to appear) differs from standard usage, and does not always allow variation to the same extent. Since realisers don't typically address such requirements, their use in a particular application may require the alteration of the realiser's rule-base or, in the case of statistical realisers, re-training on large volumes of appropruately annotated data.

This paper describes SimpleNLG, a realisation engine which grew out of recent experiences in building large-scale data-to-text NLG systems, whose goal is to summarise large volumes of numeric and symbolic data (Reiter, 2007). Sublanguage requirements and efficiency are important considerations in such systems. Although meeting these requirements was the initial motivation behind SimpleNLG, it has since been developed into an engine with significant coverage of English syntax and morphology, while at the same time providing a simple API that offers users direct programmatic control over the realisation process.

*Proceedings of the 12th European Workshop on Natural Language Generation*, pages 90–93,
Athens, Greece, 30 – 31 March 2009. 

| | Feature | Values | Applicable classes |
|---|---|---|---|
| **lexical** | ADJPOSITION | $Attrib_{1/2/3}$, PostNominal, Predicative | ADJ |
| | ADVPOSITION | Sentential, PostVerbal, Verbal | ADV |
| | AGRTYPE | Count, Mass, Group, Inv-Pl, Inv-Sg | N |
| | COMPLTYPE | AdjP, AdvP, B-Inf, WhFin, WhInf, ... | V |
| | VTYPE | Aux, Main, Modal | V |
| **phrasal** | FUNCTION | Subject, Obj, I-Obj, Prep-Obj, Modifier | all |
| | SFORM | B-Inf, Gerund, Imper, Inf, Subj | S |
| | INTERROGTYPE | Yes/No, How, What, ... | S |
| | NUMBERAGR | Plural, Singular | NP |
| | TENSE | Pres, Past, Fut | VP |
| | TAXIS (boolean) | `true` (=perfective), `false` | VP |
| | POSSESSIVE (boolean) | `true` (=possessive), `false` | NP |
| | PASSIVE (boolean) | `true`, `false` | VP |

Table 1: Features and values available in SimpleNLG

## 2 Overview of SimpleNLG

SimpleNLG is a Java library that provides interfaces offering direct control over the realisation process, that is, over the way phrases are built and combined, inflectional morphological operations, and linearisation. It defines a set of lexical and phrasal types, corresponding to the major grammatical categories, as well as ways of combining these and setting various feature values. In constructing a syntactic structure and linearising it as text with SimpleNLG, the following steps are undertaken:

1. Initialisation of the basic constituents required, with the appropriate lexical items;
2. Using the operations provided in the API to set features of the constituents, such as those in bottom panel of Table 1;
3. Combining constituents into larger structures, again using the operations provided in the API which apply to the constituents in question;
4. Passing the resulting structure to the lineariser, which traverses the constituent structure, applying the correct inflections and linear ordering depending on the features, before returning the realised string.

Constituents in SimpleNLG can be a mixture of canned and non-canned representations. This is useful in applications where certain inputs can be mapped to an output string in a deterministic fashion, while others require a more flexible mapping to outputs depending, for example, on semantic features and context. SimpleNLG tries to meet these needs by providing significant syntactic coverage with the added option of combining canned and non-canned strings.

Another aim of the engine is robustness: structures which are incomplete or not well-formed will not result in a crash, but typically will yield infelicitous, though comprehensible, output. This is a feature that SimpleNLG shares with YAG (McRoy et al., 2000). A third design criterion was to achieve a clear separation between morphological and syntactic operations. The lexical component of the library, which includes a wide-coverage morphological generator, is distinct from the syntactic component. This makes it useful for applications which do not require complex syntactic operations, but which need output strings to be correctly inflected.

### 2.1 Lexical operations

The lexical component provides interfaces that define a `Lexicon`, a `MorphologicalRule`, and a `LexicalItem`, with subtypes for different lexical classes (`Noun`, `Preposition` etc). Morphological rules, a re-implementation of those in MORPHG (Minnen et al., 2001), cover the full range of English inflection, including regular and irregular forms[1]. In addition to the range of morphological operations that apply to them, various features can be specified for lexical items. For example, as shown in the top panel of Table 1, adjectives and adverbs can be specified for their typical syntactic positions. Thus, an adjective such as *red* would have the values $Attrib_2$, indicating that it usually occurs in attribute position 2 (following $Attrib_1$ adjectives such as *large*), and *Predicative*. Similarly, nouns are classified to indicate

[1]Thanks are due to John Carroll at the University of Sussex for permission to re-use these rules.

their agreement features (count, mass, etc), while verbs can be specified for the range of syntactic complement types they allow (e.g. bare infinitives and WH-complements).

A typical development scenario involves the creation of a `Lexicon`, the repository of the relevant items and their properties. Though this can be done programmatically, the current distribution of SimpleNLG provides an interface to a database constructed from the NIH Specialist Lexicon[2], a large (> 300,000 entries) repository of lexical items in the medical and general English domains, which incorporates information about lexical features such as those in Table 1.

### 2.2 Syntactic operations

The syntactic component of SimpleNLG defines interfaces for `HeadedPhrase` and `CoordinatePhrase`. Apart from various phrasal subtypes (referred to as `PhraseSpecs`) following the usage in Reiter and Dale (2000)), several grammatical features are defined, including `Tense`, `Number`, `Person` and `Mood` (see Table 1). In addition, a `StringPhraseSpec` represents a piece of canned text of arbitrary length.

A complete syntactic structure is achieved by initialising constituents with the relevant features, and combining them using the operations specified by the interface. Any syntactic structure can consist of a mixture of `Phrase` or `CoordinatePhrase` types and canned strings. The input lexical items to phrase constructors can themselves be either strings or lexical items as defined in the lexical component. Once syntactic structures have been constructed, they are passed to a lineariser, which also handles basic punctuation and other orthographic conventions (such as capitalisation).

The syntactic component covers the full range of English verbal forms, including participals, compound tenses, and progressive aspect. Subtypes of `CoordinatePhrase` allow for fully recursive coordination. As shown in the bottom panel of Figure 1, subjunctive forms and different kinds of interrogatives are also handled using the same basic feature-setting mechanism.

The example below illustrates one way of constructing the phrase *the boys left the house*, initialising a sentence with the main verb *leave* and setting a `Tense` feature. Note that the `SPhraseSpec` interface allows the setting of the main verb, although this is internally represented as the head of a `VPPhraseSpec` dominated by the clause. An alternative would be to construct the verb phrase directly, and set it as a constituent of the sentence. Similarly, the direct object, which is specified directly as a constituent of the sentence, is internally represented as the object of the verb phrase. In this example, the direct object is an `NPPhraseSpec` consisting of two words, passed as arguments and internally rendered as lexical items of type `Determiner` and `Noun` respectively. By contrast, the subject is defined as a canned string.

(1)
```
Phrase s1 =
  new SPhraseSpec('leave');
s1.setTense(PAST);
s1.setObject(
  new NPPhraseSpec('the', 'house'));
Phrase s2 =
  new StringPhraseSpec('the boys');
s1.setSubject(s2);
```

Setting the INTERROGATIVETYPE feature of sentence (1) turns it into a question. Two examples, are shown below. While (2) exemplifies a simple yes/no question, in (3), a WH-constituent is specified as establishing a dependency with the direct object (*the house*).

(2) `s1.setInterrogative(YES_NO);`
(Did the boys leave home?)

(3) `s1.setInterrogative(WHERE, OBJECT);`
(Where did the boys leave?)

In summary, building syntactic structures in SimpleNLG is largely a question of feature setting, with no restrictions on whether representations are partially or exclusively made up of canned strings.

#### 2.2.1 Interaction of lexicon and syntax

The phrasal features in the bottom panel of Table 1 determine the form of the output, since they are automatically interpreted by the realiser as instructions to call the correct morphological operations on lexical items. Hence, the syntactic and morphological components are closely integrated (though distinct). Currently, however, lexical features such as ADJPOSITION are not fully integrated with the syntactic component. For example, although adjectives in the lexicon are specified for their position relative to other modifiers, and nouns are

[2] `http://lexsrv3.nlm.nih.gov/SPECIALIST/index.html`

specified for whether they take singular or plural agreement, this informaiton is not currently used automatically by the realiser. Full integration of lexical features and syntactic realisation is currently the focus of ongoing development.

### 2.3 Efficiency

As an indication of efficiency, we measured the time taken to realise 26 summaries with an average text length of 160.8 tokens (14.4 sentences), and sentences ranging in complexity from simple declaratives to complex embedded clauses[3]. The estimates, shown below, average over 100 iterations per text (i.e. a total of 2600 runs of the realiser) on a Dell Optiplex GX620 machine running Windows XP with a 3.16 GHz Pentium processor. Separate times are given for the initialisation of constituents based on semantic representations, along the lines shown in (1), (SYN), and linearisation (LIN). These figures suggest that a medium-length, multiparagraph text can be rendered in under a second in most cases.

| | MEAN (ms) | SD | MIN | MAX |
|---|---|---|---|---|
| SYN | 280.7 | 229.7 | 13.8 | 788.34 |
| LIN | 749.38 | 712.6 | 23.26 | 2700.38 |

## 3 Conclusions and future work

This paper has described SimpleNLG, a realisation engine which differs from most tactical generators in that it provides a transparent API to carry out low-level tasks such as inflection and syntactic combination, while making no commitments about input specifications or input-output mappings.

The simplicity of use of SimpleNLG is reflected in its community of users. The currently available public distribution[4], has been used by several groups for three main purposes: (a) as a front-end to NLG systems in projects where realisation is not the primary research focus; (b) as a simple natural language component in user interfaces for other kinds of systems, by researchers who do not work in NLG proper; (c) as a teaching tool in advanced undergraduate and postgraduate courses on Natural Language Processing.

SimpleNLG remains under continuous development. Current work is focusing on the inclusion of output formatting and punctuation modules, which are currently handled using simple defaults. Moreover, an enhanced interface to the lexicon is being developed to handle derivational morphology and a fuller integration of complementation frames of lexical items with the syntactic component.

[3]The system that generates these summaries is fully described by Portet *et al.* (to appear).

[4]SimpleNLG is available, with exhaustive documentation, at the following URL: `http://www.csd.abdn.ac.uk/~ereiter/simplenlg/`.

## References


J. A. Bateman. 1997. Enabling technology for multilingual natural language generation: the KPML development environment. *Natural Language Engineering*, 3(1):15–55.

J. Coch. 1996. Overview of AlethGen. In *Proceedings of the 8th International Natural Language Generation Workshop.*

M. Elhadad and J. Robin. 1996. An overview of SURGE: A reusable comprehensive syntactic realization component. In *Proceedings of the 8th International Natural Language Generation Workshop.*

I. Langkilde. 2000. Forest-based statistical language generation. In *Proceedings of the 1st Meeting of the North American Chapter of the Association for Computational Linguistics.*

B. Lavoie and O. Rambow. 1997. A fast and portable realizer for text generation systems. In *Proceedings of the 5th Conference on Applied Natural Language Processing.*

S.W. McRoy, S. Channarukul, and S. Ali. 2000. YAG: A template-based generator for real-time systems. In *Proceedings of the 1st International Conference on Natural Language Generation.*

G. Minnen, J. J. Carroll, and D. Pearce. 2001. Applied morphological processing of English. *Natural Language Engineering*, 7(3):207–223.

F. Portet, E. Reiter, A. Gatt, J. Hunter, S. Sripada, Y. Freer, and C. Sykes. to appear. Automatic generation of textual summaries from neonatal intensive care data. *Artificial Intelligence.*

E. Reiter and R. Dale. 2000. *Building Natural Language Generation Systems.* Cambridge University Press, Cambridge, UK.

E. Reiter, S. Sripada, J. Hunter, J. Yu, and I. Davy. 2005. Choosing words in computer-generated weather forecasts. *Artificial Intelligence*, 167:137–169.

E. Reiter. 2007. An architecture for Data-to-Text systems. In *Proceedings of the 11th European Workshop on Natural Language Generation.*

M. White. 2006. Chart realization from disjunctive inputs. In *Proceedings of the 4th International Conference on Natural Language Generation.*

# A Wizard-of-Oz environment to study Referring Expression Generation in a Situated Spoken Dialogue Task

**Srinivasan Janarthanam**
School of Informatics
University of Edinburgh
Edinburgh EH8 9AB
s.janarthanam@ed.ac.uk

**Oliver Lemon**
School of Informatics
University of Edinburgh
Edinburgh EH8 9AB
olemon@inf.ed.ac.uk

**Abstract**

We present a Wizard-of-Oz environment for data collection on Referring Expression Generation (REG) in a real situated spoken dialogue task. The collected data will be used to build user simulation models for reinforcement learning of referring expression generation strategies.

## 1 Introduction

In this paper, we present a Wizard-of-Oz (WoZ) environment for data collection in a real situated spoken dialogue task for referring expression generation (REG). Our primary objective is to study how participants (hereafter called users) with different domain knowledge and expertise interpret and resolve different types of referring expressions (RE) in a situated dialogue context. We also study the effect of the system's lexical alignment due to priming (Pickering and Garrod, 2004) by the user's choice of REs. The users follow instructions from an implemented dialogue manager and realiser to perform a technical but realistic task – setting up a home Internet connection. The dialogue system's utterances are manipulated to contain different types of REs - descriptive, technical, tutorial or lexically aligned REs, to refer to various domain objects in the task. The users' responses to different REs are then logged and studied.

(Janarthanam and Lemon, 2009) presented a framework for reinforcement learning of optimal natural language generation strategies to choose appropriate REs to users with different domain knowledge expertise. For this, we need user simulations with different domain knowledge profiles that are sensitive to the system's choice of REs. A WoZ environment is an ideal tool for data collection to build data-driven user simulations. However, our study requires a novel WoZ environment.

In section 2, we present prior related work. Section 3 describes the task performed by participants. In section 4, we describe the WoZ environment in detail. Section 5 describes the data collected in this experiment and section 6 presents some preliminary results from pilot studies.

## 2 Related Work

(Whittaker et al., 2002) present a WoZ environment to collect data concerning dialogue strategies for presenting restaurant information to users. This study collects data on strategies used by users and human expert wizards to obtain and present information respectively. (van Deemter et al., 2006) present methods to collect data (the TUNA corpus) for REG using artificially constructed pictures of furniture and photographs of real people. (Arts, 2004) presents a study choosing between technical and descriptive expressions for instruction *writing*.

In contrast to the above studies, our study is novel in that it collects data from users having different levels of expertise in a real situated task domain, and for spontaneous spoken dialogue. Our focus is on choosing between technical, descriptive, tutorial, and lexically aligned expressions rather than selecting different attributes for generating descriptions.

## 3 The Domain Task

In this experiment, the task for each user is to listen to and follow the instructions from the WoZ system and set up their home broadband Internet connection. We provide the users with a home-like environment with a desktop computer, phone socket and a Livebox package from Orange containing cables and components such as the modem, broadband filters and a power adaptor. During the experiment, they set up the Internet connection by connecting these components to each other. Prior to the task, the users are informed that they are interacting with a spoken dialogue system

*Proceedings of the 12th European Workshop on Natural Language Generation*, pages 94–97,
Athens, Greece, 30 – 31 March 2009. ©2009 Association for Computational Linguistics

that will give them instructions to set up the connection. However, their utterances are intercepted by a human wizard. The users are requested to have a conversation as if they were talking to a human operator, asking for clarifications if they are confused or fail to understand the system's utterances. The system's utterances are converted automatically to speech using the Cereproc Speech Synthesiser and played back to the user. The user follows the instructions and assembles the components. The setup is examined by the wizard at the end of the experiment to measure the percentage of task success. The user also fills in questionnaires prior to and after the task answering questions on his background, quality of the system during the task and the knowledge gained during the task.

## 4 The Wizard-of-Oz environment

The Wizard-of-Oz environment facilitates the entire experiment as described in the section above. The environment consists of the Wizard Interaction Tool, the dialogue system and the wizard. The users wear a headset with a microphone. Their utterances are relayed to the wizard who then annotates it using the Wizard Interaction Tool (shown in figure 1) and sends it to the dialogue system. The system responds with a natural language utterance which is automatically converted to speech and is played back to the user and the wizard.

### 4.1 Wizard Interaction Tool (WIT)

The Wizard Interaction Tool (WIT) (shown in figure 1) allows the wizard to interact with the dialogue system and the user. The GUI is divided in to several panels.

a. System Response Panel - This panel displays the dialogue system's utterances and RE choices for the domain objects in the utterance. It also displays the strategy adopted by the system currently and a visual indicator of whether the system's utterance is being played to the user.

b. Confirmation Request Panel - This panel lets the wizard handle issues in communication (for e.g. noise). The wizard can ask the user to repeat, speak louder, confirm his responses, etc using appropriate pre-recorded messages or build his own custom messages.

c. Confirmation Panel - This panel lets the wizard handle confirmation questions from the user. The wizard can choose 'yes' or 'no' or build a custom message.

| | |
|---|---|
| yes | "Yes it is on" |
| no | "No, its not flashing" |
| ok | "Ok. I did that" |
| req_description | "Whats an ethernet cable?" |
| req_location | "Where is the filter?" |
| req_verify_jargon | "Is it the ethernet cable?" |
| req_verify_desc | "Is it the white cable?" |
| req_repeat | "Please repeat" |
| req_rephrase | "What do you mean?" |
| req_wait | "Give me a minute?" |

Table 1: User Dialogue Acts.

d. Annotation panel - This panel lets the wizard annotate the content of participant's utterances. User responses (dialogue acts and example utterances) that can be annotated using this panel are given in Table 1. In addition to these, other behaviours, like remaining silent or saying irrelevant things are also accommodated.

e. User's RE Choice panel - The user's choice of REs to refer to the domain objects are annotated by the wizard using this panel.

### 4.2 The Instructional Dialogue Manager

The dialogue manager drives the conversation by giving instructions to the users. It follows a deterministic dialogue management policy so that we only study variation in the decisions concerning the choice of REs. It should be noted that typical WoZ environments (Whittaker et al., 2002) do not have dialogue managers and the strategic decisions will be taken by the wizard. Our dialogue system has three main responsibilities - choosing the RE strategy, giving instructions and handling clarification requests.

The dialogue system, initially randomly chooses the RE strategy at the start of the dialogue. The list of strategies are as follows.

1. Jargon: Choose technical terms for every reference to the domain objects.

2. Descriptive: Choose descriptive terms for every reference to the domain objects.

3. Tutorial: Use technical terms, but also augment the description for every reference.

The above three strategies are also augmented with an *alignment feature*, so that the system can either align or not align with the user's prior choice of REs. In aligned strategies, the system abandons the existing strategy (jargon, descriptive or tutorial) for a domain object reference when the user

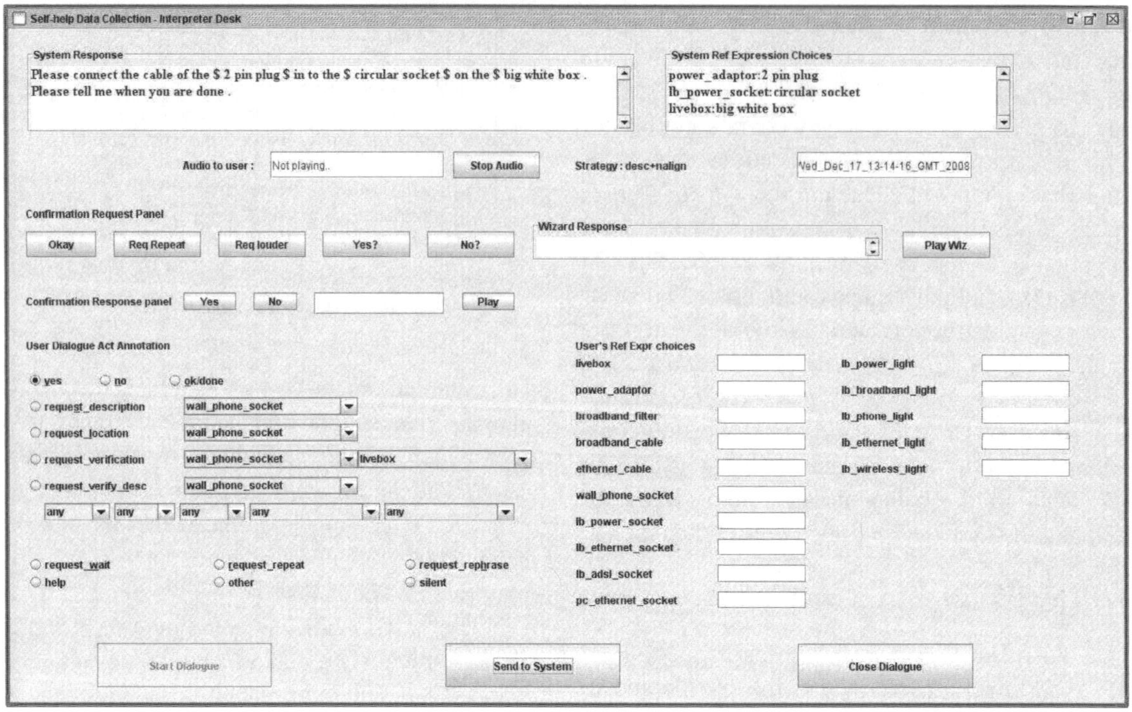


Figure 1: Wizard Interaction Tool

uses a different expression from that of the system to refer to the domain object. For instance, under the descriptive strategy, the ethernet cable is referred to as "the thick cable with red ends". But if the user refers to it as "ethernet cable", then the system uses "ethernet cable" in subsequent turns instead of the descriptive expression. In case of non-aligned strategies, the system simply ignores user's use of novel REs and continues to use its own strategy.

The step-by-step instructions to set up the broadband connection are hand-coded as a dialogue script. The script is a simple deterministic finite state automaton, which contains execution instruction acts(e.g. Plug in the cable in to the socket) and observation instruction acts(e.g. Is the ethernet light flashing?) for the user. Based on the user's response, the system identifies the next instruction. However, the script only contains the dialogue acts. The dialogue acts are then processed by a built-in realiser component to create the system utterances. The realiser uses templates in which references to domain objects are changed based on the selected strategy to create final utterances. By using a fixed dialogue management policy and by changing the REs, we only explore users' reactions to various RE strategies. The utterances are finally converted to speech and are played back to the user.

The dialogue system handles two kinds of clarification requests - open requests and closed requests. With open CRs, users request the system for location of various domain objects (e.g. "where is the ethernet cable?") or to describe them. With closed CRs, users verify the intended reference, in case of ambiguity (e.g. "Do you mean the thin white cable with grey ends?", "Is it the broadband filter?", etc.). The system handles these requests using a knowledge base of the domain objects.

### 4.3 Wizard Activities

The primary responsibility of the wizard is to understand the participant's utterance and annotate it as one of the dialogue acts in the Annotation panel, and send the dialogue act to the dialogue system for response. In addition to the primary responsibility, the wizard also requests confirmation from the user (if needed) and also responds to confirmation requests from the user. The wizard also observes the user's usage of novel REs and records them in the User's RE Choice panel. As mentioned earlier, our wizard neither decides on which strategy to use to choose REs nor chooses the next task instruction to give the user.

## 5 Data collected

Several different kinds of data are collected before, during and after the experiment. This data will be used to build user simulations and reward functions for learning REG strategies and language models for speech recognition.

1. WIT log - The WIT logs the whole conversation as an XML file. The log contains system and user dialogue acts, time of system utterance, system's choice of REs and its utterance at every turn. It also contains the dialogue start time, total time elapsed, total number of turns, number of words in system utterances, number of clarification requests, number of technical, descriptive and tutorial REs, number of confirmations etc.
2. Background of the user - The user is asked to fill in a pre-task background questionnaire containing queries on their experience with computers, Internet and dialogue systems.
3. User satisfaction survey - The user is requested to fill in a post-task questionnaire containing queries on the performance of the system during the task. Each question is answered in a four point Likert scale on how strongly the user agrees or disagrees with the given statement. Statements like, "Conversation with the system was easy", "I would use such a system in future", etc are judged by the user which will be used to build reward functions for reinforcement learning of REG strategies.
4. Knowledge pre-test - Users' initial domain knowledge is tested by asking them to match a list of technical terms to their respective descriptive expressions.
5. Knowledge gain post-test - Users' knowledge gain during the dialogue task is measured by asking them to redo the matching task.
6. Percentage of task completion - The wizard examines the final set up on the user's table to determine the percentage of task success using a form containing declarative statements describing the ideal broadband set up (for e.g. "the broadband filter is plugged in to the phone socket on the wall"). The wizard awards one point to every statement that is true of the user's set up.
7. User's utterances WAV file - The user's utterances are recorded in WAV format for building language models for automatic speech recognition.

## 6 Results from pilot studies

We are currently running pilot studies (with 6 participants so far) and have collected around 60 minutes of spoken dialogue data. We found that in the jargon strategy, some users take a lot longer to finish the task than others (max 59 turns, min 26 turns). We found that besides requesting clarifications, sometimes novice users assume incorrect references to some domain objects, affecting their task completion rates.

## 7 Conclusion

We have presented a novel Wizard-of-Oz environment to collect spoken data in a real situated task environment, and to study user reactions to a variety of REG strategies, including system alignment. The data will be used for training user simulations for reinforcement learning of REG strategies to choose between technical, descriptive, tutorial, and aligned REs based on a user's expertise in the task domain.

## Acknowledgements

The research leading to these results has received funding from the European Community's Seventh Framework (FP7) under grant agreement no. 216594 (CLASSiC Project www.classic-project.org), EPSRC project no. EP/E019501/1, and the British Council (UKIERI PhD Scholarships 2007-08).

## References

A. Arts. 2004. *Overspecification in Instructive Text.* Ph.D. thesis, Tilburg University, The Netherlands.

S. Janarthanam and O. Lemon. 2009. Learning Lexical Alignment Policies for Generating Referring Expressions for Spoken Dialogue Systems. In *Proc. ENLG'09.*

M. J. Pickering and S. Garrod. 2004. Toward a mechanistic psychology of dialogue. *Behavioral and Brain Sciences*, 27:169–225.

K. van Deemter, I. van der Sluis, and A. Gatt. 2006. Building a semantically transparent corpus for the generation of referring expressions. In *Proc. INLG'06.*

S. Whittaker, M. Walker, and J. Moore. 2002. Fish or Fowl: A Wizard of Oz Evaluation of Dialogue Strategies in the Restaurant Domain. In *Language Resources and Evaluation Conference.*

# A Hearer-oriented Evaluation of Referring Expression Generation *

**Imtiaz H. Khan, Kees van Deemter, Graeme Ritchie, Albert Gatt, Alexandra A. Cleland**
University of Aberdeen, Aberdeen, Scotland, United Kingdom
{i.h.khan,k.vdeemter,g.ritchie,a.gatt,a.cleland}@abdn.ac.uk

**Abstract**

This paper discusses the evaluation of a Generation of Referring Expressions algorithm that takes structural ambiguity into account. We describe an ongoing study with human readers.

## 1 Introduction

In recent years, the NLG community has seen a substantial number of studies to evaluate Generation of Referring Expressions (GRE) algorithms, but it is still far from clear what would constitute an optimal evaluation method. Two limitations stand out in the bulk of existing work. Firstly, most existing evaluations are essentially speaker-oriented, focussing on the degree of "human-likeness" of the generated descriptions, disregarding their effectiveness (e.g. Mellish and Dale (1998), Gupta and Stent (2005), van Deemter et al. (2006), Belz and Kilgarriff (2006), Belz and Reiter (2006), Paris et al. (2006), Viethen and Dale (2006), Gatt and Belz (2008)). The limited number of exceptions to this rule indicate that the differences between the two approaches to evaluation can be substantial (Gatt and Belz, 2008). Secondly, most evaluations have focussed on the semantic content of the generated descriptions, as produced by the Content Determination stage of a GRE algorithm; this means that linguistic realisation (i.e. the choice of words and linguistic constructions) is usually not addressed (exceptions are: Stone and Webber (1998), Krahmer and Theune (2002), Siddharthan and Copestake (2004)).

Our aim is to build GRE algorithms that produce referring expressions that are of optimal benefit to a hearer. That is, we are interested in generating descriptions that are easy to read and understand. But the readability and intelligibility of a description can crucially depend on the way in which it is worded. This happens particularly when there is potential for misunderstanding, as can happen in the case of attachment and scope ambiguities.

Suppose, for example, one wants to make it clear that all radical students and all radical teachers are in agreement with a certain idea. It might be risky to express this as *'the radical students and teachers are agreed'*, since the reader[1] might be inclined to interpret this as pertaining to all teachers rather than only the radical ones. For this reason, a GRE program might opt for the longer noun phrase *'the radical students and the radical teachers'*. But because this expression is lengthier, the choice involves a compromise between comprehensibiliity and brevity, a special case of a difficult trade-off that is typical of generation as well as interpretation of language (van Deemter, 2004).

We previously reported the design of an algorithm (based on an earlier work on expressions referring to sets (Gatt, 2007)), which was derived from experiments in which readers were asked to express their preference between different descriptions and to respond to instructions which used a variety of phrasings (Khan et al., 2008). Here we discuss the issues that arise when such an algorithm is evaluated in terms of its benefits for readers.

## 2 Summary of the algorithm

In order to study specific data, we have focussed on the construction illustrated in Section 1 above: potentially ambiguous Noun Phrases of the general form *the Adj* $Noun_i$ *and* $Noun_j$. For such phrases, there are potentially two interpretations: *wide scope* (Adj modifies both $\text{Noun}_i$ and $\text{Noun}_j$) or *narrow scope* (Adj modifies $\text{Noun}_i$ but not $\text{Noun}_j$).

Our algorithm starts from an unambiguous set-theoretic formula over lexical items (i.e. words

* This work is supported by a University of Aberdeen Sixth Century Studentship, and EPSRC grant EP/E011764/1.

[1] In this paper, we use the word reader and hearer interchangeably.

*Proceedings of the 12th European Workshop on Natural Language Generation*, pages 98–101,
Athens, Greece, 30 – 31 March 2009. ©2009 Association for Computational Linguistics

have already been chosen), and thus has to choose between a number of different realisations. The possible phrasings for the wide scope meaning are: (1) *the Adj* $Noun_1$ *and* $Noun_2$, (2) *the Adj* $Noun_2$ *and* $Noun_1$, (3) *the Adj* $Noun_1$ *and the Adj* $Noun_2$, and (4) *the Adj* $Noun_2$ *and the Adj* $Noun_1$. For narrow scope, the possibilities are: (1) *the Adj* $Noun_1$ *and* $Noun_2$, (2) *the* $Noun_2$ *and Adj* $Noun_1$, (3) *the Adj* $Noun_1$ *and the* $Noun_2$, and (4) *the* $Noun_2$ *and the Adj* $Noun_1$. For our purposes, (1) and (2) are designated as 'brief', (3) and (4) as 'non-brief' (that is, 'brevity' has a specialised sense involving the presence/absence of '*the*' and possibly *Adj* before the second *Noun*). Importantly, the 'non-brief' expressions are syntactically unambiguous, but the 'brief' NPs are potentially ambiguous, and hence are the focus of attention in this work.

Our algorithm is based on certain specific hypotheses (from the earlier experiments) which make crucial use of corpus data concerning the frequency of two types of collocations: the collocation between an adjective and a noun, and the collocation between two nouns. At a broader level, we hypothesise: *the most likely reading of an* NP *can be predicted using corpus data (Word Sketches (Kilgarriff, 2003))*. The more specific hypotheses derive from earlier work by Kilgarriff (2003) and Chantree et al. (2006), and were further developed and tested in our previous experiments. The central idea is that this statistical information can be used to predict a 'most likely' scoping (and hence interpretation) for the adjective in the 'brief' (i.e. potentially ambiguous) NPs. We define an NP to be *predictable* if our model predicts a single reading for it; otherwise it is *unpredictable*. Hence, all 'non-brief' NPs are predictable (being unambiguous), but only some of the 'brief' ones are predictable.

In a nutshell, *the model underlying our algorithm prefers predictable expressions to unpredictable ones, but if several of the expressions are predictable then brief expressions are preferred over non-brief.*

## 3 Aims of the study

We want to find out whether our generator makes the best possible choices (for hearers) from amongst the different ways in which a given description can be realised. But although our algorithm uses sophisticated strategies for avoiding noun phrases that it believes to be liable to misunderstanding, misunderstandings cannot be ruled out, and if a hearer misunderstands a noun phrase then secondary aspects such as reading (and/or comprehension) speed are of little consequence. We therefore plan first to find out the likelihood of misunderstanding. For this reason, we will report on the degree of accuracy, as a percentage of times that a participant's understanding of an expression that we label as predictable fails to match the interpretation assigned by our model. Additionally, we shall statistically test two hypotheses:

**Comprehension Accuracy 1:** Predictable expressions are more often interpreted in agreement than in disagreement with the model.

**Comprehension Accuracy 2:** There is more agreement among participants on the interpretation of predictable expressions than of unpredictable expressions.

We will not only test the comprehensibility of the expressions generated by our algorithm, but their readability and intelligibility as well. This is necessary because the experiments which led to the algorithm design considered only certain aspects of the hearer's reaction to NPs (e.g. metalinguistic judgements about a participant's *preferences*) and we wish to check these comprehensibility/brevity facets from a different, perhaps psycholinguistically more valid, perspective. It is also necessary because avoidance of misunderstandings is not the only decisive factor: if several of the expressions are predictable then our algorithm chooses between them by preferring brevity. But why is brief better than non-brief? Taking readability and intelligibility together as 'processing speed', our third hypothesis is:

**Processing speed:** Subjects process predictable brief expressions more quickly than predictable non-brief ones.

Confirmation of this hypothesis would be a strong indication that our algorithm is on the right track, particularly if the degree of accuracy (see above) turns out to be high. Processing speed is a complex concept, but we could decompose it as 'reading speed' and 'comprehension speed', permitting us to examine reading and comprehension separately. We intend to see what evidence there is for the following additional propositions, which will be tested solely to aid our understanding.

**Reading Speed:**
**RS1:** Subjects read predictable brief NPs more quickly than unpredictable brief ones.
**RS2:** Subjects read unpredictable brief NPs more quickly than predictable non-brief ones.
**RS3:** Subjects read predictable brief NPs more quickly than predictable non-brief ones.

**Comprehension Speed:**
**CS1:** Subjects comprehend predictable brief NPs more quickly than unpredictable brief ones.
**CS2:** Subjects comprehend predictable non-brief NPs more quickly than unpredictable brief ones.
**CS3:** Subjects do not comprehend predictable non-brief NPs more quickly than predictable brief ones.
(Remember that, in our restricted set of NPs, a phrase cannot be both 'unpredictable' and 'non-brief'.) Rejection of any of these statements will not count against our algorithm.

## 4 Sketch of experimental procedure

Participants will be presented with a sequence of trials (on a computer screen), each of which consists of a lead-in sentence followed by a target sentence and a comprehension question that relates to the two sentences together. The target sentence might for example say *'the radical students and teachers were waving their hands'*. The comprehension question in this case could be *'Were the moderate teachers waving their hands?'*. As both the target sentence and the comprehension question make use of definite NPs (e.g. *'the moderate teachers'*), it is necessary to ensure any presuppositions about the existence of the referent set are met, without biasing the answer. For this reason, the target sentence is preceded by a lead-in sentence to establish the existence of the sets within the discourse (here, *'there were radical and moderate people in a rally'*).

Given this set-up we are confident that we can identify, from a participant's yes/no answer, whether the NP in the target sentence was assigned a narrow-scope or a wide-scope reading for the adjective. The computer will record the participant's response as well as the length of time that the participant took to answer the question. We will use Linger[2] for presentation of stimuli. Pilots suggest that the complexity of the trials makes it advisable to use *masked sentence-based* self-paced reading, in which every press of the space bar reveals the next sentence and the previous sentence is replaced by dashes.

The choice of nouns and adjectives (to construct NPs) is motivated by the fact that there is a balanced distribution of NPs in each of the following three classes. Wide scope class is the one for which our model predicts a wide-scope reading; narrow scope class is the one for which our model predicts a narrow-scope reading; and ambiguous class is the one for which our model fails to predict a single reading (Khan et al., 2008).

## 5 Issues emerging from this study

The design of this experiment raised some difficult questions, some quite unexpected:

1. The quality of the output of a generation algorithm might appear to be a simple and well-understood concept. However, output quality is multi-faceted, because an expression may be easy to read but difficult to process semantically, or the other way round. A thorough output evaluation should address both aspects of quality, in our view.

2. If both reading and understanding are addressed, this raises the question of how these two dimensions should be traded off against each other. If one algorithm's output was read more quickly than that of another, but understood more slowly than the second, which of the two should be preferred? Perhaps there is a legitimate role here for metalinguistic judgments after all, in which participants are asked to express their preference between expressions (see Paraboni et al. (2006) for discussion)? An alternative point of view is that these questions are impossible to answer independent of a realistic setting in which participants utter sentences with a concrete communicative purpose in mind. If utterances were made in order to accomplish a concrete task (e.g., to win a game) then *task-based* evaluation would be possible.

3. Even though this paper has not focussed on details of experimental design and analysis, one difficulty is worth mentioning: given the grammatical options between which the generator is choosing, only three types of situations are represented: a description can be brief and predictable (e.g. using 'the old men and women' to convey wide scope, since the adjective is predicted by our algorithm to have wide scope), brief and unpredictable (e.g. 'the rowing boats and ships' for wide scope, given

[2] http://tedlab.mit.edu/~dr/Linger/

a prediction of narrow scope), or non-brief and predictable (e.g. 'the old men and the old women' for wide scope). It might appear that there exists a fourth option: non-brief and unpredictable. But this is ruled out by our technical sense of 'non-brief': as noted earlier, 'non-brief' NPs do not have the scope ambiguity. Because of this "missing cell", it will not be possible to analyse our data using an ANOVA test, which would have automatically taken care of all possible interactions between comprehensibility and brevity. A number of different tests will be used instead, with Bonferroni corrections where necessary.

## 6 Conclusion

Human-based evaluation is gaining considerable popularity in the NLG community. Whereas evaluation of GRE has mostly been speaker-oriented, the present paper has explored a plan for an experimental hearer-oriented evaluation. The main conclusion is that hearer-based evaluation is difficult because the quality of a generated expression can be measured in different ways, whose results cannot be assumed to match. One factor we have not examined is the notion of *fluency*: it is possible that our algorithm will sometimes choose a word order (e.g. 'the women and old men') that is relatively infrequent, and therefore lacking in fluency. Such situations might lead to longer reading times.

## References


A. Belz and A. Kilgarriff. 2006. Shared-task evaluations in HLT: Lessons for NLG. In *Proceedings of the 4th International Conference on Natural Language Generation*, pages 133–135.

A. Belz and E. Reiter. 2006. Comparing automatic and human evaluation of NLG systems. In *Proceedings of the 11th Conference of the European Chapter of the Association for Computational Linguistics*, pages 313–320, Trento, Italy, 3-7 April.

F. Chantree, B. Nuseibeh, A. de Roeck, and A. Willis. 2006. Identifying nocuous ambiguities in requirements specifications. In *Proceedings of 14th IEEE International Requirements Engineering conference (RE'06)*, Minneapolis/St. Paul, Minnesota, U.S.A.

A. Gatt and A. Belz. 2008. Attribute selection for referring expression generation: New algorithms and evaluation methods. In *Proceedings of the 5th International Conference on NLG*.

A. Gatt. 2007. *Generating Coherent References to Multiple Entities*. Ph.D. thesis, University of Aberdeen, Aberdeen, Scotland.

S. Gupta and A. Stent. 2005. Automatic evaluation of referring expression generation using corpora. In *Proceedings of the Workshop on Using Corpora for Natural Language Generation*, pages 1–6.

I. H. Khan, K. van Deemter, and G. Ritchie. 2008. Generation of referring expressions: Managing structural ambiguities. In *Proceedings of the 22nd International Conference on Computational Linguistics (COLING-8)*, pages 433–440, Manchester.

A. Kilgarriff. 2003. Thesauruses for natural language processing. In *Proceedings of NLP-KE*, pages 5–13, Beijing, China.

E. Krahmer and M. Theune. 2002. Efficient context-sensitive generation of referring expressions. In K. van Deemter and R. Kibble, editors, *Information Sharing: Reference and Presupposition in Language Generation and Interpretation, CSLI Publications*, pages 223–264.

C. Mellish and R. Dale. 1998. Evaluation in the context of natural language generation. *Computer Speech and Language*, 12(4):349–373.

I. Paraboni, J. Masthoff, and K. van Deemter. 2006. Overspecified reference in hierarchical domain: measuring the benefits for readers. In *Proceedings of the Fourth International Conference on Natural Language Generation(INLG)*, pages 55–62.

C. Paris, N. Colineau, and R. Wilkinson. 2006. Evaluations of NLG systems: Common corpus and tasks or common dimensions and metrics? In *Proceedings of the 4th International Conference on Natural Language Generation*, pages 127–129.

A. Siddharthan and A. Copestake. 2004. Generating referring expressions in open domains. In *Proceedings of the 42nd Meeting of the Association for Computational Linguistics Annual Conference (ACL-04)*.

M. Stone and B. Webber. 1998. Textual economy through close coupling of syntax and semantics. In *Proceedings of the Ninth International Workshop on Natural Language Generation*, pages 178–187, New Brunswick, New Jersey.

K. van Deemter, I. van der Sluis, and A. Gatt. 2006. Building a semantically transparent corpus for the generation of referring expressions. In *Proceedings of the 4th International Conference on Natural Language Generation*, pages 130–132.

K. van Deemter. 2004. Towards a probabilistic version of bidirectional OT syntax and semantics. *Journal of Semantics*, 21(3):251–281.

J. Viethen and R. Dale. 2006. Towards the evaluation of referring expression generation. In *Proceedings of the 4th Australasian Language Technology Workshop*, pages 115–122, Sydney, Australia.

# Towards a game-theoretic approach to content determination

**Ralf Klabunde**
Ruhr-Universität Bochum
Bochum, Germany
klabunde@linguistics.rub.de

**Abstract**

This paper argues for a game-theoretic approach to content determination that uses text-type specific strategies in order to determine the optimal content for various user types. By means of content determination for the description of numerical data the benefits of a game-theoretic treatment of content determination are outlined.

## 1 Introduction

This is a programmatic paper on the principles of content determination in natural language generation (NLG). It arose from the insight that we do not know much about the underlying principles and computational properties of several tasks in NLG. Especially conceptualization – the selection of the information to be conveyed in a natural language text, and the adaptation of this information to the language-specific requirements – is still a white spot on the generation map (Guhe, 2007). Content determination is that sub-process during conceptualization that is responsible for the selection of the information to be conveyed and its ordering. Several authors assume that establishing rhetorical relations between informational units and the successive construction of tree structures for the overall information should also be considered as a content determination task (see, e.g. Reiter and Dale (2000)), but I will ignore this task in this paper and confine my considerations to the selection and ordering of informational units, in particular propositions.

Content determination is coupled with the linguistic domain in two ways, since the content does not only need to be expressible in the target language, but the determination process is already affected by pragmatic organisation principles for specific text types. I am convinced that game theory is the appropriate tool for a formulation of these principles.

In what follows, I will first explain why content determination should be viewed as a game played by the speaker/system $\mathcal{S}$ and the speaker's/system's representation of a listener/user $\mathcal{L}$ – the 'user model'. After that I will outline the different strategies relevant for content determination by means of the content for user-tailored descriptions of numerical data.

## 2 Appproaches to content determination in NLG

The various approaches to content determination proposed in the literature may be classified in a two-dimensional way, viz. with respect to information flow (top down vs. bottom-up), and with respect to the methods used (reasoning or the use of schemas).

From an engineering perspective – the dominant view in NLG – a top-down approach, focusing on the communicative goal and using schemas which determine where to realize which information, is the most attractive and most often method used, although it lacks of a theoretical grounding. A deep reasoning approach would thus be more attractive, but is not always feasible in practice.

One of the problems in content determination is that the amount and quality of the information to be conveyed depends on the interests and cognitive abilities of the respective user and the coherence requirement. Content determination is selecting material from the domain in the hope that it will permit a coherent realization as a text. Hence, this sub-task should be viewed as a process that is also constrained by pragmatic principles for establishing coherence.

I proceed on the assumption that a theoretically well-founded reasoning approach can be established within the framework of analytic game theory (see, e.g., Shoham and Leyton-Brown (2009)).

*Proceedings of the 12th European Workshop on Natural Language Generation*, pages 102–105,
Athens, Greece, 30 – 31 March 2009. ©2009 Association for Computational Linguistics

The benefit of a game theoretic treatment is its focus on interacting agents and the reasoning mechanisms associated with games: If we are able to show that the content to be conveyed is determined by concepts of rational interaction, then we get insights into the principles that guide the overall content determination process.

The basic ideas are as follows: First, the random device – used in game-theoretic pragmatics to provide $\mathcal{S}$ with some meaning – must be replaced by a function that maps informational units of the domain to propositions. Additionally, $\mathcal{L}$'s reasoning capabilities are taken into account. The interplay of both components reflects $\mathcal{S}$'s cognitive effort to construct the proposition and represents some of the adaptive cognitive mechanisms of $\mathcal{S}$. It is well known from pragmatic and psycholinguistic studies that speakers do not only try to minimize their own effort in the production process, but that they take into account features of the listener and adopt content and form of their utterance to the listener's assumed cognitive and linguistic capabilities. Hence, the process of content determination is guided by speaker-strategies and adaptation processes which should be modelled as adopted addressee-strategies. Under this view, the ultimate goal of content determination is to find a coherent catenation of propositions that is tailored to the addressee: $\mathcal{S}$ is a decision-maker and she is already playing with $\mathcal{L}$ at pre-linguistic stages.

## 3 Game theoretic pragmatics

Jäger (2007) describes the conception of game-theoretic pragmatic analyses as follows: A game is an utterance situation with a speaker $\mathcal{S}$ and a hearer $\mathcal{L}$ as players. The actions performed by these players are the production and interpretation of utterances, and the payoffs represent the cognitive and linguistic expenses of both players. If a set $M$ of meanings is given and a set $F$ of linguistic forms, a speaker strategy $s$ is a function from $M$ to $F$. Accordingly, a hearer strategy $h$ is a function from $F$ to $M$. In this paper, I assume that $M$ is a set of propositions, i.e. a set of situative, truth-functional, concepts.

Within this framework, the production process is treated in a simplifying way. A random device assigns some meaning $m \in M$ to $\mathcal{S}$ who has to select an appropriate form $f \in F$. Successful communication is given if $\mathcal{L}$ is able to reconstruct $m$ from $f$. The $\delta$-function defines just this:

$$\delta_m(s,h) = \begin{cases} 1 & \text{iff } h(s(m)) = m \\ 0 & \text{otherwise} \end{cases} \quad (1)$$

$\mathcal{S}$ has a choice between simple or more complex expressions to express the meaning $m$. In order to measure this complexity, a function $cost$ from $F$ to the nonnegative real numbers is given whose exact shape is of no interest for this paper. The speaker utility $u_s$ refers to the $cost$-function in addition to some positive coefficient $k$ that represents the speaker's priorities. A low value of $k$ indicates that communicative success is more important than minimal effort, and a high value of $k$ means that effort is more important than success.

$$u_s(m,s,h) = \delta_m(s,h) - k \times cost(s(m)) \quad (2)$$

The addressee's utility can be identified with the $\delta$-function:

$$u_h(m,s,h) = \delta_m(s,h) \quad (3)$$

In order to adopt Jäger's characterization of a game-theoretic model of communication to NLG purposes, one has to modify it into two directions. The minor change concerns the random device that assigns meanings to the speaker. I replace this device by a function $i$ that maps informational units $d$ of the domain $D$ to propositions $p \in M$. The production grammar $s$ picks up these propositions and transforms them into linguistic forms $f$.

The more substantial change concerns the hearer strategy. From an NLG perspective, one is not primarily interested in a hearer strategy that maps forms to meanings, but in the effect of the conveyed information w.r.t. the hearer's information state $T_{\mathcal{L}}$. The aim of $\mathcal{S}$ is to modify $T_{\mathcal{L}}$, but it is $\mathcal{L}$ who decides how to process the information conveyed by $\mathcal{S}$. In general, $\mathcal{L}$'s interpretation task is to find an explanation for $p$ on the basis of his own beliefs. In other words, interpretation is abductive reasoning (Hobbs et al., 1993). Suppose $\mathcal{S}$ conveys a set of propositions $A$. Then the actions available to $\mathcal{L}$ – if $A$ is new information for him – are several update mechanisms $up(T_{\mathcal{L}}, A)$. He may just add $A$ to $T_{\mathcal{L}}$ and accept $A$ as new information without finding any explanation for $A$: $up(T_{\mathcal{L}}, A) = (T_{\mathcal{L}} \cup A) \neq T_{\mathcal{L}}$. The other extreme would be to compute the set of all logical consequences of $T_{\mathcal{L}} \cup A$, i.e. $up(T_{\mathcal{L}}, A) = Cn(T_{\mathcal{L}} \cup A)$.[1] However, this set is just the ideal state of a logically omniscient person; a more realistic view is to characterize the strategies of $\mathcal{L}$ by different depths in reasoning, starting from depth = 0 (i.e. $T_{\mathcal{L}} \cup A$) up to some information state close to $Cn(T_{\mathcal{L}} \cup A)$. I use $up(T_{\mathcal{L}}, A) \prec Cn(T_{\mathcal{L}} \cup A)$ to represent this state. Note that $up(T_{\mathcal{L}}, A) \prec Cn(T_{\mathcal{L}} \cup A)$ is not a fixed information state but depends on the user type. If the players want to be communicatively successful, $\mathcal{L}$ should ideally try to find an explanation for $A$ that results in that mentioned information state. Hence, communicative success with respect to a single proposition $p$ may now be defined by:

$$\delta_d(s,h,i,up) = \begin{cases} 1 & \text{iff } h(s(i(d))) = i(d) = p \\ & \text{and} \\ & up(T_{\mathcal{L}}, p) \prec Cn(T_{\mathcal{L}} \cup \{p\}) \\ 0 & \text{otherwise} \end{cases} \quad (4)$$

The speaker utility is defined as:

$$u_s(s,h,i,up) = \delta_d(s,h,i,up) - k \times cost(i(d)) \quad (5)$$

and the hearer utility is

$$u_h(s,h,i,up) = \delta_d(s,h,i,up) \quad (6)$$

Within this overall picture of information exchange and communicative success, content determination is the interplay of $i$ with $up(T_{\mathcal{L}}, ran(i))$, i.e. the update of $\mathcal{L}$'s information state with the range of $i$. In the rest of this paper I will show by means of an example how this interplay can be spelled out in detail. As will hopefully become apparent, the approach amounts to some sort of game – a game that takes into account specific strategies of $\mathcal{S}$ and the abductive inference strategies of $\mathcal{L}$ to create a content that is optimal for both.

## 4 Content determination for reports of numerical data

Let us assume that the content underlying reports of performance data shall be tailored to an expert and a layman, respectively. The essential conceptualization process for content of this type is the summarization of numerical data to propositional units that are tailored to the addressee's needs. I use normal form games for this task in which the expertises of the users are reflected in different Nash equilibria. $\mathcal{L}$ as expert requires content with a different equilibrium than $\mathcal{L}$ as layman does.

[1]Consider that abduction in its simplest form can be reformulated in deductive terms.

The basic scenario is as follows: A speedometer $f$ provides data about speed and the distance covered during a cycling tour. These numerical data shall be transformed into propositional units that are optimal for the respective user types. For reasons of clarity, let us assume two different user types only, a training expert and a layman who want to receive a detailed and a more shallow description, respectively. In both cases the actual values recorded by the speedometer will be compared with ideal training values, and the deviations from these ideal values shall be reported in the generated text.

Of course, the main task for $\mathcal{S}$ is to summarize these numerical data in single propositions, but how to determine the amount of data to be put into one proposition? I assume that $\mathcal{S}$'s side of the coin is an approximation problem. The grade of detail required for the expert and the layman shall be given by an approximation $a$ of the function $f$. Let us assume that the approximation is 1/10 for the expert and 1/5 for the layman ($\forall x \in dom(f)$ : $a(x) = x \pm x/10$ or $a(x) = x \pm x/5$). Table 1 shows an exemplary function for the first seven measure points and the approximations used.

| distance | speed n | ideal value | approx. 1/10 | approx. 1/5 |
|---|---|---|---|---|
| 1 | 25.3 | 25 | 22.5 - 27.5 | 20.0 - 30.0 |
| 2 | 28.2 | 26 | 23.4 - 28.6 | 20.8 - 31.2 |
| 3 | 31.7 | 27 | 24.3 - 29.7 | 21.6 - 32.4 |
| 4 | 30.5 | 28 | 25.2 - 30.8 | 22.4 - 33.6 |
| 5 | 32.8 | 29 | 26.1 - 31.9 | 23.2 - 34.8 |
| 6 | 31.1 | 30 | 27.0 - 33.0 | 24.0 - 36.0 |
| 7 | 25.8 | 30 | 27.0 - 33.0 | 24.0 - 36.0 |
| ⋮ | ⋮ | ⋮ | ⋮ | ⋮ |

Table 1: Some numerical data

In addition to the values that are outside of the approximations, the *degree* of exceeding or going below the ideal value should be taken into account as well. We do not just want to generate a sentence like *at kilometer 3 you went too fast* if the actual values were outside the approximation hull and much higher than the ideal one, but *at kilometer 3 you went much too fast*. Therefore, we define a threshold such that every value above that threshold will be classified as being much higher than the ideal value, and all values below that threshold are classified as being an exiguous deviation from that ideal value. Then the six relevant speaker actions are N-0, N-1, 1/10-0, 1/10-1, 1/5-0 and 1/5-1 with 0 and 1 indicating no use of a threshold and the use of one relevant threshold, respectively.

According to section 3, the strategies of $\mathcal{L}$ concern the interpretation grammar, i.e. the mapping from linguistic forms to propositions ($h : F \rightarrow P$) and an update of $\mathcal{L}$'s information state that may include (abductive) reasoning. The abductive inferences drawn by the layman differ from those of the expert by the profundity of the explanation: While the layman is primarily interested in increasing his fitness, the expert should be interested in a more profound explanation. Let us assume three update strategies: NOINFERENCES, i.e. $up(T_{\mathcal{L}}, P) = T_{\mathcal{L}} \cup P$, EXHAUSTIVEREASONING, i.e. $up(T_{\mathcal{L}}, P) = (T_{\mathcal{L}} \cup P) \prec Cn(T_{\mathcal{L}} \cup P)$, and MUNDANEREASONING, i.e. reasoning with only a very limited number of inferences involved.

The payoffs for the players may be motivated as follows. For $\mathcal{S}$ holds: A more detailed content requires more effort in providing that content. Furthermore, realizing the degree of exceeding the value requires additional cognitive effort. Since $\mathcal{S}$ pursues to reduce her efforts, the highest payoff will be associated with the lowest effort. The more detailed the content is, the lesser is $\mathcal{L}$'s effort to reason. However, a text that explains everything violates the Gricean maxim of quantity. Therefore, $\mathcal{L}$ should prefer at least mundane reasoning, and we could motivate the listener's payoffs by the number of inferences to be drawn.

The utility matrix in Table 2 shows the action combinations of $\mathcal{S}$ and $\mathcal{L}$ as layman. The Nash equilibrium is the strategy (1/5-0, MUNDANEREASONING); $\mathcal{S}$ will generate propositions that comprise the numerical data outside of the widest approximation hull, and without any further differentiation w.r.t. the degree of exceeding the ideal values. $\mathcal{S}$ knows that $\mathcal{L}$'s interpretation of the propositions is an abductive proof graph that represents a simple explanation of them.

With $\mathcal{L}$ as expert the payoffs must be swapped. Since the expert is able to find a more profound explanation, he strives for exhaustive reasoning. $\mathcal{S}$, in turn, knows this and will therefore select the smaller approximation. Hence, we get the utility matrix in Table 3 with (1/10-0, EXHAUSTIVEREASONING) as Nash equilibrium.

| | NOINF. | MUNDANER. | EXH.R. |
|---|---|---|---|
| N-0 | 1,5 | 1,7 | 1,1 |
| N-1 | 0,6 | 0,8 | 0,2 |
| 1/10-0 | 3,5 | 3,7 | 3,1 |
| 1/10-1 | 2,6 | 2,8 | 2,2 |
| 1/5-0 | 6,5 | 6,7 | 6,1 |
| 1/5-1 | 5,6 | 5,8 | 5,2 |

Table 2: Utility matrix with $\mathcal{L}$ as layman

| | NOINF. | MUNDANER. | EXH.R. |
|---|---|---|---|
| N-0 | 1,5 | 1,1 | 1,7 |
| N-1 | 0,6 | 0,2 | 0,8 |
| 1/10-0 | 6,5 | 6,1 | 6,7 |
| 1/10-1 | 5,6 | 5,2 | 5,8 |
| 1/5-0 | 3,5 | 3,1 | 3,7 |
| 1/5-1 | 2,6 | 2,2 | 2,8 |

Table 3: Utility matrix with $\mathcal{L}$ as expert

## 5 Outlook

Due to the programmatic status of this paper, several issues have been omitted we will deal with in our future work. The most pressing tasks concern the action sets of $\mathcal{S}$ and $\mathcal{L}$ that must be refined, and the payoffs must be based on empirical observations. However, as sketchy as the given example may be, it shows that NLG stands to benefit from Game Theory.

## References


Markus Guhe. 2007. *Incremental Conceptualization for Language Production*. Lawrence Erlbaum, Mahwah, NJ.

Jerry Hobbs, Mark Stickel, Douglas Appelt, and Paul Martin. 1993. Interpretation as Abduction. *Artificial Intelligence*, 63, 69-142.

Gerhard Jäger. 2007. Evolutionary Game Theory and typology: a case study. *Language*, 83, 74–109.

Ehud Reiter and Robert Dale. 2000. *Building Natural Language Generation Systems*. Cambridge University Press, Cambridge.

Yoav Shoham and Kevin Leyton-Brown. 2009. *Multiagent Systems: Algorithmic, Game-theoretic and Logical Foundations*. Cambridge University Press, Cambridge.

# Generating Natural Language Descriptions of Ontology Concepts

**Niels Schütte**
Dublin Institute of Technology
Dublin, Ireland
niels.schutte@student.dit.ie

**Abstract**

This paper gives an overview of ongoing work on a system for the generation of NL descriptions of classes defined in OWL ontologies. We present a general structuring approach for such descriptions. Since OWL ontologies do not by default contain the information necessary for lexicalization, lexical information has to be added to the data via annotations. A rule-based mechanism for automatically deriving these annotations is presented.

## 1 Overview

There exists a body of works regarding the verbalization of content from RDF data or ontologies like OWL. Some approaches (such as (Galanis and Androutsopoulos, 2007)) rely on rich domain dependent resources, while other approaches try to do away with such resources as much as possible and derive information such as lexicalization data that is not explicitly included in the ontology from the available data.

## 2 Data Model and Message Definition

The goal of the system is to generate natural language texts from class definitions in an OWL ontology that serve as a description of the class.

To generate textual descriptions, linguistic representations for the contents of the ontology have to be found. Since OWL ontologies do not by default contain the information necessary for lexicalization, lexical information has to be added to the data. In the current system, classes are assumed to represent simple objects of the world and therefore to be realizable as noun phrases that can be lexicalized with the name of the class.

Attributes of classes are described in OWL by defining **restrictions** that apply to so called **properties**. Properties are binary relations among ontology objects. They are realized as syntactic structures that connect objects. During annotation, each property is assigned a certain **relation type** that determines the syntactic structure that is used to realize the property.

### 2.1 Relation types

The relation types form an abstraction over the possible structural realizations of properties by providing a specification of a surface structure that can be used to realize the property. Depending on the type of the relation, a number of other attributes of the relation may be specified to determine details of the realization, such as lexicalizations for some elements of the structure and a specification about how to fill the parameters of the configuration with the parameters of the property. At the moment there exists a small set of relation types that covers most of the relations in the example ontologies that were considered for the system. This approach corresponds with the results presented in (Hewlett et al, 2005) where the authors affirm to have found a small set of patterns that covers most of the properties in a number of major ontologies.

The relation type of a property also determines whether a property can be expressed as an adjective modifier. This information can be exploited in aggregation operations to create more concise text.

The two most important relation types are the ones called *simple* and *roleplaying*.

*simple* specifies that the properties should be realized as a simple configuration of two participants that are connected with a verb in the active form. This type fits preferably for properties like "eats" or "produces". The objects in the domain and range position of the property are most often mapped straight to domain and range parameters of the relation. Apart from this, it has to be determined which word to use to lexicalize the verb that

*Proceedings of the 12th European Workshop on Natural Language Generation*, pages 106–109,
Athens, Greece, 30 – 31 March 2009. 

appears in the realization of the property. A typical sentence formed with a property of this type (in this example the property "eats") would be

*A mouse eats only cheese.*

*roleplaying* specifies that the property should be realized as a configuration in which one participant fulfills a certain role for another participants. This relation is typically used to realize properties like "hasColor" or "hasHabitat", since even though the property itself is a binary relation, its name suggests to express it as a configuration that involves, apart from the domain and range objects, a third object whose lexicalization is derived from the name of the property. A sentence for the property "hasParent" of this type would be:

*A child has at most 2 humans as parent.*

## 2.2 Automatic Annotation

In this section we describe our approach to automatically generating annotations using rules based on a part of speech analysis of the property name. A rule consists of a pattern and a specification of the relation that is to be used to realize the property. The pattern is a sequence of part of speech elements. A pattern fits a property, if the property name can be split into words whose part of speech are equal to the sequence specified by the pattern [1].

If the pattern fits, the relation is instantiated according to the specification associated in the rule with the pattern. Keywords can be used to assign the objects in the domain or range position to the domain or range slot of the relation. Names of parts of speech detected in the pattern can also be used to assign parts of the property name as lexicalization to elements of the relation. The following rule is currently used in the system:

```
VP -> Simple (SUBJ, OBJ, VP)
```

It assigns properties like "eats" to *simple* relations that use the domain object of the property as domain object and the range subject likewise. The element of the property name "VP" (in the example for "eats", simply "eats") is used to lexicalize the verb of the relation. Detected elements are always reduced to their stem before assigning lexicalizations (e.g. "eat" is actually assigned instead of "eats"). The following rule currently assigns properties like "hasColor" to *roleplaying* relations.

[1] We are currently exploring if this approach should be extended to regular expressions instead of sequences.

```
VP NP -> RolePlaying(SUBJ, OBJ, VP, NP)
         COND has(VP)
```

The *COND* part specifies an additional condition where certain parts of the pattern have to be filled with special words. The inclusion of special conditions for the rules allows it to create more specific patterns.

At this stage, the automatic assignment is only performed for annotating properties. It is however possible to extend this approach to classnames to create linguistically more complex lexicalizations for classes.

# 3 Structuring

The description texts generated by our system are structured based on analysis of texts from encyclopedia entries and the possible relations among the available pieces of information. The information available in the definition is dissected into discrete message objects. Before structuring begins, the system attempts to summarize some of the information from the definition.For example it is possible to combine cardinality restrictions without losing information.

The structure of the descriptions consists of an introductory passage, whose main purpose it is to give a quick burst of information about the class, and a sequence of subsequent sections that presents the remaining information about the class structured according to the properties of the class. The description is closed with the presentation of the classes the subject class is disjoint with. In general each element is realized as one complex sentence.

The introduction starts off with information about *what kind of thing* the class is. This is realized by introducing the messages presenting the immediate superclasses of the class. To set the class apart from the superclasses the introduction is enriched with as much additional information as possible and textually sensible. This information is linked as closely as possible to the superclass message. This is realized by adding messages that can be transformed into adjective modifiers to the reference to the subject class in the first sentence, and adding more information as a relative sentence. This results in sentences such as:

*A grizzly bear is a large bear that lives only in North America.*

This phrase consists of three distinct pieces of information from the ontology: the immediate superclass of the class "grizzly bear" and two restrictions for a property named "hasSize" (e.g. $\exists$ hasSize {Large}) and "livesIn" (e.g. $\forall$ livesIn NorthAmerica). The first restriction was chosen for this position because it can be expressed as an adjective. Whether and how a message can be transformed into an adjective is determined by the attributes of the relation type of the property of the restriction that is the source of the message. In this case, a manual annotator has decided that the values of the "hasSize" property can be alternatively be directly used as adjectives of the subject of the description instead of using the default realization of the *roleplaying* relation. This decision can just as well be made heuristically in the automatic annotation generation process. The criterion here would be that the word "Size" that specifies the role played by the range object refers to an immediate quality of the class. Other candidates for a class of such words are "Color" or "Gender". However there exists a great number of properties that fit the *roleplaying* pattern for which such a transformation would not be appropriate. Examples include the properties "hasParents" or "hasMaker". In these properties the role refers to an object external to the class rather than to an immediate quality of it.

The rest of the available information is ordered into groups according to the property (**property groups**) that is restricted by the restriction that is contained in the message. This produces groups of messages that all pertain to the same property. Those property groups are the first step towards text sections that deal with one particular attribute of the class that is described through restrictions on each property addressed.

## 4 Microplanning

In the next step, microplanning is performed to derive complete text specifications. Most of the structuring that is left to be done is performed in the property groups and is linked with microplanning operations such as aggregation and is therefore performed at this stage.

Depending on the types of the restrictions in the messages, rhetorical structures are formed inside each group. Figure 1 gives an overview of possible structures inside a group. The boxes represent complexes of messages based on groups of restrictions. The names refer to the names for restriction types used in the Manchester Syntax for OWL, with CARD summarizing all cardinality restrictions. The labels on the arcs represent rhetorical relations that connect the complexes.

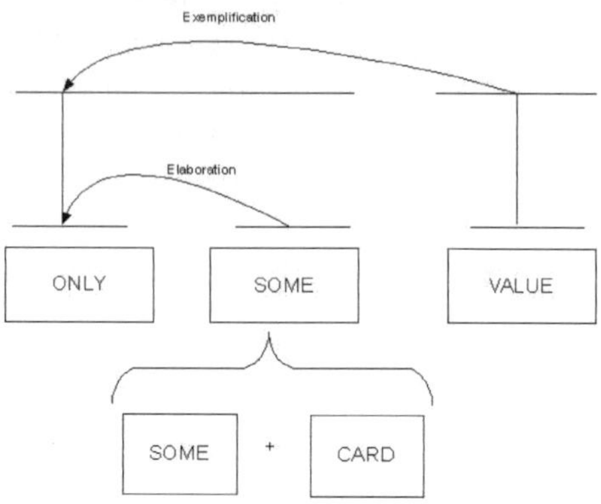


Figure 1: Structure inside groups

The SOME restrictions and CARD restrictions can be combined, since both make statements about the positive existence of objects. This combination is linked to the ONLY restrictions via an elaboration. VALUE restrictions finally can be connected to this complex via an exemplification relation since they make a statement about concrete objects as opposed to the statements about possible objects made by the other restrictions.

An example for a statement generated from a moderately complex structure containing an ONLY restriction and an EXACTLY restriction would be this sentence:

*A gizzly bear has only bears as parents and it has exactly two bears as parents.*

The semantic content behind this sentence is a group of messages concerning the property "hasParent", that contains messages derived from the restrictions $\forall$ *parent bear* and $=$ *hasParent 2*. Figure 2 presents the structure that is formed inside the group. The SOME block formed from the cardinality restrictions and the SOME restrictions which are not present in this example. The resulting block is then connected to the ONLY block. It should be noted that the ONLY restriction is exploited to determine the term that is used to lexicalize the range object of the message from the cardinality restriction, since the restrictions given through it are normally more specific than the normal range defined for the property.

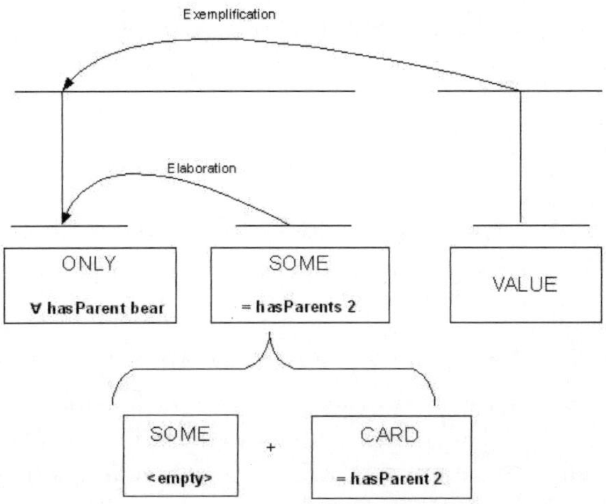


Figure 2: Example of structure inside a group in action

The task of Referring Expression Generation stage in this system currently only makes sure an appropiate pronoun is used in subsequent reference to the subject of the description. In general the neutral pronoun "it" is used, unless a restriction is found that can be interpreted as an information about the gender of the class.

A complete description text for the concept of a grizzly bear taking reference expressions into account may be:

*A grizzly bear is a large bear that lives only in north america. It has only bears as parents and it has exactly two bears as parents. A grizzly bear can not be an ice bear or a brown bear.*

The first sentence is the introduction of the description. The second sentence is the realization of the property group of the property "hasParent". The last sentence finally presents the classes the subject class is disjoint with and closes the description.

Surface Generation is performed by the KPML language generation system (Bateman, 1997). The structural relations of the text plan, the linguistic relations inside the messages and the representations of classes are enriched with SPL plan fragments that combine to form a complete specification for a text. The type of a restriction is realized as a modification of the message.

## 5 Conclusion

The system generates sensible texts for a number of classes in a number of ontologies. The proposed schema for the structure of the text appears to produce natural sounding introductions to the text as well a sensible organization for the remaining bulk of the information. We are not aware of a system that performs the same task to the same degree without relying on more domain specific resources. The system does not and can not cover all imaginable ontologies. Problems especially arise from complex class definitions that contain nested class definitions, since they can require quite complex linguistic structures. For evaluation, testers familiar with the OWL formalism will be asked to judge whether the produced texts accurately represent the specified information, and whether the texts appear natural.

The structure-based annotation mechanism profits from well organized approaches to naming classes and properties, but runs into problems if names cannot be fitted into the expected patterns. In this case, the generated annotations have to be checked manually and need to be corrected. If formal patterns like simple grammars for naming can be agreed upon during the design of the ontology, these patterns can be exploited directly to generate annotations. This might be worth considering as a step in ontology development.

## Acknowledgements

The author would like to thank John Bateman for his input to the work and his help with this paper, and John Kelleher for his reviewing and comments.

## References

Dimitrios Galanis and Ion Androutsopoulos 2007. *Generating Multilingual Personalized Descriptions from OWL Ontologies on the Semantic Web: the NaturalOWL System*

Xiantang Sun and Chris Mellish 2006. *Domain Independent Sentence Generation from RDF Representations for the Semantic Web*

Daniel Hewlett and Aditya Kalyanpur and Vladimir Kolovski and Christian Halaschek-Wiener 2005. *Effective NL Paraphrasing of Ontologies on the Semantic Web.*

Ehud Reiter and Robert Dale 2000. *Building natural language generation systems.* Cambridge Press.

Bateman, J. A. 1997. *Enabling technology for multilingual natural language generation: the KPML development environment* Journal of Natural Language Engineering 3(1)

# A Japanese corpus of referring expressions used in a situated collaboration task

**Philipp Spanger   Yasuhara Masaaki   Iida Ryu   Tokunaga Takenobu**
Department of Computer Science
Tokyo Institute of Technology
{philipp, yasuhara, ryu-i, take}@cl.cs.titech.ac.jp

## Abstract

In order to pursue research on generating referring expressions in a situated collaboration task, we set up a data-collection experiment based on the Tangram puzzle. For a pair of participants we recorded every utterance in synchronisation with the current state of the puzzle as well as all operations by the participants. Referring expressions were annotated with their referents in order to build a referring expression corpus in Japanese. We provide preliminary results on the analysis of the corpus from various standpoints, focussing on *action-mentioning expressions*.

## 1 Introduction

Referring expressions are a linguistic device to refer to a certain object, enabling smooth collaboration between humans and agents where physical operations are involved. Previous research often either selectively focussed only on a limited number of expression-types or set up overly controlled experiments. In contrast, we intend to work towards analysing the whole breadth of referring expressions in a situated domain. For this purpose we created a corpus (in Japanese) and analysed it from various standpoints.

From very early on in referring expression research, there has been some interest in the collaborative aspect of the reference process (Clark and Wilkes-Gibbs, 1986). This has more recently developed into creating situated corpora in order to analyse the referring expressions occurring in situated collaborative tasks. The *COCONUT* corpus (Di Eugenio et al., 2000) is collected from keyboard-input dialogues between two participants who are collaboratively working on a simple 2-D design task (buying and arranging furniture for two rooms). In contrast, the *QUAKE* corpus (Byron et al., 2005) – as well as the more recent *SCARE* corpus (Stoia et al., 2008), which is an extension of *QUAKE* – is based on an interaction captured in a 3-D virtual reality (VR) world where two participants collaboratively carry out a treasure hunting task. There has been ongoing work to exploit these two resources for research on different aspects of referring expressions (Pamela W. Jordan, 2005; Byron, 2005).

However, while these resources have inspired new research into different aspects of referring expressions, at the same time they have clear limitations. The *COCONUT* corpus is collected from dialogues in which participants refer to symbol-like objects in a 2-D world. It thus resembles the more recent (non-collaborative) TUNA-corpus (van Deemter, 2007) in tending to encourage very simple types of expressions. Furthermore, limiting participants' interaction to keyboard input makes the dialogue less natural. While the *QUAKE* corpus deals with a more complex domain (3-D virtual world), the participating subjects were only able to carry out limited kinds of actions (pushing buttons, picking up or dropping objects) as compared with the complexity of the three-dimensional target domain.

In contrast to these two corpora, we set up a comparatively simple collaborative task (Tangram Puzzle) allowing participants to freely communicate via speech and to perform actions various enough to accomplish the given task, e.g. picking, moving, turning and rotating pieces. All utterances by participants were recorded in synchronisation with operations on objects and the object arrangement. The utterances were transcribed and all referring expressions found were annotated together with their referents. Thus, this corpus allows us to study in detail human-human interaction, particularly referring expressions in a situated setting. In what follows, we first describe details of the building of the corpus and then provide

*Proceedings of the 12th European Workshop on Natural Language Generation*, pages 110–113,
Athens, Greece, 30 – 31 March 2009. 

results of our preliminary analysis. This analysis reveals a novel type of referring expression mentioning an action on objects, which we call *action-mentioning expressions*.

## 2 Building the corpus

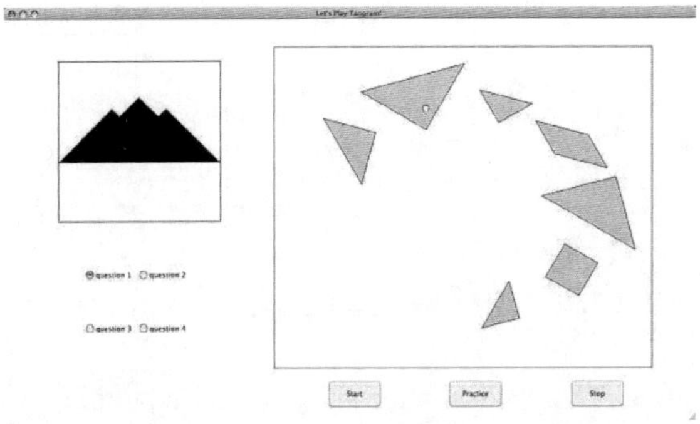

Figure 1: Screenshot of the Tangram simulator

### 2.1 Experimental setting

We recruited 12 Japanese graduate students (4 females, 8 males) and split them into 6 pairs. Each pair was instructed to solve the Tangram puzzle (an ancient Chinese geometrical puzzle) cooperatively. The goal of Tangram is to construct a given shape by arranging seven pieces of simple figures as shown in Figure 1.

In order to record detailed information of the interaction (position of pieces, participants' actions), we implemented a Tangram simulator in which the pieces on the computer display can be moved, rotated and flipped with simple mouse operations. Figure 1 shows the simulator interface in which the left shows the goal shape area and the right the working area. We assigned two different roles to participants, a *solver* and an *operator*; the solver thinks of the arrangement of the pieces to make the goal shape and gives instructions to the operator, while the operator manipulates the pieces with the mouse according to the solver's instructions.

A solver and an operator sit side by side in front of their own computer display. Both participants share the same working area of the simulator. The operator can manipulate the pieces, but cannot see the goal shape. In contrast, the solver sees the goal shape but cannot move pieces. A shield screen was set between the participants in order to prevent them from peeking at their partner's display. In this asymmetrical interaction, we can expect many referring expressions during the interaction.

Each pair is assigned four exercises and the participants exchanged roles after two exercises. We set a time limit of 15 minutes for an exercise. Utterances by the participants are recorded separately in stereo through headset microphones in synchronisation with the position of the pieces and the mouse actions. In total, we collected 24 dialogues of about four hours. The average length of a dialogue was 10 minutes 43 seconds.

### 2.2 Annotation

Recorded dialogues were transcribed with a time code attached to each utterance. Since our main concern is collecting referring expressions, we defined an utterance to be a complete sentence to prevent a referring expression being split into several utterances. Referring expressions were annotated together with their referents by using the multi-purpose annotation tool SLAT (Noguchi et al., 2008). Two annotators (two of the authors) annotated four dialogue texts separately. We annotated all 24 dialogue texts and corrected discrepancies by discussion between the annotators.

## 3 Analysis of the corpus

We collected a total of 1,509 tokens and 449 types of referring expressions in 24 dialogues. Our asymmetric experimental setting tended to encourage referring expressions from the solver, while the operator was constrained to confirming his understanding of the solver's instructions. This is reflected in the number of referring expressions by the solver (1,287) largely outnumbering those of the operator (222). There are a number of expressions (215 expressions; 15% of the total) referring to multiple objects (referring to 2 or more pieces) and we excluded them from our current analysis. We exclusively deal here with expressions referring to a specific single piece or indefinite expressions, i.e. those that have no definite referent (in total 1,294 tokens).

We found the following syntactic/semantic features used in the expressions: i) demonstratives (adjectives and pronouns), ii) object attribute-values, iii) spatial relations, iv) actions on an object and v) others. The number of these features is summarised in Table 1. (Note that multiple features can be used in a single expression.) The right-most column shows an example with its En-

Table 1: Features of referring expressions

| | Feature | types | tokens | Example |
|---|---|---|---|---|
| i) | *demonstrative* | 118 | 745 | |
| | *adjective* | 100 | 196 | "*ano migigawa no sankakkei* (that triangle at the right side)" |
| | *pronoun* | 19 | 551 | "*kore* (this)" |
| ii) | *attribute* | 303 | 641 | |
| | *size* | 165 | 267 | "*tittyai sankakkei* (the small triangle)" |
| | *shape* | 271 | 605 | "*ôkii sankakkei* (the large triangle)" |
| | *direction* | 6 | 6 | "*ano sita muiteru dekai sankakkei* (that large triangle facing to the bottom)" |
| iii) | *spatial relations* | 129 | 148 | |
| | *projective* | 125 | 144 | "*hidari no okkii sankakkei* (the small triangle on the left)" |
| | *topological* | 2 | 2 | "*ôkii hanareteiru yatu* (the big distant one)" |
| | *overlapping* | 2 | 2 | "*sono sita ni aru sankakkei* (the triangle underneath it)" |
| iv) | *action-mentioning* | 78 | 85 | "*migi ue ni doketa sankakkei* (the triangle you put away to the top right)" |
| v) | *others* | 29 | 30 | |
| | *remaining* | 15 | 15 | "*nokotteiru ôkii sankakkei* (the remaining large triangle)" |
| | *similarity* | 14 | 15 | "*sore to onazi katati no* (the one of the same shape as that one)" |

glish translation. The identified feature in the referring expression is underlined.

We note here a tendency to employ object attributes, particularly the attribute "shape" as well as use of demonstratives, particularly demonstrative pronouns. These kinds of referring expressions are quite general and appear in a variety of other non-situated settings as well. In addition, we found another kind of expression not usually employed by humans outside of situated collaboration tasks; referring expressions mentioning an action on an object. We have 85 expressions (over 6% of the total) of this type in our corpus.

## 4 Action-mentioning expressions

We further analysed those expressions that mention an action on an object, which we call *action-mentioning expressions* hereafter. Although there was significant variation in usage of action-mentioning expressions among the pairs, all 6 pairs of participants used at least one action-mentioning expression, indicating that it is a fundamental type of expression for this task setting. *Action-mentioning expressions* are different from *haptic-ostensive* referring expressions (Foster et al., 2008) since *action-mentioning expressions* are not necessarily accompanied by simultaneous physical operation on an object.

Action-mentioning expressions can be again divided into three categories: i) combination of a temporal adverbial with a verb indicating an action ("turned", "put", "moved", etc) (55 tokens or about 65% of action-mentioning expression), ii) use of temporal adverbials without a verb, i.e. verb ellipsis (22 tokens or about 26%) and iii) expressions with a verb without temporal adverbials (8 tokens or about 9%). The second category including verb ellipsis would be rare in English, but it is quite natural in Japanese.

Only less than 10% of this kind of expression did not include any temporal adverbial, indicating that humans tend to describe the temporal aspect of an action. This needs to be integrated into any generation algorithm for this task domain. The temporal adverbials used by the participants were the Japanese "*sakki no NP* (the NP [*verb*-ed] just before)" or "*ima no NP* (the current NP/the NP [you are *verb*-ing] now/the NP [*verb*-ed] just before)". "*Ima*" generally refers to the current time point ("now"). It can, however, refer to a past time point as well, thus it is ambiguous.

Participants tended to use "*ima*" largely in its perfect meaning (completed action). The frequency of use of "*ima*" in its perfect meaning in comparison to its progressive meaning was about 2:1. The distribution of the two types of temporal adverbials "*sakki*" and "*ima*" was about 2:3. The slight preference here for "*ima*" might be explained by its dual meanings (progressive and perfect) in contrast to the exclusive use of "*sakki*" for past actions.

Figure 2 shows the distribution of "*sakki* (just before)" and past-cases of "*ima* (now)" dependent on the time-distance to the action they refer to. For actions occurring within a timeframe of about 10 seconds previous to uttering an expression, participants had an overwhelming preference for "*ima*". The frequency of "*ima*" decreases quickly for actions that occurred 10-20 seconds prior to the utterance. In contrast, after 20 seconds from the ac-

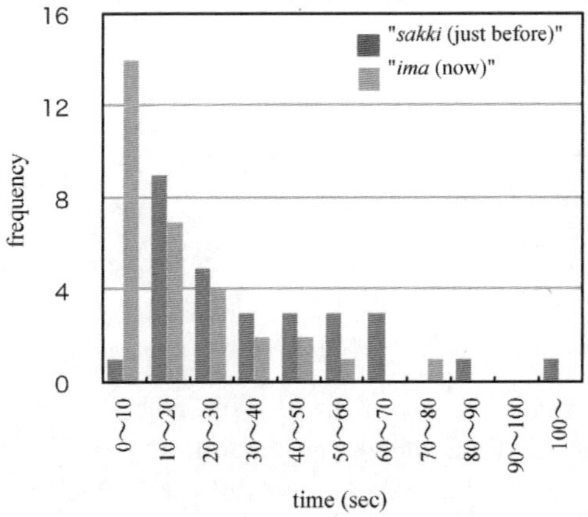


Figure 2: Frequency of "*sakki*" and "*ima*" over the time-distance to referenced action

tion, participants prefered "*sakki*".

In addition, we investigated what actions occurred in between the utterance and the action mentioned. The actions we take into account here are basic manipulations of an object like "move", "flip", "click" and so on. Referring to an immediately preceding action, participants had a strong preference for using "*ima*". Interestingly, with only one other action in between, the participants' preference becomes opposite (i.e. "*sakki*" is preferred.). For referring to actions further in the past (i.e. more actions in between), there was a continous preference for "*sakki*" over "*ima*". Further analysis should also investigate the phenomenon of the difference in use of temporal adverbials for other languages and whether this is related to characteristics of the Japanese language or rather an inherent property of the use of temporal adverbials in natural language.

## 5 Conclusion and future work

We collected a corpus of Japanese referring expressions as a first step towards developing algorithms for generating referring expressions in a situated collaboration. We carried out an initial analysis of the collected expressions, focussing on expressions that include a mention of an action on an object. We noted that they are often combined with temporal adverbials with participants seeking to make a temporal ordering of actions. In addition, we intend to further analyse other types of expressisons (demonstratives, etc) and work on developing generation algorithms for this domain. In future work, we intend to generalise this experiment in the Tangram-domain to other domains. Furthermore, information such as gestures and eye movements should be incorporated in data collection. This will lay the basis for the development of more general models for the generation of referring expressions in a situated collaborative task.

## References


Donna Byron, Thomas Mampilly, Vinay Sharma, and Tianfang Xu. 2005. Utilizing visual attention for cross-modal coreference interpretation. In *CONTEXT 2005*, pages 83–96.

Donna K. Byron. 2005. The OSU Quake 2004 corpus of two-party situated problem-solving dialogs. Technical report, Department of Computer Science and Enginerring, The Ohio State University.

H. H. Clark and D. Wilkes-Gibbs. 1986. Referring as a collaborative process. *Cognition*, 22:1–39.

B. Di Eugenio, P. W. Jordan, R. H. Thomason, and J. D Moore. 2000. The agreement process: An empirical investigation of human-human computer-mediated collaborative dialogues. *International Journal of Human-Computer Studies*, 53(6):1017–1076.

Mary Ellen Foster, Ellen Gurman Bard, Markus Guhe, Robin L. Hill, Jon Oberlander, and Alois Knoll. 2008. The roles of haptic-ostensive referring expressions in cooperative, task-based human-robot dialogue. In *Proceedings of 3rd Human-Robot Interaction*, pages 295–302.

Masaki Noguchi, Kenta Miyoshi, Takenobu Tokunaga, Ryu Iida, Mamoru Komachi, and Kentaro Inui. 2008. Multiple purpose annotation using SLAT – Segment and link-based annotation tool. In *Proceedings of 2nd Linguistic Annotation Workshop*, pages 61–64.

Marilyn A. Walker Pamela W. Jordan. 2005. Learning content selection rules for generating object descriptions in dialogue. *Journal of Artificial Intelligence Research*, 24:157–194.

Laura Stoia, Darla Magdalene Shockley, Donna K. Byron, and Eric Fosler-Lussier. 2008. SCARE: A situated corpus with annotated referring expressions. In *Proceedings of the Sixth International Conference on Language Resources and Evaluation (LREC 2008)*.

Kees van Deemter. 2007. TUNA: Towards a UNified Algorithm for the generation of referring expressions. Technical report, Aberdeen University. www.csd.abdn.ac.uk/research/tuna/pubs/TUNA-final-report.pdf.

# The effect of linguistic devices in information presentation messages on comprehension and recall

**Martin I. Tietze and Andi Winterboer and Johanna D. Moore**
University of Edinburgh, Edinburgh, United Kingdom
mtietze@inf.ed.ac.uk, A.Winterboer@ed.ac.uk, J.Moore@ed.ac.uk

## Abstract

In this paper we examine the effect of linguistic devices on recall and comprehension in information presentation using both recall and eye-tracking data. In addition, the results were validated via an experiment using Amazon's *Mechanical Turk* micro-task environment.

## 1 Introduction

In this paper, we present two experiments designed to examine the impact of linguistic devices, such as discourse cues and connectives, on comprehension and recall in information presentation for natural language generation (NLG) as used in spoken dialogue systems (SDS).

Spoken dialogue systems have traditionally used simple templates to present options (e.g., flights, restaurants) and their attributes to users (Walker et al., 2004). Recently, however, researchers have proposed approaches to information presentation that use linguistic devices (e.g., but, however, moreover, only, just, also etc.) in order to highlight specific properties of and relations between items presented to the user, e.g. associations (Polifroni and Walker, 2006) and contrasts (Winterboer and Moore, 2007). Previous research indicates that linguistic devices such as connectives facilitate comprehension (see Ben-Anath, 2005, for a review). However, to our knowledge, no empirical validation has been performed to test whether using linguistic devices has an effect on comprehension and recall of the information presentated.

## 2 Experiment 1: Recall of written materials

In order to test whether there are differences in recall, we performed a within-participants reading experiment comparing recall for experiment material presented with or without linguistic devices[1] A total of 24 participants, native English speakers and mostly students of the University of Edinburgh, were paid to participate in the study. They were naive to the purpose of the experiment but were told that they were about to be presented with a number of consumer products and that they were supposed to answer questions about these. Each participant read 14 short texts describing consumer products from 14 domains, see Table 1 and Table 2 for examples. The texts are the type of presentation typically produced by spoken dialogue systems designed to help users select an entity from a set of available options. Participants' eye-movements during reading were recorded as described in section 3.

> Messina's price is £22. It has very good food quality, attentive service, and decent décor.
> Ray's price is £34. It has very good food quality, excellent service, and impressive décor.
> Alhambra's price is £16. It has good food quality, bad service, and plain décor.

Figure 1: *Experiment material without discourse cues*

> Messina's price is £22. It has very good food quality, attentive service, and decent décor.
> Ray's price is £34. It has **also** very good food quality, **but** excellent service, and **moreover** impressive décor.
> Alhambra's price is **only** £16. It has good food quality, **but** bad service, and **only** plain décor.

Figure 2: *Experiment material with discourse cues*

There were two types of messages, one containing linguistic devices to point out similari-

[1]This experiment has been presented as an one-page abstract, (Winterboer et al., 2008)

*Proceedings of the 12th European Workshop on Natural Language Generation*, pages 114–117,
Athens, Greece, 30 – 31 March 2009. 

ties and differences among the options, and one without these linguistic markers. Each participant read seven texts of each type, alternating between types. Ordering of both the domains and the text type was controlled for. We took particular care to add discourse devices without modifying the propositions in any other way. After each message, the participant had to answer three questions testing different levels of recall. Examples of each type of question are given in figure 3.

1. Verbatim questions: *Which restaurant's price is £34?*
2. Comparison questions: *Which restaurant is the cheapest?*
3. Evaluation questions: *Which restaurant would you like to go to and why?*

Figure 3: *The three types of evaluation questions with examples*

### 2.1 Experimental procedure

In each trial, participants read a text presented for up to 45 seconds on the screen. Users could press *Enter* on the keyboard when they were finished reading. They were then presented with the questions, which they had to answer one after the other. After a question was presented, the participant pressed *Enter* to be prompted to type in an answer.

### 2.2 Results

Overall, we found a consistent numerical trend indicating that items in messages containing linguistic devices could be recalled more easily (see Table 2.2). In particular, answers to comparison questions were correctly recalled significantly more often when linguistic markers were present.

| | Verb. Q. | Comp. Q. | Eval. Q. |
|---|---|---|---|
| w/o cues | 0.79 | 0.68* | 0.73 |
| with cues | 0.82 | 0.79* | 0.81 |

Figure 4: *Average recall on a scale from 0 to 1 for the 3 questions. $t$-test, "*" indicates a significant difference with $p < 0.5$.*

## 3 Comprehension of written materials

In this experiment we used an eye-tracker in order to measure reading times, because reading times are considered to be sensitive to people's ongoing discourse processing/comprehension (Haviland and Clark, 1974). We found that reading the presentation messages containing linguistic devices took generally slightly longer, with participants reading messages containing discourse cues taking 37.93 seconds per message on average, and messages without discourse cues taking 35.28 seconds on average to read. The question, however, was whether this difference could be attributed exclusively to the number of additional words or whether readers also spent more time to build a mental representation of the presentation's content by reading the parts marked by discourse cues more carefully. Alternatively, sentence complexity might also increase with the introduction of linguistic cues, which in turn increases reading times. In order to answer this question, we compared the reading times of interest areas (IA) located directly (one word) after the (potential) location of the discourse marker. In total, we determined 46 IAs within the 14 messages, each one consisting of two words or around nine characters on average.

### 3.1 Results

The results of the different reading time measures, established with linear-mixed effects model (LME) analyses in R[2] (see Table 1), do not reveal any significant differences between the two conditions, although, surprisingly, IAs had a numerically shorter reading time when linguistic markers were used. In this repeated measures design experiment, participant, IA, and item were random-effect factors and the fixed-effect factor was whether the presentation contained linguistic devices. We compared first pass and remaining pass reading times per IA, the total number of passes, and regressions in and out of the IA.

Although sentences containing linguistic devices are more complex and thus should incur longer reading times, our analyses do not any differences in reading times for the words directly following the linguistic devices. The differences in the overall reading times noted above are therefore due to the additional words (the linguistic devices) and not caused by differences in sentence complexity or increased effort towards the marked parts of the text.

[2] www.r-project.org

| | RT | FPRT | NoP | RegrIn | RegrOut |
|---|---|---|---|---|---|
| with cues | 473.83 | 1055.56 | 3.639 | 0.430 | 0.322 |
| w/o cues | 510.24 | 1150.70 | 3.567 | 0.494 | 0.350 |
| | $t = -1.511$ | $t = -0.820$ | $t = 0.625$ | $t = -1.002$ | $t = -0.519$ |
| | $p = 0.131$ | $p = 0.412$ | $p = 0.5321$ | $p = 0.3164$ | $p = 0.6039$ |

Table 1: *Eye-tracking data per IA (first pass reading times, remaining time reading times, number of passes, regressions out and in) for messages with and without discourse cues*

## 4 Experiment 2: Web-based recall of written materials

We carried out a web-based user study on Amazon's *Mechanical Turk*[3] (MT) platform both in order to verify the results obtained in the previous recall experiment and in order to test whether results obtained from casual website users are comparable to those obtained from laboratory participants who focus exclusively on performing the experiment in the lab. We recruited native English speakers online to carry out the same experiment previously conducted in the lab. MT is a web-based micro-task platform that allows researchers and developers to put small tasks requiring human intelligence on the web. Deploying MT is advantageous because it attracts many visitors due to its affiliation with the well established Amazon website and thus eases recruitment of new participants especially from outside the usual student population. In addition, conducting experiments online significantly reduces the effort involved in data collection for the experimenter. Moreover, the website allows for convenient payment for both participants and the experimenter. For these reasons, MT has recently been used in a number of language experiments (e.g., Kaisser et al., 2008; Kittur et al., 2008).

### 4.1 Participants

We had 60 participants reading the same materials that were used in experiment 1. MT does allow to place restrictions on participant location (only users from the US were allowed to participate to ensure English language skills), for instance, or the number of trials (each participant was only allowed to participate once). However, one cannot balance gender of participants or control for age and literacy reliably, as user provided data cannot be verified. Also, one does not know whether participants are conducting another task simultaneously, or are otherwise distracted. We paid \$ 2.50 for participation, which was, given that we expected the experiment to last less than 30 minutes, considerably more than participants would receive for most other tasks available. We hoped that the higher reward would encourage participants to take the task more seriously.

[3] `https://www.mturk.com/mturk/`

### 4.2 Experimental setup and procedure

In order to resemble the interface that was used in the previous experiment as closely as possible in terms of the general "look and feel", a web-based interface was implemented using Adobe's Flash format. We chose the widely used Flash format because it can be integrated into the MT environment easily and allows for tighter user control in comparison with standard HTML pages. For example, we made it impossible for users to reread the presented information once they read the corresponding question. With standard HMTL users would have been able to use their browser's back button to do just that. The experiment was then made available to the users on Amazon's MT website. The procedure was otherwise exactly the same as in experiment 1.

### 4.3 Results

The first thing we noticed when evaluating the data was that it took only a couple of hours from making the tasks available on the MT website to receiving the results. In addition, we learnt from the submitted answers that the general answer quality was comparable to answers obtained in the lab-based experiment. Average recall rate was nearly identical with 0.76 (web-based) and 0.77 (lab-based). In addition, the average answer time was also almost identical 23 minutes (web-based) and 26 minutes (lab-based) per participant. However, the results from three of the 60 participants had to be excluded from the analysis (and payment withheld), as they answered less than 50% of the questions while performing the task in less than half of the average time.

We did not find an effect on the comparison questions. Instead, this time the difference between the two conditions was significant in terms of correct answers to the evaluation question. Thus, we again found that using linguistic markers facilitates recall of information.

| | Verb. Q. | Comp. Q. | Eval. Q. |
|---|---|---|---|
| w/o cues | 0.83 | 0.62 | 0.83* |
| with cues | 0.80 | 0.65 | 0.88* |

Figure 5: *Average recall on a scale from 0 to 1 for the 3 questions in the web-based experiment. t-test, "*" indicates a significant difference with* $p < 0.5$.

## 5 Discussion and outlook

Taken together, we found a small but significant effect of discourse cues on recall. The combination of eye-tracking and recall data seems to provide a relatively clear picture: Although sentences with linguistic devices took more time to read, this is exclusively due to the additional words and not caused by a differences in the construction of the internal representation. While these findings are in line with results from psycholinguistics which demonstrated that linguistic devices may improve comprehension and recall (Ben-Anath, 2005), given the small effect, it does not fully explain the improvements in terms of task effectiveness found in information presentation for SDS (Winterboer and Moore, 2007).

We additionally validated the results using participants recruited online. The similar results show that this method is applicable to the evaluation of written language materials and adds further strength to its establishment as an alternative to lab-based experiments.

Nonetheless, in real-world SDSs users are presented with information about different options auditorily. Listening to auditory stimuli should be more difficult than reading the same stimuli, because readers can always re-read a problematic word or sentence, whereas auditory stimuli are presented sequentially and are transient. However, research on the differences between reading and listening comprehension seems to suggest that the findings found in reading can also be applied to spoken stimuli due to the commonality of processing between the two modalities (Sinatra, 1990). However, to confirm this, we are repeating the experiments in order to examine whether linguistic devices also facilitate recall and comprehension in auditorily presented messages, using stimuli created with a speech synthesiser. We plan to use the auditory moving window paradigm (Ferreira et al., 1996) to assess the impact of lingustic devices in this modality in more detail.

## References

D. Ben-Anath. 2005. The Role of Connectives in Text Comprehension. *Working Papers in TESOL and Applied Linguistics*, 5(2):1–27.

F. Ferreira, JM Henderson, MD Anes, PA Weeks, and DK McFarlane. 1996. Effects of Lexical Frequency and Syntactic complexity in Spoken-Language Comprehension: Evidence From the Auditory Moving-Window Technique. *Journal of experimental psychology. Learning, memory, and cognition*, 22(2):324–335.

S.E. Haviland and H.H. Clark. 1974. What's new? acquiring new information as a process in comprehension. *Journal of Verbal Learning and Verbal Behaviour*, 13:512–521.

Michael Kaisser, Marti Hearst, and John Lowe. 2008. Improving Search Result Quality by Customizing Summary Lengths. In *Proceedings of the 46th Annual Meeting of the Association for Computational Linguistics*.

Aniket Kittur, Ed H. Chi, and Bongwon Suh. 2008. Crowdsourcing user studies with Mechanical Turk. In *Proceeding of the twenty-sixth annual SIGCHI conference on Human factors in computing systems*.

J. Polifroni and M. Walker. 2006. Learning database content for spoken dialogue system design. In *5th International Conference on Language Resources and Evaluation (LREC)*.

G.M. Sinatra. 1990. Convergence of listening and reading processing. *Reading Research Quarterly*, 25:115–130.

Marilyn A. Walker, Steve Whittaker, Amanda Stent, Preetam Maloor, Johanna D. Moore, Michael Johnston, and Gunaranjan Vasireddy. 2004. Generation and evaluation of user tailored responses in multimodal dialogue. *Cognitive Science*, 28:811–840.

Andi Winterboer and Johanna D. Moore. 2007. Evaluating information presentation strategies for spoken recommendations. In *Proceedings of the ACM conference on Recommender Systems (RecSys '07)*.

Andi Winterboer, Johanna D. Moore, and Fernanda Ferreira. 2008. Do discourse cues facilitate recall in information presentation messages? In *Proceedings of the 9th International Conference on Spoken Language Processing*.

# Precision and mathematical form in first and subsequent mentions of numerical facts and their relation to document structure

**Sandra Williams and Richard Power**
The Open University
Walton Hall, Milton Keynes MK7 6AA, U.K.
s.h.williams@open.ac.uk; r.power@open.ac.uk

## Abstract

In a corpus study we found that authors vary *both* mathematical form and precision[1] when expressing numerical quantities. Indeed, within the same document, a quantity is often described vaguely in some places and more accurately in others. Vague descriptions tend to occur early in a document and to be expressed in simpler mathematical forms (e.g., fractions or ratios), whereas more accurate descriptions of the same proportions tend to occur later, often expressed in more complex forms (e.g., decimal percentages). Our results can be used in Natural Language Generation (1) to generate repeat descriptions within the same document, and (2) to generate descriptions of numerical quantities for different audiences according to mathematical ability.

## 1 Introduction

This study is part of the NumGen project[2], which aims (a) to investigate how numerical quantity descriptions vary in English, (b) to specify a grammar that covers these variations, and (c) to develop an algorithm that selects appropriate descriptions for people with different levels of mathematical ability. We collected, from newspapers, popular science magazines and scientific journals, examples of numerical facts that were mentioned more than once, so that first mentions could be compared with subsequent mentions. For example in the following text, two mentions of the same numerical fact – the proportion of A grades in UK A-level examinations in 2008 – are underlined:

> ***A-level results show record number of A grades***
> ***Record numbers of teenagers have received top A-level grades***
> *By Graeme Paton, Education Editor*
> *<u>More than a quarter</u> of papers were marked A as results in the so-called gold standard examination reach a new high.*
> ...
> *According to figures released today by the Joint Council for Qualifications, <u>25.9 per cent</u> of A-level papers were awarded an A grade this summer...*
> (Daily Telegraph, 14 August 2008)

Comparing the two, (a) the first (*More than a quarter*) is less precise than the second (*25.9 per cent*), (b) its mathematical form, a common fraction, is less complex than the decimal percentage form of the second, and (c) its string has more characters (i.e., it is *not* shorter in length as might be expected if it were a summary). Also, the two mentions occur in different parts of the document – the first paragraph, and the fifth paragraph.

### 1.1 What do we mean by precision?

To compare the **precision** of numerical expressions we needed a more exact definition of the concept. We derived the following rules to determine precision:

- Precision increases with the number of significant figures
- Round numbers imply vagueness (implicit approximation)
- Modifiers increase the precision of round numbers when they indicate the direction of approximation (> or <)
- Common proportional quantities imply vagueness (implicit approximation similar to round numbers)

[1] Our use of the term *precision* has nothing to do with precision in information retrieval (i.e., the percentage of documents retrieved that are relevant).

[2] http://mcs.open.ac.uk/sw6629/numgen

*Proceedings of the 12th European Workshop on Natural Language Generation*, pages 118–121,
Athens, Greece, 30 – 31 March 2009. ©2009 Association for Computational Linguistics

Our first rule concerns arithmetical precision — i.e., the number of significant figures. Thus 344 with three significant figures is more precise than 340 with only two and *56%* with two significant figures is more precise than *50%* with one.

Second, we adhere to Krifka's RNRI (round number round interpretation) theory that when speakers or writers mention a round figure such as *sixty*, they mean that the actual figure is slightly less than or more than the round number unless they explicitly modify it with (say) *exactly*, and similarly, hearers or readers interpret it as rounded (Krifka, 2007). As a consequence, *sixty* and *around sixty* have the same level of precision, while *exactly sixty* is more precise than *sixty*.

Third, we take into account modifiers (or numerical hedges) such as *under*, *over*, *more than*, and verbs such as *topped*. So we say that *over sixty* and *topped sixty* are more precise than *sixty* since they give more information.

Finally, we extend Krifka's ideas (2007) to cover common proportional quantities. Krifka confined his ideas to scalar and numerical quantities, but we propose that they can also be applied to common proportions such as *half*, *two thirds* and *three quarters* and their ratio, decimal, percentage and multiple equivalents. We hypothesise that when speakers or writers use a common proportion, they implicitly round up or down just the same as with round whole numbers, so we would argue that *around a half* is the same level of precision as *a half*, whereas *more than half* is more precise than *half*. When comparing different types, we take the implied vagueness of common proportions into account, so that we consider *25%* to be more precise than *one quarter*.

### 1.2 Maths form and conceptual complexity

Numerical proportions may be expressed by different **mathematical forms**, e.g., fractions, ratios, percentages. Complexity of mathematical form denotes the amount of effort and numerical skill required by readers to interpret a numerical quantity; as complexity of mathematical concepts increases, the amount of effort required for comprehension also increases.

As a convenient measure of the complexity of mathematical forms, we employ a scale corresponding to the levels at which they are introduced in the Mathematics Curriculum for Schools (1999); that is, we assume that simple concepts are taught before difficult ones, so that a child learns whole numbers up to ten at Level 1, then much later learns standard index form (e.g., $4.12 \text{x} 10^6$) at Level 8 (table 1).

| **Maths Form** | **Level or Complexity** |
|---|---|
| Whole numbers 1–10 | Level 1 |
| Whole numbers 1–100 | Level 2 |
| Whole numbers 1–1000 | Level 3 |
| 1-place decimals | Level 3 |
| Common fractions | Level 3 |
| Money and temperature | Level 3 |
| Whole numbers $> 1000$ | Level 4 |
| 3-place decimals | Level 4 |
| Multiples | Level 4 |
| Percentages | Level 4 |
| Fractions | Level 5 |
| Ratios | Level 5 |
| Decimal Percentages | Level 6 |
| Standard index form | Level 8 |

Table 1: Scale of Level/Complexity extracted from the Maths Curriculum for Schools (1999)

## 2 Hypotheses

Our hypotheses about repeated mentions of numerical facts are as follows:

- Precision will increase from first to subsequent mentions.
- Level of complexity of mathematical forms will increase from first to subsequent mentions.
- Changes in precision and mathematical form are related to document structure.

## 3 Empirical Study

### 3.1 The NumGen Corpus

The corpus has 97 articles on ten topics, where each topic describes the same underlying numerical quantities, e.g., 19 articles on the discovery of a new planet all published in the first week of May 2007 (from Astronomy and Astrophysics, Nature, Scientific American, New Scientist, Science, 11 newspapers and three Internet news sites). In total, the corpus has 2,648 sentences and 54,684 words.

### 3.2 Corpus analysis and annotation

The articles were split into sentences automatically, then checked and corrected manually. We annotated 1,887 numerical quantity expressions (788 integers, 319 dates, 140 decimals, 87 fractions, 107 multiples, 66 ordinals, 336 percentages and 44 ratios).

In this study, we looked for coreferring phrases containing numerical quantities, such as the sentences *... of papers were marked A* and *... of A-level papers were awarded an A grade* in the above text, and compared the numerical expressions associated with them.[3] Then, for each fact, we noted the linguistic form of first and subsequent mentions in each text and their document positions.

### 3.3 Judgements on precision and mathematical level

Two readers (the authors) judged whether precision had changed from first to subsequent mentions of a numerical fact in a text, and if so, whether it had increased or decreased, according to the rules set out in the list in section 1.1. We also judged the conceptual complexity of mathematical forms, ranging from 1 to 8 (as defined in table 1). For precision, the judges agreed on 94% of cases (Cohen's kappa is 0.88). Differences were resolved by discussion.

### 3.4 Results

Table 2 shows results for binomial tests on 88 cases of repeated numerical facts. They show a clear trend towards *unequal precision* between first and subsequent mentions and, in the 62 cases where it is unequal, an overwhelming trend for precision to *increase*. Regarding mathematical level (i.e., the complexity scale for mathematical form), the trend is for subsequent mentions to have a level *equal* to that of first mentions, but in the 31 cases where it is unequal, they show a significant trend towards an *increase in level* — i.e., subsequent mentions are conceptually more difficult.

Our first hypothesis (precision increases from first to subsequent mentions) is thus clearly supported. Our second hypothesis (level of conceptual complexity increases from first to subsequent mentions) is supported by significant increases in level only where the level changed. Note that by our definition, complexity of mathematical concepts is distinct from precision: for example, 59 is more precise than 60 but equally complex (both are taught at Level 2 – whole numbers up to 100). Further investigation revealed that mathematical level tended to remain the same where both mentions were at the beginning of a document (n=14, $p < 0.005$, in a 2-tailed binomial test, as above).

Hypothesis three (changes in precision and mathematical form are related to document structure) is partially validated in that precision and mathematical level both increase from early to later positions in the document structure.

| Observation | n | Prop. | Sig. |
|---|---|---|---|
| Precision: Equal | 26 | .30 | .0002 |
| Unequal | 62 | .70 | |
| Precision: Increase | 56 | .90 | |
| Decrease | 6 | .10 | .00001 |
| Maths Level: Equal | 57 | .65 | |
| Unequal | 31 | .35 | .007 |
| Maths Level: Increase | 25 | .81 | |
| Decrease | 6 | .19 | .0009 |

Table 2: Binomial tests on repeated mentions, based on .5 probability, 2-tailed, Z approximation.

## 4 Discussion

Are these results surprising? We believe they show that appropriate presentation of numerical information requires surprising sophistication. It is usual to *summarise* information early in an article, but with numerical facts, summarisation cannot be equated with lower precision or with simpler mathematical form. If summarisation means identifying important facts and presenting them in a condensed form, then why are early mentions of numerical facts *not* condensed? A surprisingly large proportion of first mentions (45%) had longer (or equally long) strings than subsequent mentions (see the text in the introduction, where *More than a quarter* is longer than *25.9 per cent*). Also, why change the mathematical form? It is not obvious that 25.9% should be converted to a common fraction. Intuitively we might reason that *25.9%* is close to *25%* which can be expressed by the simpler mathematical form *a quarter*, but it is far from obvious how this reasoning should be generalised so that it applies to all cases.

A side-effect of our analysis is that it provides some empirical evidence in support of

[3]Note that the numerical facts themselves do not corefer, since they are merely properties of coreferring sets or scales (Deemter and Kibble, 2000).

Krifka's RNRI theory (2007); however, the data is sparse. Ten repeated mentions of numerical facts had round, whole number first mentions and subsequent mentions that were more precise, e.g., *200,000...207,000*. Thus demonstrating that authors do indeed write round numbers which they intend readers to interpret as being approximate. There is similar evidence from 22 examples demonstrating that RNRI can be extended to common proportions.

## 5 Related work

Communicating numerical information is important in Natural Language Generation (NLG) because input data is wholly or partially numerical in *nearly every* NLG system, but the problem has received little attention. For example, SUMTIME summarises weather prediction data for oil rig personnel e.g., *1.0-1.5 mainly SW swell falling 1.0 or less mainly SSW swell by afternoon* (Reiter et al., 2005) but would require much greater flexibility to present the same numerical facts to non-professionals.

The difficulty of communicating numerical information has been highlighted in educational and psychological research. Hansen *et al.*'s book (2005) provides ample evidence of confusions that many children have about e.g., decimal places; indeed, they demonstrate that many believe *68.95%* is larger than *70.1%* -- misconceptions that often persist into adulthood. Even professionals misunderstand the mathematics of risk. Gingerenzer and Edwards (2003) found doctors calculate more reliably with reference sets than with proportions.

We are not aware of any research on linguistic variation in proportions; in fact, a recent special issue on numerical expressions contained *no* papers on proportions (Corver et al., 2007).

## 6 Conclusions and Future Work

In this paper we presented:

- A set of rules for determining precision in numerical quantities that is sufficient to cover the examples in our corpus
- A scale for conceptual complexity in numerical expressions derived from the Mathematics Curriculum for Schools.
- A corpus of sets of articles whose main message is to present numerical facts
- Empirical results demonstrating trends towards increasing precision and complexity in repeat mentions of numerical facts with position in document structure.

Our results identify an interesting and well-defined problem that will be addressed in the final stage of NUMGEN: how to derive appropriate simplified expressions (less precise, simpler mathematical form) for use in contexts like the openings of articles, or communications intended for readers with lower levels of mathematical ability.

## Acknowledgements

Our thanks to members of The Open University NLG Group. NUMGEN is supported by ESRC[4] Small Grant RES-000-22-2760.

## References

N. Corver, J. Doetjes, and J. Zwarts. 2007. Linguistic perspectives on numerical expressions: Introduction. *Lingua, Special issue on Linguistic perspectives on numerical expressions*, 117(5):751–775.

K. Van Deemter and R. Kibble. 2000. On Coreferring: coreference in MUC and related annotation schemes. *Computational Linguistics*, 26:629–637.

G. Gigerenza and A. Edwards. 2003. Simple tools for understanding risks: from innumeracy to insight. *British Medical Journal*, 327:714–744.

A. Hansen, D. Drews, J. Dudgeon, F. Lawton, and L. Surtees. 2005. *Children's Errors in Maths: Understanding Common Misconceptions in Primary Schools*. Learning Matters Ltd, Exeter, UK.

M. Krifka. 2007. Approximate interpretation of number words: A case for strategic communication. In G. Bouma, I. Kraer, and J. Zwarts, editors, *Cognitive foundations of interpretation*, pages 111–126, Amsterdam. Koninklijke Nederlandse Akademie van Wetenschapen.

Qualification and Curriculum Authority. 1999. *Mathematics: the National Curriculum for England*. Department for Education and Employment, London.

E. Reiter, S. Sripada, J. Hunter, J. Yu, and I. Davy. 2005. Choosing words in computer-generated weather forecasts. *Artificial Intelligence*, 167(1-2):137–169.

[4] Economic and Social Research Council

# Clustering and Matching Headlines for Automatic Paraphrase Acquisition

**Sander Wubben, Antal van den Bosch, Emiel Krahmer, Erwin Marsi**
Tilburg centre for Creative Computing
Tilburg University
The Netherlands
{s.wubben,antal.vdnbosch,e.j.krahmer,e.c.marsi}@uvt.nl

**Abstract**

For developing a data-driven text rewriting algorithm for paraphrasing, it is essential to have a monolingual corpus of aligned paraphrased sentences. News article headlines are a rich source of paraphrases; they tend to describe the same event in various different ways, and can easily be obtained from the web. We compare two methods of aligning headlines to construct such an aligned corpus of paraphrases, one based on clustering, and the other on pairwise similarity-based matching. We show that the latter performs best on the task of aligning paraphrastic headlines.

## 1 Introduction

In recent years, text-to-text generation has received increasing attention in the field of Natural Language Generation (NLG). In contrast to traditional concept-to-text systems, text-to-text generation systems convert source text to target text, where typically the source and target text share the same meaning to some extent. Applications of text-to-text generation include summarization (Knight and Marcu, 2002), question-answering (Lin and Pantel, 2001), and machine translation.

For text-to-text generation it is important to know which words and phrases are semantically close or exchangable in which contexts. While there are various resources available that capture such knowledge at the word level (e.g., synset knowledge in WordNet), this kind of information is much harder to get by at the phrase level. Therefore, paraphrase acquisition can be considered an important technology for producing resources for text-to-text generation. Paraphrase generation has already proven to be valuable for Question Answering (Lin and Pantel, 2001; Riezler et al., 2007), Machine Translation (Callison-Burch et al., 2006) and the evaluation thereof (Russo-Lassner et al., 2006; Kauchak and Barzilay, 2006; Zhou et al., 2006), but also for text simplification and explanation.

In the study described in this paper, we make an effort to collect Dutch paraphrases from news article headlines in an unsupervised way to be used in future paraphrase generation. News article headlines are abundant on the web, and are already grouped by news aggregators such as Google News. These services collect multiple articles covering the same event. Crawling such news aggregators is an effective way of collecting related articles which can straightforwardly be used for the acquisition of paraphrases (Dolan et al., 2004; Nelken and Shieber, 2006). We use this method to collect a large amount of aligned paraphrases in an automatic fashion.

## 2 Method

We aim to build a high-quality paraphrase corpus. Considering the fact that this corpus will be the basic resource of a paraphrase generation system, we need it to be as free of errors as possible, because errors will propagate throughout the system. This implies that we focus on obtaining a high precision in the paraphrases collection process. Where previous work has focused on aligning news-items at the paragraph and sentence level (Barzilay and Elhadad, 2003), we choose to focus on aligning the headlines of news articles. We think this approach will enable us to harvest reliable training material for paraphrase generation quickly and efficiently, without having to worry too much about the problems that arise when trying to align complete news articles.

For the development of our system we use data which was obtained in the DAESO-project. This project is an ongoing effort to build a Parallel Monolingual Treebank for Dutch (Marsi

*Proceedings of the 12th European Workshop on Natural Language Generation*, pages 122–125,
Athens, Greece, 30 – 31 March 2009. ©2009 Association for Computational Linguistics

| |
|---|
| Placenta sandwich? No, urban legend! |
| Tom wants to make movie with Katie |
| Kate's dad not happy with Tom Cruise |
| Cruise and Holmes sign for eighteen million<br>Eighteen million for Tom and Katie |
| Newest mission Tom Cruise not very convincing<br>Latest mission Tom Cruise succeeds less well<br>Tom Cruise barely succeeds with MI:3 |
| Tom Cruise: How weird is he?<br>How weird is Tom Cruise really? |
| Tom Cruise leaves family<br>Tom Cruise escapes changing diapers |

Table 1: Part of a sample headline cluster, with sub-clusters

and Krahmer, 2007) and will be made available through the Dutch HLT Agency. Part of the data in the DAESO-corpus consists of headline clusters crawled from Google News Netherlands in the period April–August 2006. For each news article, the headline and the first 150 characters of the article were stored. Roughly 13,000 clusters were retrieved. Table 1 shows part of a (translated) cluster. It is clear that although clusters deal roughly with one subject, the headlines can represent quite a different perspective on the content of the article. To obtain only paraphrase pairs, the clusters need to be more coherent. To that end 865 clusters were manually subdivided into sub-clusters of headlines that show clear semantic overlap. Subclustering is no trivial task, however. Some sentences are very clearly paraphrases, but consider for instance the last two sentences in the example. They do paraphrase each other to some extent, but their relation can only be understood properly with world knowledge. Also, there are numerous headlines that can not be sub-clustered, such as the first three headlines shown in the example.

We use these annotated clusters as development and test data in developing a method to automatically obtain paraphrase pairs from headline clusters. We divide the annotated headline clusters in a development set of 40 clusters, while the remainder is used as test data. The headlines are stemmed using the porter stemmer for Dutch (Kraaij and Pohlmann, 1994).

Instead of a word overlap measure as used by Barzilay and Elhadad (2003), we use a modified $TF{*}IDF$ word score as was suggested by Nelken and Shieber (2006). Each sentence is viewed as a document, and each original cluster as a collection of documents. For each stemmed word $i$ in sentence $j$, $TF_{i,j}$ is a binary variable indicating if the word occurs in the sentence or not. The $TF{*}IDF$ score is then:

$$\text{TF.IDF}_\text{i} = TF_{i,j} \cdot \log \frac{|D|}{|\{d_j : t_i \in d_j\}|}$$

$|D|$ is the total number of sentences in the cluster and $|\{d_j : t_i \in d_j\}|$ is the number of sentences that contain the term $t_i$. These scores are used in a vector space representation. The similarity between headlines can be calculated by using a similarity function on the headline vectors, such as cosine similarity.

### 2.1 Clustering

Our first approach is to use a clustering algorithm to cluster similar headlines. The original Google News headline clusters are reclustered into finer grained sub-clusters. We use the $k$-means implementation in the CLUTO[1] software package. The $k$-means algorithm is an algorithm that assigns $k$ centers to represent the clustering of $n$ points ($k < n$) in a vector space. The total intra-cluster variances is minimized by the function

$$V = \sum_{i=1}^{k} \sum_{x_j \in S_i} (x_j - \mu_i)^2$$

where $\mu_i$ is the centroid of all the points $x_j \in S_i$.

The PK1 cluster-stopping algorithm as proposed by Pedersen and Kulkarni (2006) is used to find the optimal $k$ for each sub-cluster:

$$PK1(k) = \frac{Cr(k) - mean(Cr[1...\Delta K])}{std(Cr[1...\Delta K])}$$

Here, $Cr$ is a criterion function, which measures the ratio of withincluster similarity to betweencluster similarity. As soon as $PK1(k)$ exceeds a threshold, $k-1$ is selected as the optimum number of clusters.

To find the optimal threshold value for cluster-stopping, optimization is performed on the development data. Our optimization function is an $F$-score:

$$F_\beta = \frac{(1+\beta^2) \cdot (\text{precision} \cdot \text{recall})}{(\beta^2 \cdot \text{precision} + \text{recall})}$$

[1] http://glaros.dtc.umn.edu/gkhome/views/cluto/

We evaluate the number of aligments between possible paraphrases. For instance, in a cluster of four sentences, $\binom{4}{2} = 6$ alignments can be made. In our case, precision is the number of alignments retrieved from the clusters which are relevant, divided by the total number of retrieved alignments. Recall is the number of relevant retrieved aligments divided by the total number of relevant alignments.

We use an $F_\beta$-score with a $\beta$ of 0.25 as we favour precision over recall. We do not want to optimize on precision alone, because we still want to retrieve a fair amount of paraphrases and not only the ones that are very similar. Through optimization on our development set, we find an optimal threshold for the PK1 algorithm $th_{pk1} = 1$. For each original cluster, $k$-means clustering is then performed using the $k$ found by the cluster stopping function. In each newly obtained cluster all headlines can be aligned to each other.

### 2.2 Pairwise similarity

Our second approach is to calculate the similarity between pairs of headlines directly. If the similarity exceeds a certain threshold, the pair is accepted as a paraphrase pair. If it is below the threshold, it is rejected. However, as Barzilay and Elhadad (2003) have pointed out, sentence mapping in this way is only effective to a certain extent. Beyond that point, context is needed. With this in mind, we adopt two thresholds and the Cosine similarity function to calculate the similarity between two sentences:

$$cos(\theta) = \frac{V1 \cdot V2}{\|V1\|\|V2\|}$$

where $V1$ and $V2$ are the vectors of the two sentences being compared. If the similarity is higher than the upper threshold, it is accepted. If it is lower than the lower theshold, it is rejected. In the remaining case of a similarity between the two thresholds, similarity is calculated over the contexts of the two headlines, namely the text snippet that was retrieved with the headline. If this similarity exceeds the upper threshold, it is accepted. Threshold values as found by optimizing on the development data using again an $F_{0.25}$-score, are $Th_{lower} = 0.2$ and $Th_{upper} = 0.5$. An optional final step is to add alignments that are implied by previous alignments. For instance, if headline $A$ is paired with headline $B$, and headline $B$ is aligned to headline $C$, headline $A$ can be aligned to $C$ as well. We do not add these alignments, because in particular in large clusters when one wrong alignment is made, this process chains together a large amount of incorrect alignments.

| Type | Precision | Recall |
|---|---|---|
| $k$-means clustering clusters only | 0.91 | 0.43 |
| $k$-means clustering all headlines | 0.66 | 0.44 |
| pairwise similarity clusters only | 0.93 | 0.39 |
| pairwise similarity all headlines | 0.76 | 0.41 |

Table 2: Precision and Recall for both methods

| |
|---|
| Playstation 3 more expensive than competitor<br>Playstation 3 will become more expensive than Xbox 360 |
| Sony postpones Blu-Ray movies<br>Sony postpones coming of blu-ray dvds |
| Prices Playstation 3 known: from 499 euros<br>E3 2006: Playstation 3 from 499 euros |
| Sony PS3 with Blu-Ray for sale from November 11th<br>PS3 available in Europe from November 17th |

Table 3: Examples of correct (above) and incorrect (below) alignments

## 3 Results

The 825 clusters in the test set contain 1,751 subclusters in total. In these sub-clusters, there are 6,685 clustered headlines. Another 3,123 headlines remain unclustered. Table 2 displays the paraphrase detection precision and recall of our two approaches. It is clear that $k$-means clustering performs well when all unclustered headlines are artificially ignored. In the more realistic case when there are also items that cannot be clustered, the pairwise calculation of similarity with a back off strategy of using context performs better when we aim for higher precision. Some examples of correct and incorrect alignments are given in Table 3.

## 4 Discussion

Using headlines of news articles clustered by Google News, and finding good paraphrases within these clusters is an effective route for obtaining pairs of paraphrased sentences with reasonable precision. We have shown that a cosine similarity function comparing headlines and using a back off strategy to compare context can be used to extract paraphrase pairs at a precision of 0.76. Although we could aim for a higher precision by assigning higher values to the thresholds, we still want some recall and variation in our paraphrases. Of course the coverage of our method is still somewhat limited: only paraphrases that have some words in common will be extracted. This is not a bad thing: we are particularly interested in extracting paraphrase patterns at the constituent level. These alignments can be made with existing alignment tools such as the GIZA++ toolkit.

We measure the performance of our approaches by comparing to human annotation of subclusterings. The human task in itself is hard. For instance, is we look at the incorrect examples in Table 3, the difficulty of distinguishing between paraphrases and non-paraphrases is apparent. In future research we would like to investigate the task of judging paraphrases. The next step we would like to take towards automatic paraphrase generation, is to identify the differences between paraphrases at the constituent level. This task has in fact been performed by human annotators in the DAESO-project. A logical next step would be to learn to align the different constituents on our extracted paraphrases in an unsupervised way.

### Acknowledgements

Thanks are due to the Netherlands Organization for Scientific Research (NWO) and to the Dutch HLT Stevin programme. Thanks also to Wauter Bosma for originally mining the headlines from Google News. For more information on DAESO, please visit daeso.uvt.nl.

### References

Regina Barzilay and Noemie Elhadad. 2003. Sentence alignment for monolingual comparable corpora. In *Proceedings of the 2003 conference on Empirical methods in natural language processing*, pages 25–32.

Chris Callison-Burch, Philipp Koehn, and Miles Osborne. 2006. Improved statistical machine translation using paraphrases. In *Proceedings of the main conference on Human Language Technology Conference of the North American Chapter of the Association of Computational Linguistics*, pages 17–24.

Bill Dolan, Chris Quirk, and Chris Brockett. 2004. Unsupervised construction of large paraphrase corpora: exploiting massively parallel news sources. In *COLING '04: Proceedings of the 20th international conference on Computational Linguistics*, page 350.

David Kauchak and Regina Barzilay. 2006. Paraphrasing for automatic evaluation. In *Proceedings of the Human Language Technology Conference of the NAACL, Main Conference*, pages 455–462, June.

Kevin Knight and Daniel Marcu. 2002. Summarization beyond sentence extraction: a probabilistic approach to sentence compression. *Artif. Intell.*, 139(1):91–107.

Wessel Kraaij and Rene Pohlmann. 1994. Porters stemming algorithm for dutch. In *Informatiewetenschap 1994: Wetenschappelijke bijdragen aan de derde STINFON Conferentie*, pages 167–180.

Dekang Lin and Patrick Pantel. 2001. Dirt: Discovery of inference rules from text. In *KDD '01: Proceedings of the seventh ACM SIGKDD international conference on Knowledge discovery and data mining*, pages 323–328.

Erwin Marsi and Emiel Krahmer. 2007. Annotating a parallel monolingual treebank with semantic similarity relations. In *he Sixth International Workshop on Treebanks and Linguistic Theories (TLT'07)*.

Rani Nelken and Stuart M. Shieber. 2006. Towards robust context-sensitive sentence alignment for monolingual corpora. In *Proceedings of the 11th Conference of the European Chapter of the Association for Computational Linguistics (EACL-06)*, 3–7 April.

Ted Pedersen and Anagha Kulkarni. 2006. Automatic cluster stopping with criterion functions and the gap statistic. In *Proceedings of the 2006 Conference of the North American Chapter of the Association for Computational Linguistics on Human Language Technology*, pages 276–279.

Stefan Riezler, Alexander Vasserman, Ioannis Tsochantaridis, Vibhu O. Mittal, and Yi Liu. 2007. Statistical machine translation for query expansion in answer retrieval. In *ACL*.

Grazia Russo-Lassner, Jimmy Lin, and Philip Resnik. 2006. A paraphrase-based approach to machine translation evaluation. Technical report, University of Maryland, College Park.

Liang Zhou, Chin-Yew Lin, and Eduard Hovy. 2006. Re-evaluating machine translation results with paraphrase support. In *Proceedings of the 2006 Conference on Empirical Methods in Natural Language Processing*, pages 77–84, July.

# A Situated Context Model for Resolution and Generation of Referring Expressions

**Hendrik Zender** and **Geert-Jan M. Kruijff** and **Ivana Kruijff-Korbayová**
Language Technology Lab, German Research Center for Artificial Intelligence (DFKI)
Saarbrücken, Germany
{zender, gj, ivana.kruijff}@dfki.de

## Abstract

The background for this paper is the aim to build robotic assistants that can "naturally" interact with humans. One prerequisite for this is that the robot can correctly identify objects or places a user refers to, and produce comprehensible references itself. As robots typically act in environments that are larger than what is immediately perceivable, the problem arises how to identify the appropriate context, against which to resolve or produce a referring expression (RE). Existing algorithms for generating REs generally bypass this problem by assuming a given context. In this paper, we explicitly address this problem, proposing a method for context determination in large-scale space. We show how it can be applied both for resolving and producing REs.

## 1 Introduction

The past years have seen an extraordinary increase in research on robotic assistants that help users perform daily chores. Autonomous vacuum cleaners have already found their way into people's homes, but it will still take a while before fully conversational robot "gophers" will assist people in more demanding everyday tasks. Imagine a robot that can deliver objects, and give directions to visitors on a university campus. This robot must be able to verbalize its knowledge in a way that is understandable by humans.

A conversational robot will inevitably face situations in which it needs to refer to an entity (an object, a locality, or even an event) that is located somewhere outside the current scene, as Figure 1 illustrates. There are conceivably many ways in which a robot might refer to things in the world, but many such expressions are unsuitable in most

Figure 1: Situated dialogue with a service robot

human-robot dialogues. Consider the following set of examples:

1. "position $P = \langle 45.56, -3.92, 10.45 \rangle$"
2. "Peter's office no. 200 at the end of the corridor on the third floor of the Acme Corp. building 3 in the Acme Corp. complex, 47 Evergreen Terrace, Calisota, Earth, (...)"
3. "the area"

These REs are valid descriptions of their respective referents. Still they fail to achieve their *communicative goal*, which is to specify the right amount of information that the hearer needs to uniquely identify the referent. The next REs *might* serve as more appropriate variants of the previous examples (*in certain contexts!*):

1. "the IT help desk"
2. "Peter's office"
3. "the large hall on the first floor"

The first example highlights a requirement on the knowledge representation to which an algorithm for generating referring expressions (GRE) has access. Although the robot needs a robot-centric representation of its surrounding space that allows it to safely perform actions and navigate its world, it should use human-centric qualitative descriptions when talking about things in the world. We

*Proceedings of the 12th European Workshop on Natural Language Generation*, pages 126–129,
Athens, Greece, 30 – 31 March 2009. ©2009 Association for Computational Linguistics

do not address this issue here, but refer the interested reader to our recent work on multi-layered spatial maps for robots, bridging the gap between robot-centric and human-centric spatial representations (Zender et al., 2008).

The other examples point out another important consideration: how much information does the human need to single out the intended referent among the possible entities that the robot could be referring to? According to the seminal work on GRE by Dale and Reiter (1995), one needs to distinguish whether the intended referent is already in the hearer's *focus of attention* or not. This focus of attention can consist of a local visual scene (visual context) or a shared workspace (spatial context), but also contains recently mentioned entities (dialogue context). If the referent is already part of the current context, the GRE task merely consists of singling it out among the other members of the context, which act as distractors. In this case the generated RE contains *discriminatory* information, e.g. "the red ball" if several kinds of objects with different colors are in the context. If, on the other hand, the referent is not in the hearer's focus of attention, an RE needs to contain what Dale and Reiter call *navigational*, or *attention-directing* information. The example they give is "the black power supply in the equipment rack," where "the equipment rack" is supposed to direct the hearers attention to the rack and its contents.

In the following we propose an approach for context determination and extension that allows a mobile robot to produce and interpret REs to entities outside the current visual context.

## 2 Background

Most GRE approaches are applied to very limited, visual scenes – so-called *small-scale space*. The domain of such systems is usually a small visual scene, e.g. a number of objects, such as cups and tables, located in the same room), or other closed-context scenarios (Dale and Reiter, 1995; Horacek, 1997; Krahmer and Theune, 2002). Recently, Kelleher and Kruijff (2006) have presented an incremental GRE algorithm for situated dialogue with a robot about a table-top setting, i.e. also about small-scale space. In all these cases, the context set is assumed to be identical to the visual scene that is shared between the interlocutors. The intended referent is thus already in the hearer's *focus of attention*.

In contrast, robots typically act in *large-scale space*, i.e. space "larger than what can be perceived at once" (Kuipers, 1977). They need the ability to understand and produce references to things that are beyond the current visual and spatial context. In any situated dialogue that involves entities beyond the current focus of attention, the task of *extending the context* becomes key.

Paraboni et al. (2007) present an algorithm for *context determination* in hierarchically ordered domains, e.g. a university campus or a document structure. Their approach is mainly targeted at producing textual references to entities in written documents (e.g. figures, tables in book chapters). Consequently they do not address the challenges that arise in physically and perceptually situated dialogues. Still, the approach presents a number of good contributions towards GRE for situated dialogue in large-scale space. An appropriate context, as a subset of the full domain, is determined through Ancestral Search. This search for the intended referent is rooted in the "position of the speaker and the hearer in the domain" (represented as *d*), a crucial first step towards situatedness. Their approach suffers from the shortcoming that spatial relationships are treated as one-place attributes by their GRE algorithm. For example they transform the spatial containment relation that holds between a room entity and a building entity ("the library in the Cockroft building") into a property of the room entity (BUILDING NAME = COCKROFT) and not a two-place relation (`in(library,Cockroft)`). Thus they avoid recursive calls to the algorithm, which would be needed if the intended referent is related to another entity that needs to be properly referred to.

However, according to Dale and Reiter (1995), these related entities do not necessarily serve as discriminatory information. At least in large-scale space, in contrast to a document structure that is conceivably transparent to a reader, they function as *attention-directing elements* that are introduced to build up *common ground* by incrementally extending the hearer's focus of attention. Moreover, representing some spatial relations as two-place predicates between two entities and some as one-place predicates is an arbitrary decision.

We present an approach for context determination (or *extension*), that imposes less restrictions on its knowledge base, and which can be used as a sub-routine in existing GRE algorithms.

## 3 Situated Dialogue in Large-Scale Space

Imagine the situation in Figure 1 did not take place somewhere on campus, but rather inside building 3B. Certainly the robot would not have said "the IT help desk is on the 1st floor in building 3B." To avoid confusing the human, an utterance like "the IT help desk is on the 1st floor" would have been appropriate. Likewise, if the IT help desk happened to be located on another site of the university, the robot would have had to identify its location as being "on the 1st floor in building 3B on the new campus." The hierarchical representation of space that people are known to assume (Cohn and Hazarika, 2001), reflects upon the choice of an appropriate context when producing REs.

In the above example the physical and spatial situatedness of the dialogue participants play an important role in determining which related parts of space come into consideration as potential distractors. Another important observation concerns the verbal behavior of humans when talking about remote objects and places during a complex dialogue (i.e. more than just a question and a reply). Consider the following example dialogue:

> Person A: "Where is the exit?"
>
> Person B: "You first go down this corridor. Then you turn right. After a few steps you will see the big glass doors."
>
> Person A: "And the bus station? Is it to the left?"

The dialogue illustrates how utterances become grounded in previously introduced discourse referents, both temporally and spatially. Initially, the physical surroundings of the dialogue partners form the context for anchoring references. As a dialogue unfolds, this point can conceptually move to other locations that have been explicitly introduced. Discourse markers denoting spatial or temporal cohesion (e.g. "then" or "there") can make this move to a new anchor explicit, leading to a "mental tour" through large-scale space.

We propose a general principle of *Topological Abstraction* (TA) for context extension which is rooted in what we will call the *Referential Anchor* $a$.[1] TA is designed for a multiple abstraction hierarchy (e.g. represented as a lattice structure rather than a simple tree). The Referential Anchor $a$, corresponding to the current focus of attention, forms the nucleus of the context. In the simple case, $a$ corresponds to the hearer's physical location. As illustrated above, $a$ can also move along the "spatial progression" of the most salient discourse entity during a dialogue. If the intended referent is outside the current context, TA extends the context by incrementally ascending the spatial abstraction hierarchy until the intended referent is an element of the resulting sub-hierarchy, as illustrated in Figure 2. Below we describe two instantiations of the TA principle, a TA algorithm for reference generation (TAA1) and TAA2 for reference resolution.

[1]similar to Ancestral Search (Paraboni et al., 2007)

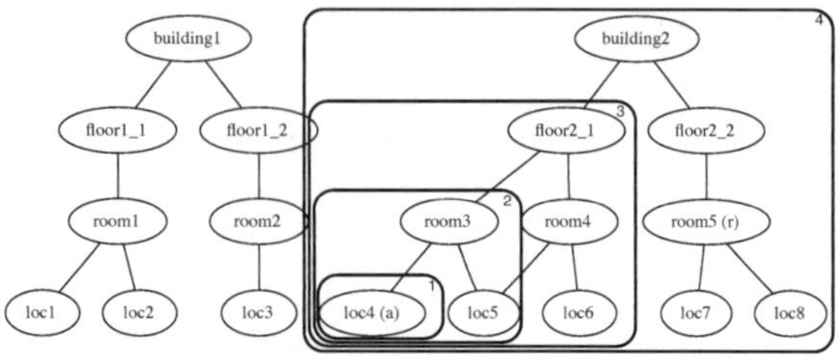


Figure 2: Incremental TA in large-scale space

**Context Determination for GRE** TAA1 constructs a set of entities dominated by the Referential Anchor $a$ (and $a$ itself). If this set contains the intended referent $r$, it is taken as the current utterance context set. Else TAA1 moves up one level of abstraction and adds the set of all child nodes to the context set. This loop continues until $r$ is in the context set. At that point TAA1 stops and returns the constructed context set (cf. Algorithm 1).

TAA1 is formulated to be neutral to the kind of GRE algorithm that it is used for. It can be used with the original Incremental Algorithm (Dale and Reiter, 1995), augmented by a recursive call if a relation to another entity is selected as a discriminatory feature. It could in principle also be used with the standard approach to GRE involving relations (Dale and Haddock, 1991), but we agree with Paraboni et al. (2007) that the mutually qualified references that it can produce[2] are not easily resolvable if they pertain to circumstances where a confirmatory search is costly (such as in large-scale space). More recent approaches to avoiding infinite loops when using relations in GRE make use of a graph-based knowledge representation (Krahmer et al., 2003; Croitoru and van Deemter, 2007). TAA1 is compatible with these approaches, as well as with the salience based approach of (Krahmer and Theune, 2002).

[2]An example for such a phenomenon is the expression "the ball on the table" in a context with several tables and several balls, but of which only one is on a table. Humans find such REs natural and easy to resolve in visual scenes.

**Algorithm 1** TAA1 (for reference generation)

```
Require: a = referential anchor; r = intended referent
  Initialize context: C = {}
  C = C ∪ topologicalChildren(a) ∪ {a}
  if r ∈ C then
    return C
  else
    Initialize: SUPERNODES = {a}
    for each n ∈ SUPERNODES do
      for each p ∈ topologicalParents(n) do
        SUPERNODES = SUPERNODES ∪ {p}
        C = C ∪ topologicalChildren(p)
      end for
      if r ∈ C then
        return C
      end if
    end for
    return failure
  end if
```

**Algorithm 2** TAA2 (for reference resolution)

```
Require: a = ref. anchor; desc(x) = description of referent
  Initialize context: C = {}
  Initialize possible referents: R = {}
  C = C ∪ topologicalChildren(a) ∪ {a}
  R = desc(x) ∩ C
  if R ≠ {} then
    return R
  else
    Initialize: SUPERNODES = {a}
    for each n ∈ SUPERNODES do
      for each p ∈ topologicalParents(n) do
        SUPERNODES = SUPERNODES ∪ {p}
        C = C ∪ topologicalChildren(p)
      end for
      R = desc(x) ∩ C
      if R ≠ {} then
        return R
      end if
    end for
    return failure
  end if
```

**Resolving References to Elsewhere** Analogous to the GRE task, a conversational robot must be able to understand verbal descriptions by its users. In order to avoid overgenerating possible referents, we propose TAA2 (cf. Algorithm 2) which tries to select an appropriate referent from a relevant subset of the full knowledge base. It is initialized with a given semantic representation of the referential expression, $desc(x)$, in a format compatible with the knowledge base. Then, an appropriate entity satisfying this description is searched for in the knowledge base. Similarly to TAA1, the description is first matched against the current *context set* $C$ consisting of $a$ and its child nodes. If this set does not contain any instances that match $desc(x)$, TAA2 increases the context set along the spatial abstraction axis until at least one possible referent can be identified within the context.

## 4 Conclusions and Future Work

We have presented two algorithms for context determination that can be used both for resolving and generating REs in large-scale space.

We are currently planning a user study to evaluate the performance of the TA algorithms. Another important item for future work is the exact nature of the spatial progression, modeled by "moving" the referential anchor, in a situated dialogue.

## Acknowledgments

This work was supported by the EU FP7 ICT Project "CogX" (FP7-ICT-215181).

## References

A. G. Cohn and S. M. Hazarika. 2001. Qualitative spatial representation and reasoning: An overview. *Fundamenta Informaticae*, 46:1–29.

M. Croitoru and K. van Deemter. 2007. A conceptual graph approach to the generation of referring expressions. In *Proc. IJCAI-2007*, Hyderabad, India.

R. Dale and N. Haddock. 1991. Generating referring expressions involving relations. In *Proc. of the 5th Meeting of the EACL*, Berlin, Germany, April.

R. Dale and E. Reiter. 1995. Computational interpretations of the Gricean Maxims in the generation of referring expressions. *Cognitive Science*, 19(2):233–263.

H. Horacek. 1997. An algorithm for generating referential descriptions with flexible interfaces. In *Proc. of the 35th Annual Meeting of the ACL and 8th Conf. of the EACL*, Madrid, Spain.

J. Kelleher and G.-J. Kruijff. 2006. Incremental generation of spatial referring expressions in situated dialogue. In *In Proc. Coling-ACL 06*, Sydney, Australia.

E. Krahmer and M. Theune. 2002. Efficient context-sensitive generation of referring expressions. In K. van Deemter and R.Kibble, editors, *Information Sharing: Givenness and Newness in Language Processing*. CSLI Publications, Stanford, CA, USA.

E. Krahmer, S. van Erk, and A. Verleg. 2003. Graph-based generation of referring expressions. *Computational Linguistics*, 29(1).

B. Kuipers. 1977. *Representing Knowledge of Large-scale Space*. Ph.D. thesis, Massachusetts Institute of Technology, Cambridge, MA, USA.

I. Paraboni, K. van Deemter, and J. Masthoff. 2007. Generating referring expressions: Making referents easy to identify. *Computational Linguistics*, 33(2):229–254, June.

H. Zender, O. Martínez Mozos, P. Jensfelt, G.-J. Kruijff, and W. Burgard. 2008. Conceptual spatial representations for indoor mobile robots. *Robotics and Autonomous Systems*, 56(6):493–502, June.

# Investigating Content Selection for Language Generation using Machine Learning

**Colin Kelly**
Computer Laboratory
University of Cambridge
15 JJ Thomson Avenue
Cambridge, UK

**Ann Copestake**
Computer Laboratory
University of Cambridge
15 JJ Thomson Avenue
Cambridge, UK

**Nikiforos Karamanis**
Department of Computer Science
Trinity College Dublin
Dublin 2
Ireland

{colin.kelly,ann.copestake,nikiforos.karamanis}@cl.cam.ac.uk

## Abstract

The content selection component of a natural language generation system decides which information should be communicated in its output. We use information from reports on the game of cricket. We first describe a simple factoid-to-text alignment algorithm then treat content selection as a collective classification problem and demonstrate that simple 'grouping' of statistics at various levels of granularity yields substantially improved results over a probabilistic baseline. We additionally show that holding back of specific types of input data, and linking database structures with commonality further increase performance.

## 1 Introduction

Content selection is the task executed by a natural language generation (NLG) system of deciding, given a knowledge-base, which subset of the information available should be conveyed in the generated document (Reiter and Dale, 2000).

Consider the task of generating a cricket match report, given the scorecard for that match. Such a scorecard would typically contain a large number of statistics pertaining to the game as a whole as well as individual players (e.g. see Figure 1). Our aim is to identify which statistics should be selected by the NLG system.

Much work has been done in the field of content selection, in a diverse range of domains e.g. weather forecasts (Coch, 1998). Approaches are usually domain specific and predominantly based on structured tables of well-defined input data.

Duboue and McKeown (2003) attempted a statistical approach to content selection using a substantial corpus of biographical summaries paired with selected content, where they extracted rules and patterns linking the two. They then used machine learning to ascertain what was relevant.

Barzilay and Lapata (2005) extended this approach but applying it to a sports domain (American football), similarly viewing content selection as a classification task and additionally taking account of contextual dependencies between data, and found that this improved results compared to a content-agnostic baseline. We aim throughout to extend and improve upon Barzilay and Lapata's methods.

We emphasise that content selection through statistical machine learning is a relatively new area – approaches prior to Duboue and McKeown's are, in principle, much less portable – and as such there is not an enormous body of work to build upon.

This work offers a novel algorithm for data-to-text alignment, presents a new 'grouping' method for sharing knowledge across similar but distinct learning instances and shows that holding back certain data from the machine learner, and reintroducing it later on can improve results.

## 2 Data Acquisition & Alignment

We first must obtain appropriately aligned cricket data, for the purposes of machine learning.

Our data comes from the online Wisden almanack (Cricinfo, 2007), which we used to download 133 match report/scorecard pairs. We employed an HTML parser to extract the main text from the match report webpage, and the match data-tables from the scorecard webpage. An example scorecard can be found in Figure 1[1].

[1] Cricket is a bat-and-ball sport, contested by two opposing teams of eleven players. Each side's objective is to score more 'runs' than their opponents. An 'innings' refers to the collective performance of the batting team, and (usually) ends when all eleven players have batted.

In Figure 1, in the batting section R stands for 'runs made', M for 'minutes played on the field', B for 'number of balls faced'. 4s and 6s are set numbers of runs awarded for hitting balls that reach the boundary. SR is the number of runs per 100 balls. In the bowling section, O stands for 'overs

*Proceedings of the 12th European Workshop on Natural Language Generation*, pages 130–137,
Athens, Greece, 30 – 31 March 2009. ©2009 Association for Computational Linguistics

**Result** India won by 63 runs

| **India innings** (50 overs maximum) | | **R** | **M** | **B** | **4s** | **6s** | **SR** |
|---|---|---|---|---|---|---|---|
| SC Ganguly∗ | run out (Silva/Sangakarra†) | 9 | 37 | 19 | 2 | 0 | 47.36 |
| V Sehwag | run out (Fernando) | 39 | 61 | 40 | 6 | 0 | 97.50 |
| D Mongia | b Samaraweera | 48 | 91 | 63 | 6 | 0 | 76.19 |
| SR Tendulkar | c Chandana b Vaas | 113 | 141 | 102 | 12 | 1 | 110.78 |
| ... | | | | | | | |
| Extras | (lb 6, w 12, nb 7) | **25** | | | | | |
| **Total** | (all out; 50 overs; 223 mins) | **304** | | | | | |

**Fall of wickets** 1-32 (Ganguly, 6.5 ov), 2-73 (Sehwag, 11.2 ov), 3-172 (Mongia, 27.4 ov), 4-199 (Dravid, 32.1 ov), ..., 10-304 (Nehra, 49.6 ov)

| **Bowling** | **O** | **M** | **R** | **W** | **Econ** | |
|---|---|---|---|---|---|---|
| WPUJC Vaas | 10 | 1 | 64 | 1 | 6.40 | (2w) |
| DNT Zoysa | 10 | 0 | 66 | 1 | 6.60 | (6nb, 2w) |
| ... | | | | | | |
| TT Samaraweera | 8 | 0 | 39 | 2 | 4.87 | (2w) |

Figure 1: Statistics in a typical cricket scorecard.

### 2.1 Report Alignment

We use a supervised method to train our data, and thus need to find all 'links' between the scorecard and match report. We execute this alignment by first creating tags with tag attributes according to the common structure of the scorecards, and tag values according to the data within a particular scorecard. We then attempt to automatically align the values of those tags with factoids, single pieces of information found in the report.

For example, from Figure 1 the fact that Tendulkar was the fourth player to bat on the first team is captured by constructing a tag with tag attribute *team1_player4*, and tag value 'SR Tendulkar'. The fact he achieved 113 runs is encapsulated by another tag, with tag attribute as *team1_player4_R* and tag value as '113'. Then if the report contained the phrase 'Tendulkar made 113 off 102 balls' we would hope to match the 'Tendulkar' factoid with our tag value 'SR Tendulkar', the '113' factoid with our tag value '113' and replace both factoids with their respective tag attributes, in this case *team1_player4* and *team1_player4_R* respectively. Similar methods for this problem have been employed by Barzilay and Lapata (2005) and Duboue and McKeown (2003).

The basic idea behind our 6-step process for alignment is that we align those factoids we are most certain of first. The main obstacle we face when aligning is the large incidence of repeated numbers occurring within the scorecard, as this would imply we have multiple, different tags all with the same tag values. It is wholly possible (and quite typical) that single figures will be repeated many times within a single scorecard[2].

Therefore it would be advantageous for us to have some means to differentiate amongst tags, and hopefully select the correct tag when encountering a factoid which corresponds to repeated tag values. Our algorithm is as follows:

**Preprocessing** We began by converting all verbalised numbers to their cardinal equivalents, e.g. 'one', 'two' to '1', '2', and selected instances of 'a' into '1'.

**Proper Nouns** In the first round of tagging we attempt to match proper names from the scorecard with strings within the report. Additionally, we maintain a list of all players referenced thus far.

**Player-Relevant Details** Using the list of players we have accumulated, we search the report for matches on tag values relating to only those players. This step was based on the assumption that a factoid about a specific player is unlikely to appear unless that player has been named.

**Non-Player-Relevant Details** The next stage involves attempting to match factoids to tag values whose attributes don't refer to a particular player e.g., more general match information as well as team statistics.

bowled', M for 'maiden overs', R for 'runs conceded' and W for 'wickets taken'. Econ is 'economy rate', or number of runs per over.

It is important to note that Figure 1 omits the opposing team's innings (comprising new instances of the 'Batting', 'Fall of Wickets' and 'Bowling' sections), and some additional statistics found at the bottom of the scorecard.

[2]For example in Figure 1 we can see the number 6 appearing four times: twice as the number of 4s for two different players, once as an *lb* statistic and once as an *nb* statistic.

**Anchor-Based Matching** We next use surrounding text anchor-based matching: for example, if a sentence contains the string 'he bowled for 3 overs' we will preferentially attempt to match the factoid '3' with tag values from tags which we know refer to overs.

**Remaining Matches** The final step acts as our 'catch-all' – we proceed through all remaining words in the report and try to match each potential factoid with the first (if any) tag found whose tag value is the same.

### 2.2 Evaluation

The output of our program is the original text with all aligned figures and strings (factoids) replaced with their corresponding tag attributes. We can see an extract from an aligned report in Figure 2 where we show the aligned factoids in bold, and their corresponding tag attributes in italics. We also note at this point that much of commentary shown does not in fact appear in the scorecard, and therefore additional knowledge sources would typically be required to generate a full match report – this is beyond the scope of our paper, but Robin (1995) attempts to deal with this problem in the domain of basketball using revision-based techniques for including additional content.

We asked a domain expert to evaluate five of our aligned match reports – he did this by creating his own 'gold standard' for each report, a list of aligned tags. Compared to our automatically aligned tags, we obtained 79.0% average precision, 75.8% average recall and a mean F of 77.0%.

> **NatWest Series** *(series)*, match **9** *(team1_player1_R)*
>
> **India v Sri Lanka** *(matchtitle)*
>
> At **Bristol** *(venue_town)*, **July 11** *(date)* **(day/night** *(daynight)*).
> **India** *(team1)* won by **63 runs** *(winmethod)*.
> **India** *(team1)* **5** *(team1_points)* pts.
> Toss: **India** *(team1)*.
>
> The highlight of a meaningless match was a sublime innings from **Tendulkar** *(team1_player4)*, who resumed his fleeting love affair with Nevil Road to the delight of a flag-waving crowd. On **India** *(team1)*'s only other visit to **Bristol** *(venue_town)*, for a World Cup game in 1999 against Kenya, **Tendulkar** *(team1_player4)* had creamed an unbeaten 140, and this time he drove with elan to make **113** *(team1_player4_R)* off just **102** *(team1_player4_B)* balls with **12** *(team1_player4_4s)* fours and **a** *(team1_player4_6s)* six.
> ...

Figure 2: Aligned match report extract

## 3 Categorization

We are using the methods of Barzilay and Lapata (henceforth B&L) as our starting point, so we describe what we did to emulate and extend them.

### 3.1 Barzilay and Lapata's Method

B&L's corpus was composed of a relational database of football statistics. Within the database were multiple tables, which we will refer to as 'categories' (actions within a game, e.g. touchdowns and fumbles). Each category was composed of 'groups' (the rows within a category table), with each row referring to a distinct player, and each column referring to different types of action within that category ('attributes').

B&L's technique for the purposes of the machine learning was to assign a '1' or '0' to each row, where a row would receive the value '1' if one or more of the entries in the row was verbalised in the report. In the context of our data we could apply a similar division, for example, by constructing a category entitled 'Batting' with attributes (columns) 'Runs', 'Balls', 'Minutes', '4s' and '6s' etc., and rows corresponding to players. In this case a group within that category would correspond to one line of the 'Innings' table in Figure 1.

We note that B&L were selecting content on a row basis, while we are aiming to select individual tag attributes (i.e., specific row/column cell references) within the categories, a more difficult task. We discuss this further in Section 6.

The technique above allows the machine learning algorithm to be aware that different statistics are semantically related – i.e., each group within a category contains the same 'type' of information. We therefore think this is a logical starting point for our work, and we aim to expand upon it.

### 3.2 Classifying Tags

The key step was deciding upon an appropriate division of our scorecard into various categories and the groups for each category in the style of B&L. As can be seen from Figure 1 our input information is a mixture of structured (e.g. Bowling, Batting sections), semi-structured (Fall of Wickets section) and almost unstructured (Result) information. This is somewhat unlike B&L's data, which was fully structured in database form. We deal

| Category | Attributes | Verb |
|---|---|---|
| **Batting** | 9 | 47.0 |
| **Bowling** | 11 | 10.2 |
| **Fall of Wickets** | 8 | 46.4 |
| **Match Details** | 11 | 75.2 |
| **Match Result** | 8 | 45.1 |
| **Officials** | 8 | 6.0 |
| **Partnerships** | 11 | 75.5 |
| **Team Statistics** | 13 | 46.2 |

Table 1: Number of attributes per category with percent verbalised (Verb)

with this by enforcing a stronger structure – dividing the information into eight of our own 'categories', based roughly on the formatting of the webpages. These are outlined in Table 1.

The first three categories in the table are quite intuitive and implicit from the respective sections of the scorecard. There is additional information in a typical scorecard (not shown in Figure 1), which we must also categorise. The 'Team Statistics' category contains details about the 'extras'[3] scored by each team, as well as the number of points gained by the team towards that particular series[4]. We divide the remaining tag attributes as follows into three categories: 'Officials' – persons participating in the match, other than the teams (e.g. umpires, referees); 'Match Details' – information that would have been known before the match was played (e.g. venue, date, season); and 'Match Result' – data that could only be known once the match was over (e.g. final result, player of the match).

Finally we have an additional 'Partnerships'[5] category which is given explicitly on a separate webpage referenced from each scorecard, but is also implicit from information contained in the 'Fall of Wickets' and 'Batting' sections. We anticipate that this category will help us manage the issue of data sparsity. For instance, in our domain we could group partnerships (which could contain a multitude of player combinations and therefore distinct tags) with the various possible binary combinations of players together for shared learning. We discuss this further in Section 8.3.

Within 5 of the categories described above, we are further able to divide the data into 'groups' - the Batting, Bowling, Fall of Wickets and Partnerships categories refer to multiple players and thus have multiple rows. The Team Statistics category contains two groups, one for each team. The other categories merely form one-line tables.

## 4 Machine Learning

Our task is to establish which tag attributes (and hence tag values) should be included in the final match report, and is a multi-label classification problem. We chose to use BoosTexter (Schapire and Singer, 2000) as it has been shown to be an effective classifier (Yang, 1999), and it is one of the few text classification tools which directly supports multi-label classification. This is also what B&L used.

Schapire and Singer's BoosTexter (2000) uses 'decision stumps', or single level decision trees to classify its input data. The predicates of these stumps are defined, for text, by the presence or absence of a single term, and, for numerical attributes, whether the attribute exceeds a given threshold, decided dynamically.

### 4.1 Running BoosTexter

BoosTexter requires two input files to train a hypothesis, 'Names' and 'Data'.

**Names** The Names file contains, for each possible tag attribute, $t$, across all scorecards, the type of its corresponding tag value. These are *continuous* for numbers and *text* for normal text. From our 133 scorecards we extracted a total of 61,063 tag values, of which 82.2% were *continuous*, the remainder being *text*.

**Data** The Data file contains, for each scorecard, a comma-delimited list of all tag values for a particular scorecard, with a '?' for unknown values, followed by a list of the verbalised tag attributes.

**Testing** We can now run BoosTexter with a user-defined number of rounds, $T$, which creates a hypothesis file. Using this hypothesis file and a test 'data' file (without the list of verbalised tag attributes), BoosTexter will give its hypothesized predictions, a value $f$ for each tag attribute $t$. The sign of $f$ determines whether the classifier believes the tag value corresponding to $t$ is relevant

[3]Additional runs awarded to the batting team for specific actions executed by the bowling team. There are four types: No Ball, Wide, Bye, Leg Bye.

[4]Each cricket game is part of a specific 'series' of games. e.g. India would receive five points for their win within the NatWest series.

[5]A 'partnership' refers to a pair of players who bat together, and usually comprises information such as the number of runs scored between them, the number of deliveries faced and so on.

to the test scorecard, while $|f|$ is a measure of the confidence the classifier has in its assertion.

### 4.2 Data Sparsity

The very nature of the data means that there are a large number of tag values which do not occur in every scorecard – the average scorecard contained 24 values, yet our 'names' file contained 1193 possible tag attributes. A lot of this was due to partnership tag attributes which formed 43.6% of the 'names' entries. This large figure is because a large number of all possible binary combinations of players existed in the training data across both teams[6]. This implies we will be unable to train for a significant number of tag attributes as many specific tag values occur very rarely. Indeed we found that of 158,669 entries, 97,666 (61.55%) were 'unknown'.

## 5 Evaluation Baselines

It is not clear what constitutes a suitable baseline so we considered multiple options. The issue of ambiguous reference baselines is not specific to the cricket domain, as there is no standardized baseline approach across the prior literature. We employ ten-fold cross validation throughout.

### 5.1 Majority Baseline

B&L created a 'majority baseline' whereby they returned those categories (i.e., tables) which were verbalised more than half of the time in their aligned reports.

As explained in Section 3.2 we divided our tag attributes into 8 categories. We emulated B&L's baseline method as follows: For each category, if any of the tag values within a particular 'group' was tagged as verbalised, we counted that as a 'vote' for that particular category. We then calculated the total number of 'votes' divided by the total number of 'groups' within each category. All categories which had a ratio of 50% or greater in this calculation were considered to be 'majority categories'. Our baseline $B_{\mathrm{maj}}$ then consisted of all tag attributes forming part of those majority categories. As shown in Table 1 there were only two categories which exceeded the 50% threshold, 'Match Details' and 'Partnerships'.

We can see that this baseline performs abysmally. The reason for this poor behaviour is

[6] 93 of the possible $2\sum_{i=1}^{10} i = 110$ combinations occurred.

| $B_{\mathrm{maj}}$ | $\mu$ | min | max | $\sigma$ |
|---|---|---|---|---|
| **Precision** | 0.0966 | 0.0333 | 0.1583 | 0.0250 |
| **Recall** | 0.4879 | 0.2727 | 0.7895 | 0.0977 |
| **F** | 0.1603 | 0.0620 | 0.2568 | 0.0384 |

Table 2: Majority Baseline, $B_{\mathrm{maj}}$

that since so many tag attributes contribute to the categories we are including far too many possibilities in our baseline.

### 5.2 Probabilistic Baseline

This baseline is based on the premise that those tag attributes which occur with highest frequency across the training data refer to those tag values which will often occur in a typical match report. To create our baseline set of tag attributes $B_{\mathrm{prob}}$ we extract the $a$ most frequently verbalised tag attributes across all the training data where $a$ is the average length of the verbalised tag attribute lists for each report/scorecard pair.

| $B_{\mathrm{prob}}$ | $\mu$ | min | max | $\sigma$ |
|---|---|---|---|---|
| **Precision** | 0.5157 | 0.2174 | 0.7391 | 0.1010 |
| **Recall** | 0.5157 | 0.1389 | 0.7647 | 0.0990 |
| **F** | 0.5100 | 0.1695 | 0.6939 | 0.0852 |

Table 3: Probabilistic Baseline, $B_{\mathrm{prob}}$

This baseline achieves a mean F score of 51%, however the tag attributes being returned are very inconsistent with a typical match report – they correspond in the majority to player names but not one refers to any other tag attributes relevant to those players. This renders the output mostly meaningless in terms of our aim to select content for an NLG system.

### 5.3 No-Player Probabilistic Baseline

Taking the above into account we create a baseline which derives its choice of tag attributes from match statistics *only*. This baseline is similar to the Probabilistic Baseline above, with the exception that when summing the numbers of tag attributes in the sets we do not consider player-name tag attributes in our counts. Instead, we extract the $a'$ most frequent tag attributes, where $a'$ is the average size of the sets *excluding* player-name tag attributes. To finally obtain our baseline set $B_{\mathrm{nops}}$ we merge our $a'$ most frequent tag attributes with any and all corresponding player-name tag attributes[7].

| $B_{\text{nops}}$ | $\mu$ | min | max | $\sigma$ |
|---|---|---|---|---|
| **Precision** | 0.4923 | 0.1765 | 0.6875 | 0.0922 |
| **Recall** | 0.3529 | 0.1111 | 0.5625 | 0.0842 |
| **F** | 0.4064 | 0.1538 | 0.5946 | 0.0767 |

Table 4: No-Player Probabilistic Baseline, $B_{\text{nops}}$

As can be seen from Table 4, this method suffers an absolute F-score drop of more than 10% from the previous method. However if we analyse the output more closely we can see that although the accuracy has dropped, the returned tag attributes are more thematically consistent with the training data. This is our preferred baseline.

## 6 Evaluation Paradigm

The main difficulty we encountered arose when we came to assessing the Precision and Recall figures as we have yet to decide on what level we are considering the output of our system to be correct. We see three possibilities for the level:

**Category** We could simply count the 'votes' predicted on a per category basis (as described in sections 3.1 and 5.1), and evaluate categories based on the number of votes given for each. We would expect this to generate very good results as we are effectively overgrouping, once on a group basis (grouping together all attributes) and once on a category basis (unifying all groups within a category), but the output would be so general and trivial (effectively stating something to the effect that "a match report should contain information about batting, bowling and team statistics") that it would be of no use in an NLG system.

**Groups** Here we compare which 'groups' were verbalised within each category, and which were predicted to be verbalised (as we did for the Majority Baseline of Section 5.1). Our implicit grouping means that we do not have to necessarily return the correct statistic pertaining to a group since each group acts as a basket for the statistics contained within it, and is susceptible to 'false positives'. This method is most similar to B&L's.

**Tags** Since we are trying to establish which *tag attributes* should be included rather than which *groups* are likely to contain verbalised tag attributes, we could say that even the above method is too liberal in its definition of correctness. Thus we also evaluate our groups on the basis of their component parts, i.e., if a particular group of tag attributes is estimated to be verbalised by BoosTexter, then we include all attributes from that group.

[7] e.g., if *team1_player4_R* is in $a'$ then we would also include *team1_player4* in our final set.

## 7 Initial Results

Our 'categorized' results are derived from presenting BoosTexter with each individual category as described in Section 3.2, then merging the selected tag attributes together and evaluating based on the criteria described above. We then show BoosTexter's performance 'as is', by running the program on the full output of our alignment stage with no categorization/grouping.

### 7.1 Categorized – Groups Level

Our 'Categorized Groups' results can be found in Figure 3 and Table 5. For each of our tests we vary the value of $T$ (the number of rounds) to see how it affects our accuracy.

Here we see we have a maximum F score of 0.7039 for $T = 25$. This is a very high result, performing far better than all our baselines, however we feel the 'basketing' mentioned in Section 6 means that the results are not particularly instructive – instead of specific 'interesting' tag attributes, we return a grouped list of tag attributes, only some of which are likely to be 'interesting'. Thus we decide to no longer pursue 'grouping' as a valid evaluation method, and evaluate all our methods at the 'tag attribute' level.

| | | Best | $\mu$ | $\sigma$ |
|---|---|---|---|---|
| | **Precision** | 0.7620 | 0.7473 | 0.0320 |
| CG | **Recall** | 0.6795 | 0.6680 | 0.0322 |
| | **F** | 0.7039 | 0.6897 | 0.0106 |

Table 5: Categorized Groups with Best value for $T = 25$.

### 7.2 Categorized – Tags Level

What is notable here is that, for all values of $T$ which we ran our tests on (ranging from 1 to 3000), we obtained just one set of results for 'Categorized Tags', displayed in Table 6.

This behaviour indicates that the boosting is not helping to improve the results. Rather, it is repeatedly producing the same hypotheses, with varying confidence levels. The low F score is due to

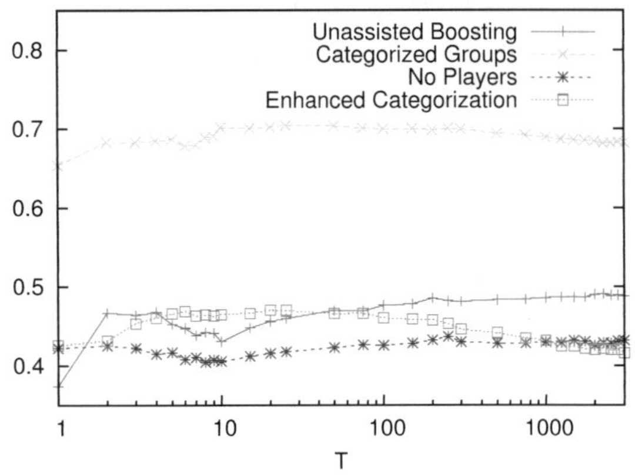


Figure 3: All F scores Results

| | $\mu$ | min | max | $\sigma$ |
|---|---|---|---|---|
| **Precision** | 0.0880 | 0.0496 | 0.1933 | 0.0223 |
| **Recall** | 0.7872 | 0.5417 | 1.0000 | 0.1096 |
| **F** | 0.1575 | 0.0924 | 0.3151 | 0.0361 |

Table 6: Categorized Tags Results

the very low Precision value. This method is effectively a direct application of B&L's method to our domain, however because of our strict accuracy measurement, it does not perform particularly well. In fact it is even worse than $B_{\mathrm{maj}}$, our worst-performing baseline. We believe this is because the Majority Baseline is limited in the breadth of tags returned, whereas this method returns very large sets of over 200 tag attributes (due to the many contributing tag attributes of each category) while the average size of the training sets is 24.

Ideally we want to strike a balance between the improved granularity of the Categorized Tags evaluation (without the low accuracy) with the excellent performance of the Categorized Groups evaluation (without the too-broad basketing).

### 7.3 Unassisted Boosting

Our results are in Table 7 (row UB) and Figure 3. We can see F values are increasing on the whole, and that we have nearly reached our Probabilistic Baseline. Inspecting the contents of the sets returned by BoosTexter, we see they are slightly more in line with a typical training set, but still suffer from an over-emphasis on player names. We also believe the high number of rounds required for our best result ($T = 2250$) is caused by the sparsity issue described in Section 4.2.

| | | Best | $\mu$ | $\sigma$ |
|---|---|---|---|---|
| UB | **Precision** | 0.4965 | 0.4730 | 0.0253 |
| | **Recall** | 0.4961 | 0.4723 | 0.0252 |
| | **F** | 0.4907 | 0.4673 | 0.0249 |
| NP | **Precision** | 0.4128 | 0.3976 | 0.0094 |
| | **Recall** | 0.4759 | 0.4633 | 0.0126 |
| | **F** | 0.4367 | 0.4227 | 0.0091 |
| EC | **Precision** | 0.4440 | 0.4318 | 0.0136 |
| | **Recall** | 0.5127 | 0.4753 | 0.0271 |
| | **F** | 0.4703 | 0.4467 | 0.0194 |

Table 7: Unassisted Boosting (UB), No Players (NP) and Enhanced Categorization (EC). Best values for $T = 2250$, 250 and 20 respectively.

## 8 No-Players & Enhanced Categorization

We now consider alternative, novel methods for improving our results.

### 8.1 Player Exclusion

We have thus far ignored coherency in our data – for example we want to make sure that player statistics will be accompanied by their corresponding player name.

One problem so far with our approach has been that we are effectively double-counting the players. Our methods inspect which player names should appear at the same time as finding appropriate match statistics, whereas we believe we should instead be finding relevant statistics in the first instance, holding back player names, then including only those players to whom the statistics refer. Thus we restate our task in this way.

This is also sensible as in previous incarnations the learning algorithm had been learning from the literal strings of the player names. Although a player could be more likely to be named for various reasons, these reasons would not appear in the scorecard and we feel the strings are best ignored.

Thus we decide to remove all player names from the machine learning input, reinstating only relevant ones once BoosTexter has selected its chosen tag attributes.

### 8.2 Player Exclusion Results

As can be seen from Table 7 (row NP) and Figure 3, we have a maximum F value of 0.4367 when $T = 250$, and have achieved a 3% absolute increase, over our $B_{\mathrm{nops}}$ baseline, a static implementation of the above ideas.

### 8.3 Enhanced Categorization

Our final method combines the ideas of Section 8.1 above with the benefits of categorization, and handles data sparsity issues.

The method is identical to that of Section 3.1, with two important exceptions: The first is that we reintroduce player names after the learning, as above. The second is that instead of just a binary include/don't-include decision for each tag attribute, we offer a list of verbalised tag attributes to the learner, but *anonymising them with respect to the group in which they appear*. This enables the learner to, given any group, predict which tag attributes should be returned, independent of the group in question. This means groups with often-empty tag values are able to leverage the information from groups with usually populated tag values, hence solving our data-sparsity issues. For example, this will solve the issue, referenced in Section 4.2 of a lack of training data for particular player-combination partnerships.

Having held back the group to which the tag attributes belong, we reintroduce them enabling discovery of the original tag attribute. This offers the benefits of categorization, but with a finer-grained approach to the returned sets of tag attributes.

### 8.4 Enhanced Categorization Results

Our results are in Table 7 (row EC) and Figure 3. We achieved our best F score result of 0.4703 for a relatively low value of $T = 20$, and we can clearly see that boosting establishes a reasonable ruleset after a small number of iterations – we believe we have resolved the issue of data sparsity. The fact that this grouping has improved our results compared to feeding the information in 'flat' (as in Section 7.3) emphasises that the construction and make-up of the categories play a key role in defining performance.

## 9 Conclusions & Future Work

This paper has presented an exploration of various methods which could prove useful when selecting content given a partially structured database of statistics and output text to emulate. We began by acquiring the necessary domain data, in the form of scorecards and reports, and employed a six-step process to align scorecard statistics verbalised in the reports. We next categorised our statistics based on the scorecard format. We established three baselines – one 'unthinking' probabilistic baseline, a 'sensible' probabilistic one, and another using categorization.

We found that unassisted boosting actually performed worse than our comparable probabilistic baseline, $B_{\text{prob}}$, but its output was marginally more in line with the typical training data. We explored how categorization affected our results, and showed that by grouping similar sets of tag attributes together we achieved a 7.4% improvement over the comparable baseline value, $B_{\text{nops}}$ (Table 4). We further improved this technique in a novel way by sharing structural information between learning instances, and by holding back certain information from the learner. Our final best F-value marked a relative 15.7% increase on $B_{\text{nops}}$.

There are multiple avenues still available for exploration. One possibility would be to further investigate the effects of categorization from Section 3.2, for example by varying the size and number of categories. We would also like to apply our methods to another domain (e.g. rugby games) to establish the relative generality of our approach.

## Acknowledgments

This paper is based on Colin Kelly's M.Phil. thesis, written towards his completion of the University of Cambridge Computer Laboratory's *Computer Speech, Text and Internet Technology* course. Grateful thanks go to the EPSRC for funding.

## References

Regina Barzilay and Mirella Lapata. 2005. Collective Content Selection for Concept-To-Text Generation. In *HLT '05*, pages 331–338. Association for Computational Linguistics.

Jose Coch. 1998. Multimeteo: multilingual production of weather forecasts. *ELRA Newsletter*, 3(2).

Cricinfo. 2007. Wisden Almanack. *http://cricinfo.com/wisdenalmanack*. Retrieved 28 April 2007. Registration required.

Pablo A. Duboue and Kathleen R. McKeown. 2003. Statistical Acquisition of Content Selection Rules for Natural Language Generation. *EMNLP '03*, pages 121–128.

Ehud Reiter and Robert Dale. 2000. *Building Natural Language Generation Systems*. Cambridge University Press.

Jacques Robin. 1995. *Revision-based generation of natural language summaries providing historical background: corpus-based analysis, design, implementation and evaluation*. Ph.D. thesis, Columbia University.

Robert E. Schapire and Yoram Singer. 2000. BoosTexter: A boosting-based system for text categorization. *Machine Learning*, 39(2/3):135–168.

Yiming Yang. 1999. An evaluation of statistical approaches to text categorization. *Information Retrieval*, 1(1/2):69–90.

# Generating clausal coordinate ellipsis multilingually: A uniform approach based on postediting

**Karin Harbusch**
Computer Science Department
University of Koblenz-Landau
PO Box 201602, 56016 Koblenz/DE
harbusch@uni-koblenz.de

**Gerard Kempen**
Max Planck Institute for Psycholinguistics
PO Box 310, 6500AH Nijmegen/NL
& Cognitive Psychology Unit, Leiden University
gerard.kempen@mpi.nl

## Abstract

Present-day sentence generators are often incapable of producing a wide variety of well-formed elliptical versions of coordinated clauses, in particular, of combined elliptical phenomena (Gapping, Forward and Backward Conjunction Reduction, etc.). The applicability of the various types of clausal coordinate ellipsis (CCE) presupposes detailed comparisons of the syntactic properties of the coordinated clauses. These nonlocal comparisons argue against approaches based on local rules that treat CCE structures as special cases of clausal coordination. We advocate an alternative approach where CCE rules take the form of postediting rules applicable to nonelliptical structures. The advantage is not only a higher level of modularity but also applicability to languages belonging to different language families. We describe a language-neutral module (called Elleipo; implemented in JAVA) that generates as output all major CCE versions of coordinated clauses. Elleipo takes as input linearly ordered nonelliptical coordinated clauses annotated with lexical identity and coreferentiality relationships between words and word groups in the conjuncts. We demonstrate the feasibility of a single set of postediting rules that attains multilingual coverage.

## 1 Introduction

In present-day Natural-Language Generation (NLG) architectures, elision rules typically form part of the *Aggregation* component, i.e. of the module that decides how to group conceptual messages into a sentence—a module belonging to the *Microplanner* (cf. Reiter & Dale, 2000, for an authoritative overview of sentence and text generation technology). In such generators, the computation of coordinate structures takes place at a relatively early stage of syntactic processing. However, many types of clausal coordinate ellipsis (CCE) require detailed comparisons of the final syntactic shape of the coordinated clauses (*conjuncts*). This is even more true when it is desirable to combine elision constructions, as in German example (1a), where Subgapping—a form of Gapping—combines with Backward Conjunction Reduction (for definitions and examples see Table 1). Example (1) also illustrates that often more than one elliptical option is available: (1b) shows a variant with Subgapping alone. If the nonelliptical sentence generator would choose a different Verb order in the second conjunct (*'gestutzt werden sollen'* as in (1d)), then Subgapping would be the sole alternative.

(1) a. *Die Bäume sollen gefällt ~~werden~~ und*
The trees should cut-down be and
*die Sträucher ~~sollen~~ gestutzt werden*
the shrubs should pruned be
'The trees should be cut down and the shrubs pruned'

b. *Die Bäume sollen gefällt werden und die Sträucher ~~sollen~~ gestutzt ~~werden~~*

c. **Die Bäume sollen gefällt ~~werden~~ und gestutzt werden ~~sollen~~ die Sträucher*

d. *Die Bäume sollen gefällt werden und gestutzt ~~werden~~ ~~sollen~~ die Sträucher*

The comparisons between the clausal conjuncts mainly pertain to the linear order of their major constituents and to identity relations between the lexical material contained in them. For instance, if a right-peripheral string of lexical items in the anterior conjunct is identical to such a string in the posterior conjunct, then Backward Conjunction Reduction licenses elision of the former string. In (1a), the two one-word strings '*werden*' meet this requirement.

Language-typological work, e.g. the recent survey by Haspelmath (2007), provides another argument for a "late" CCE component. The main phenomena can be categorized into a small number of basic types, which have been attested in languages belonging to different language

*Proceedings of the 12th European Workshop on Natural Language Generation*, pages 138–145,
Athens, Greece, 30 – 31 March 2009. ©2009 Association for Computational Linguistics

families. This suggests the possibility of a multilingual approach to CCE where the main CCE processes are defined as procedures that are isolated from the "normal" grammar rules for nonelliptical structures, and are independent from each other (see Section 4).

Instead of having an aggregation component where the rules for nonelliptical clausal coordinate structures are intermingled with rules for elliptical variants, we consider an alternative approach where the application of the ellipsis rules is deferred until the nonelliptical structures have been completed. That is, the elision options are calculated and executed during a *postediting* stage, after the strategic and tactic components of the generator have delivered the nonelliptical versions. We claim that this modular approach facilitates the development of multilingual CCE components for different languages by switching on and off the individual CCE procedures (e.g. no Gapping in Japanese).

The structure of the paper is as follows. In Section 2, we introduce the four main CCE phenomena and informally define their treatment in a procedural manner. Section 3 lays out the basic postediting rules that we implemented in JAVA as a language-neutral algorithm (nicknamed *Elleipo*, which means 'I leave out' in classical Greek). In Section 4, we present some findings from language-typological studies and explore their implications for potential multilingual applicability of Elleipo. Finally, in section 5, we draw some conclusions.

The Elleipo version described here embodies several important improvements to a version described briefly in Harbusch & Kempen (2006), particularly with respect to *Subject Gap in clauses with Finite/Fronted Verbs (SGF)*. Moreover, the space allowed here enables us to explain Elleipo's inner workings in more detail, and to demonstrate its multilingual potential.

## 2 Clausal coordinate ellipsis (CCE)

### 2.1 Clausal coordinate ellipsis in linguistic theories and in NLG: State of the art

Treatments of the phenomena of clausal coordination and CCE are provided by all major grammar formalisms. Some representative studies are Sarkar & Joshi (1996) for Tree Adjoining Grammar; Steedman (2000) for Combinatory Categorial Grammar; Bresnan (2000) and Frank (2002) for Lexical-Functional Grammar; Crysmann (2003) and Beavers & Sag (2004) for Head-driven Phrase-Structure Grammar; and te Velde (2005) for the Minimalist Program. Their treatments of CCE take the form of special declarative coordination rules, in contrast with the modular and procedural approach we propose.

In the NLG community, modular treatments of CCE—implemented as programs that take unreduced coordinations expressed in the system's grammar formalism as input and return elliptical versions as output—have been elaborated in several projects (Shaw, 1998; Dalianis, 1999; Hielkema, 2005). These systems are limited in that that they do not cover all of the four CCE processes and are monolingual.

### 2.2 Clausal coordinate ellipsis types

In the linguistic literature on clausal coordinate ellipsis, four main CCE processes are often distinguished, as shown in Table 1.

In the theoretical framework by Kempen (2009) and its implementations (Harbusch & Kempen (2006) for German and Dutch; Harbusch *et al.* (2009) for Estonian), the elision process is guided by *identity constraints* and *linear order* (cf. column 4 in Table 1). We distinguish three basic types of identity relations between words or word groups (constituents) belonging to different conjuncts[1]:

(1) *Lemma identity:* two different words belong to the same inflectional paradigm; e.g. the Verbs '*live*' and '*lives*' in example (2).
(2) *Form identity:* two words have the same spelling/sound and are lemma-identical; e.g., two tokens of '*want*' are form-identical if they are both Verbs, but not if one is a Verb and the other is a Noun.
(3) *Coreferentiality:* two words/constituents denote the same entity or entities in the external context, i.e. have the same reference.

[1] Very often, lemma- and form identity coincide with coreference, but not necessarily. For instance, in '*John bought a car in July, and Peter ~~bought a car~~ in August,*' the two tokens of '*a car*' are not, in all likelihood, coreferential. Nevertheless, elision of '*a car*' is allowed in this Gapping example. In the semantic literature, this relation is called *sloppy identity*. On the other hand, in '*Who wants coffee and who wants tea?,*' the two tokens of '*who*' are not coreferential, and the second token cannot be elided. We assume that the strategic and/or the tactical component of the generator assigns differing identity tags (see Section 3.1) to lemma- or form-identical constituents if and only if their reference is strictly non-identical. Also note that, in the following, the three identity relationships will not only be applied to individual words but also to constituents entirely consisting of words that meet the respective criteria (cf. the numerical subscripts in Figure 1 in Section 3).

Table 1. Clausal coordinate ellipsis (CCE) types. Column 2 lists the abbreviations for the types mentioned in column 1 (see Elleipo's algorithm in Section 3). Column 3 illustrates the CCE types. Column 4 summarizes the elision conditions explained in Section 3.

| CCE type | Abbr. | Examples | Elision conditions |
|---|---|---|---|
| *Gapping* | *g* | (2) *Ulf* ***lives*** *in Leipzig and*<br>*his children* ***~~live~~***$_g$ *in Ulm* | Lemma identity of Verb & contrastiveness of remnants |
| *Long-Distance Gapping (LDG)* | *g(g)*$^+$ | (3) *My wife* ***wants to buy*** *a car and*<br>*my son* ***~~wants~~***$_g$ ***[~~to buy~~]***$_{gg}$ *a motorcycle* | Gapping conditions in *superclause* (Section 3.2.1) |
| *Subgapping* | *sg* | (4) *The driver* ***was*** *killed and*<br>*the passengers* ***~~were~~***$_{sg}$ *severely wounded* | Gapping conditions & VP remnant in second conjunct |
| *Stripping* | *str* | (5) *My sister* ***lives in Narva*** *and*<br>*her children* ***[~~live in Narva~~]***$_{str}$ ***too*** | Gapping conditions & only one non-Verb remnant |
| *Forward Conjunction Reduction (FCR)* | *f* | (6) ***Since two years, my sister*** *lives in Delft and*<br>***[~~since two years, my sister~~]***$_f$ *works in Leiden*<br>(7) *Tokyo is the city [S* ***where*** *Ota lives and*<br>***~~where~~***$_f$ *Kusuke works]* | Form identity & left-peripherality (within clause boundaries) of major clausal constituents |
| *Backward Conjunction Reduction (BCR)* | *b* | (8) *John wrote one* ***~~article~~***$_b$ *and*<br>*Mary edited two* ***articles****.*<br>(9) *Anja arrived before three* ***[~~o'clock~~]***$_b$ *and*<br>*Maria* *~~arrived~~*$_g$ *after four* ***o'clock*** | Lemma identity & right-peripherality, possibly disregarding major constituent boundaries |
| *Subject Gap in clauses with Finite/Fronted Verbs (SGF)* | *s* | (10) *Into the wood went* ***the hunter*** *and*<br>***[~~the hunter~~]***$_s$ *shot a hare* | Form-identical Subject & first conjunct starting with Verb/Modifier/Adjunct & FCR applied if licensed |

As summarized in column 4 of Table 1, all forms of *Gapping* (i.e. including *LDG, Subgapping* and *Stripping*) are characterized by elision of the posterior member of a paired lemma-identical Verb. The position of this Verb need not be peripheral but is often medial, as in examples (2) through (5), and (9). Non-elided constituents in the posterior conjunct are called *remnants*. All remnants should pair up with a constituent in the anterior conjunct that has the same grammatical function but is not coreferential. Stated differently, the members of such a pair are *contrastive*—in (2): the Subjects '*Ulf*' vs. '*his children*', and the locative Modifiers '*in Leipzig*' vs. '*in Ulm.*' (Notice that although two tokens of '*my*' in (3) occupy comparable positions in the two conjuncts, it is not possible to elide any of them. On the other hand, '*were*' in (4) can be elided from the posterior conjunct although it has no literal anterior counterpart.)

In *LDG*, the remnants originate from different clauses (more precisely: different clauses that belong to the same *superclause*; term defined in Section 3.2.1). In (3), '*my son*' belongs to the main clause but '*a motorcycle*' to the infinitival complement clause. In *Subgapping*, the posterior conjunct includes a remnant in the form of a nonfinite complement clause (VP; '*severely wounded*' in (4)). In *Stripping*, the posterior conjunct is left with one non-Verb remnant, often supplemented by the Adverb '*too.*'

In *Forward Conjunction Reduction (FCR)*, elision affects the posterior token of a pair of left-peripheral strings consisting of one or more form-identical major constituents. In (6) and (7), the posterior tokens of '*since two years, my sister*' and '*where,*' respectively, belong to such pairs and are eligible for FCR.

*Backward Conjunction Reduction (BCR)* is *almost* the mirror image of FCR as it deletes the anterior member of a pair of right-peripheral lemma-identical word strings ('*o'clock*' in (9)); however, BCR may elide part of a major constituent—e.g. only the part '*article*' of the Direct Object in (8) and '*o'clock*' of the temporal Modifier '*before three o'clock*' in (9). In addition, it requires only lemma identity—witness examples like (8).[2]

*Subject Gap in clauses with Finite/Fronted Verbs (SGF)* can elide the Subject of the posterior conjunct when in the anterior conjunct the form-identical Subject follows the Verb (Subject-Verb inversion); moreover, the Head Verbs of the conjoined clauses—both with main or interrogative clause word order—are different. (FCR cannot have caused the absence of the posterior Subject since the anterior Subject is not left-peripheral.) The examples in (11)

[2]However, case-identity is required as well, at least in German: *?Hilf ~~[dem Patienten]~~*$_{DAT}$ *und reanimier [den Patient]*$_{ACC}$ 'Help and reanimate the patient'.

through (14) show that the first constituents of the unreduced clauses must meet certain special requirements, which extend the rule proposed in our previous publications. In particular, these constituents *are* allowed to be non-form-identical finite Head Verbs (11) or form-identical Modifiers (12) but *not* form-identical arguments, e.g. Direct Objects (13) or Complements (14). Additionally, if FCR is licensed, as in (12), it should actually be realized in order to allow SGF.

(11) *Stehen die Leute noch am Eingang und*
Stand the people still at-the entrance and
*rufen [~~die Leute~~]$_s$ Parolen?*
shout the people slogans
'Are the people still standing at the entrance (and are they) shouting slogans?'

(12) *Warum/Gestern bist du gegangen und*
Why/Yesterday have you left and
*[~~warum/gestern~~]$_f$ hast ~~du~~$_s$ nichts gesagt*
why/yesterday have you nothing said
'Why did you leave and didn't you tell me anything?' / 'Yesterday you left and ...'

(13) **Diesen Wein trinke ich nicht mehr und*
This wine drink I not anymore and
*[~~diesen Wein~~]$_f$ gieße ~~ich~~$_s$ weg*
this wine throw I away
'I don't drink this wine anymore and throw it away'

(14) **Das Examen bestehen will er und*
The exam pass will he and
*[~~das Examen bestehen~~]$_f$ kann ~~er~~$_s$ auch*
the exam pass can he too/as-well
'He wants to pass the exam and will be able to as well'

## 3 Language-neutral CCE generation

In this Section, we describe Elleipo's algorithm in more detail than we were able to in Harbusch & Kempen (2006), again using the German example (15). Moreover, we elaborate on SGF, given the new, more detailed rules. We limit ourselves to '*and*'-coordinations of only $n$=2 conjuncts. Actually, Elleipo can handle $n$-ary coordinations consisting of $n \geq 2$ conjuncts by processing $n$–1 consecutive pairs of conjuncts (1+2, 2+3, etc.), together with an asyndeton rule that replaces non-final *'and'*-s by commas.

(15) *Heute wird Hans sein Auto putzen und*
Today will Hans his car clean and
*~~heute wird~~ Susi ihr Fahrrad ~~putzen~~*
today will Susi her bike clean
'Today, Hans will clean his car and today, Susi will clean her bike'

Elleipo's functioning is based on the assumption that CCE does not result from the application of local declarative grammar rules for clause formation but from a procedural component that inspects nonelliptical (unreduced) sentences produced by the sentence generator and may block the overt expression of certain constituents. Due to this feature, Elleipo can be combined, at least in principle, with various generators. However, the module needs a formalism-dependent interface that converts generator output to a (simple) canonical form.

### 3.1 Elleipo's input

Elleipo takes as input nonelliptical syntactic trees in *canonical form*, supplied with *identity tags* (cf. Figure 1). Every categorial node of an input tree is immediately dominated by a functional node. Each conjunct is rooted in a categorial node whose daughter nodes (immediate constituents) are grammatical functions (Subject, Direct Object, Head, Subordinating Conjunction, Expr(ession), etc.). Within a conjunct, all major constituents are represented at the same hierarchical level ("flat" trees).

Categorial nodes are adorned with numerical identity tags (ID-tags) which express lemma identity. In Figure 1, the ID "2" is attached to the head node of both exemplars of AP '*heute*' 'today', thus marking their lemma identity. In contrast, the Subject NPs '*Hans*' and '*Susi*' carry different ID-tags, indicating that they are not lemma-identical and cannot be elided by any CCE process.

### 3.2 The three stages of Elleipo

Elleipo is called for every coordination domain within a non-elliptical input clause. We define a *coordination domain* as a (sub)tree rooting in a grammatical function node that dominates two or more categorial S-nodes separated by coordinating conjunctions ('*and*'). For any given coordination domain, Elleipo's task consists of three consecutive stages: *Preparation, Diagnosis, and ReadOut.*

#### 3.2.1 Preparation

The first job within *Preparation* is the demarcation of *superclauses*. Kempen (2009) introduced this notion in the treatment of Gapping, in particular LDG. A *superclause* is either a simple finite or non-finite clause (rooting in an S-node, without any subordinate clauses), or a hierarchy of finite or non-finite clauses where every embedded clause is an immediate daughter of an embedding clause; moreover, none of the participating clauses begins with a subordinating

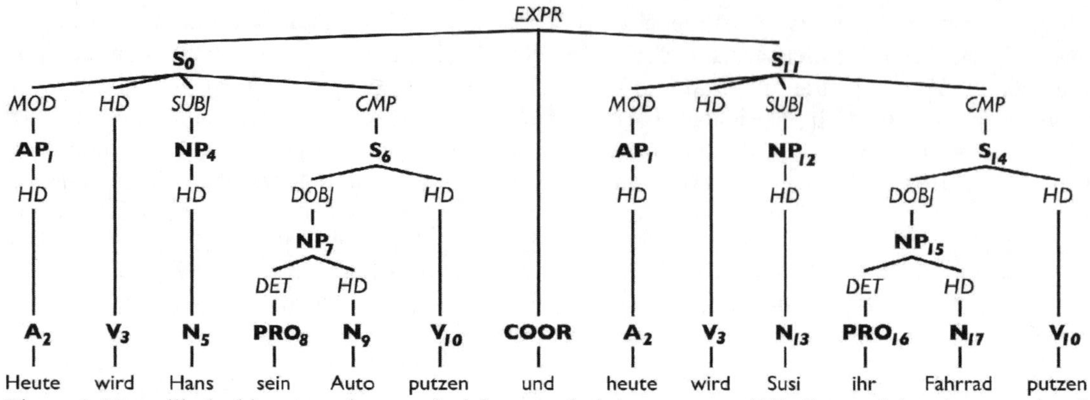

Figure 1. Non-elliptical input tree in canonical form, underlying sentence (15). Categorial nodes are printed in bold, functional nodes in italics. The numerical subscripted tags denote lemma identity or coreference.

conjunction, with the possible exception of the topmost member of the hierarchy.[3]

Next, Elleipo inspects and compares the content of the conjoined clauses by assembling four lists: FUNC-PAIRS, LI-FUNC-PAIRS, LPERIPH and RPERIPH (see Table 2). The lists FUNC-PAIRS and LI-FUNC-PAIRS are crucial not only in calculating whether a form of Gapping is applicable but also in the determination of *contrastiveness* of Gapping remnants. We presuppose a division of MODifier constituents into MOD types—locative (LMOD), temporal (TMOD, causal (CMOD), etc.—which are recorded in the two lists of pairs. Gapping requires the set of grammatical functions, including MOD types, in the anterior and posterior conjuncts to be identical. If so, and if FUNC-PAIRS includes at least one pair of non-coreferential members (carrying different ID-tags), the Boolean variable CONTRAST is set to *true*. In the example, FUNC-PAIRS($S_0$, $S_{11}$) includes two pairs of non-coreferential major constituents (the Subjects and the Complements); hence, CONTRAST = *true*. LPERIPH is crucial in FCR, where only complete form-identical major constituents may be elided. RPERIPH is used in BCR, which sometimes leaves incomplete constituents behind, as exemplified by (8) and (9).

[3] The "embedded" clauses referred to in the definition of superclause fulfill the grammatical function of Subject or Object Complement within the embedding clause, or they are adverbial clauses fulfilling the function of Modifier within the embedding clause. In Figure 1, the Complement clauses $S_6$ and $S_{14}$ are major constituents of $S_0$ and $S_{11}$, respectively. The hierarchy spanning $S_0$ and $S_6$ is a superclause, and so is the hierarchy consisting of $S_{11}$ and $S_{14}$. In '*Hans sagte, dass Susi ihr Fahrrad putzen wird*' 'Hans said that Susi will clean her bike,' the Complement clause does not belong to the same superclause as the main clause '*Hans sagte ...*,' but instead starts up its own superclause. Gapping and its varieties can only be applied to two coordinated superclauses.

### 3.2.2 Diagnosis

For each of the four CCE processes, Elleipo inspects all coordination domains for elision options. This requires interpreting the lists collected during the Preparation stage. Any licensed elision option for a word or constituent causes the current value of the parameter CCE-TYPE to be added as a tag to that word or constituent (cf. the subscripts in examples (2) through (10)). Different elliptical variants (cf. examples (1a/b)) are represented by multiple tags and yield alternative realizations, to be spelled out during the final ReadOut stage. If the Boolean variable CONTRAST is *true*, Gapping runs recursively within the current coordination domain. Figure 2 shows pseudocode for Gapping, with input parameters LC = left conjunct, RC=right conjunct, and CCE-TYPE=*g*). In the example: GAPPING($S_0$, $S_{11}$, "*g*").

Lemma identity of the Head Verbs of the clausal conjuncts licenses Gapping. So, the temporal Adverbial Modifier and the Head Verb of the posterior conjunct can both be marked for elision: '*Heute wird Hans sein Auto putzen und ~~heute~~$_g$ ~~wird~~$_g$ Susi ihr Fahrrad putzen*' (steps 8 and 9). Earlier on, in step 3 and 4, Elleipo has already noticed that one of the non-lemma-identical pairs—$S_6$ and $S_{14}$—consists of Complement clauses belonging to the same superclause as the coordinated main clauses (i.e. they do not start up a new superclause hierarchy). In step 6, Elleipo is called recursively for this coordinate subdomain, with argument CCE-TYPE set to "*gg*". As the Head Verbs of these complement clauses are lemma-identical and the contrastiveness condition holds (i.e. the grammatical function DOBJ occurs in both the anterior and the posterior complement and the exemplars are not lemma-identical), the posterior Verb is marked for elision, yielding '*Heute wird*

Table 2. Definitions of the (possibly empty) lists of paired major clause constituents calculated during Elleipo's Preparation stage. Column 3 shows the content of the lists for example (15), i.e. the superclauses $S_0$ and $S_{11}$.

| List | Definition | Content of lists for example (15) |
|---|---|---|
| FUNC-PAIRS | All constituent pairs *LCAT–RCAT* with same grammatical function, dominated by an S-node pair; if (LCAT, RCAT) is an S-node pair, then FUNC-PAIRS is assembled recursively for this pair as well. | FUNC-PAIRS($S_0$,$S_{11}$)={$AP_1$–$AP_1$,$V_3$–$V_3$, $NP_4$–$NP_{12}$, $S_6$–$S_{14}$} Due to recursive application: FUNC-PAIRS($S_6$,$S_{14}$)={$NP_7$–$NP_{15}$,$V_{10}$–$V_{10}$} |
| LI-FUNC-PAIRS | Lemma-Identical pairs of corresponding FUNC-PAIRS (i.e., LI-FUNC-PAIRS $\subseteq$ FUNC-PAIRS). | LI-FUNC-PAIRS($S_0$,$S_{11}$)={$AP_1$–$AP_1$,$V_3$–$V_3$} LI-FUNC-PAIRS($S_6$,$S_{14}$)={$V_{10}$–$V_{10}$} |
| LPERIPH | Left-peripheral form-identical complete major constituents shared by the conjuncts. | LPERIPH($S_0$,$S_{11}$)={$A_2$,$V_3$} |
| RPERIPH | Right-peripheral lemma-identical lexical string shared by the conjuncts. | RPERIPH($S_0$,$S_{11}$) ={$V_{10}$} |

```
proc GAPPING(LC, RC, CCE-TYPE) {
 for all pairs (LCAT, RCAT) in FUNC-PAIRS(LC, RC) {
  if (LCAT is an S-node) & (LCAT doesn't begin a new superclause) then {// call GAPPING recursively//
     if NOT (LCAT and RCAT are lemma-identical)
       then {attach "g" to CCE-TYPE; //LDG//
             call GAPPING(LCAT, RCAT, CCE-TYPE);}
       else mark RCAT for elision, with CCE-TYPE}
  if (LCAT and RCAT are lemma-identical) & NOT(LCAT is an S-node)
    then mark RCAT for elision, with CCE-TYPE}}
```

Figure 2. Pseudocode for the GAPPING procedure

*Hans sein Auto putzen und ~~heute~~$_g$ ~~wird~~$_g$ Susi ihr Fahrrad ~~putzen~~$_{gg}$.'*

FCR and BCR are both executed by one procedure, called CR. In FCR mode, CR is called with the value of LPERIPH as input; in BCR mode, it takes RPERIPH's value as input. Recall that these lists were computed in the Preparation stage and may contain a form-identical (LPERIPH) or a lemma-identical (RPERIPH) lexical string. In calls to CR (see the pseudocode in Figure 3), parameter PERIPH is set to LPERIPH or RPERIPH, and *CCE-TYPE* to "*b*" or "*f*" depending on whether BCR or FCR is to be executed. In our example, the main program calls are:

CR($S_0$, $S_{11}$, LPERIPH($S_0$, $S_{11}$), "*f*"), and
CR($S_0$, $S_{11}$, RPERIPH($S_0$, $S_{11}$), "*b*").

FCR and BCR are attempted after, and fully independently from, Gapping, irrespective of whether the latter was successful or not. As Modifier '*heute*' and Head Verb '*wird*' are both listed in *LPERIPH*($S_0$, $S_{11}$), both major constituents are marked as eligible for elision from the posterior conjunct (line 6 of Figure 3)—an effect which happens to coincide with the effects of Gapping:

*'Heute wird Hans sein Auto putzen und ~~heute~~$_{g\text{-}f}$ ~~wird~~$_{g\text{-}f}$ Susi ihr Fahrrad ~~putzen~~$_{gg}$'.*

```
1 proc CR(LC, RC, PERIPH, CCE-TYPE) {
2 while PERIPH ≠ ∅ {
3    set (LCAT, RCAT) to PERIPH's first element;
4    PERIPH =PERIPH minus first element;
5    if CCE-TYPE = "f"
6      then mark RCAT else LCAT for elision,
         with CCE-TYPE}}
```

Figure 3. Pseudocode for procedure CR (executing FCR or BCR).

When attempting BCR, Elleipo discovers the lemma-identical '*putzen*' ($V_{10}$), and marks the anterior exemplar with "*b*": *'Heute wird Hans sein Auto ~~putzen~~$_b$ und ~~heute~~$_{g\text{-}f}$ ~~wird~~$_{g\text{-}f}$ Susi ihr Fahrrad ~~putzen~~$_{gg}$'.*

Elleipo's fourth check concerns SGF (Figure 4; see section 2.1 for the rules), here with negative result. In example (15), Subject-Verb-inversion is realized in the first conjunct. However, the two Subjects *'Peter'* and *'Susi'* are not coreferential.

```
1 proc SGF(LC, RC) {
2   if (Head Verb precedes SUBJ in LC)
      & (coreferential SUBJs in LI-FUNC-PAIRS)
      & (Head Verb or MOD in 1st position in LC)
      & (1st position in RC is occupied by SUBJ or a
         major constituent already marked for FCR)
3     then mark RC's SUBJ for elision "s";}
```

Figure 4. Pseudocode for SGF

### 3.2.3 ReadOut

The resulting terminal string annotated with elision marks is handed over to the *ReadOut* stage. As ReadOut assumes that all elisions are optional, it may deliver more than one elliptical output string. However, not every possible combination of elisions is legitimate; certain combinations have to be ruled out. We mention four important restrictions here. First, Gapping and BCR cannot elide both tokens of a lexical item. For instance, if *'putzen'* in the anterior conjunct of (15) is elided due to BCR, then its posterior counterpart *'putzen,'* which could be Gapped, should remain—and vice-versa. Second, in LDG, if a Verb with *n* subscripts "*g*" is elided, then all Verbs with *m*>*n* subscripts "*g*" should be elided as well. Third, in Gapping, if only one non-Head-Verb constituent remains (i.e. Stripping), then (the language-specific equivalent of) the Adverb *'too'* is added. Fourth, SGF requires that FCR, if licensed, is actually executed. Moreover, the ReadOut stage performs certain types of embellishments, e.g. it applies an asyndeton rule that replaces all but the last token of the coordinating conjunction by commas.

## 3.4 Elleipo evaluated for German

A detailed evaluation of Elleipo is currently only available for the German version (Harbusch & Kempen, 2007). In the TIGER corpus with 50,000 sentences, 99 percent of the CCE sentences conform to Elleipo's CCE rules. Nevertheless, we are aware that these rules do not handle SGF in conjoined subordinate clauses where the first conjunct has the standard Verb-final word order but the second conjunct (with SGF) embodies Verb-second order. Furthermore, Elleipo does not take into account certain semantic constraints ("one-event semantics"; Reich, in press; see also Frank, 2002; Kempen, 2009). Another insufficiency concerns the rules for asyndeton, which are more complicated than simply converting prefinal *'and'*-s to commas (see Borsley (2005) for pertinent examples).

# 4 Multilingual CCE generation

## 4.1 CCE rules in typological studies

The four CCE processes have been attested in two Germanic languages (German and Dutch) and in a Finno-Ugric language (Estonian; Harbusch *et al.*, 2009), where they account for a wide range of CCE phenomena. This invites the prediction that CCE obeys the same rules in many other languages as well. However, Haspelmath's (2007) survey immediately falsifies this prediction: Other CCE processes may be at work in other languages, and/or some of the above four main processes may be absent.

Japanese may provide illustrations of both points. On the one hand, it is uncontroversial that it does not have Gapping. On the other hand, it may have a form of CCE that stands midway between FCR and BCR. Yatabe (2001) interprets (16) as *Left Node Raising*, i.e. as the mirror image of BCR. Like FCR, it elides a left-peripheral string of the posterior conjunct; like BCR, the elided string need not be a complete major constituent. The elided Verb *yonde* is part of the prenominal Relative clause *yonde agenakatta* which is a major constituent (immediate daughter) of the NP headed by the Noun *hito*. But notice that (16) embodies coordination of NPs rather than clauses. If Japanese indeed exhibits *partial* elision of left-peripheral major constituents at the *clausal* level, thus violating our FCR definition, then we obviously need to define an additional CCE type.

(16) *Yonde ageta hito to*
read$_{gerund}$ give$_{past}$ person and
*~~yonde~~*$_{f}$ *agenakatta hito ga ita*
read$_{gerund}$ give$_{neg\text{-}past}$ person NOM be$_{past}$
'There were people who gave (him/her) the favor of reading (it) (to him/her) and people who didn't'

In contrast, Abe & Hoshi (1997) analyze Japanese example (17) in terms of *Preposition Stranding*. As far as we can see, this structure does not require a special CCE process because Elleipo treats it as BCR, which allows partial elision of the PP Modifier in the anterior conjunct, hence stranding of the Preposition.

(17) *John-ga Bill[-~~nituite hanasita~~]*$_{b}$, *sosite*
John-Nom Bill -about talked and
*Mary-ga Susan-nituite hanasita*
Mary-Nom Susan-about talked
'John talked about Bill and Mary about Susan'

Haspelmath (2007) also discusses certain languages with Subject–Object–Verb (SOV) as basic word order (Turkish and Korean) which allow Object deletion from non-peripheral positions in the posterior conjunct; i.e., they license the pattern SOV&S_V, as in *'The-boy the-cart pulled and the-girl ~~the-cart~~ pushed.'* Elleipo cannot handle this CCE structure: FCR and BCR require peripherality of the elided constituent; SGF only applies to Subjects; and Gapping presupposes elision of the Head Verb. In order to encompass the problematic pattern, we may need to define a new CCE process. However, at least in Turkish SOV&S_V cases, the elision may be due to pragmatic factors. Göksel & Kerslake (2005) show that major clause constituents fulfilling diverse grammatical functions can be elided as long their referents are recoverable on the basis of the accompanying linguistic or nonlinguistic context. Because the anterior conjunct may provide such a context, one first needs to rule out contextual recoverability as the licensing factor.

At the same time, Haspelmath also shows that Elleipo's four CCE processes cover a high proportion of CCE patterns occurring cross-linguistically. (However, he does not discuss SGF.) A typical illustration is the set of nine "more widely attested patterns" of CCE that he enumerates with respect to elision of Objects or Verbs in four language groups with different basic word orders of S, O and V (Table 2 in Haspelmath, 2007). All these patterns are covered by our four CCE processes, except SOV&S_V.

## 5 Discussion

We conclude that a software module embodying Elleipo's four main CCE processes—maybe with relatively minor adjustments—will be able to generate a great deal of CCE structures for many different languages.

As for possible practical applications, Elleipo's status as a postprocessor working on input specifications of unreduced syntactic structures facilitates combinability with sentence generators based on various grammar formalisms. Even template-based message generators, such as used in car navigation and weather forecast systems, can attain higher levels of fluency and conciseness if the templates are annotated with syntactic structure and ID-tags.

## References


Abe, J. & Hoshi, H. 1997. Gapping and P-Stranding. *Journal of East Asian Linguistics, 6*.

Beavers, J. & Sag, I.A. 2004. Coordinate Ellipsis and Apparent Non-Constituent Coordination *Procs. of 11th Int. Conf. on HPSG*, Louvain.

Borsley, R.D. 2005. Against ConjP. *Lingua, 115*.

Bresnan, J.W. 2000. *Lexical-Functional Syntax*. Blackwell, Oxford, UK.

Crysmann, B. 2003. An asymmetric theory of peripheral sharing in HPSG: Conjunction reduction and coordination of unlikes. *Procs. of 8th Conf. on Formal Grammar*, Vienna.

Dalianis, H. 1999. Aggregation in natural language generation. *Computational Intelligence, 15*.

Göksel, A. & Kerslake, C. 2005. *Turkish: A comprehensive Grammar*. Routledge, Abington, Oxon, UK.

Frank, A. 2002. A (discourse) functional analysis of asymmetric coordination. *Procs. of LFG02 Conf.*, Athens.

Harbusch, K. & Kempen, G. 2006. Elleipo: A module that computes coordinative ellipsis for language generators that don't. *Procs. of 11th EACL*, Trento.

Harbusch, K. & Kempen, G. 2007. Clausal coordinate ellipsis in German. *Procs. of 16th NODALIDA*, Tartu.

Harbusch, K., Koit, M. & Õim, H. 2009. A comparison of clausal coordinate ellipsis in Estonian and German. *Procs. of 12th EACL*, Athens.

Hielkema, F. 2005. *Performing syntactic aggregation using discourse structures*. Unpublished Master's thesis, AI Unit, University of Groningen.

Haspelmath, M. 2007. Coordination. In: Shopen, T. (Ed.), *Language typology and linguistic description*. Cambridge University Press [2nd Ed.], Cambidge UK.

Kempen, G. 2009. Clausal coordination and coordinate ellipsis in a model of the speaker. *Linguistics, 47(3)*.

Reich, I. In press. From discourse to "odd coordinations"—On Asymmetric Coordination and Subject Gaps in German. In: Fabricius-Hansen, C. & Ramm, W. (Eds.), *'Subordination' vs. 'Coordination' in Sentence and Text*. Benjamins, Amsterdam.

Reiter, E. & Dale, R. 2000. *Building natural language generation systems*. Cambridge University Press, Cambridge, UK.

Sarkar, A. & Joshi, A. 1996. Coordination in Tree Adjoining Grammars. *Procs. of 16th COLING*, Copenhagen.

Shaw, S. 1998. Segregatory coordination and ellipsis in text generation. *Procs. of 17th COLING*, Montreal.

Steedman, M. 2000. *The syntactic process*. MIT Press, Cambridge MA.

te Velde, J.R. 2006. *Deriving Coordinate Symmetries*. Benjamins, Amsterdam.

Yatabe, S. 2001. The syntax and semantics of left-node raising in Japanese. *Procs. of the 7th Int. HPSG Conf.*, Berkeley. CSLI Publications, Stanford CA.

# Towards Empirical Evaluation of Affective Tactical NLG

**Ielka van der Sluis**
Trinity College Dublin
Dublin
ielka.vandersluis@cs.tcd.ie

**Chris Mellish**
University of Aberdeen
Aberdeen
c.mellish@abdn.ac.uk

## Abstract

One major aim of research in affective natural language generation is to be able to use language intelligently to induce effects on the emotions of the reader/ hearer. Although varying the *content* of generated language ("strategic" choices) might be expected to change the effect on emotions, it is not obvious that varying the *form* of the language ("tactical" choices) can do this. Indeed, previous experiments have been unable to show emotional effects of tactical variations. Building on what has been discovered in previous experiments, we present a new experiment which does demonstrate such effects. This represents an important step towards the empirical evaluation of affective NLG systems.

## 1 Introduction

This paper is about developing techniques for the empirical evaluation of affective natural language generation (NLG). Affective NLG has been defined as "NLG that relates to, arises from or deliberately influences emotions or other non-strictly rational aspects of the Hearer" (De Rosis and Grasso, 2000). It currently covers two main strands of work, the portrayal of non-rational aspects in an artificial speaker/writer (e.g. the work of Mairesse and Walker (2008) on projecting personality) and the use of NLG in ways sensitive to the non-rational aspects of the hearer/reader and calculated to achieve effects on these aspects (e.g. the work of De Rosis et al. (1999) on generating instructions in an emotionally charged situation and that of Moore et al. (2004) on producing appropriate tutorial feedback). Although there has been success in evaluating work of the first kind, it remains more problematic to evaluate whether work of the second type directly affects emotion or mood, or whether it influences task performance for other reasons.

Since the work of Thompson (1977), NLG tasks have been considered to divide mainly into those involving *strategy* ("deciding what to say") and *tactics* ("deciding how to say it"). It seems clear that one can affect a reader's emotion differently by making different strategic decisions about content (e.g. telling someone that they have passed an exam will make them happier than telling them that they have failed), but it is less clear that tactical alternations (e.g. involving ordering of material, choice of words or syntactic constructions) can have these kinds of effects. Unfortunately, the exact dividing line between strategy and tactics remains a matter of debate. For the purpose of this paper, we take "strategic" to cover matters of basic propositional content (the basic information to be communicated) and "tactical" to include most linguistic issues, including matters of emphasis and focus, inasmuch as they can be influenced by linguistic formulation. It is important to know whether tactical choices can influence emotions because to a large extent NLG research concentrates on tactical issues (partly because strategic NLG remains a rather domain-specific activity).

Some light on the effects of tactical variations in text is shed by work in Psychology, where there has been a great deal of work on the effects of the "framing" of a text (Moxey and Sanford, 2000; Teigen and Brun, 2003). Some of this has been industrially funded, as there are considerable applications, for instance, in advertising. The alternative texts considered differ in ways that NLG researchers would call tactical. For instance, a piece of meat could be described as "75% lean" or "25% fat", and arguably these are alternative truthful descriptions of the same situation. However, evaluation of this work has been primarily in terms of whether it affects people's *choices* or *evaluations*

*Proceedings of the 12th European Workshop on Natural Language Generation*, pages 146–153,
Athens, Greece, 30 – 31 March 2009. ©2009 Association for Computational Linguistics

of options available (Levin et al., 1998), or other aspects of task performance (O'Hara and Sternberg, 2001; Brown and Pinel, 2003; Cadinu et al., 2005). As far as we know it is unknown whether emotions can be affected in this way. There is therefore an open question about whether it is possible to detect the non-rational effects of different tactical decisions on readers. We believe that achieving this is important for the further scientific development of affective NLG.

In the rest of this paper, we discuss previous (unsuccessful) attempts to measure emotional effects of tactical decisions in texts (section 2), the particular linguistic choices we have focussed on, including a text validation experiment (section 3) and our choice of a method for measuring emotions (section 4). In section 5 we then present a new study which for the first time demonstrates significant differences in emotions evoked in readers associated with tactical textual variations. We then briefly reflect on this result in a concluding section.

## 2 Background for the Present Study

In (van der Sluis and Mellish, 2008) we described several experiments investigating different methods of measuring the effects of texts on emotions to demonstrate that tactical differences would lead to differences in effects. Our method was to present participants with texts about cancer-causing chemicals in foods or unexpected health-giving properties of drinking water and to attempt to measure the emotions invoked by different variations of these texts. However, we were unable to show statistically significant results of tactical variations. We mentioned the following possible explanations for this:

- We used methods where participants reported on their own emotions. However, it could be that (in this context) participants were unwilling or unable to report accurately.
- The self-reporting methods used were perhaps not fine grained enough to register the differences between the effects of similar texts.
- The texts themselves were perhaps too subtly different or not long enough to induce strong emotions.
- The participants were perhaps not involved enough in the task to get strong emotions.

We believe that of these, the final reason is the most compelling. The self-reporting methods used had been validated and used in multiple previous studies in Psychology, and so there was no reason to suggest that they would fundamentally fail in this new context. The granularity of the measurement methods can be improved relatively simply (see section 4 below). But it is very believable that the participants would fail to be really concerned by the texts in the experiments reported since the source was unclear, the message a general one not addressed to them individually and the topic (healthy and unhealthy food) one that occurs often enough in newspapers to fail to overcome natural boredom.

The main innovation of the experiment we describe below was in our method of seeking the emotional involvement of the participants. The texts that the participants read took the form of "feedback" on a (fake) IQ test that they undertook as part of the experiment. We selected university students as the participants, as they would likely be concerned about their intelligence, especially as compared to their peers. The texts appeared to be written individually for the participants and so sought to engage them directly.

## 3 Linguistic Choice and Framing

As in (van der Sluis and Mellish, 2008), the study we present here sought to evoke positive emotions to differing extents in a reader by tactical manipulations to "slant" the tasks positively to varying degrees. This section describes the text variations used and their validation.

### 3.1 Tactical Methods

The two texts produced for this experiment were written by hand, but used the following methods to give a more "positive slant" to a text. These are all methods that could be implemented straightforwardly in an NLG system[1]. In the following, the word "positive polarity" is used to refer to propositions giving good news to the reader or attributes which give good news to the reader if they have high values (such as the reader's intelligence). Similarly "negative polarity" refers to items that represent bad news, e.g. failing a test. For ethical reasons, negative polarity items did not arise in this experiment.

**A. Sentence emphasis** - include explicit emphasis in sentences expressing positive polarity propositions (e.g. exclamation marks and phrases such as "on top of this").

[1]Though the choice about *when* to apply them might not be so straightforward.

**B. Choice of vague evaluative adjectives** - when evaluating positive polarity attributes, choose vague evaluative adjectives that are more positive over ones that are less positive (e.g. "excellent", rather than "ok").

**C. Choice of vague adverbs** - provide explicit emphasis to positive polarity propositions by including vague adverbs expressing great extent (e.g. "significantly", rather than "to some extent" or no adverb).

**D. Choice of verbs** - for a positive polarity proposition, choose a verb that emphasises the great extent of the proposition (e.g. "outperformed", rather than "did better than").

**E. Choice of realisation of rhetorical relations** - when realising a concession/contrast relation between a positive polarity proposition and one that is negative or neutral, word it so that the positive polarity proposition is in the nucleus (more emphasised) position (e.g. say "although you did badly on X, you did well on Y" instead of "although you did well on Y, you did badly on X").

The idea is that an NLG system would employ methods of this kind in order to "slant" a message positively, rather that to present a message in a more neutral way. This might be done, for instance, to induce positive emotions in a reader who needs encouragement.

We claim that these choices can be viewed as tactical, i.e. that they are "allowable" alternative realisations of the same underlying content. For instance, we believe a teacher could use such methods in giving feedback to a student needing encouragement without fear of prosecution for misrepresenting the same truth that would be expressed without the use of these methods.

Whenever one words a proposition in different ways, it can be claimed that a (perhaps subtle) change of meaning is involved. However, in these cases we claim that it is the *writer's attitudes* that are being manipulated (and reflected in the text). We can therefore choose between these alternatives by varying the writer, not the underlying message. Our view is supported by a number of current accounts of the semantics of vague adjectives (though this is not an area without controversy). Many accounts of vagueness appeal to the idea that there is a norm which an adjective like "tall" implicitly refers to, and some of these argue both that the norm itself can be contextually determined and also that the amount by which the norm has to be exceeded has to be "significant" to a degree which is "relativized to some agent" (Kennedy, 2007). For instance, with the phrase "John is tall"

> "the property [...] attributed to John is not an intrinsic property, but rather a relational one. Moreover, it is not a property the possession of which depends only on the difference between Johns height and some norm, but also on whether that difference is a significant one. I take it that whether or not a difference is a significant difference does not depend only on its magnitude, but also on what our interests are" (Graff, 2000)

It is compatible with these accounts that different agents, with different interests and notions of what is noteworthy, can use vague adjectives in different ways[2].

Another reason for considering these methods as tactical is that in an NLG system, they would likely be implemented somewhere late in the "pipeline".

Probably the best way to check that we are using tactical alternations (according to our definition) is via some kind of text validation experiment with human participants. Section 3.3 below describes such an experiment, which provides strong support for this position.

### 3.2 Test Texts

For the experiment, we produced two feedback texts describing the same set of intelligence test results, one relatively neutral and one "positively slanted" using the above methods. In the experiment, they were given to participants in two groups, named "0" and "+" respectively. Each text consisted of 7 sentences, with a direct correspondance between the sentences of the two texts. Figure 1 presents the variations used in the feedback used in the experiment for group + (i.e. positively slanted) and group 0 (i.e. neutrally slanted). Note that the actual numbers are the same in both texts.

### 3.3 Text validation

A text validation study was conducted in which 15 colleagues participated. The participants were asked to comment on 12 sentence pairs, the 7 shown in Figure 1 and 5 additional filler pairs. The following analysis reports on our findings on the 7 sentence pairs shown in Figure 1 only.

In order that we could test our intuitions about the tactical nature of the linguistic alternations (discussed in section 3.1 above), the participants were presented with a scenario where there were two different teachers, Mary Jones and Gordon

[2] Though there are certainly *some* limits on the situations where a word like "tall" can be truthfully used to describe a height

+1: Your Baumgartner score of 7.38 is excellent!

01: Your Baumgartner score of 7.38 is ok.

+2: You did distinctively better than the average score obtained by other people in your age group.

02: You did somewhat better than the average score obtained by other people in your age group.

+3: Especially your scores on Imagination/Creativity and on Clarity of Thought were great and considerably higher than average.

03: Your scores on Imagination/Creativity and on Clarity of Thought were good and a little higher than average.

+4: A factor analyses of your Baumgartner score results in an overall excellent performance.

04: A factor analyses of your Baumgartner score results in an overall reasonable performance.

+5: Although, compared to your peers, you have only slightly higher Spatial Intelligence (7.5 vs 7.0) and Visual Intelligence (7.2 vs 6.8) scores, your Clarity of Thought Score is very much better (7.2 vs 6.3).

05: Compared to your peers, you have a somewhat better Clarity of Thought Score (7.2 vs 6.3), but you have only slightly higher Spatial Intelligence (7.5 vs 7.0) and Visual Intelligence (7.2 vs 6.8) scores.

+6: On top of this you also outperformed most people in your age group with your exceptional scores for Imagination and Creativity (7.9 vs 7.2) and Logical-Mathematical Intelligence (7.1 vs. 6.5).

06: You did better than most people in your age group with your scores for Imagination and Creativity (7.9 vs 7.2) and Logical-Mathematical Intelligence (7.1 vs. 6.5).

+7: There is a lot of variation in your age group, but your score is significantly higher than average.

07: Your score is higher than average, but there is a lot of variation in your age group.

Figure 1: Linguistic variation used in the IQ test feedback

Smith, both completely honest but with very different ideas about teaching (Mary believing that any pupil can succeed, given encouragement, but Gordon believing that most pupils are lazy and have overinflated ideas about their abilities). Given a positively slanted sentence (e.g. +7) from Mary and a corresponding more neutrally slanted one (e.g. 07) from Gordon, addressed to one or more pupils, participants were asked to indicate:

1. "Is it possible that Mary and Gordon might actually be (honestly) giving different feedback to the *same* pupil on the same task?"

2. "If the two pieces of feedback were given to the same pupil (for the same task) and the pupil's parents found out, do you think they would have grounds to make a complaint that one of the teachers is lying?"

The hypothesis was that (for the 7 pairs of sentences from Figure 1) in general participants would answer "yes" to question 1 and "no" to question 2. Indeed, for 6 pairs at least 14 out of the 15 participants answered as we had predicted. For the other pair (+4/04), 12 out of 15 agreed with both predictions. We see this as very strong evidence for our position (the participants gave different answers for the filler pairs, and so were not just producing these answers blindly).

No alterations were made to the two feedback texts on the basis of the text validation results.

## 4 Measuring Emotions

There are two broad ways of measuring the emotions of human subjects – physiological methods and self-reporting. Physiological methods unfortunately tend to have the problems of complex setup and calibration, which mean that it is hard to transport them between tasks or individuals. In addition, although emotional states are undoubtedly connected to physiological variables, it is not always clear what is being measured by these methods (cf. (Lazarus et al., 1980); (Cacioppo et al., 2000) ).

Because of these problems, we have opted to investigate self-reporting methods, as validated and used widely in psychological experiments. Three well-established methods that are used frequently in the field of psychology are the Russel Affect Grid (Russell et al., 1989), the Self Assessment Manikin (SAM) (Lang, 1980) and the Positive and Negative Affect Scale (PANAS) (Watson et al., 1988). In our previous study (van der Sluis and Mellish, 2008), we had problems with participants understanding how to use the Russel Affect Grid and SAM and so now we opted to use a version of the PANAS test.

The PANAS test is a scale using affect terms that describe positive and negative feelings and emotions. Participants in the experiment read the terms and indicate to what extent they experience(d) the emotions indicated by each of them using a five point scale ranging from (1) very slightly/not at all, (2) a little, (3) moderately, (4) quite a bit to (5) extremely. A total score for positive affect is calculated by simply adding the scores for the positive terms, and similarly for negative affect.

As before, we used a simplified version of the PANAS scale in order not to overburden the participants with questions and to avoid bored answering. In this test, which has been fully validated (Mackinnon et al., 1999), participants have to rate only 10 instead of 20 terms: 5 for positive affect (i.e. alert, determined, enthusiastic, excited, inspired) and 5 for negative affect (i.e. afraid, scared, nervous, upset, distressed).

Our use of the simplified PANAS in this study differed from our previous study, however, by having participants respond to the PANAS questions using a slider, rather than a five point scale. This means that only two terms were put at the extreme ends of the slider (i.e. 'very slightly/not at all' and 'extremely' were presented but not 'a little', 'moderately' or 'quite a bit'). The change to use a slider was because van der Sluis and Mellish (2008) observed partipants only using a small part of the possible scale for answers, and within this the five point scale might have lost useful information.

Although our particular experiment focussed on positive affect, we included the negative affect terms partly so that we could detect outliers in our participant set – people who were perhaps extremely nervous about the test or sensitive about their IQ. In fact, we did not find any such outliers.

## 5 Experiment to Measure Emotional Effects of Positive Feedback

### 5.1 Set Up of the Study

As stated above, the texts that we presented to our participants were portrayed as giving feedback on an IQ test that the participants had just taken. The IQ test was set up as a web experiment in which participants could linearly traverse through the various phases of the test. An outline of the set up is given in Figure 2. In the general introduction to the experiment, participants were told that the experiment was 'an assessment of a new kind of intelligence test which combines a number of well-established methods that are used as indicators of human brain power'. To make it more difficult for the participant to keep track of how well/poorly she performed over the course of the test, it also said that the test consisted of open and multiple choice questions that had different weight factors in the calculation of the overall score and that would assess various aspects of their intelligence. Subsequently, the participant was asked to tick a consent form to participate in the study. Then a questionnaire followed in which the participant was asked about her age, gender and the quality of her English. She was also asked if she had any experience with IQ tests and how she expected to score on this one. These questions were interleaved with an emotion assessment test (reduced PANAS) in which the participant was asked 'how do you feel right now?'.

After filling out the questionnaire, the participant could start the "IQ test" whenever she was ready. The "IQ test" consisted of 30 questions which she had to answer one at a time. The participant could not skip a question and also had to indicate for each of the questions how confident she was about her answer. The questions that were used for the test were carefully collected from the internet and included items from various tests and games. Different types of questions were used: questions about logical truths, mathematical questions that required some calculations, questions about words and letter sequences, questions including pictures and questions about the participant's personality. They were ordered randomly (but with the same order for each participant).

When the participant had finished the test, she was asked to wait patiently while the system calculated the test scores. When enough calculation time had passed the participant was presented with the test feedback (one of the two texts, regardless of their actual performance). This feedback first explained the test and its type of scoring:

> The Baumgartner test which you have just undertaken tests various kinds of intelligence, for instance, your visual intelligence, your logical-mathematical intelligence and your spatial intelligence. These various aspects of your intelligence contribute to an overall Baumgartner Score. The Baumgartner Score rates your intelligence on a 10-point scale with 10 as the highest possible score. Note that your Baumgartner Score can change over time dependent on experience and practice. Below your test score is presented in comparison with the average score in your age group.

The introduction to the test was followed by either the positively (+1..+7, Figure 1) or the relatively neutrally (01..07, Figure 1) phrased test results. After the participant had processed the feedback, she was asked to fill out one more questionnaire to assess her emotions (i.e. 'How do you feel right now knowing your scores on the test'). This time the simplified PANAS test was interleaved with questions about the participant's results, (e.g. were they as expected and how did she value them), the test (e.g. was it difficult, doable or easy?) and space for comments on the test and the experiment. Finally the participant was debriefed about the experiment and about the goal of the study.

1. General introduction to the experiment;
2. Consent form;
3. Questionnaire on participant's background and familiarity with IQ-test interleaved with a PANAS test to assess the participant's current emotional state;
4. Message: 'Please press the next button at the bottom of this page whenever you are ready to start the intelligence test';
5. IQ test questions;
6. Message: Please be patient while your answers are being processed and your test score is computed. After the result page, you will be asked another set of questions about the test, your performance and the way you feel about it. This information is very important for this study, so please answer the questions as honestly as possible.';
7. Feedback + or 0;
8. Questionnaire: PANAS test to assess how the participants felt after reading the test feedback interleaved with questions about the test, their expectations and space for comments;
9. Debriefing which informed participants about the study's purpose and stated that the IQ test was not real and that their test results did not contain any truth.

Figure 2: Phases in the experiment set up

### 5.2 Pilot Experiment

A pilot of the experiment was carried out by asking a number of people to try the experiment via the web interface. The main outcomes of this study, in which 11 colleagues participated, was that the experiment was too long. Accordingly, the questionnaires before and after the IQ test (phase 3 and 8 in Figure 2) were shortened. Also the IQ test itself was shortened from 40 to 30 questions.

### 5.3 Main Experiment: participants and experimental setting

30 participants, all female university students, took the IQ test. All participants except two were in age band 18-24. The exceptions were in age band 25-29 (group +) and 30-34 (group 0). The participants were randomly distributed over group + and group 0 and (for ethical reasons) did the test one by one in a one-person experiment room while the experimenter was waiting outside the room. As soon as the participant indicated that she had finished the task (i.e. stepped out of the experiment room), she was debriefed about the study by the experimenter and was paid with a voucher worth 5 pounds.

### 5.4 Hypotheses

Since the message of the feedback texts was relatively positive and there is no necessary correlation between positive and negative PANAS scores (Watson and Clark, 1999), we expected the main effects of the texts to be on the average evaluation of the positive PANAS terms. In order to cater for the fact that individuals might differ in their initial positive PANAS scores, we decided to look at the difference of the scores (score after minus score before). Therefore the hypothesis for this study was that participants who received the positively phrased feedback would show a larger change in their positive emotions than the participants who received the neutrally phrased feedback.

| | *0-group* | *+-group* |
|---|---|---|
| **Negative PANAS terms Before** | 1.60(.76) | 1.58(.68) |
| **Negative PANAS terms After** | 1.57(.68) | 1.31(.45) |
| **Positive PANAS terms Before** | 3.25(.78) | 3.32(.55) |
| **Positive PANAS terms After** | 3.13(.58) | 3.75(.55) |

Table 1: Means and Standard deviations (between brackets) for the negative and positive PANAS terms as indicated before and after the IQ test undertaken by participants that received neutral and participants that received positive feedback on their performance.

### 5.5 Results

Table 1 indicates that on average after they had received their test results, participants in the +-group were more positively tuned than participants in the 0-group. Participants in the +-group also rated the positive emotion terms higher than they had done before they undertook the IQ test. No such results were found for the 0-group. In contrast, compared to their responses before the IQ test, participants in the 0-group rated the positive terms slightly lower after they had processed their neutrally phrased feedback. With respect to the negative PANAS terms, participants in the +-group report slightly less negative emotions after they read their test scores, but none of the differences found in the negative PANAS scores were significant.

A 2 (feedback type) * 2 (before/after) * 2 (positive/negative mean) repeated measures ANOVA was carried out on the average PANAS scores. This showed no main effect of feedback type (+ vs 0) and no main effect of before/after on average PANAS scores. However, there was a highly significant interaction between feedback type and before/after, which indicates that the change in PANAS mean before and after the text was strongly dependent on feedback type[3] ($F(1, 28) = 10.246$, $p < .003$). We interpret this to mean that the (after minus before) value is significantly

[3] An ANOVA test on the positive means only produces a similar result.

| | 0-group | +-group |
|---|---|---|
| **Alert Before** | 3.96(.80) | 3.17(.99) |
| **Alert After** | 3.45(.76) | 3.65(.75) |
| **Determined Before** | 3.49(1.02) | 3.60(.50) |
| **Determined After** | 3.50(1.13) | 3.74(.61) |
| **Enthusiastic Before** | 3.52(1.05 | 3.49(.72) |
| **Enthusiastic After** | 2.97(.81) | 3.84(.66) |
| **Excited Before** | 2.74(.97) | 3.28(.61) |
| **Excited After** | 2.64(.75) | 3.69(.83) |
| **Inspired Before** | 2.56(1.21) | 3.06(.77) |
| **Inspired After** | 3.06(1.05) | 3.81(.78) |

Table 2: Means and Standard deviations (between brackets) for the positive PANAS terms as indicated after the IQ test undertaken by participants that received positive and participants that received neutral feedback on their performance.

| | | 0-group | +-group |
|---|---|---|---|
| *ER* | | | |
| | **not disclosed** | 1 | 0 |
| | **not so good** | 0 | 1 |
| | **ok** | 9 | 4 |
| | **well** | 4 | 10 |
| | **extremely well** | 1 | 0 |

Table 3: Participant responses when questioned about the results they expected (*ER*) .

greater for the +-group. A two-tailed, two sample t-test verifies this (t = 3.2, $p < 0.004$). We did some post-hoc investigation in an attempt to understand the main result more fully. When looking at the positive PANAS scores in more detail (see Table 2), it turns out that only three of the five positive PANAS terms included in the simplified PANAS test render promising results. Interactions were found for the terms 'alert' ($F(1, 28) = 10.291$, $p < .003$) and 'enthusiastic' ($F(1, 28) = 5.651$, $p < .025$). No interactions were found for the terms 'determined' and 'inspired'. For 'inspired' however, we found a main effect of feedback type : ($F(1, 28) = 8.755$, $p < .006$), which indicates that participants in the +-group could have been more inspired because of their test scores than participants in the 0-group. Not all of these results would be significant if Bonferroni corrections were made.

### 5.6 The Role of Expectations

It is possible that this result could have been caused by other (systematic but unanticipated) differences between the two groups. In particular, perhaps the result could be caused by a difference in how well the two groups of participants *expected to* perform. As it happens, participants were asked: 'How do you expect to score on an intelligence test?' before they did the test. The answers to this question are summarised in Table 3. This data suggests that participants in the +-group initially had higher expectations. It is difficult to get a consensus from the psychological literature about how this might have affected the results. On the one hand, some studies have shown that positive expectations can have an accelerating effect on a person's actual positive emotional experience (Wilson et al., 2003; Wilson and Klaaren, 1992). Such results might suggest an alternative explanation of the fact that the +-group showed a greater change in positive emotions. On the other hand, it might be argued that subjects with lower expectations would be more surprised (since both texts presented good results) and so their emotions would have been influenced more significantly. That is, if a subject already expects to do well then one would not expect that finding that they actually did well would cause much of a change in their emotions. This would predict that it should be the 0-group that shows the greatest emotion change. Overall, it is hard to know whether the data about expectations should affect our confidence in the experiment result, though it would be worthwhile controlling for initial expectations in further experiments of this kind.

## 6 Discussion and Future Directions

### 6.1 Discussion

Compared with the previous study of van der Sluis and Mellish (2008), we expected participants to indicate stronger emotional effects, because the text participants were asked to read was about their own capabilities instead of about something in the world around them which they could think would not affect them. Indeed, this seems to have been the case. In van der Sluis and Mellish (2008), all responses used the lower half of the scale, whereas with the slider our participants indicated values up to both extremes of the range available. Unfortunately, the fact that one set of values is discrete and the other continuous means that it is hard to carry out a simple statistical comparison.

### 6.2 Future Work

In the study described in the paper, a number of different techniques (e.g. emphasis, vague adjectives and adverbs) were used to phrase the various propositions in the feedback. In future work we aim to identify the relative importance of the individual techniques.

### 6.3 Conclusion

The fact that we have been able to show a significant difference in the emotions induced by the two texts is very encouraging. It suggests that there *is* a possible methodology for directly evaluating affective NLG and that the tactical concerns with which much of NLG research is occupied are relevant to affective NLG. A similar methodology could perhaps now be used to determine the effectiveness of specific NLG methods and mechanisms in terms of inducing emotions. Although we have now shown that NLG tactical decisions can affect emotions, it remains to be seen what kind of changes in strategy, learning, motivation, etc., can be induced by positive affect and thus how these framing decisions would best be made by an NLG system.

## Acknowledgments

This work was supported by the EPSRC platfrom grant 'Affecting people with natural language' (EP/E011764/1) and also in part by Science Foundation Ireland under a CSET grant (NGL/CSET). We would like to thank the people who contributed to this study, most notably Judith Masthoff, Albert Gatt and Kees van Deemter and Nikiforos Karamanis.

## References

R. Brown and E. Pinel. 2003. Stigma on my mind: Individual differences in the experience of stereotype threat. *Journal of Experimental Social Psychology*, 39:626–633.

J. Cacioppo, G. Bernston, J. Larson, K. Poehlmann, and T. Ito. 2000. The psychophysiology of emotion. In M. Lewis and J. Haviland-Jones, editors, *Handbook of Emotions*, pages 173–191. New York: Guilford Press.

M. Cadinu, A. Maass, A. Rosabianca, and J. Kiesner. 2005. Why do women underperform under stereotype threat? *Psychological Science*, 16(7):572–578.

D. Graff. 2000. Shifting sands: An interest-relative theory of vagueness. *Philosophical Topics*, 20:45–81.

C. Kennedy. 2007. Vagueness and grammar: the semantics of relative and absolute gradable adjectives. *Linguistics and Philosophy*, 30:1–45.

P. Lang. 1980. Behavioral treatment and bio-behavioral assessment: Computer applications. In J. Sidowske, J. Johnson, and T. Williams, editors, *Technology in Mental Health Care Delivery Systems*, pages 119–137. Norwood, NJ: Ablex.

R. Lazarus, A. Kanner, and S. Folkman. 1980. Emotions: A cognitive-phenomenological analysis. In R. Plutchik and H. Kellerman, editors, *Emotion, theory, research, and experience*. New York: Academic Press.

I. Levin, S. Schneider, and G. Gaeth. 1998. All frames are not created equal: A typology and critical analysis of framing effects. *Organizational behaviour and human decision processes*, 76(2):149–188.

A. Mackinnon, A. Jorm, H. Christensen, A. Korten, P. Jacomb, and B. Rodgers. 1999. A short form of the positive and negative affect schedule: evaluation of factorial validity and invariance across demographic variables in a community sample. *Personality and Individual Differences*, 27(3):405–416.

F. Mairesse and M. Walker. 2008. Trainable generation of big-five personality styles through data-driven parameter estimation. In *Proc. of the 46th Annual Meeting of the ACL*.

J. Moore, K. Porayska-Pomsta, S. Varges, and C. Zinn. 2004. Generating tutorial feedback with affect. In *Proceedings of the 7th International Florida Artificial Intelligence Research Symposium Conference (FLAIRS)*.

L. Moxey and A. Sanford. 2000. Communicating quantities: A review of psycholinguistic evidence of how expressions determine perspectives. *Applied Cognitive Psychology*, 14(3):237–255.

L. O'Hara and R. Sternberg. 2001. It doesn't hurt to ask: Effects of instructions to be creative, practical, or analytical on essay-writing performance and their interaction with students' thinking styles. *Creativity Research Journal*, 13(2):197–210.

F. De Rosis and F. Grasso. 2000. Affective natural language generation. In A. Paiva, editor, *Affective Interactions*. Springer LNAI 1814.

F. De Rosis, F. Grasso, and D. Berry. 1999. Refining instructional text generation after evaluation. *Artificial Intelligence in Medicine*, 17(1):1–36.

J. Russell, A. Weiss, and G. Mendelsohn. 1989. Affect grid: A single-item scale of pleasure and arousal. *Journal of Personality and Social Psychology*, 57:493–502.

K. Teigen and W. Brun. 2003. Verbal probabilities: A question of frame. *Journal of Behavioral Decision Making*, 16:53–72.

H. Thompson. 1977. Strategy and tactics: A model for language production. In *Proceedings of the Chicago Linguistics Society*, Chicago.

I. van der Sluis and C. Mellish. 2008. Using tactical NLG to induce affective states: Empirical investigations. In *Proceedings of the fifth international natural language generation conference*, pages 68–76.

D. Watson and L. Clark, 1999. *Manual for the Positive and Negative Affect Schedule - Expanded Form*. The University of Iowa.

D. Watson, L. Clark, and A. Tellegen. 1988. Development and validation of brief measures of positive and negative affect: The PANAS scales. *Journal of Personality and Social Psychology*, 54(1063-1070).

T. Wilson and K. Klaaren. 1992. The role of affective expectations in affective experience. In M. Clark, editor, *Review of Personality and Social Psychology*, volume 14: Emotion and Social Behaviour, pages 1–31. Newbury Park, CA: Sage.

T. Wilson, D Gilbert, and D. Centerbar. 2003. Making sense: The causes of emotional evanescence. In I. Brocas and J. Carrillo, editors, *The Psychology of Economic Decisions*, volume 1: Rationality and Well Being, pages 209–233. New York: Oxford University Press.

# What Game Theory can do for NLG: the case of vague language

**Kees van Deemter**
University of Aberdeen
k.vdeemter@abdn.ac.uk

## Abstract

This informal position paper brings together some recent developments in formal semantics and pragmatics to argue that the discipline of *Game Theory* is well placed to become the theoretical backbone of Natural Language Generation. To demonstrate some of the strengths and weaknesses of the Game-Theoretical approach, we focus on the utility of *vague* expressions. More specifically, we ask what light Game Theory can shed on the question when an NLG system should generate vague language.

## 1 NLG as a choice problem

Natural Language Generation (NLG) is the area of computational linguistics that is concerned with the mapping from non-linguistic to linguistic expressions (e.g. Reiter and Dale 2000). This formulation might be taken to suggest that NLG is best viewed as a kind of *translation* problem, where the challenge is to find a way to convert a formal expression into (for example) an English one. In its early years, this may have been a fruitful way to think about NLG but, these days, a better perspective is of NLG as a *choice* problem. For after the advances of recent years, the problem is no longer such much "How on Earth can this information be expressed in English?", but rather "From all the possible ways to express this information in English, which one is the most effective choice?"

Let us try to say this a bit more precisely. It is usually fair to assume that the formal expressions from which NLG takes its departure are themselves clear and unambiguous. Let us call the inputs to the generator *Meanings*. Now suppose we have a grammar that tells us how each given Meaning can be expressed in a language such as English. The task for NLG now is to choose, for each of these Meanings, which of all the different linguistic Forms that can express it (according to the grammar) is the *best* expression of this particular Meaning. Ultimately, this choice is likely to depend on a number of other parameters, such as the identity of the hearer, and the words that have earlier been used. In the present paper, these "contextual" issues will largely be ignored, allowing us to simplify by thinking in terms of a mapping from Meanings to Forms.

The perspective that views NLG as a choice problem is far from new (see e.g. McDonald 1987, where it takes a central position); in fact, it forms the methodological spine of Systemic-Functional Grammar, with its AND/OR graphs (Bateman 1997). Given this perspective, the question comes up what factors determine the choice between different linguistic Forms. This question is difficult to answer in detail, but at the most abstract level, the answer is likely to have something to do with the "utility"of the different Forms that can be generated, and perhaps such additional factors as the *cost* to the speaker of generating them, and the *cost* to the hearer of processing (e.g., parsing and interpreting) them. To utter a sentence is to perform an action, and the choice between different actions is naturally thought of as governed by utility, understood in the broadest possible sense.

## 2 Game Theory

The analysis of NLG as driven by the *utility* of utterances feels natural to people familiar with practical applications of NLG, where texts are generated for a real-life setting. More generally, this type of analysis suits anyone who is interested in the effects of an utterance on an audience (e.g., Mellish and Van der Sluis 2009). To see how NLG systems could be amenable to a decision-theoretical analysis, in which the expected payoffs associated with different texts are compared, consider an NLG system that informs roadgrit-

*Proceedings of the 12th European Workshop on Natural Language Generation*, pages 154–161,
Athens, Greece, 30 – 31 March 2009. 

ters' decisions about the condition of the roads in Scotland, to help them decide which ones are icy enough to require treatment (e.g. Turner et al. 2008).

Computerised weather forecasts can tell road gritters which roads are likely to be icey, and hence dangerous. There can be thousands of dangerous roads on a given night, and it is often impossible to say in a few words *exactly* which road are dangerous (Turner et al. 2008). One summary produced by the generator might approximate the data by saying 'Roads *in the Highlands* are icey' while another might say 'Roads *above 500 metres* are icey' (assume this covers a larger set of roads). It matters which of these summaries is generated, because each summary will lead to a different set of roads being treated with salt (i.e., gritted). The first summary may have 10 false positives (i.e., roads gritted unnecessarily) and 10 false negatives (i.e., dangerous roads not gritted); the second summary might have 100 false positives and only 2 false negatives. In a situation of this kind, which involves a tradeoff between safety on the one hand, and money and environmental damage (from salt) on the other, decision theory would be a natural framework in which to compare the utility of the two summaries. If a false positive has a negative utility of $-0.1$ and a false negative one of $-0.5$, for example, then the first summary wins the day. (Needless to say, the choice of these constants is crucial, and tricky to justify.)

More specifically, many NLG systems invite a *game-theoretical* analysis – or an Optimality-Theoretic analysis, which can come down to the same thing (Dekker and Van Rooij 2000; Van Deemter 2004 for an application to NLG). Suppose I want to state that all old people are entitled to certain benefits (cf. Khan et al. 2009):

a. Old men and old women are entitled to benefits.

b. Old men and women are entitled to benefits.

Which of these two linguistic Forms should I choose? This depends on the strategy of the hearer. If the hearer interprets (b) as concerning *all* women (rather only the old ones) then my utterance will have misfired to an extent. The success (for speaker and/or hearer!) of the speaker's generation strategy, in other words, depends on the hearer's interpretation strategy.[1]

This interaction means that decision theory is not the best tool for analysing the situation, for whereever different agents' strategies interact, *Decision Theory* gives way to *Game Theory*. Game Theory was conceived in the nineteen fourties (Von Neumann and Morgenstern 1944) and has since come to be used extensively by economists, sociologists, biologists, and others. Far from being limited to games in a limited sense of the word, Game Theory is the mathematical study of rational social interaction and, as such, it is reasonable to expect it to be able to shed light on language use as well. Perhaps more than anything, it promises to have the potential to explain *why* communication works the way it does. For if we could show that people's linguistic behaviour conforms with what it would be rational for them to do, then this would have substantial explanatory value.

Work by David Lewis and other on communication and *coordination games* helped to make Game Theory relevant for situations where the players are not in conflict with each other (Lewis 1969). A classic example is where two generals are both intent on attacking an enemy, but while each general individually is weaker than the enemy, they can beat him if they attack at the same time. Communication ("I am going to attack now!") can help the generals to cooperate and win the battle. Essentially the same things happens when you try to meet a friend: neither of you may care where and when to meet, as long as the two of you end up in the same place at the same time; communication, of course, can help you achieve this goal.

Applications of Game Theory to language now come in many flavours (see e.g. Klabunde 2009, this conference). In this paper I want to engage in a small case study: the expression of *quantitative information* in English. More specifically, I will focus on the fact that quantitative information is often only communicated *vaguely*. When a thermometer, for example, measures your body temperature as 39.82 Celcius, your doctor might express this by saying that your temperature is '39.8 degrees', but he might also round this off even further, saying that it is 'approximately 40 degrees'. Even more vaguely, she might tell you that you have 'a high fever'. Which of these linguistic Forms is preferable, and why?

Questions of this kind have led to a lively dis-

[1]For a game-theoretical perspective on the generation of referring expressions, where success depends on alignment between hearer and speaker strategies, see Kibble 2003.

cussion among linguists, philosophers, and theoretical economists (Lipman 2000, 2006; De Jaegher 2003; Van Rooij 2003), focussing on the question under what circumstances vagueness can lead to a higher utility than crispness. The question is important for understanding human communication, because vagueness plays such a central role in it. Vague adjectives, for example, are prevalent among the words first learned by a typical infant (Peccei 1994) and many of their subtleties are understood by children of only 24 months old (Ebeling and Gelman 1994). In my opinion, the understanding of vagueness is equally important for the NLG community, and particularly for those of us who work on "data to speech" (Theune 2001) or "data to text" (Reiter 2008) systems, where the expression of quantitative data plays such a crucial role. For this reason, I have chosen it as the topic of an informal case study on the relevance of game theory for NLG.

## 3 Vagueness in situations of conflict

First, let us focus on a type of situations where it is relatively easy to understand what the differential benefits of vagueness can be. We start by examining a game-theoretic study of a different phenomenon: ambiguity.

### 3.1 The utility of ambiguity: Aragonès and Neeman

Like others who have discussed these issues, we take *vagueness* to arise if an expression allows borderline cases. The word 'tall', for example, is vague because in a typical context there can be people who are difficult to categorise as either tall or not tall: they are somewhat in between, one is tempted to say. *Ambiguity* is something else. It arises when an expression can be meant in a limited number of different ways. The word 'letter', for example, is ambiguous because it can refer to one individual character or to the sort of meaningful arrangement of characters that people once used to communicate long distance. In 1994, two game theorists asked whether a Game Theoretical explanation might be given for strategic use of ambiguity (i.e., where ambiguity is used on purpose), and they came up with the following answer (Aragonès and Neeman 1994).

Suppose two unscrupulous politicians position themselves for an election. Not burdened with any convictions, they are free to choose between three different idiologies (left, right, center), depending on what gives them the highest utility; additionally, they can choose between two *commitment*[2] levels, $c_{high}$ and $c_{low}$, both representable as real numbers with $c_{high} > c_{low}$. Unfortunately, Aragonès and Neeman do not say what a commitment level is, but one might think of a more and a less extreme version of their chosen ideology.

What combination of an ideology and an commitment level should each politician choose? This depends on the electorate, of course. Suppose there are three blocs of voters: V(left), V(right) and V(center). A leftist voter prefers a leftist politician, and preferably one with a high commitment level. Confronted with a choice between two rightwing politicians, our leftist voter will prefer one with a low commitment. A rightwing voter behaves as the mirror-image of the leftist voter, while the neutral voter is neutral between the two idiologies but, weary of ideology, she prefers low commitment over high commitment. Commitment, in other words, is only relevant for a choice between politicians of the same ideology.

If this is the whole story then politicians will choose an ideology and commitment level based on their estimates of the numbers of voters in each bloc, trying to maximise their expected payoff, formulated solely in terms of the likelihood of winning the election. The task for Game Theory is to work out what *combination* of strategies might give both politicians the highest possible payoff, for example in the sense that a policy change by just one of the two politicans can never improve his expected payoff.

But Aragonès and Neeman's model allows politicians to look beyond the election, towards their anticipated time in government. Surely, a low commitment is easier to fulfil than a high commitment, particularly in view of unforeseen contingencies, so it is nicer to be elected on a low-commitment platform that does not tie one's hands too much. To model this, Aragonès and Neeman formulate utility in a way that multiplies the probability of a politician's winning the elections with a constant that is negatively correlated to his commitment. Let $U_i(I_1, c_1; I_2, c_2)$ be the utility for politician $i$ given that politician 1 chooses ideology $I_1$ with commitment level $c_1$,

[2]Aragonès and Neeman call these *ambiguity* levels, but since the relation with ambiguity is debatable we opt for a more neutral term. Low commitment equals high ambiguity and conversely.

while politician 2 chooses $I_2$ with level $c_2$. Furthermore, $P_i(I_1, c_1; I_2, c_2)$ represents the probability of $i$ winning the elections given this same constellation of choices. Let $k \geq c_{high}$.

Utility formula: $U_i(I_1, c_1; I_2, c_2) = P_i(I_1, c_1; I_2, c_2)(k - c_i)$

Under these assumptions one can show that a low commitment level (i.e., $c_{low}$) can sometimes give a politician a slightly *lower* probability of winning the elections (because his core voters will be less inclined to vote for him), yet a *higher* overall utility (because his time in office will be easier). For details see Aragonès and Neeman (1994).

### 3.2 The utility of vagueness

It is often thought that Aragonès and Neeman's model demonstrates how ambiguity can be used strategically, but that it fails to shed light on *vagueness* (e.g. De Jaegher 2003). I do not see, however, how this view stands up to linguistic scrutiny. To see why, let me construct what strikes me as a possible example.

Suppose the ideology in question – a leftist, or perhaps a populist one – is to take away money from the 10% of richest people and give it to the 10% poorest. Commitment level, in this case, could be a way of making explicit *what percentage* of the top 10% to give away. One position might assert that this has to be, say, 50% of their income, while another position might put this figure at 5%. But if we identified high commitment with the 50% position and low commitment with the 5% position then none of the two commitment levels would be ambiguous. To make one of them ambiguous, we would need something like the following:

The ambiguous politicians' game:
– $I$: take money from the 10% of richest people and divide it equally over the 10% poorest.
– $c_{50}$: do $I$ with 50% of the money of each of the richest people.
– $c_{ambiguous}$: do $I$ with either 5% or 50% of the money of each of the richest people.

But this must be a simplification, for we are dealing with a continuum: there is nothing to exclude percentages in between 25% and 5%, for example. It seems, therefore, perfectly possible to construct a version of Aragonès and Neeman's game – an even more plausible version, I believe – that hinges on vagueness. For example:

The vague politicians' game:
– $I$ and $c_{50}$: (as above).
– $c_{vague}$: do $I$ with a *large* portion of the money of each of the richest people

Clearly, $c_{vague}$ involves vagueness, because 'a large portion' admits borderline cases. In all important respects the vague politicians' game is isomorphic to the ambiguous politicians' game: fierce advocates of redistribution would favour $c_{50}$ over $c_{vague}$, for example, because the latter leaves them uncertain over the amount of redistribution. It is also plausible that politicians would prefer to avoid a commitment as clear as $c_{50}$, because future contingencies might make it difficult for them to honour this promise. In fact, one could extend the game with a second election, in which the electorate could give their verdict on a politician's time in office, and to adapt the utility formula with a third term which represents the probability of winning that second election. Surely, the breaking of promises doesn't do much for a politician's changes of being re-elected, and a precise promise is easier to break than a vague one.

With help from Aragonès and Neeman, we have found a situation in which vagueness has a higher utility than precision.[3] It should be noted, however, that this model (and that of De Jaegher 2003 likewise) hinges on the fact that the interests of the speaker and the hearer differ: what's good for the politician may be bad for his voters. NLG systems can be faced with similar asymmetries, for example when an artificial doctor decides to keep its predictions vague to avoid being contradicted by the facts; a doctor who says "These symptoms will disappear fairly soon" is less likely to get complaints than one who says "These symptoms will have disappeared by midnight next Sunday". Something similar holds for a roadgritting system (like the one in Turner et al. 2008), which might easily face lawsuits if it gets things too evidently wrong. Advertisements also come to mind, be-

[3] Another game with this property was described in De Jaegher (2003), involving a more complex version of the game of the *two generals* (section 2). De Jaegher's game lets one general tell the other about the *preparedness* of the enemy. The utility of vagueness hinges on a subtle asymmetry between the generals, only one of whom will suffer if the enemy turns out to be *prepared*. Intriguing though it is, I find it difficult to see how De Jaegher's game is relevant to everyday communication or NLG.

cause the interests of the advertiser may not coincide with those of the customer. – Examples where vagueness can save money or face are plentiful, yet one wonders whether vagueness can also be advantageous in situations where it is one's honest aim to inform an audience as well as one can.

## 4 Vagueness when there is no conflict

So, let us investigate the advantages of vagueness in situations that are typical for today's NLG systems, where the system tries, unselfishly, to assist a user to the best of its ability.

### 4.1 Lipman's questions

The question why vagueness is used strategically in situations where the interests of speakers and hearers are essentially aligned was asked perhaps most forcefully by the economist Barton Lipman. First he did this in a brief response to an essay by the famous game theorist Ariel Rubinstein (Lipman 2000), and later in a growing but still unfinished discussion paper (Lipman 2006). Lipman uses what we shall call an *airport scenario*, where player 1 asks player 2 to go to the airport to pick up an acquaintance of player 1. In its simplest form, the scenario lets player 1 know the referent's height with full precision (assuming that such a thing is possible), while player 2 carries a perfect measuring device. There are two other people at the airport, and it is assumed that heights are distributed uniformly between a maximum denoted by 1 and a minimum denoted by 0. The payoff for both players – please note the symmetry! – is 1 if player 2 successfully picks the referent, while it is 0 if she fails (i.e., the first person she addresses turns out to be someone else).

Lipman observes that, under these assumptions, vagueness would be bad: why would player 2 say 'He is tall', for example, if he can say 'He is 183.721cm'? By stating his acquaintance's exact height, player 1 will allow player 2 to identify this person with almost complete certainty, given that the chance of two people having the exact same height is almost nil. Lipman also wonders what would happen if only one predicate was available to player 1. He proves that, under these assumptions, optimal communication arises if a word is used in accordance with the following rule:

> Say 'the tall person' if height(person) $>$ $1/2$, else say 'the short person'.

Lipman observes that this concept of 'tall' does not involve vagueness, because the rule does not allow any borderline cases: everyone is either tall or short. In other words, no *rationale* for vagueness has yet been found.

Note that Lipman is not questioning that vague utterances can be useful, which they evidently can be (see e.g. Parikh 1994 for a convincing demonstration using a game-theoretic approach). He is asking whether vague expressions can be *more* useful than any non-vague expression.

### 4.2 Answering Lipman

*First*, let us consider a possible modification of Lipman's scenario. In this *modified airport scenario* the speaker knows the heights of all three people at the airport. Suddenly it becomes easier to understand why vagueness can be useful. For suppose your acquaintance happens to be the tallest person of the three. You can then identify him as *'the tall guy'*. Arguably, this is safer than citing the person's height in centimeters, because 'the tall guy' (meaning, in this case, the same as *tallest* guy) does not require the players to make any measurements: *comparisons* between heights can often be made in an instant, and with more confidence than absolute measurements. I dealt with cases of this type in my paper on vague descriptions (van Deemter 2006), where a generator takes numerical height measurements to produce noun phrases that involve gradable adjectives: 'the tall guy', 'the fastest one of the three heavy tortoises'. In cases like this, one can argue that vagueness is only *local*, in the same way that ambiguity can be merely local, for example when the sentence as a whole allows one to disambiguate an ambiguous word in it (e.g. when a pronoun gets resolved or a lexical item disambiguated). In the modified airport scenario, the noun phrase as a whole (e.g., 'the tall guy') allows no borderline cases, so there is no *global* vagueness here.

Local vagueness is wide-spread and can make use of different "precisification" mechanisms. When I say of a gymnastic exercise, for example, that it is 'good for young and old', for example, then there is nothing vague about my description of the people involved: I am using vague words to say that this exercise is good for *everyone*, regardless of age. Although local vagueness constitutes some kind of answer to Lipman, most linguists assume that *globally* vague utterances exist as well (even when the interests of the speaker and the hearer are aligned). Let us assume they are right and continue to look for a *rationale*.

*Secondly*, it has been suggested that strategic vagueness can arise from a desire to reduce the "cost" of the utterances involved (e.g. Van Rooij 2003, Jäger 2008). One might amplify this idea by arguing that vague words are part of a highly efficient mechanism that makes their meaning dependent on the context in which they are used. The size constraints on 'a small elephant', for example, are very different from those on 'a small mouse'; this suggests that vague words may not only be efficient to use but also efficient to learn (Van Deemter, in preparation). All this seems true enough but, as an answer to the question "Why vagueness?" it does not stand up to Lipman-style scrutiny. Let me explain why not.

Consider the earlier-mentioned doctor, who measures your body temperature as 39.82 Celcius. By stating that you have 'a high fever' (instead of 'thirty eight point eighty two degrees') the doctor is pruning away details that are of questionable relevance in the situation at hand. But this does not force him to use language that is *vague*: language that allows borderline cases, in other words. He could have achieved a similar economy by rounding, saying that your temperature is '(about) forty degrees'; in this way, he would have reduced information without being vague. The benefits of information reduction can be modelled in a game where communication informs action: if '38.82 Celcius' and '39 Celcius' are associated with the same medical action (e.g., to take an aspirin) then the fact that '39 Celcius' is "cheaper" to produce and to process will tend to give this expression a better utility than '38.82 Celcius'. But information reduction does not imply vagueness, so we are back at square one: Why vagueness?

It might be thought that things change when uncertainty is taken into account: a measurement of 39.82 Celcius is not as exact as it sounds, for example, because errors are likely. The result of the measurement is perhaps best conveyed by a normal distribution of which 39.82 is the mean value, and such a complex curve is difficult to put in just a few words. Still, the argument of the previous paragraph continues to apply, because the curve can be summarised without vagueness: the figure of 38.82 Celcius is one such summary.

A *third* suggestion (e.g. Veltman 2002) is that vague expressions such as 'high fever' do more than just *reduce* the information obtained from a measurement. The expression 'high fever' also *adds* bias or evaluation to the raw data, namely the information that the temperature in question is worrisome. You do not need domain knowledge to understand the medical implications: hearing that something medical is 'high' tells you that you should be worried.

Once again, this sounds like an excellent reason for using vagueness, particularly in situations where an understanding of the metric in question cannot be taken for granted (such as oxygen saturation, the metrics for which mean little to most of us). Still, it is not evident that this justifies the use of vagueness. If bias needs to be expressed, then why not simply add it? Why not state the exact temperature (or an approximation of it) *and* say that this reading should be considered worrisome? One might respond that this would have been time and space consuming, but if that is a problem then why have no conventions arisen for expressing quantities in two ways, a worrisome and a non-worrisome one? Why should bias necessarily be coupled with vagueness only, given that it is as easy to think of a crisp expression that contains bias as it is to think of a vague expression that does not (e.g., in the case of an adjective like 'tall')? A good example of *crispness* + *bias* is the word 'obese', in the sense of having a Body Mass Index of over 30. For the reason why obesity was defined in this way is precisely that this degree of overweight is considered medically worrisome.

## 5 Discussion: vagueness and game theory

### 5.1 Vagueness is harder to justify than you think

Let us first summarise our findings about vagueness, some of which will be discussed more fully in Van Deemter (in preparation).

It is often easy to see why vague *words* come in handy; the modified airport scenario demonstrates how vague words can create an information loss that is only local: by making a vague word part of a referring expression, a crisp borderline is enforced on a vague concept, resulting in a beautifully efficient description (e.g., 'the tall guy') that is arguably clearer than any expression that relies on absolute values. This means that the utterance *as a whole* is not vague at all: it is only locally vague. Whether we speak of vagueness in such situations seems a matter of taste.

It is also clear why vagueness can have differential benefits in communication between agents whose interests differ more than just minimally (cf., Horton and Keysar 1996 for experimental evidence of speaker's laziness in situations where their interests are approximately aligned), such as a politician and his potential voters, or like a professional who does not wish to be sued by his clients. In situations of this kind it can be beneficial for a speaker or an NLG system to obfuscate, exploiting the borderline cases inherent in vague expressions.

Beyond this, it is suprisingly difficult to see how vagueness can be advantageous for NLG. This is partly because there appear to exist some linguistic issues that NLG researchers are able to disregard. It seems plausible, for example, that vagueness is unavoidable in situations where no commonly understood metrics are available, for instance when we judge how beautiful a sunset is, how wise a person, or how dismal the weather. As long as NLG systems use tangible input data (about millimetres rainfall, for example, or body temperature), these reasons for vagueness seem irrelevant. Similarly, there is much that is unknown about the working of perception even in simple domains. What is it that allows me to talk about the height of someone I see, for example? The input to my personal "generator" (as opposed to the input to a typical NLG system) might not be equivalent to a tidy number. (Could it be some inherently vague percept, perhaps?) These difficult questions (see also Lipman 2006) must remain unanswered here.

### 5.2 The utility of utility

Confronted with the claim that Game Theory should be the theoretical backbone to NLG, some people might respond that no new backbone is needed, because the theory of formal languages, conjoined with a properly expressive variant of Symbolic Logic, provides sufficient backbone already. I believe this objection to be misguided. Admittedly, the disciplines in question are well suited for saying which Forms can express which Meanings. But it is far less clear that these disciplines have anything to say about the key problem of NLG: how to choose the most effective way to express a given Meaning in (for example) English. This is a vacancy that Game Theory would be well placed to fulfill, in my opinion. The present paper has illustrated this claim by discussing the question when and why a generator should choose a vague expression. The fact that this discussion has yet to produce a clear conclusion is, in my opinion, not due to any shortcomings of Game Theory, but to the intrinsic difficulty of the problem.

There is, of course, a *caveat*. The use of game theory in empirical sciences has, with proper modestly, been described as "modelling by example" (e.g. Rasmussen 2001): a mathematical game shows us an example of how things *might* be, not necessarily how things are. The situation is familiar to linguists, of course, and from applications of mathematics more generally. By inspecting a formal grammar, for example, one does not learn much about language, unless there exists evidence that the lingistic Forms and Meanings pair up as specified by the grammar. In similar fashion, one learns little from a Game Theoretical model unless one has reason to accept the assumptions that were built into it: the choices that it assumes available to the players, and the payoffs related to each outcome of the game, for example. This means that Game Theory can come to the aid of linguistic pragmatics and NLG, but that only empirical research can tell us what games people *actually* play when they communicate.


### Acknowledgments

Thanks are due to my colleagues Ehud Reiter, Albert Gatt and Hans van Ditmarsch, for useful discussions on the theme of this paper. Funding from the EPSRC under the Platform Grant "Affecting People with Natural Language" (EP/E011764/1) is gratefully acknowledged.


## References


Aragonès and Neeman 2000. Enriqueta Aragonès and Zvika Neeman. Strategic ambiguity in electoral competition. *Journal of Theoretical Politics* **12**, pp.183-204.

Bateman 1997. John Bateman. Sentence generation and systemic grammar: an introduction. Iwanami Lecture Series: Language Sciences. Iwanami Shoten Publishers, Tokyo.

de Jaegher 2003. Kris de Jaegher. A game-theoretical rationale for vagueness. *Linguistics and Philosophy* **26**: pp.637-659.

Dekker and Van Rooij 2000. Bi-directional Optimality Theory: an application of Game Theory.

*Journal of Semantics* **17**: 217-242.

Ebeling and Gelman 1994. K.S.Ebeling and S.A.Gelman. Children's use of context in interpreting "big" and "little". *Child Development* **65** (4): 1178-1192.

Horton and Keysar 1996. William S. Horton and Boaz Keysar. When do speakers take into account common ground? *Cognition* **59**, pp.91-117.

Jäger 2008. Gerhard Jäger. Applications of Game Theory in Linguistics. *Language and Linguistics Compass* **2/3**.

Khan et al 2009. Imtiaz Khan, Kees van Deemter, Graeme Ritchie, Albert Gatt, and Alexandra A.Cleland. A hearer oriented evaluation of referring expression generation. Proc. of 12th European Workshop on Natural Language Generation (ENLG-2009).

Kibble 2003. Rodger Kibble. Both sides now: predictive reference resolution in generation and resolution. Proc. of Fifth International Workshop on Computational Semantics (IWCS-2003). Tilburg, The Netherlands.

Klabunde 2009. Ralph Klabunde. Towards a game-theoretic approach to content determination. Proc. of 12th European Workshop on Natural Language Generation (ENLG-2009).

Lewis 1969. David Lewis. *Convention – A Philosophical Study*. Harvard University Press.

Lipman 2000. Barton L.Lipman. Economics and Language. "Comments" section, Rubinstein (2000).

Lipman 2006. Barton L.Lipman. Why is language vague? Working paper, December 2006, Department of Economics, Boston University.

McDonald 1987. Natural Language Generation. In S.Shapiro *Encyclopaedia of Artificial Intelligence*, Volume 1. John Wiley, New York.

Mellish and Van der Sluis 2009. Chris Mellish and Ielka van der Sluis. Towards empirical evaluation of affective tactical NLG. Proc. of 12th European Workshop on Natural Language Generation (ENLG-2009)

Von Neumann and Morgenstern 1944. John von Neumann and Oskar Morgenstern. *Theory of games and economic behavior.* Wiley & Sons, Princeton, New Jersey.

Parikh 1994. Rohit Parikh. Vagueness and utility: the semantics of common nouns. *Linguistics and Philosophy* **17**: 521-535.

Peccei 1994. Jean Stilwell Peccei. *Child Language*. Routledge.

Rasmussen 2001. Eric Rasmussen. *Games & Information: an introduction to game theory.* Third Edition. Blackwell Publishing.

Reiter and Dale 2000. Ehud Reiter and Robert Dale. *Building natural language generation systems*. Cambridge University Press. Cambridge.

Reiter 2007. Ehud Reiter. An architecture for data-to-text systems. In Procs. of 11th European Workshop on Natural Language Generation (ENLG-2007): pp.97-104.

Rubinstein 1998. Ariel Rubinstein. *Modeling Bounded Rationality*. MIT Press, Cambridge Mass.

Rubinstein 2000. Ariel Rubinstein. *Economics and Language: Five Essays.* Cambridge University Press. Cambridge.

Theune et al. 2001. M.Theune, E.Klabbers, J.R. de Pijper and E.Krahmer. From data to speech a general approach. *Natural Languag Engineering* **7** (1): 47-86.

Turner et al. 2008. R.Turner, S.Sripada, E.Reiter and I.P.Davy. Using spatial reference frames to generate grounded textual summaries of georeferenced data. In Proceedings of INLG-2008. Salt Fork, Ohio, USA.

Van Deemter 2004. Kees van Deemter. Towards a probabilistic version of bidirectional OT syntax and semantics. *Journal of Semantics* **21** (3).

Van Deemter 2006. Kees van Deemter. Generating referring expressions that involve gradable properties. *Computational Linguistics* **32** (2).

Van Deemter (in preparation). Kees van Deemter. *Not Exactly: in Praise of Vagueness.* To appear with Oxford University Press.

Van Rooij 2003. Robert van Rooij. Being polite is a handicap: towards a game theoretical analysis of polite linguistic behavior. In Procs. of Theoretical Aspects of Rationality and Knowledge (TARK-9), Bloomington, Indiana.

Veltman 2002. Frank Veltman. Het verschil tussen 'vaag' en 'niet precies'. (The difference between 'vague' and 'not precise'.) Inaugural lecture. Vossiuspers, University of Amsterdam.

# Generation Challenges 2009

*Proceedings of the 12th European Workshop on Natural Language Generation*, pages 162–164,
Athens, Greece, 30 – 31 March 2009. ©2009 Association for Computational Linguistics

# Preface

Generation Challenges 2009 was the third round of shared-task evaluation competitions (STECs) that involve the generation of natural language, and followed the Pilot Attribute Selection for Generating Referring Expressions Challenge in 2007 (ASGRE'07) and Referring Expression Generation Challenges in 2008 (REG'08). More information about all these NLG STEC activities can be found via the links on the Generation Challenges homepage: http://www.nltg.brighton.ac.uk/research/genchal09

Generation Challenges 2009 brought together four STECs: the TUNA Referring Expression Generation Task (TUNA-REG) organised by Albert Gatt, Anja Belz and Eric Kow; the two GREC Challenges, GREC Main Subject Reference Generation (GREC-MSR) and GREC Named Entity Generation (GREC-NEG), organised by Anja Belz, Eric Kow, Jette Viethen and Albert Gatt; and the Giving Instructions in Virtual Environments Challenge (GIVE) organised by Donna Byron, Justine Cassell, Robert Dale, Alexander Koller, Johanna Moore, Jon Oberlander, and Kristina Striegnitz.

In the GIVE Challenge, participating teams developed systems which generate natural-language instructions to users navigating a virtual 3D environment and performing computer-game-like tasks. The four participating systems were evaluated by measuring how quickly, accurately and efficiently users were able to perform tasks with a given system's instructions. The evaluation report for the GIVE Challenge can be found in this volume; the participants' reports will be made publicly available at a later stage.

The TUNA-REG Task was the end-to-end referring expression generation task (combining the attribute selection and realisation subtasks) which was first introduced in REG'08, and which used the TUNA corpus of paired descriptions and pictures of entities. This year's TUNA-REG Task had an open call for participation, but it was also organised in the spirit of a progress check which would give participants from TUNA-REG'08 an opportunity to submit improved systems, the results for which could be compared to last year's results. Of five registered teams from five countries, four teams submitted a total of 6 systems to TUNA-REG. These, along with two sets of human outputs, were evaluated by automatic intrinsic and human-based intrinsic and extrinsic evaluations. The results report and the participants' reports can be found in this volume.

The GREC-MSR Task was the same as in REG'08 and used a corpus of introductory sections from Wikipedia articles on geographic entities and people. The task was to generate referring expressions for mentions of the main subject of the article in the context of the full text of the article. The new GREC-NEG Task used a separate corpus of introductory sections from Wikipedia articles on people, and the task was to generate referring expressions for all mentions of all people in an article.

Eight teams from seven countries registered for each of the GREC-MSR and GREC-NEG tasks. As the system submission deadline approached, it became clear that just two teams were certain that they were going to complete their systems in time. For this reason, and also because of a moving camera-ready deadline, we decided, after careful consideration and consultation with participants, to extend the system development period for the GREC Tasks and to hold the GREC'09 results meeting at the ACL-IJCNLP'09 Workshop on Language Generation and Summarisation in Singapore on 6 August 2009, and to publish all GREC'09 reports in the proceedings of that workshop.

In addition to the four shared tasks, Generation Challenges 2009 offered (i) an open submission track in which participants could submit any work involving the data from any of the shared tasks, while opting out of the competetive element, (ii) an evaluation track, in which proposals for new evaluation methods for the shared task could be submitted, and (iii) a task proposal track in which proposals for new shared tasks could be submitted. We believe that these types of open-access tracks are important because they allow the wider research community to shape the focus and methodologies of STECs directly. We received one submission in the open submission track, involving the TUNA data, and none in the other tracks.

We successfully applied (with the help of support letters from many of last year's participants and other HLT colleagues) for funding from the Engineering and Physical Sciences Research Council (EPSRC), the main funding body for HLT in the UK. This support helped with all aspects of organising Generation Challenges 2009, and enabled us to create the new GREC-People corpus and to carry out extensive human evaluations, as well as to employ a dedicated research fellow (Eric Kow) to help with all aspects of Generation Challenges 2009.

Preparations are already underway for a fourth NLG shared-task evaluation event next year, Generation Challenges 2010, which is likely to include a further run of the GREC-NEG Task with an extended training/development corpus, a new task which links GREC-NEG to a named-entity recognition preprocessing stage, and a second run of the GIVE Challenge. We are hoping that results will be presented at INLG'10.

Like our previous STECs, Generation Challenges 2009 would not have been possible without the contributions of many different people. We would like to thank the faculty and staff of Brighton University, and the students of UCL, Brighton and Sussex Universities who participated in the evaluation experiments as well as all other participants in our online data elicitation and evaluation exercises; the ENLG'09 organisers, Mariet Theune and Emiel Krahmer; the research support team at Brighton University and the EPSRC for help with obtaining funding; and last but not least, the participants in the shared tasks for making the most of the short available time to build some very successful systems.

*February 2009* *Anja Belz and Albert Gatt*

# Report on the First NLG Challenge on Generating Instructions in Virtual Environments (GIVE)

**Donna Byron**
Northeastern University
dbyron@ccs.neu.edu

**Alexander Koller**
Saarland University
koller@mmci.uni-saarland.de

**Kristina Striegnitz**
Union College
striegnk@union.edu

**Justine Cassell**
Northwestern University
justine@northwestern.edu

**Robert Dale**
Macquarie University
Robert.Dale@mq.edu.au

**Johanna Moore**
University of Edinburgh
J.Moore@ed.ac.uk

**Jon Oberlander**
University of Edinburgh
J.Oberlander@ed.ac.uk

### Abstract

We describe the first installment of the Challenge on Generating Instructions in Virtual Environments (GIVE), a new shared task for the NLG community. We motivate the design of the challenge, describe how we carried it out, and discuss the results of the system evaluation.

## 1 Introduction

This paper reports on the methodology and results of the First Challenge on Generating Instructions in Virtual Environments (GIVE-1), which we ran from March 2008 to February 2009. GIVE is a new shared task for the NLG community. It provides an end-to-end evaluation methodology for NLG systems that generate instructions which are meant to help a user solve a treasure-hunt task in a virtual 3D world. The most innovative aspect from an NLG evaluation perspective is that the NLG system and the user are connected over the Internet. This makes it possible to cheaply collect large amounts of evaluation data.

Five NLG systems were evaluated in GIVE-1 over a period of three months from November 2008 to February 2009. During this time, we collected 1143 games that were played by users from 48 countries. As far as we know, this makes GIVE-1 the largest evaluation effort in terms of experimental subjects ever. We have evaluated the five systems both on objective measures (success rate, completion time, etc.) and subjective measures which were collected by asking the users to fill in a questionnaire.

GIVE-1 was intended as a pilot experiment in order to establish the validity of the evaluation methodology and understand the challenges involved in the instruction-giving task. We believe that we have achieved these purposes. At the same time, we provide evaluation results for the five NLG systems which will help their developers improve them for participation in a future challenge, GIVE-2. GIVE-2 will retain the successful aspects of GIVE-1, while refining the task to emphasize aspects that we found to be challenging. We invite the ENLG community to participate in designing GIVE-2.

**Plan of the paper.** The paper is structured as follows. In Section 2, we will describe and motivate the GIVE Challenge. In Section 3, we will then describe the evaluation method and infrastructure for the challenge. Section 4 reports on the evaluation results. Finally, we conclude and discuss future work in Section 5.

## 2 The GIVE Challenge

In the GIVE scenario, subjects try to solve a treasure hunt in a virtual 3D world that they have not seen before. The computer has a complete symbolic representation of the virtual world. The challenge for the NLG system is to generate, in real time, natural-language instructions that will guide the users to the successful completion of their task.

Users participating in the GIVE evaluation start the 3D game from our website at `www.give-challenge.org`. They then see a 3D game window as in Fig. 1, which displays instructions and allows them to move around in the world and manipulate objects. The first room is a tutorial room where users learn how to interact with the system; they then enter one of three evaluation worlds, where instructions for solving the treasure hunt are generated by an NLG system. Users can either finish a game successfully, lose it by triggering an alarm, or cancel the game. This result is stored in a database for later analysis, along with a complete log of the game.

Complete maps of the game worlds used in the evaluation are shown in Figs. 3–5: In these worlds, players must pick up a trophy, which is in a wall safe behind a picture. In order to access the tro-

*Proceedings of the 12th European Workshop on Natural Language Generation*, pages 165–173,
Athens, Greece, 30 – 31 March 2009. 

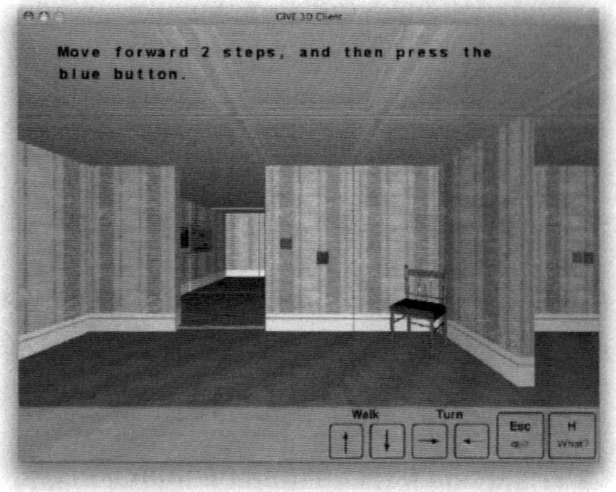


Figure 1: What the user sees when playing with the GIVE Challenge.

phy, they must first push a button to move the picture to the side, and then push another sequence of buttons to open the safe. One floor tile is alarmed, and players lose the game if they step on this tile without deactivating the alarm first. There are also a number of distractor buttons which either do nothing when pressed or set off an alarm. These distractor buttons are intended to make the game harder and, more importantly, to require appropriate reference to objects in the game world. Finally, game worlds contained a number of objects such as chairs and flowers that did not bear on the task, but were available for use as landmarks in spatial descriptions generated by the NLG systems.

### 2.1 Why a new NLG evaluation paradigm?

The GIVE Challenge addresses a need for a new evaluation paradigm for natural language generation (NLG). NLG systems are notoriously hard to evaluate. On the one hand, simply comparing system outputs to a gold standard using automatic comparison algorithms has limited value because there can be multiple generated outputs that are equally good. Finding metrics that account for this variability and produce results consistent with human judgments and task performance measures is difficult (Belz and Gatt, 2008; Stent et al., 2005; Foster, 2008). Human assessments of system outputs are preferred, but lab-based evaluations that allow human subjects to assess each aspect of the system's functionality are expensive and time-consuming, thereby favoring larger labs with adequate resources to conduct human subjects studies. Human assessment studies are also difficult to replicate across sites, so system developers that are geographically separated find it difficult to compare different approaches to the same problem, which in turn leads to an overall difficulty in measuring progress in the field.

The GIVE-1 evaluation was conducted via a client/server architecture which allows any user with an Internet connection to provide system evaluation data. Internet-based studies have been shown to provide generous amounts of data in other areas of AI (von Ahn and Dabbish, 2004; Orkin and Roy, 2007). Our implementation allows smaller teams to develop a system that will participate in the challenge, without taking on the burden of running the human evaluation experiment, and it provides a direct comparison of all participating systems on the same evaluation data.

### 2.2 Why study instruction-giving?

Next to the Internet-based data collection method, GIVE also differs from other NLG challenges by its emphasis on generating instructions in a virtual environment and in real time. This focus on instruction giving is motivated by a growing interest in dialogue-based agents for situated tasks such as navigation and 3D animations. Due to its appeal to younger students, the task can also be used as a pedagogical exercise to stimulate interest among secondary-school students in the research challenges found in NLG or Computational Linguistics more broadly.

Embedding the NLG task in a virtual world encourages the participating research teams to consider communication in a *situated* setting. This makes the NLG task quite different than in other NLG challenges. For example, experiments have shown that human instruction givers make the instruction follower move to a different location in order to use a simpler referring expression (RE) (Stoia et al., 2006). That is, RE generation becomes a very different problem than the classical non-situated Dale & Reiter style RE generation, which focuses on generating REs that are single noun phrases in the context of an unchanging world.

On the other hand, because the virtual environments scenario is so open-ended, it – and specifically the instruction-giving task – can potentially be of interest to a wide range of NLG researchers. This is most obvious for research in sentence planning (GRE, aggregation, lexical choice) and realization (the real-time nature of the task imposes high demands on the system's efficiency). But if extended to two-way dialog, the task can also involve issues of prosody generation (i.e., research on text/concept-to-speech generation), discourse generation, and human-robot interaction. Finally, the game world can be scaled to focus on specific issues in NLG, such as the generation of REs or the generation of navigation instructions.

## 3 Evaluation Method and Logistics

Now we describe the method we applied to obtain experimental data, and sketch the software infrastructure we developed for this purpose.

### 3.1 Software architecture

A crucial aspect of the GIVE evaluation methodology is that it physically separates the user and the NLG system and connects them over the Internet. To achieve this, the GIVE software infrastructure consists of three components (shown in Fig. 2):

1. the *client*, which displays the 3D world to users and allows them to interact with it;
2. the *NLG servers*, which generate the natural-language instructions; and
3. the *Matchmaker*, which establishes connections between clients and NLG servers.

These three components run on different machines. The client is downloaded by users from our website and run on their local machine; each NLG server is run on a server at the institution that implemented it; and the Matchmaker runs on a central server we provide. When a user starts the client, it connects to the Matchmaker and is randomly assigned an NLG server and a game world. The client and NLG server then communicate over the course of one game. At the end of the game, the client displays a questionnaire to the user, and the game log and questionnaire data are uploaded to the Matchmaker and stored in a database. Note that this division allows the challenge to be conducted without making any assumptions about the internal structure of an NLG system.

The GIVE software is implemented in Java and available as an open-source Google Code project. For more details about the software, see (Koller et al., 2009).

### 3.2 Subjects

Participants were recruited using email distribution lists and press releases posted on the internet.

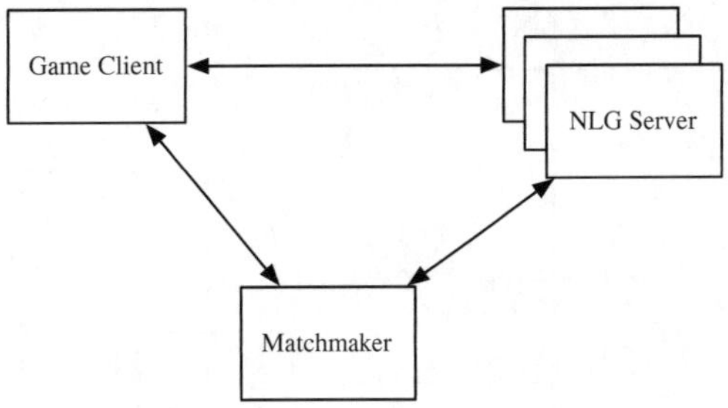


Figure 2: The GIVE architecture.

Collecting data from anonymous users over the Internet presents a variety of issues that a lab-based experiment does not. An Internet-based evaluation skews the demographic of the subject pool toward people who use the Internet, but probably no more so than if recruiting on a college campus. More worrisome is that, without a face-to-face meeting, the researcher has less confidence in the veracity of self-reported demographic data collected from the subject. For the purposes of NLG software, the most important demographic question is the subject's fluency in English. Players of the GIVE 2009 challenge were asked to self-report their command of English, age, and computer experience. English proficiency did interact with task completion, which leads us to conclude that users were honest about their level of English proficiency. See section 4.4 below for a discussion of this interaction. All-in-all, we feel that the advantage gained from the large increase in the size of the subject pool offsets any disadvantage accrued from the lack of accurate demographic information.

### 3.3 Materials

Figs. 3–5 show the layout of the three evaluation worlds. The worlds were intended to provide varying levels of difficulty for the direction-giving systems and to focus on different aspects of the problem. World 1 is very similar to the development world that the research teams were given to test their system on. World 2 was intended to focus on object descriptions - the world has only one room which is full of objects and buttons, many of which cannot be distinguished by simple descriptions. World 3, on the other hand, puts more emphasis on navigation directions as the world has many interconnected rooms and hallways.

The difference between the worlds clearly bears out in the task completion rates reported below.

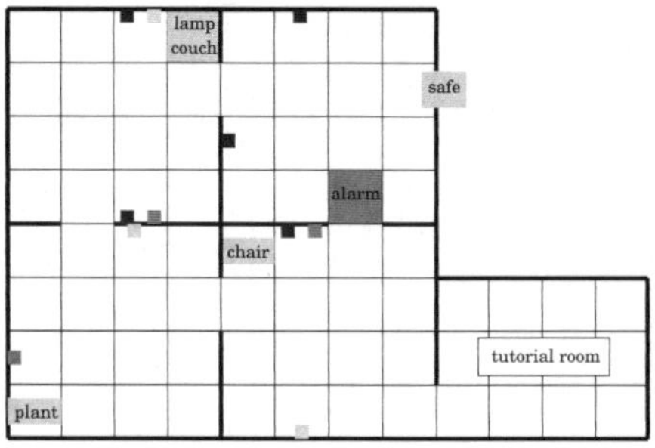


Figure 3: World 1

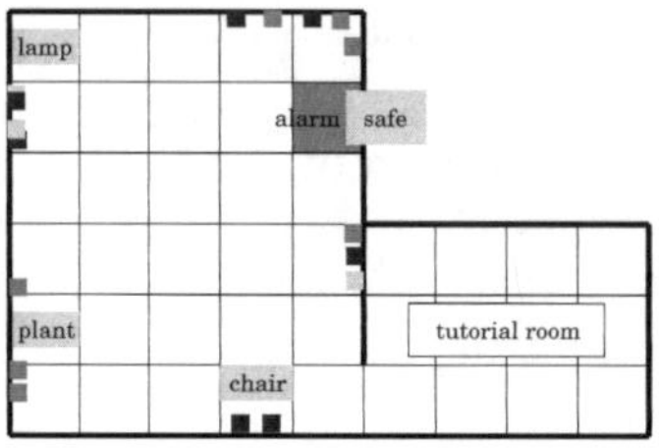


Figure 4: World 2

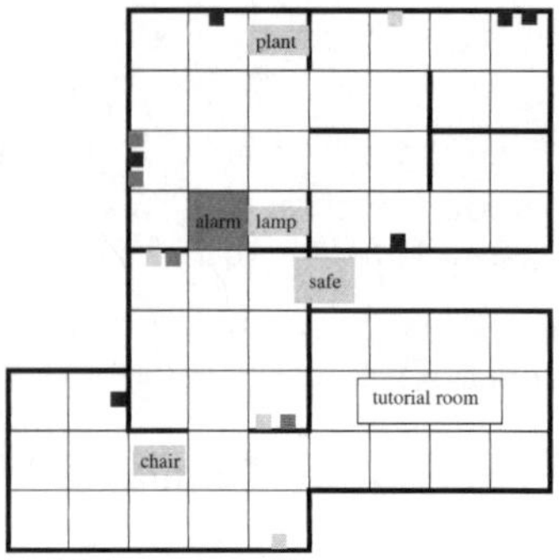


Figure 5: World 3

### 3.4 Timeline

After the GIVE Challenge was publicized in March 2008, eight research teams signed up for participation. We distributed an initial version of the GIVE software and a development world to these teams. In the end, four teams submitted NLG systems. These were connected to a central Matchmaker instance that ran for about three months, from 7 November 2008 to 5 February 2009. During this time, we advertised participation in the GIVE Challenge to the public in order to obtain experimental subjects.

### 3.5 NLG systems

Five NLG systems were evaluated in GIVE-1:

1. one system from the University of Texas at Austin ("Austin" in the graphics below);
2. one system from Union College in Schenectady, NY ("Union");
3. one system from the Universidad Complutense de Madrid ("Madrid");
4. two systems from the University of Twente: one serious contribution ("Twente") and one more playful one ("Warm-Cold").

Of these systems, "Austin" can serve as a baseline: It computes a plan consisting of the actions the user should take to achieve the goal, and at each point in the game, it realizes the first step in this plan as a single instruction. The "Warm-Cold" system generates very vague instructions that only tell the user if they are getting closer ("warmer") to their next objective or if they are moving away from it ("colder"). We included this system in the evaluation to verify whether the evaluation methodology would be able to distinguish such an obviously suboptimal instruction-giving strategy from the others.

Detailed descriptions of these systems as well as each team's own analysis of the evaluation results can be found at `http://www.give-challenge.org/research/give-1`.

## 4 Results

We now report on the results of GIVE-1. We start with some basic demographics; then we discuss objective and subjective evaluation measures.

Notice that some of our evaluation measures are in tension with each other: For instance, a system which gives very low-level instructions ("move forward"; "ok, now move forward"; "ok, now turn left"), such as the "Austin" baseline, will lead the user to completing the task in a minimum number of steps; but it will require more instructions than a system that aggregates these. This is intentional, and emphasizes both the pilot experiment character of GIVE-1 and our desire to make GIVE a friendly comparative challenge rather than a competition with a clear winner.

### 4.1 Demographics

Over the course of three months, we collected 1143 valid games. A game counted as valid if the game client didn't crash, the game wasn't marked as a test game by the developers, and the player completed the tutorial.

Of these games, 80.1% were played by males and 9.9% by females; a further 10% didn't specify their gender. The players were widely distributed over countries: 37% connected from an IP address in the US, 33% from an IP address in Germany, and 17% from China; Canada, the UK, and Austria also accounted for more than 2% of the partic-

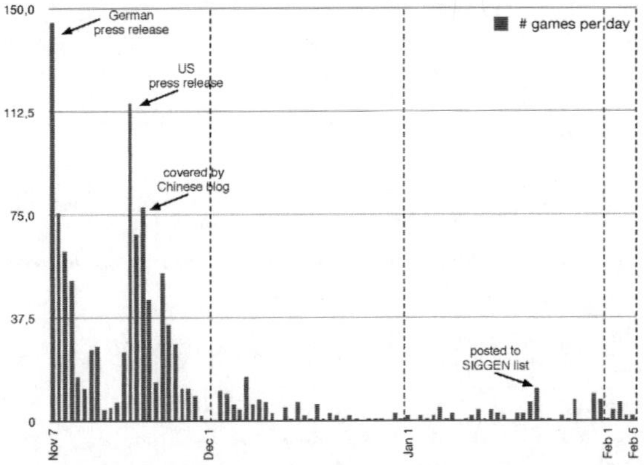


Figure 6: Histogram of the connections per day.

ipants each, and the remaining 2% of participants connected from 42 further countries. This imbalance stems from very successful press releases that were issued in Germany and the US and which were further picked up by blogs, including one in China. Nevertheless, over 90% of the participants who answered this question self-rated their English proficiency as "good" or better. About 75% of users connected with a client running on Windows, with the rest split about evenly among Linux and Mac OS X.

The effect of the press releases is also plainly visible if we look at the distribution of the valid games over the days from November 7 to February 5 (Fig. 6). There are huge peaks at the very beginning of the evaluation period, coinciding with press releases through Saarland University in Germany and Northwestern University in the US, which were picked up by science and technology blogs on the Web. The US peak contains a smaller peak of connections from China, which were sparked by coverage in a Chinese blog.

## 4.2 Objective measures

We then extracted objective and subjective measurements from the valid games. The objective measures are summarized in Fig. 7. For each system and game world, we measured the percentage of games which the users completed successfully. Furthermore, we counted the numbers of instructions the system sent to the user, measured the time until task completion, and counted the number of low-level steps executed by the user (any key press, to either move or manipulate an object) as well as the number of task-relevant actions (such as pushing a button to open a door).

- task success (Did the player get the trophy?)
- instructions (Number of instructions produced by the NLG system.*)
- steps (Number of all player actions.*)
- actions (Number of object manipulation action.*)
- second (Time in seconds.*)

* Measured from the end of the tutorial until the end of the game.

Figure 7: Objective measurements

| | Austin | Madrid | Twente | Union | Warm-Cold |
|---|---|---|---|---|---|
| task success | 40%<br>B | 71%<br>A | 35%<br>B | 73%<br>A | 18%<br>C |
| instructions | 83.2<br>B | 58.3<br>A | 121.2<br>C | 80.3<br>B | 190.0<br>D |
| steps | 103.6<br>A | 124.3<br>B | 160.9<br>C | 117.5<br>A B | 307.4<br>D |
| actions | 11.2<br>B | 8.7<br>A | 14.3<br>C | 9.0<br>A | 14.3<br>C |
| seconds | 129.3<br>A | 174.8<br>B | 207.0<br>C | 175.2<br>B | 312.2<br>D |

Figure 8: *Objective* measures by system. Task success is reported as the percentage of successfully completed games. The other measures are reported as the mean number of instructions/steps/actions/seconds, respectively. Letters group indistinguishable systems; systems that don't share a letter were found to be significantly different with $p < 0.05$.

To ensure comparability, we only counted successfully completed games for all these measures, and only started counting when the user left the tutorial room. Crucially, all objective measures were collected completely unobtrusively, without requiring any action on the user's part.

Fig. 8 shows the results of these objective measures. This figure assigns systems to groups A, B, etc. for each evaluation measure. Systems in group A are better than systems in group B, etc.; if two systems don't share the same letter, the difference between these two systems is significant with $p < 0.05$. Significance was tested using a $\chi^2$-test for task success and ANOVAs for instructions, steps, actions, and seconds. These were followed by post-hoc tests (pairwise $\chi^2$ and Tukey) to compare the NLG systems pairwise.

Overall, there is a top group consisting of the Austin, Madrid, and Union systems: While Madrid and Union outperform Austin on task success (with 70 to 80% of successfully completed games, depending on the world), Austin significantly outperforms all other systems in terms of task completion time. As expected, the Warm-Cold system performs significantly worse than all others in almost all categories. This confirms the ability of the GIVE evaluation method to distinguish between systems of very different qualities.

### 4.3 Subjective measures

The subjective measures, which were obtained by asking the users to fill in a questionnaire after each game, are shown in Fig. 9. Most of the questions were answered on 5-point Likert scales ("overall" on a 7-point scale); the "informativity" and "timing" questions had nominal answers. For each question, the user could choose not to answer.

The results of the subjective measurements are summarized in Fig. 10, in the same format as above. We ran $\chi^2$-tests for the nominal variables informativity and timing, and ANOVAs for the scale data. Again, we used post-hoc pairwise $\chi^2$- and Tukey-tests to compare the NLG systems to each other one by one.

Here there are fewer significant differences between different groups than for the objective measures: For the "play again" category, there is no significant difference at all. Nevertheless, "Austin" is shown to be particularly good at navigation instructions and timing, whereas "Madrid" outperforms the rest of the field in "informativity". In the overall subjective evaluation, the earlier top group of Austin, Madrid, and Union is confirmed, although the difference between Union and Twente is not significant. However, "Warm-Cold" again performs significantly worse than all other systems in most measures. Furthermore, although most systems perform similarly on "informativity" and "timing" in terms of the number of users who judged them as "just right", there are differences in the tendencies: Twente and Union tend to be overinformative, whereas Austin and Warm-Cold tend to be underinformative; Twente and Union tend to give their instructions too late, whereas Madrid and Warm-Cold tend to give them too early.

**7-point scale items:**

overall: What is your overall evaluation of the quality of the direction-giving system? (very bad 1 . . . 7 very good)

**5-point scale items:**

task difficulty: How easy or difficult was the task for you to solve? (very difficult 1 2 3 4 5 very easy)

goal clarity: How easy was it to understand what you were supposed to do? (very difficult 1 2 3 4 5 very easy)

play again: Would you want to play this game again? (no way! 1 2 3 4 5 yes please!)

instruction clarity: How clear were the directions? (totally unclear 1 2 3 4 5 very clear)

instruction helpfulness: How effective were the directions at helping you complete the task? (not effective 1 2 3 4 5 very effective)

choice of words: How easy to understand was the system's choice of wording in its directions to you? (totally unclear 1 2 3 4 5 very clear)

referring expressions: How easy was it to pick out which object in the world the system was referring to? (very hard 1 2 3 4 5 very easy)

navigation instructions: How easy was it to navigate to a particular spot, based on the system's directions? (very hard 1 2 3 4 5 very easy)

friendliness: How would you rate the friendliness of the system? (very unfriendly 1 2 3 4 5 very friendly)

**Nominal items:**

informativity: Did you feel the amount of information you were given was: too little / just right / too much

timing: Did the directions come ... too early / just at the right time / too late

Figure 9: Questionnaire items

| | Austin | Madrid | Twente | Union | Warm-Cold |
|---|---|---|---|---|---|
| task difficulty | 4.3 A | 4.3 A | 4.0 A | 4.3 A | 3.5 B |
| goal clarity | 4.0 A | 3.7 A | 3.9 A | 3.7 A | 3.3 B |
| play again | 2.8 A | 2.6 A | 2.4 A | 2.9 A | 2.5 A |
| instruction clarity | 4.0 A | 3.6 A B | 3.8 A B | 3.6 B | 3.0 C |
| instruction helpfulness | 3.8 A | 3.9 A | 3.6 A | 3.7 A | 2.9 B |
| informativity | 46% B | 68% A | 51% B | 56% B | 51% B |
| overall | 4.9 A | 4.9 A | 4.3 B | 4.6 A B | 3.6 C |
| choice of words | 4.2 A | 3.8 B C | 4.1 A B | 3.7 C | 3.5 C |
| referring expressions | 3.4 B | 3.9 A | 3.7 A B | 3.7 A B | 3.5 B |
| navigation instructions | 4.6 A | 4.0 B | 4.0 B | 3.7 B | 3.2 C |
| timing | 78% A | 62% B | 60% B C | 62% B | 49% C |
| friendliness | 3.4 A B | 3.8 A | 3.1 B | 3.6 A | 3.1 B |

Figure 10: *Subjective* measures by system. Informativity and timing are reported as the percentage of successfully completed games. The other measures are reported as the mean rating received by the players. Letters group indistinguishable systems; systems that don't share a letter were found to be significantly different with $p < 0.05$.

### 4.4 Further analysis

In addition to the differences between NLG systems, there may be other factors which also influence the outcome of our objective and subjective measures. We tested the following five factors: evaluation world, gender, age, computer expertise, and English proficiency (as reported by the users on the questionnaire). We found that there is a significant difference in task success rate for different evaluation worlds and between users with different levels of English proficiency.

The interaction graphs in Figs. 11 and 12 also suggest that the NLG systems differ in their robustness with respect to these factors. $\chi^2$-tests that compare the success rate of each system in the three evaluation worlds show that while the instructions of Union and Madrid seem to work equally well in all three worlds, the performance of the other three systems differs dramatically between the different worlds. Especially World 2 was challenging for some systems as it required relational object descriptions, such as *the blue button on the left of another blue button*.

The players' English skills also affected the systems in different ways. While Austin, Madrid and Warm Cold don't manage to lead players with only basic English skills to success as often as other players, Union's and Twente's success rates do not depend on the players' English skills ($\chi^2$-tests do not find significant differences in success rate between players with different levels of English proficiency for these two systems). However, if we remove the players with the lowest level of English proficiency, language skills do not have an effect on the task success rate anymore for any of the systems.

## 5 Conclusion

In this document, we have described the first installment of the GIVE Challenge, our experimental methodology, and the results. Altogether, we collected 1143 valid games for five NLG systems over a period of three months. Given that this was the first time we organized the challenge, that it was meant as a pilot experiment from the beginning, and that the number of games was sufficient to get significant differences between systems on a number of measures, we feel that GIVE-1 was a success. We are in the process of preparing several diagnostic utilities, such as heat maps and a tool that lets the system developer replay an indi-

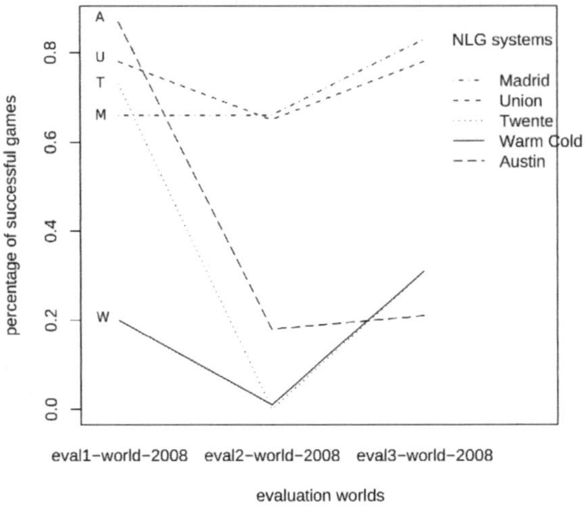


Figure 11: Effect of the evaluation worlds on the success rate of the NLG systems.

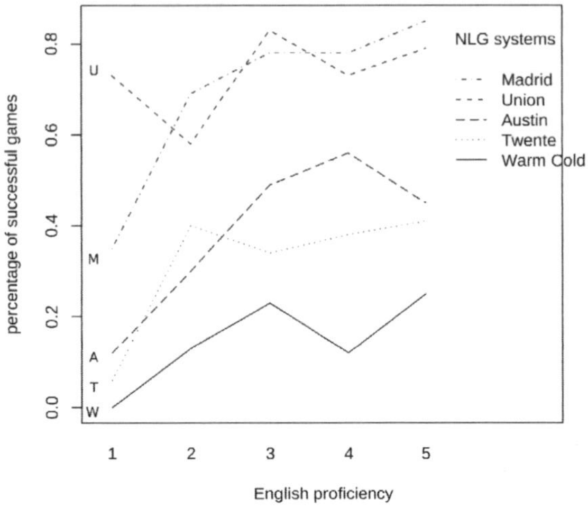


Figure 12: Effect of the players' English skills on the success rate of the NLG systems.

vidual game, which will help the participants gain further insight into their NLG systems.

Nevertheless, there are a number of improvements we will make to GIVE for future installments. For one thing, the timing of the challenge was not optimal: A number of colleagues would have been interested in participating, but the call for participation came too late for them to acquire funding or interest students in time for summer projects or MSc theses. Secondly, although the software performed very well in handling thousands of user connections, there were still game-invalidating issues with the 3D graphics and the networking code that were individually rare, but probably cost us several hundred games. These should be fixed for GIVE-2. At the same time, we are investigating ways in which the networking and matchmaking core of GIVE can be factored out into a separate, challenge-independent system on which other Internet-based challenges can be built. Among other things, it would be straightforward to use the GIVE platform to connect two human users and observe their dialogue while solving a problem. Judicious variation of parameters (such as the familiarity of users or the visibility of an instruction giving avatar) would allow the construction of new dialogue corpora along such lines.

Finally, GIVE-1 focused on the generation of navigation instructions and referring expressions, in a relatively simple world, without giving the user a chance to talk back. The high success rate of some systems in this challenge suggests that we need to widen the focus for a future GIVE-2 – by allowing dialogue, by making the world more complex (e.g., allowing continuous rather than discrete movements and turns), by making the communication multi-modal, etc. Such extensions would require only rather limited changes to the GIVE software infrastructure. We plan to come to a decision about such future directions for GIVE soon, and are looking forward to many fruitful discussions about this at ENLG.

**Acknowledgments.** We are grateful to the participants of the 2007 NSF/SIGGEN Workshop on Shared Tasks and Evaluation in NLG and many other colleagues for fruitful discussions while we were designing the GIVE Challenge, and to the organizers of Generation Challenges 2009 and ENLG 2009 for their support and the opportunity to present the results at ENLG. We also thank the four participating research teams for their contributions and their patience while we were working out bugs in the GIVE software. The creation of the GIVE infrastructure was supported in part by a Small Projects grant from the University of Edinburgh.

## References

A. Belz and A. Gatt. 2008. Intrinsic vs. extrinsic evaluation measures for referring expression generation. In *Proceedings of ACL-08:HLT, Short Papers*, pages 197–200, Columbus, Ohio.

M. E. Foster. 2008. Automated metrics that agree with human judgements on generated output for an embodied conversational agent. In *Proceedings of INLG 2008*, pages 95–103, Salt Fork, OH.

A. Koller, D. Byron, J. Cassell, R. Dale, J. Moore, J. Oberlander, and K. Striegnitz. 2009. The software architecture for the first challenge on generating instructions in virtual environments. In *Proceedings of the EACL-09 Demo Session*.

J. Orkin and D. Roy. 2007. The restaurant game: Learning social behavior and language from thousands of players online. *Journal of Game Development*, 3(1):39–60.

A. Stent, M. Marge, and M. Singhai. 2005. Evaluating evaluation methods for generation in the presence of variation. In *Proceedings of CICLing 2005*.

L. Stoia, D. M. Shockley, D. K. Byron, and E. Fosler-Lussier. 2006. Noun phrase generation for situated dialogs. In *Proceedings of INLG*, Sydney.

L. von Ahn and L. Dabbish. 2004. Labeling images with a computer game. In *Proceedings of the ACM CHI Conference*.

# The TUNA-REG Challenge 2009: Overview and Evaluation Results

**Albert Gatt**
Computing Science
University of Aberdeen
Aberdeen AB24 3UE, UK
a.gatt@abdn.ac.uk

**Anja Belz** **Eric Kow**
Natural Language Technology Group
University of Brighton
Brighton BN2 4GJ, UK
{asb,eykk10}@bton.ac.uk

## Abstract

The TUNA-REG'09 Challenge was one of the shared-task evaluation competitions at Generation Challenges 2009. TUNA-REG'09 used data from the TUNA Corpus of paired representations of entities and human-authored referring expressions. The shared task was to create systems that generate referring expressions for entities given representations of sets of entities and their properties. Four teams submitted six systems to TUNA-REG'09. We evaluated the six systems and two sets of human-authored referring expressions using several automatic intrinsic measures, a human-assessed intrinsic evaluation and a human task performance experiment. This report describes the TUNA-REG task and the evaluation methods used, and presents the evaluation results.

## 1 Introduction

This year's run of the TUNA-REG Shared-Task Evaluation Competition (STEC) is the third, and final, competition to involve the TUNA Corpus of referring expressions. The TUNA Corpus was first used in the Pilot Attribute Selection for Generating Referring Expressions (ASGRE) Challenge (Belz and Gatt, 2007) which took place between May and September 2007; and again for three of the shared tasks in Referring Expression Generation (REG) Challenges 2008, which ran between September 2007 and May 2008 (Gatt et al., 2008). This year's TUNA Task replicates one of the three tasks from REG'08, the TUNA-REG Task. It uses the same test data, to enable direct comparison against the 2008 results. Four participating teams submitted 6 different systems this year; teams and their affiliations are shown in Table 1.

| Team ID | Affiliation |
|---|---|
| GRAPH | Macquarie, Tilburg and Twente Universities |
| IS | ICSI, University of California |
| NIL-UCM | Universidad Complutense de Madrid |
| USP | University of São Paolo |

Table 1: TUNA-REG'09 Participants.

## 2 Data

Each file in the TUNA corpus[1] consists of a single pairing of a domain (a representation of 7 entities and their attributes) and a human-authored description for one of the entities (the target referent). Some domains represent sets of people, some represent items of furniture (see also Table 2). The descriptions were collected in an online elicitation experiment which was advertised mainly on a website hosted at the University of Zurich Web Experimentation List[2] (a web service for recruiting subjects for experiments), and in which participation was not controlled or monitored. In the experiment, participants were shown pictures of the entities in the given domain and were asked to type a description of the target referent (which was highlighted in the visual display). The main condition[3] manipulated in the experiment was $+/-LOC$: in the $+LOC$ condition, participants were told that they could refer to entities using any of their properties (including their location on the screen). In the $-LOC$ condition, they were discouraged from doing so, though not prevented.

The XML format we have been using in the TUNA-REG STECs, shown in Figure 1, is a variant of the original format of the TUNA corpus. The root TRIAL node has a unique ID and an indication of the $+/-LOC$ experimental condi-

[1] http://www.csd.abdn.ac.uk/research/tuna/

[2] http://genpsylab-wexlist.unizh.ch

[3] The elicitation experiment had an additional independent variable, manipulating whether descriptions were elicited in a 'fault-critical' or 'non-fault-critical' condition. For the shared tasks this was ignored by collapsing all the data in these two conditions.

*Proceedings of the 12th European Workshop on Natural Language Generation*, pages 174–182,
Athens, Greece, 30 – 31 March 2009. ©2009 Association for Computational Linguistics

tion. The DOMAIN node contains 7 ENTITY nodes, which themselves contain a number of ATTRIBUTE nodes defining the possible properties of an entity in attribute-value notation. The attributes include properties such as an object's colour or a person's clothing, and the location of the image in the visual display which the DOMAIN represents. Each ENTITY node indicates whether it is the target referent or one of the six distractors, and also has a pointer to the image that it represents. The WORD-STRING is the actual description typed by one of the human authors, the ANNOTATED-WORD-STRING is the description with substrings annotated with the attributes they realise, while the ATTRIBUTE-SET contains the set of attributes only. The ANNOTATED-WORD-STRING and ATTRIBUTE-SET nodes were provided in the training and development data only, to show how substrings of a human-authored description mapped to attributes.

```
<TRIAL CONDITION="+/-LOC" ID="...">
  <DOMAIN>
    <ENTITY ID="..." TYPE="target" IMAGE="...">
      <ATTRIBUTE NAME="..." VALUE="..." />
      ...
    </ENTITY>
    <ENTITY ID="..." TYPE="distractor" IMAGE="...">
      <ATTRIBUTE NAME="..." VALUE="..." />
      ...
    </ENTITY>
    ...
  </DOMAIN>
  <WORD-STRING>
    string describing the target referent
  </WORD-STRING>
  <ANNOTATED-WORD-STRING>
    string in WORD-STRING annotated
    with attributes in ATTRIBUTE-SET
  </ANNOTATED-WORD-STRING>
  <ATTRIBUTE-SET>
    set of domain attributes in the description
  </ATTRIBUTE-SET>
</TRIAL>
```

Figure 1: XML format of corpus items.

Apart from differences in the XML format, the data used in the TUNA-REG Task also differs from the original TUNA corpus in that it has only the singular referring expressions from the original corpus, and in that we have added to it the files of images of entities that the XML mark-up points to.

The test set, which was constructed for the 2008 run of the TUNA-REG Task, consists of 112 items, each with a different domain paired with *two* human-authored descriptions. The items are distributed equally between furniture items and people, and between both experimental conditions (+/ − *LOC*). In the following sections, the two sets of human descriptions will be referred to as HUMAN-1 and HUMAN-2.[4] The numbers of files in the training, development and test sets, as well as in the people and furniture subdomains, are shown in Table 2.

| | Furniture | People | All |
|---|---|---|---|
| *Training* | 319 | 274 | 593 |
| *Development* | 80 | 68 | 148 |
| *Test* | 56 | 56 | 112 |
| *All* | 455 | 398 | 853 |

Table 2: TUNA-REG data: subset sizes.

## 3 The TUNA-REG Task

Referring Expression Generation (REG) has been the subject of intensive research in the NLG community, giving rise to substantial consensus on the problem definition, as well as the nature of the inputs and outputs of REG algorithms. Typically, such algorithms take as input a domain, consisting of entities and their attributes, together with an indication of which is the intended referent, and output a set of attributes true of the referent which distinguish it from other entities in the domain. The TUNA-REG task adds an additional stage (realisation) in which selected attributes are mapped to a natural language expression (usually a noun phrase). Realisation has received far less attention among REG researchers than attribute selection.

The TUNA-REG task is an 'end-to-end' referring expression generation task, in the sense that it takes as input a representation of a set of entities and their properties, and outputs a word string which describes the target entity. Participating systems were not constrained to have attribute selection as a separate module from realisation.

In terms of the XML format, the items in the test set distributed to participants consisted of a DOMAIN node and ATTRIBUTE-SET, and participating systems had to generate appropriate WORD-STRINGS.

As with previous STECs involving the TUNA data, we deliberately refrained from including in the task definition any aim that would imply assumptions about quality (as would be the case if we had asked participants to aim to produce, say, minimal or uniquely distinguishing referring expressions), and instead we simply listed the evaluation criteria that were going to be used (described in Section 5).

[4]Descriptions in each set are not all by the same author.

| *Evaluation criterion* | *Type of evaluation* | *Evaluation technique* |
|---|---|---|
| Humanlikeness | Intrinsic/automatic | Accuracy, String-edit distance, BLEU-3, NIST |
| Adequacy/clarity | Intrinsic/human | Judgment of adequacy as rated by native speakers |
| Fluency | Intrinsic/human | Judgment of fluency as rated by native speakers |
| Referential clarity | Extrinsic/human | Speed and accuracy in identification experiment |

Table 3: Overview of evaluation methods.

## 4 Participating Teams and Systems

This section briefly describes this year's submissions. Full descriptions of participating systems can be found in the participants' reports included in this volume.

**IS:** The submission of the IS team, IS-FP-GT, is based on the idea that different writers use different styles of referring expressions, and that, therefore, knowing the identity of the writer helps generate REs similar to those in the corpus. The attribute-selection algorithm is an extended full-brevity algorithm which uses a nearest neighbour technique to select the attribute set (AS) most similar to a given writer's previous ASs, or, in a case where no ASs by the given writer have previously been seen, to select the AS that has the highest degree of similarity with all previously seen ASs by any writer. If multiple ASs remain, the algorithm first selects the shortest, then the most representative of the remaining REs, then the AS with the highest-frequency attributes. Individualised statistical models are used to convert the selected AS into a surface-syntactic dependency tree which is then converted to a word stirng with an existing realiser.

**GRAPH:** The GRAPH team reused their existing graph-based attribute selection component, which represents a domain as a weighted graph, and uses a cost function for attributes. The team developed a new realiser which uses a set of templates derived from the descriptions in the TUNA corpus. In order to build templates, certain subsets of attributes were grouped together, individual attributes were replaced by their type, and a preferred order for attributes was determined based on frequencies of orderings. During realisation, if a matching template exists, types are replaced with the most frequent word string for each given attribute; if no match exists, realisation is done by a simple rule-based method.

**NIL-UCM:** The three systems submitted by this group use a standard evolutionary algorithm for attribute selection where genotypes consist of binary-valued genes each representing the presence or absence of a given attribute. Realisation is done with a case-based reasoning (CBR) method which retrieves the most similar previously seen ASs for an input AS, in order of their similarity to the input. (Sub)strings are then copied from the preferred retrieved case to create the output word string. One system, NIL-UCM-EvoCBR uses both components as described above. The other two systems, NIL-UCM-ValuesCBR and NIL-UCM-EvoTAP, replace one of the components with the team's corresponding component from REG'08.

**USP:** The system submitted by this group, USP-EACH, is a frequency-based greedy attribute selection strategy which takes into account the $+/-$ $LOC$ attribute in the TUNA data. Realisation was done using the surface realiser supplied to participants in the ASGRE'07 Challenge.

## 5 Evaluation Methods and Results

We used a range of different evaluation methods, including intrinsic and extrinsic,[5] automatically computed and human-evaluated, as shown in the overview in Table 3. Participants computed automatic intrinsic evaluation scores on the development set (using the `teval` program provided by us). We performed all of the evaluations shown in Table 3 on the test data set. For all measures, results were computed both (a) overall, using the entire test data set, and (b) by entity type, that is, computing separate values for outputs in the *furniture* and in the *people* domain. Evaluation methods for each evaluation type and corresponding evaluation results are presented in the following three sections.

### 5.1 Automatic intrinsic evaluations

Humanlikeness, by which we mean the similarity of system outputs to sets of human-produced reference 'outputs', was assessed using Accuracy,

[5]Intrinsic evaluations assess properties of peer systems in their own right, whereas extrinsic evaluations assess the effect of a peer system on something that is external to it, such as its effect on human performance at some given task or the added value it brings to an application.

| | All development data | | | People | | | Furniture | | |
|---|---|---|---|---|---|---|---|---|---|
| | Accuracy | SE | BLEU | Accuracy | SE | BLEU | Accuracy | SE | BLEU |
| IS-FP-GT | 9.71% | 4.313 | 0.297 | 4.41% | 4.764 | 0.2263 | 15% | 3.863 | 0.3684 |
| GRAPH | – | 5.03 | 0.30 | – | 5.15 | 0.33 | – | 4.94 | 0.27 |
| NIL-UCM-EvoTAP | 6% | 5.41 | 0.20 | 3% | 6.04 | 0.15 | 8% | 4.87 | 0.24 |
| NIL-UCM-ValuesCBR | 1% | 5.86 | 0.19 | 1% | 5.80 | 0.17 | 1% | 5.91 | 0.20 |
| USP-EACH | – | 6.03 | 0.19 | – | 7.50 | 0.04 | – | 4.78 | 0.31 |
| NIL-UCM-EvoCBR | 3% | 6.31 | 0.17 | 1% | 6.94 | 0.16 | 4% | 5.77 | 0.18 |

Table 4: Participating teams' self-reported automatic intrinsic scores on development data set with single human-authored reference description (listed in order of overall mean SE score).

| | All test data | | | | People | | | | Furniture | | | |
|---|---|---|---|---|---|---|---|---|---|---|---|---|
| | Acc | SE | BLEU | NIST | Acc | SE | BLEU | NIST | Acc | SE | BLEU | NIST |
| GRAPH | 12.50 | 6.41 | 0.47 | 2.57 | 8.93 | 7.04 | 0.43 | 2.16 | 16.07 | 5.79 | 0.51 | 2.26 |
| IS-FP-GT | 3.57 | 6.74 | 0.28 | 0.75 | 3.57 | 7.04 | 0.37 | 0.94 | 3.57 | 6.45 | 0.13 | 0.36 |
| NIL-UCM-EvoTAP | 6.25 | 7.28 | 0.26 | 0.90 | 3.57 | 8.07 | 0.20 | 0.45 | 8.93 | 6.48 | 0.34 | 1.22 |
| USP-EACH | 7.14 | 7.59 | 0.27 | 1.33 | 0.00 | 9.04 | 0.11 | 0.46 | 14.29 | 6.14 | 0.41 | 2.28 |
| NIL-UCM-ValuesCBR | 2.68 | 7.71 | 0.27 | 1.69 | 3.57 | 8.07 | 0.23 | 0.94 | 1.79 | 7.34 | 0.28 | 1.99 |
| NIL-UCM-EvoCBR | 2.68 | 8.02 | 0.26 | 1.97 | 0.00 | 9.07 | 0.19 | 1.65 | 5.36 | 6.96 | 0.35 | 1.69 |
| HUMAN-2 | 2.68 | 9.68 | 0.12 | 1.78 | 3.57 | 10.64 | 0.12 | 1.50 | 1.79 | 8.71 | 0.13 | 1.57 |
| HUMAN-1 | 2.68 | 9.68 | 0.12 | 1.68 | 3.57 | 10.64 | 0.12 | 1.41 | 1.79 | 8.71 | 0.12 | 1.49 |

Table 5: Automatic intrinsic scores on test data set with two human-authored reference descriptions (listed in order of overall mean SE score).

string-edit distance, BLEU-3 and NIST-5. Accuracy measures the percentage of cases where a system's output word string was identical to the corresponding description in the corpus. String-edit distance (SE) is the classic Levenshtein distance measure and computes the minimal number of insertions, deletions and substitutions required to transform one string into another. We set the cost for insertions and deletions to 1, and that for substitutions to 2. If two strings are identical, then this metric returns 0 (perfect match). Otherwise the value depends on the length of the two strings (the maximum value is the sum of the lengths). As an aggregate measure, we compute the mean of pairwise SE scores.

BLEU-$x$ is an n-gram based string comparison measure, originally proposed by Papineni et al. (2001; 2002) for evaluation of Machine Translation systems. It computes the proportion of word n-grams of length $x$ and less that a system output shares with several reference outputs. Setting $x = 4$ (i.e. considering all n-grams of length $\leq 4$) is standard, but because many of the TUNA descriptions are shorter than 4 tokens, we compute BLEU-3 instead. BLEU ranges from 0 to 1.

NIST is a version of BLEU, but where BLEU gives equal weight to all n-grams, NIST gives more importance to less frequent n-grams, which are taken to be more informative. The maximum NIST score depends on the size of the test set.

Unlike string-edit distance, BLEU and NIST are by definition aggregate measures (i.e. a single score is obtained for a peer system based on the entire set of items to be compared, and this is not generally equal to the average of scores for individual items).

Because the test data has two human-authored reference descriptions per domain, the Accuracy and SE scores had to be computed slightly differently to obtain test data scores (whereas BLEU and NIST are designed for multiple reference texts). For the test data only, therefore, Accuracy expresses the percentage of a system's outputs that match at least *one* of the reference outputs, and SE is the average of the two pairwise scores against the reference outputs.

**Results:** Table 4 is an overview of the self-reported scores on the development set included in the participants' reports (not all participants report Accuracy scores). The corresponding scores for the test data set as well as NIST scores for the test data (all computed by us), are shown in Table 5. The table also includes the result of comparing the two sets of human descriptions, HUMAN-1 and HUMAN-2, to each other using the same metrics (their scores are distinct only for non-commutative measures, i.e. NIST and BLEU).

We ran[6] a one-way ANOVA for the SE scores.

[6]We used SPSS for all statistical analyses and tests.

There was a main effect of SYSTEM on SE ($F = 10.938, p < .001$). A post-hoc Tukey HSD test with $\alpha = .05$ revealed a number of significant differences: all systems were significantly better than the human-authored descriptions, and GRAPH was furthermore significantly better than NIL-UCM-EvoCBR.

We also computed the Kruskal-Wallis H value for the systems' individual Accuracy scores, using a chi square test to establish significance. By this test, the observed aggregate difference among the seven systems is significant at the .01 level ($\chi^2_7 = 20.169$).

### 5.2 Human intrinsic evaluation

The TUNA'09 Challenge was the first TUNA shared-task competition to include an intrinsic evaluation involving human judgments of quality.

**Design:** The intrinsic human evaluation involved descriptions for all 112 test data items from all six submitted systems, as well as from the two sets of human-authored descriptions.[7] Thus, each of the 112 test set items was associated with 8 different descriptions. We used a Repeated Latin Squares design which ensures that each subject sees descriptions from each system and for each domain the same number of times. There were fourteen $8 \times 8$ squares, and a total of 896 individual judgments in this evaluation, each system receiving 112 judgments (14 from each subject).

**Procedure:** In each of the 112 trials, participants were shown a system output (i.e. a WORD-STRING), together with its corresponding domain, displayed as the set of corresponding images on the screen.[8] The intended (target) referent was highlighted by a red frame surrounding it on the screen. They were asked to give two ratings in answer to the following questions (the first for *Adequacy*, the second for *Fluency*):

1. *How clear is this description?* Try to imagine someone who could see the same grid with the same pictures, but didn't know which of the pictures was the target. How easily would they be able to find it, based on the phrase given?
2. *How fluent is this description?* Here your task is to judge how well the phrase reads. Is it good, clear English?

We did not use a rating scale (where integers correspond to different assessments of quality), because it is not generally considered appropriate to apply parametric methods of analysis to ordinal data. Instead, we asked subjects to give their judgments for Adequacy and Fluency for each item by manipulating a slider like this:

The slider pointer was placed in the center at the beginning of each trial, as shown above. The position of the slider selected by the subject mapped to an integer value between 1 and 100. However, the scale was not visible to participants, whose task was to move the pointer to the left or right. The further to the right, the more positive the judgment (and the higher the value returned); the further to the left, the more negative.

Following instructions, subjects did two practice examples, followed by the 112 test items in random order. Subjects carried out the experiment over the internet, at a time and place of their choosing, and were allowed to interrupt and resume the experiment. According to self-reported timings, subjects took between 25 and 60 minutes to complete the experiment (not counting breaks).

**Participants:** We recruited eight native speakers of English from among post-graduate students currently doing a Masters degree in a linguistics-related subject.[9]

We recorded subjects' gender, level of education, field of study, proficiency in English, variety of English and colour vision. Since all subjects were native English speakers, had normal colour vision, and had comparable levels of education and academic backgrounds, as indicated above, these variables are not included in the analyses reported below.

**Results:** Table 6 displays the mean Fluency and Adequacy judgments obtained by each system. We conducted two separate 8 (SYSTEM) $\times$ 2 (DOMAIN) Univariate Analyses of Variance (ANOVAs) on Adequacy and Fluency, where DOMAIN ranges

[7] Note that we refer to all outputs, whether human or system-generated, as *system outputs* in what follows.

[8] The on-screen display of images was very similar, although not identical, to that in the original TUNA elicitation experiments.

[9] MA Linguistics and MRes Speech, Language and Cognition at UCL; MA Applied Linguistics and MRes Psychology at Sussex; and MA Media-assisted Language Teaching at Brighton.

| | All test data | | | | People | | | | Furniture | | | |
|---|---|---|---|---|---|---|---|---|---|---|---|---|
| | Adequacy | | Fluency | | Adequacy | | Fluency | | Adequacy | | Fluency | |
| | Mean | SD | Mean | SD | Mean | SD | Mean | SD | Mean | SD | Mean | SD |
| GRAPH | 84.11 | 21.07 | 85.81 | 17.52 | 85.30 | 18.10 | 87.70 | 14.42 | 82.91 | 23.78 | 83.93 | 20.11 |
| USP-EACH | 77.72 | 28.33 | 84.20 | 20.27 | 81.04 | 26.48 | 81.82 | 24.47 | 74.41 | 29.93 | 86.57 | 14.79 |
| NIL-UCM-EvoTAP | 76.16 | 28.34 | 61.95 | 26.13 | 78.66 | 27.48 | 59.13 | 29.78 | 73.66 | 29.22 | 64.77 | 21.79 |
| HUMAN-2 | 74.63 | 34.77 | 73.38 | 27.63 | 80.93 | 31.83 | 73.16 | 30.88 | 68.34 | 36.68 | 73.59 | 24.23 |
| NIL-UCM-ValuesCBR | 72.34 | 33.93 | 59.41 | 33.94 | 68.18 | 37.37 | 46.23 | 34.92 | 76.50 | 29.86 | 72.59 | 27.43 |
| HUMAN-1 | 70.38 | 34.92 | 71.52 | 30.79 | 83.39 | 24.27 | 72.39 | 28.55 | 57.36 | 39.08 | 70.64 | 33.13 |
| NIL-UCM-EvoCBR | 63.65 | 37.19 | 55.38 | 35.32 | 56.61 | 40.20 | 41.45 | 37.38 | 70.70 | 32.76 | 69.30 | 26.93 |
| IS-FP-GT | 59.46 | 40.94 | 66.21 | 30.97 | 88.79 | 19.26 | 65.27 | 32.22 | 30.14 | 35.51 | 67.16 | 29.94 |

Table 6: Human-assessed intrinsic scores on test data set, including the two sets of human-authored reference descriptions (listed in order of overall mean Adequacy score).

| Adequacy | | | | | Fluency | | | | | |
|---|---|---|---|---|---|---|---|---|---|---|
| GRAPH | A | | | | GRAPH | A | | | | |
| USP-EACH | A | B | | | USP-EACH | A | B | | | |
| NIL-UCM-EvoTAP | A | B | | | HUMAN-2 | | B | C | | |
| HUMAN-2 | A | B | C | | HUMAN-1 | | | C | D | |
| NIL-UCM-ValuesCBR | A | B | C | | IS-FP-GT | | | C | D | E |
| HUMAN-1 | | B | C | D | NIL-UCM-EvoTAP | | | | D | E |
| NIL-UCM-EvoCBR | | | C | D | NIL-UCM-ValuesCBR | | | | | E |
| IS-FP-GT | | | | D | NIL-UCM-EvoCBR | | | | | E |

Table 7: Homogeneous subsets for Adequacy and Fluency. Systems which do not share a letter are significantly different at $\alpha = .05$.

over People and Furniture Items. On Adequacy, there were main effects of SYSTEM ($F(7, 880) = 7.291, p < .001$) and DOMAIN ($F(1, 880) = 29.133, p < .001$), with a significant interaction between the two ($F(7, 880) = 15.30, p < .001$). On Fluency, there were main effects of SYSTEM ($F(7, 880) = 18.14$) and of DOMAIN ($F(7, 880) = 17.20$), again with a significant SYSTEM $\times$ DOMAIN interaction ($F(7, 880) = 5.60$), all significant at $p < .001$. Post-hoc Tukey comparisons on both dependent measures yielded the homogeneous subsets displayed in Table 7.

### 5.3 Extrinsic task-performance evaluation

As for earlier shared tasks involving the TUNA data, we carried out a task-performance experiment in which subjects have the task of identifying intended referents.

**Design:** The extrinsic human evaluation involved descriptions for all 112 test data items from all six submitted systems, as well as from the two sets of human-authored descriptions. We used a Repeated Latin Squares design with fourteen $8 \times 8$ squares, so again there were a total of 896 individual judgments and each system received 112 judgments, however this time it was 7 from each subject, as there were 16 participants; so half the participants did the first 56 items (the first 7 squares), and the other half the second 56 (the remaining 7 squares).

**Procedure:** In each of their 5 practice trials and 56 real trials, participants were shown a system output (i.e. a WORD-STRING), together with its corresponding domain, displayed as the set of corresponding images on the screen. In this experiment the intended referent was not highlighted in the on-screen display, and the participants' task was to identify the intended referent among the pictures by mouse-clicking on it.[10]

In previous TUNA identification experiments (Belz and Gatt, 2007; Gatt et al., 2008), subjects had to read the description before identifying the intended referent. In ASGRE'07 both description and pictures were displayed at the same time, yielding a single time measure that combined reading and identification times. In REG'08, subjects first read the description and then called up the pictures on the screen when they had finished reading the description, which yielded separate reading and identification times.

[10]Due to limitations related to the stimulus presentation software, the images in this experiment were displayed in strict rows and columns, whereas the display grid in the web-based TUNA elicitation experiment and the intrinsic human evalution experiment were slightly distorted. This may have affected timings in those (very rare) cases where a description explicitly referenced the column a target referent was located in, as in *the chair in column 1*.

This year we tried out a version of the experiment where subjects listened to descriptions read out by a synthetic voice[11] over headphones while looking at the pictures displayed on the screen.

Stimulus presentation was carried out using DMDX, a Win-32 software package for psycholinguistic experiments involving time measurements (Forster and Forster, 2003). Participants initiated each trial, which consisted of an initial warning bell and a fixation point flashed on the screen for 1000ms. Following this, the visual domain was displayed, and the voice reading the description was initiated after a delay of 500ms. We recorded time in milliseconds from the start of display to the mouse-click whereby a participant identified the target referent. This is hereafter referred to as the *identification speed*. The analysis reported below also uses *identification accuracy*, the percentage of correctly identified target referents, as an additional dependent variable. Trials timed out after 15,000ms.

**Participants:** The experiment was carried out by 16 participants recruited from among the faculty and administrative staff of the University of Brighton. All participants carried out the experiment under supervision in the same quiet room on the same laptop, in the same ambient conditions, with no interruptions. All participants were native speakers, and we recorded type of post, whether they had normal colour vision and hearing, and whether they were left or right-handed.

**Timeouts and outliers:** None of the trials reached time-out stage during the experiment. Outliers were defined as those identification times which fell outside the *mean* ±2SD (standard deviation) range. 44 data points (4.9%) out of a total of 896 were identified as outliers by this definition; these were replaced with the series mean (Ratliff, 1993). The results reported for identification speed below are based on these adjusted times.

**Results:** Table 8 displays mean identification speed and identification accuracy per system. A univariate ANOVA on identification speed revealed significant main effects of SYSTEM ($F(7, 880) = 4.04, p < .001$) and DOMAIN ($F(1, 880) = 11.53, p < .001$), with a significant interaction ($F(7, 880) = 6.02, p < .001$). Table 9 displays homogeneous subsets obtained following pairwise comparisons using a post-hoc Tukey HSD analysis.

[11]We used the University of Edinburgh's Festival speech generation system (Black et al., 1999) in combination with the nitech_us_slt_arctic_hts voice, a high-quality female American voice.

| | | |
|---|---|---|
| USP-EACH | A | |
| GRAPH | A | |
| NIL-UCM-EvoTAP | A | B |
| IS-FP-GT | A | B |
| NIL-UCM-ValuesCBR | A | B |
| NIL-UCM-EvoCBR | A | B |
| HUMAN-2 | | B |
| HUMAN-1 | | B |

Table 9: Homogeneous subsets for Identification Speed. Systems which do not share a letter are significantly different at $\alpha = .05$.

We treated identification accuracy as an indicator variable (indicating whether a participant correctly identified a target referent or not in a given trial). A Kruskal-Wallis test showed a significant difference between systems ($\chi^2_7 = 44.98; p < .001$).

### 5.4 Correlations

Table 10 displays the correlations between the eight evaluation measures we used. The numbers are Pearson product-moment correlation coefficients, calculated on the means (1 mean per system on each measure).

As regards the human-assessed intrinsic scores, there is no significant correlation between Adequacy and Fluency. Among the automatically computed intrinsic measures, the only significant correlation is between Accuracy and BLEU. For the extrinsic identification performance measures, there is no significant correlation between Identification Accuracy and Identification Speed.

As for correlations across the two types (human-assessed and automatically computed) of intrinsic measures, the only significant correlations are between Fluency and Accuracy, and between Adequacy and Accuracy. So, a system with a higher percentage of human-like outputs (as measured by Accurach) also tends to be scored more highly in terms of Fluency and Adequacy by humans.

We also found significant correlations between intrinsic and extrinsic measures: there was a strong and significant correlation between Identification Accuracy and Adequacy, implying that more adequate system outputs allowed people to identify target referents more correctly; there was also a significant (negative) correlation between

| | All test data | | | People | | | Furniture | | |
|---|---|---|---|---|---|---|---|---|---|
| | ID acc. | ID. speed | | ID acc. | ID. speed | | ID acc. | ID. speed | |
| | % | Mean | SD | % | Mean | SD | % | Mean | SD |
| GRAPH | 0.96 | 3069.16 | 878.89 | 0.95 | 3081.01 | 767.62 | 0.96 | 3057.31 | 984.60 |
| HUMAN-1 | 0.91 | 3517.58 | 1028.83 | 0.95 | 3323.76 | 764.59 | 0.88 | 3711.41 | 1214.55 |
| USP-EACH | 0.90 | 3067.16 | 821.00 | 0.86 | 3262.79 | 865.61 | 0.95 | 2871.53 | 730.15 |
| NIL-UCM-EvoTAP | 0.88 | 3159.41 | 910.65 | 0.88 | 3375.17 | 948.46 | 0.89 | 2943.65 | 824.17 |
| NIL-UCM-ValuesCBR | 0.87 | 3262.53 | 974.55 | 0.80 | 3447.50 | 1003.21 | 0.93 | 3077.56 | 916.87 |
| HUMAN-2 | 0.83 | 3463.88 | 1001.29 | 0.89 | 3647.41 | 1045.95 | 0.77 | 3280.35 | 927.79 |
| NIL-UCM-EvoCBR | 0.81 | 3362.22 | 892.45 | 0.75 | 3779.64 | 831.91 | 0.88 | 2944.80 | 748.69 |
| IS-FP-GT | 0.68 | 3167.11 | 964.45 | 0.89 | 2980.30 | 750.78 | 0.46 | 3353.91 | 1114.68 |

Table 8: Identification speed and accuracy per system. Systems are displayed in descending order of overall identification accuracy.

| | Human-assessed, intrinsic | | Extrinsic | | Auto-assessed, intrinsic | | | |
|---|---|---|---|---|---|---|---|---|
| | Fluency | Adequacy | ID Acc. | ID Speed | Acc. | SE | BLEU | NIST |
| Fluency | 1 | 0.68 | 0.50 | -0.89* | .85* | -0.57 | 0.66 | 0.30 |
| Adequacy | 0.68 | 1 | 0.95** | -0.65 | .83* | -0.29 | 0.60 | 0.48 |
| Identification Accuracy | 0.50 | 0.95** | 1 | -0.39 | 0.68 | -0.01 | 0.49 | 0.60 |
| Identification Speed | 0.89* | -0.65 | -0.39 | 1 | -0.79 | 0.68 | -0.51 | 0.06 |
| Accuracy | 0.85* | 0.83* | 0.68 | -0.79 | 1.00 | -0.68 | .859* | 0.49 |
| SE | -0.57 | -0.29 | -0.01 | 0.68 | -0.68 | 1 | -0.75 | -0.07 |
| BLEU | 0.66 | 0.60 | 0.49 | -0.51 | .86* | -0.75 | 1 | 0.71 |
| NIST | 0.30 | 0.48 | 0.60 | 0.06 | 0.49 | -0.07 | 0.71 | 1 |

Table 10: Correlations (Pearson's $r$) between all evaluation measures. (*significant at $p \leq .05$; **significant at $p \leq .01$)

Fluency and Identification Speed, implying that more fluent descriptions led to faster identification. While these results differ from previous findings (Belz and Gatt, 2008), in which no significant correlations were found between extrinsic measures and automatic intrinsic metrics, it is worth noting that significance in the results reported here was only observed between *human-assessed* intrinsic measures and the extrinsic ones.

## 6 Concluding Remarks

The three editions of the TUNA STEC have attracted a substantial amount of interest. In addition to a sizeable body of new work on referring expression generation, as another tangible outcome of these STECs we now have a wide range of different sets of system outputs for the same set of inputs. A particularly valuable resource is the pairing of these outputs from the submitted systems in each edition with evaluation data.

As this was the last time we are running a STEC with the TUNA data, we will now make all data sets, documentation and evaluation software from all TUNA STECs available to researchers. We are planning to add to these as many system outputs as we can, so that other researchers can perform evaluations involving these.

We are also planning to complete our evaluations of the evaluation methods we have developed. Among such experiments will be direct comparisons between the results of the three variants of the identification experiment we have tried out, and a direct comparison between different designs for human-assessed intrinsic evaluations (e.g. comparing the slider design reported here to preference judgments and rating scales).

Apart from the technological progress in REG which we hope the TUNA STECs have helped achieve, perhaps the single most important scientific result is strong evidence for the importance of extrinsic evaluations, as these do not necessarily agree with the results of much more commonly used intrinsic types of evaluations.

## Acknowledgments

We thank our colleagues at the University of Brighton who participated in the identification experiment, and the Masters students at UCL, Sussex and Brighton who participated in the quality assessment experiment. The evaluations were funded by EPSRC (UK) grant EP/G03995X/1.

## References

A. Belz and A. Gatt. 2007. The attribute selection for gre challenge: Overview and evaluation results. In

*Proceedings of UCNLG+MT: Language Generation and Machine Translation*.

A. Belz and A. Gatt. 2008. Intrinsic vs. extrinsic evaluation measures for referring expression generation. In *Proceedings of the 46th Annual Meeting of the Association for Computational Linguistics (ACL'08)*, pages 197–200.

A. Black, P. Taylor, and R. Caley, 1999. *The Festival Speech Synthesis System: System Documentation*. University of Edinburgh, 1.4 edition.

K. I. Forster and J. C. Forster. 2003. DMDX: A windows display program with millisecond accuracy. *Behavior Research Methods, Instruments, & Computers*, 35(1):116–124.

A. Gatt, A. Belz, and Eric Kow. 2008. The tuna challenge 2008: Overview and evaluation results. In *Proceedings of the 5th International Conference on Natural Language Generation (INLG'08)*.

K. Papineni, S. Roukos, T. Ward, and W.-J. Zhu. 2001. BLEU: A method for automatic evaluation of machine translation. IBM research report, IBM Research Division.

S. Papineni, T. Roukos, W. Ward, and W. Zhu. 2002. Bleu: a. method for automatic evaluation of machine translation. In *Proc. 40th Annual Meeting of the Association for Computational Linguistics (ACL-02)*, pages 311–318.

R. Ratliff. 1993. Methods for dealing with reaction time outliers. *Psychological Bulletin*, 114(3):510–532.

# Realizing the Costs: Template-Based Surface Realisation in the GRAPH Approach to Referring Expression Generation

**Ivo Brugman**
University of Twente
The Netherlands
i.h.g.brugman@student.utwente.nl

**Mariët Theune**
University of Twente
The Netherlands
m.theune@utwente.nl

**Emiel Krahmer**
Tilburg University
The Netherlands
e.j.krahmer@uvt.nl

**Jette Viethen**
Macquarie University
Australia
jviethen@ics.mq.edu.au

## Abstract

We describe a new realiser developed for the TUNA 2009 Challenge, and present its evaluation scores on the development set, showing a clear increase in performance compared to last year's simple realiser.

## 1 Introduction

The TUNA Challenge 2009 is the last in a series of challenges using the TUNA corpus of referring expressions (Gatt et al. 2007) for comparative evaluation of referring expression generation. The 2009 Challenge is aimed at *end-to-end referring expression generation*, which encompasses two subtasks: (1) *attribute selection*, choosing a number of attributes that uniquely characterize a target object, distinguishing it from other objects in a visual scene, and (2) *realisation*, converting the selected set of attributes into a word string. Our contributions to the previous Challenges focused on subtask (1), but this year we focus on subtask (2). Below, we briefly sketch how attribute selection is performed in our system, describe our newly developed realiser, and present our evaluation results on the TUNA 2009 development set.

## 2 Attribute selection

We use the Graph-based algorithm of Krahmer et al. (2003) for attribute selection. In this approach, objects and their attributes are represented in a graph as nodes and edges respectively, and attribute selection is seen as a graph search problem that outputs the cheapest distinguishing graph, given a particular *cost function* that assigns costs to attributes. By assigning zero costs to some attributes, e.g., the type of an object, the human tendency to mention redundant properties can be mimicked. For the TUNA Challenge 2009 we use the same settings as last year (Krahmer et al. 2008). The used cost function assigns a zero cost to attributes that are highly frequent in the TUNA corpus, while the other attributes have a cost of either 1 (somewhat infrequent) or 2 (very infrequent). The *order* in which attributes are added is also controlled: to ensure that the cheapest attributes are added first, they are tried in the order of their frequency in the TUNA (2008) training corpus. Using these settings, last year the GRAPH attribute selection algorithm made the top 3 on all evaluation measures (Gatt et al. 2008, Table 11).

## 3 Realisation

The main resource for realisation is a set of templates, derived from the human-produced object descriptions in the TUNA 2009 training data. To construct the templates, we first grouped the descriptions by the combination of attributes they expressed. For instance, in the domain of furniture references, all descriptions expressing the attributes colour, type and orientation were grouped together. This was done for all combinations of attributes. Next, for each description, parts of the word string were related to the attributes in the set. For instance, for the string "red couch facing left", we linked "red" to colour, "couch" to type, and "facing left" to orientation.[1] This provided us with information on how the attributes were expressed (e.g., by adjectives or prepositional phrases) and in which order they appeared in the word string. For each combination of attributes, the surface order that occurred most frequently was selected as the basis for a template. If multiple orderings were equally frequent, we chose the most natural-seeming one. This resulted in templates such as "the [colour] [type] facing [orientation]" for the attribute set {type, colour, orientation}.

During realisation, the templates are used as fol-

[1] This corresponds to the ANNOTATED-WORD-STRING nodes already present in the TUNA corpus. Unfortunately, various problems prevented us from automatically deriving our templates from those existing annotations.

*Proceedings of the 12th European Workshop on Natural Language Generation*, pages 183–184,
Athens, Greece, 30 – 31 March 2009. 

lows. When a set of attributes is input to the realiser, it checks if there is a template matching this particular attribute combination. If so, the template is selected, and the gaps in the template are filled with lexical expressions for the attribute values. The words used to express the values are those that occurred most frequently in the training data for this particular template. If no matching template is found, a description is generated in a simple rule-based fashion, based on the realiser we used last year, but with improved lexical choices. For example, the old realiser always used the word "person" to express the type attribute in descriptions of people, whereas in the TUNA corpus "man" is used most frequently. We changed the realiser to reflect such human preferences.

Template construction for the furniture domain was fairly straightforward, resulting in 25 templates. In practice, only 13 of these are used. Since the GRAPH attribute selection algorithm adds the type and colour attributes to a description for free, these attributes are always selected, making any templates lacking them irrelevant given the current settings of the algorithm.

For the more realistic people domain, template construction was more complicated. For example, when the hairColour attribute is mentioned in human descriptions it can refer either to the hair on a person's head ("white-haired") or his beard ("with a white beard"). The attribute selection algorithm does not make this distinction, leaving it unclear which of the two realisations should be used when hairColour and hasBeard attributes are both to be included in a description. We solved this by simply using the expression that occurred most frequently in the training data for each attribute combination, even allowing hairColour to be mentioned twice if this happened in most human descriptions. Another problem is that many attribute combinations occurred only once in the training data, leading to a very large number (50+) of potential templates. We reduced this number in an ad hoc manner, by ignoring combinations involving attributes (such as hasHair) that are very unlikely to be selected given the current settings of the attribute selection algorithm. This approach left us with 40 templates in the people domain.

## 4 Evaluation

System performance is measured by comparing the generated word strings to the human descriptions in the TUNA development set, comprising 80 furniture and 68 people descriptions. The evaluation measures reported here are *mean edit distance* (MED), the mean of the token-based Levenshtein edit distance between the reference word strings and the system word strings, *mean normalised edit distance* (MNED), where the edit distance is normalised by the number of tokens, and cumulative BLEU 3 score. Table 1 summarizes our evaluation results. For comparison, we also provide the results obtained when using last year's simple realiser, which we reimplemented in Java.

| | MED | MNED | BLEU 3 |
|---|---|---|---|
| **Furniture** | 4.94 (5.48) | 0.48 (0.50) | 0.27 (0.22) |
| **People** | 5.15 (7.53) | 0.46 (0.67) | 0.33 (0.07) |
| **Overall** | 5.03 (6.42) | 0.47 (0.58) | 0.30 (0.15) |

Table 1: Results on the 2009 development set (between brackets are those using last year's realiser).

We see a clear improvement when we compare the performance of the new and the old realiser, in particular in the people domain. However, further evaluation experiments are required to determine whether the improvements are mostly due to our use of templates derived from human descriptions, or to the simple improvements in lexical choice incorporated in the rules used as fall-back in case no matching templates are found.

To further improve the realiser, we need to add templates for all remaining attribute combinations found in the corpus. This should not be difficult, as the set-up of the realiser allows easy creation of templates. It should also be easily portable to other languages; in fact we intend to explore its use for the realisation of referring expressions in Dutch.

## References


Gatt, A., I. van der Sluis and K. van Deemter 2007. Evaluating algorithms for the generation of referring expressions using a balanced corpus. *Proceedings of ENLG 2007* 49-56.

Gatt, A., A. Belz and E. Kow 2008. The TUNA challenge 2008: Overview and evaluation results *Proceedings of INLG 2008* 198-206.

Krahmer, E., S. van Erk and A. Verleg 2003. Graph-based generation of referring expressions. *Computational Linguistics, 29(1)*, 53-72.

Krahmer, E., M. Theune, J. Viethen, and I. Hendrickx 2008. GRAPH: The costs of redundancy in referring expressions. *Proceedings of INLG 2008* 227-229.

# Generation of Referring Expression with an Individual Imprint

**Bernd Bohnet**
International Computer Science Institute
1947 Center Street, CA 94704 Berkeley
bohnet@icsi.berkeley.edu

## Abstract

A major outcome of the last Shared Tasks for Referring Expressions Generation was that each human prefers distinct properties, syntax and lexical units for building referring expressions. One of the reasons for this seems to be that entities might be identified faster since the conversation partner has already some knowledge about how his conversation partner builds referring expressions. Therefore, artificial referring expressions should provide such individual preferences as well so that they become human like. With this contribution to the shared task, we follow this idea again. For the development set, we got a very good DICE score of 0.88 for the furniture domain and of 0.79 for the people domain.

## 1 Introduction

We expect that the test set does not provide the information to which human a referring expression belongs. Therefore, we implemented a fall back strategy in order to get still acceptable DICE scores. In such cases, we select among all sets the set of referring expressions which is most similar to all others. We compute the similarity between two sets as the average DICE score between all referring expression of two sets. The basis for our algorithm is an extended full brevity implementation, cf. (Bohnet and Dale, 2005). IS-FP uses also the nearest neighbor technique like the IS-FBN algorithm that was introduced by Bohnet (2007).

With the nearest neighbor technique, IS-FP selects the expressions which are most similar to the referring expressions of the same human and a human that builds referring expressions similar or in the case that the human is unknown it uses the most similar one to all others referring expressions. The similarity is computed as the average of all DICE scores between all combinations of the available trails for two humans. From the result of the nearest neighbor evaluation, FP selects the shortest and if still more than one expressions remain then it computes the similarity among them and chooses the most typical and finally, if still alternatives remain, it selects one with the attributes having the highest frequency. Table 1 shows the results for IS-FP trained on the training set and applied to the development set.

| Set | Dice | MASI | Accuracy . |
|---|---|---|---|
| Furniture | 0.880 | 0.691 | 51.25% |
| People | 0.794 | 0.558 | 36.8% |
| Total | 0.837 | 0.625 | 44% |

Table 1: Results for the IS-FP algorithm

## 2 IS-GT: Realization with Graph Transducers

We build the input dependency tree for the text generator due to the statistical information that we collect from the training data for each person. This procedure is consistent with our referring expression generator IS-FP that reproduces the individual imprint in a referring expression for the target person. We start with the realization of the referring expressions from a surface syntactic dependency tree, cf. (Mel'čuk, 1988). For the realization of the text, we use the Text Generator and Linguistic Environment MATE.

*Proceedings of the 12th European Workshop on Natural Language Generation*, pages 185–186,
Athens, Greece, 30 – 31 March 2009. 

## 3 The Referring Expression Models

An algorithm learns a Referring Expression Model for each person that contributed referring expression to the corpus. The model contains the following information:

(1) The lexicalization for the values of a attribute such as couch for the value sofa, man for value person, etc.

(2) The preferred usage of determiners for the type that can be definite (*the*), indefinite (*a*), no article.

(3) The syntactic preferences such as *the top left chair*, *the chair at the bottom to the left*, etc.

The information about the determiner and the lexicalization is collected from the annotated word string and the word string itself. We collect the most frequent usage for each person in the corpus. In order to collect the preferred syntax, we annotated the word strings with syntactic dependency trees. Each of the dependency tress contains additional attributes, which describe the information content of a branch outgoing from the root as well as the possible value of the attribute at the nodes which carry the information. The learning program cuts the syntactic tree at edges starting at the root node and stores the branches in the referring expression model for the person.

## 4 Realization

For the realization, we use a handcrafted grammar that generates out of the dependency trees topologic graphs. The main task of the grammar is to determine the word order. The system was developed only by using the training data without any consideration of the development data. We used as guide for the optimization cross validation of training data.

## 5 IS-FP-GT: The Combination of Attribute Selection and Realization

For the combination of the both methods, we combine the two procedure in a pipeline architecture. Table 2 shows the results.

## 6 Conclusion

The IS-FP algorithm reproduces the imprint of human referring expressions. When the test set contains the reference to the human then the scores are exceptional high.

| Set | Accuracy | String ED | Mean SED | Blue 3 |
|---|---|---|---|---|
| Furniture | 15 % | 3,8625 | 0.3826 | 0.3684 |
| People | 4,41 % | 4,764 | 0.4817 | 0.2263 |
| Total | 9,71 | 4,313 | 0.4321 | 0.297 |

Table 2: Results for the TUNA-REG Task

## References

B. Bohnet and R. Dale. 2005. Viewing referring expression generation as search. In *IJCAI*, pages 1004–1009.

B. Bohnet. 2007. IS-FBN, IS-FBS, IS-IAC: The Adaptation of Two Classic Algorithms for the Generation of Referring Expressions in order to Produce Expressions like Humans Do. In *MT Summit XI, UCNLG+MT*, pages 84–86.

I.A. Mel'čuk. 1988. *Dependency Syntax: Theory and Practice*. State University of New York Press, Albany.

# Evolutionary and Case-Based Approaches to REG: NIL-UCM-EvoTAP, NIL-UCM-ValuesCBR and NIL-UCM-EvoCBR

**Raquel Hervás and Pablo Gervás**
Natural Interaction based on Language (NIL)
Universidad Complutense de Madrid
raquelhb@fdi.ucm.es, pgervas@sip.ucm.es

## 1 Evolutionary Approach to Attribute Selection

We propose the use of evolutionary algorithms (EAs) (Holland, 1992) to deal with the attribute selection task of referring expression generation. Evolutionary algorithms operate over a population of individuals (possible solutions for a problem) that evolve according to selection rules and genetic operators. The fitness function is a metric that evaluates each of the possible solutions, ensuring that the average adaptation of the population increases each generation. Repeating this process hundreds or thousands of times leads to very good solutions for the problem.

We encode as a fitness function the specific constraints required for the reference to be acceptable. The crossover and mutation genetic operators ensure a reasonable variation between the different options much as a human-generated text would.

Each individual is represented by a set of genes that are the list of possible attributes in the reference. Each gene has an associated value of 0 (if the attribute is not included in the reference), or 1 (if the attribute is included in the reference). The initial population should have a low number of genes set to 1, because references tend to be short and the use of all the possible attributes should be avoided.

For the *crossover operator*, two individuals are selected randomly and crossed by a random point of their structure. For the *mutation operator*, some of the genes are chosen randomly to be mutated from 1 to 0, or vice versa.

The fitness function must find a balance between the univocal identification of a referent, and a natural use of attributes. The formula used as fitness function is defined in Equation 1:

$$fit_{ind_i} = f_{att_i} * weight_{att} + ident * weight_{id} \quad (1)$$

where *ident* represents whether the reference is univocally identifying the target among the distractors, and $f_{att_i}$ computes the role of attributes as the normalised sum of the weight (depending on its absolute frecuency in ATTRIBUTE-SET elements in the corpus) of all attributes present (gene=1), as defined by Equation 2:

$$f_{att_i} = \frac{\sum gene_{att_i} * weight_{att_i}}{\#attsRef} \quad (2)$$

## 2 Case-Based Reasoning for Realization

Template-based solutions for natural language generation rely on reusing fragments of text extracted from typical texts in a given domain, applying a process of abstraction that identifies which part of them is common to all uses, and leaving certain gaps to be filled with details corresponding to a new use. A case-based solution (Aamodt and Plaza, 1994) to reference realization can obtain the information needed to realize a reference from the original examples of appropriate use that originated the templates.

In our approach, a case consists of a description of the problem (`ATTRIBUTE-SET`) and a solution (`ANNOTATED-WORD-STRING` interpreted as a template). Cases are stored in a Case Retrieval Net (CRN) (Lenz and Burkhard, 1996), a memory model developed to improve the efficiency of the retrieval tasks of the CBR cycle. Each attribute-value pair from the `ATTRIBUTE-SET` is a node in the net. Templates in `ANNOTATED-WORD-STRING` are considered as solutions to the cases. Similarities between the nodes are established for the retrieval stage of the CBR process. For example, we have considered that 'back' and 'right' orientation values have a higher similarity than 'back' and 'front' that are exactly the opposite.

The attribute-value pairs of `ATTRIBUTE-SET` that must be realized in a final string are used to query the net, which returns the more similar cases. Only one of them must be chosen to be adapted for the solution. We consider four different types of retrieved cases: *preferred* (cases with exactly the same attributes than the query), *more* (cases with the same attributes as the query and

*Proceedings of the 12th European Workshop on Natural Language Generation*, pages 187–188,
Athens, Greece, 30 – 31 March 2009. ©2009 Association for Computational Linguistics

| | | String Acc. | Edit Dist. | Norm. Edit Distance | BLEU 1 Score | BLEU 2 Score | BLEU 3 Score | BLEU 4 Score |
|---|---|---|---|---|---|---|---|---|
| EvoTAP | **Furniture** | 0,08 | 4,87 | 0,51 | 0,44 | 0,33 | 0,24 | 0,18 |
| | **People** | 0,03 | 6,04 | 0,59 | 0,39 | 0,25 | 0,15 | 0,00 |
| | **Both** | 0,06 | 5,41 | 0,55 | 0,41 | 0,29 | 0,20 | 0,13 |
| ValuesCBR | **Furniture** | 0,01 | 5,91 | 0,55 | 0,44 | 0,31 | 0,20 | 0,13 |
| | **People** | 0,01 | 5,80 | 0,56 | 0,43 | 0,28 | 0,17 | 0,08 |
| | **Both** | 0,01 | 5,86 | 0,55 | 0,44 | 0,30 | 0,19 | 0,11 |
| EvoCBR | **Furniture** | 0,04 | 5,77 | 0,58 | 0,39 | 0,26 | 0,18 | 0,13 |
| | **People** | 0,01 | 6,94 | 0,61 | 0,41 | 0,25 | 0,16 | 0,08 |
| | **Both** | 0,03 | 6,31 | 0,59 | 0,41 | 0,26 | 0,17 | 0,11 |

Table 1: Results over development data for the three systems

some more), *lessExtra* (cases that lack some attribute from the query but have some extra ones), and *lessNoExtra* (cases that lack some attribute from the query and have no extra ones). The order given is the preferred order to chose the most suitable case for the query.

Adaptation of the chosen case depends on its type. The idea is to keep all the parts of the template that correspond to attributes common to the query and the case. Extra attributes in the case that do not appear in the query are discarded. Attributes in the query not appearing in the case are lost.

## 3 Results and Discussion

We have tested both solutions (evolutionary and case-based) separately and together in three different systems, relying on solutions presented in last year's challenge.

- **NIL-UCM-EvoTAP**. Selects attributes using the evolutionary solution and realises using the NIL-UCM-BSC solution (Gervás et al., 2008).
- **NIL-UCM-ValuesCBR**. Selects attributes using the NIL-UCM-MFVF solution (Gervás et al., 2008) and realizes using the case-based approach.
- **NIL-UCM-EvoCBR**. Selects attributes using the evolutionary solution and realizes using the case-based approach.

The results obtained by the three systems over development data are shown in Table 1.

The evolutionary approach performs poorly but might be improved by using a more refined algorithm for calculating attribute weights, such as done in the last year NIL-UCM-MFVF solution.

The reported CBR results were obtained over a case base built from a selection of the available training data (samples that relied on data not available in the input were omitted). This approach could be further refined by generating style-specific subsets of the case base.


## Acknowledgments

This research is funded by the Spanish Ministry of Education and Science (TIN2006-14433-C02-01).


## References


Aamodt, A. and Plaza, E.. 1994. Case-based reasoning: Foundational issues, methodological variations, and system approaches *AI Communications, 7(1).*

Gervás, P. and Hervás, R. and León, C. 2008. NIL-UCM: Most-Frequent-Value-First Attribute Selection and Best-Scoring-Choice Realization. *Referring Expression Generation Challenge 2008*, INGL-08, USA.

Holland, J.H. 1992. Adaptation in Natural and Artificial Systems. An Introductory Analysis with Applications to Biology, Control and Artificial Intelligence. MIT Press, Cambridge, Massachusetts, Second Edition.

M. Lenz and H. Burkhard 1996. Case Retrieval Nets: Basic Ideas and Extensions. *Kunstliche Intelligenz.*

# USP-EACH: Improved Frequency-based Greedy Attribute Selection

**Diego Jesus de Lucena**
University of São Paulo
São Paulo - Brazil
diego.si@usp.br

**Ivandré Paraboni**
University of São Paulo
São Paulo - Brazil
ivandre@usp.br

## Abstract

We present a follow-up of our previous frequency-based greedy attribute selection strategy. The current version takes into account also the instructions given to the participants of TUNA trials regarding the use of location information, showing an overall improvement on string-edit distance values driven by the results on the Furniture domain.

## 1 Introduction

In previous work (Lucena & Paraboni, 2008) we presented a frequency-based greedy attribute selection strategy submitted to the TUNA Challenge 2008. Presently we further the issue by taking additional information into account - namely, the trial condition information available from the TUNA data - and report improved results for string-edit distance as required for the 2009 competition.

## 2 Background

In Lucena & Paraboni (2008) we presented a combined strategy based on attribute frequency and certain aspects of a greedy attribute selection strategy for referring expressions generation. A list P of attributes sorted by frequency is the centre piece of the following selection strategy:

- select all attributes whose relative frequency falls above a threshold value t (t was estimated to be 0.8 for both Furniture and People domains.)
- if the resulting description uniquely describes the target object, then finalizes.
- if not, starting from the most frequent attribute in P, search exhaustively for an attribute g such that g, if selected, would rule out all remaining distractors in the context.

The overall effect obtained is twofold: on the one hand, in a complex situation of reference (in which many attributes may rule out many distractors, but more than one will be required to achieve uniqueness) the algorithm simply selects *frequent* attributes. This may be comparable to a human speaker who has to single out the target object but who does not have the means to come up with the 'right' attribute straight away.

On the other hand, as the number of distractors decreases, a single attribute capable of ruling out all distractors will eventually emerge, forcing the algorithm to switch to a *greedy* strategy and finalize. Once again, this may be comparable to what a human speaker may do when an appropriate attribute becomes sufficiently salient and all distractors in the context can be ruled out at once.

The above approach performed fairly well (at least considering its simplicity) as reported in Lucena & Paraboni (2008). However, there is one major source of information available from the TUNA data that was *not* taken into account in the above strategy: the *trial condition* represented by the +/- LOC feature. Because this feature distinguishes the very kinds of instruction given to each participant to complete the TUNA task, the information provided by -/+ LOC is likely to have a significant impact on the overall results. This clear gap in our previous work represents an opportunity for improvement discussed in the next section.

## 3 Algorithm

The present work is a refined version of the original frequency-based greedy attribute selection strategy submitted to the TUNA Challenge 2008 (Lucena & Paraboni, 2008), now taking also the trial condition (+/-LOC) into account.

*Proceedings of the 12th European Workshop on Natural Language Generation*, pages 189–190,
Athens, Greece, 30 – 31 March 2009. 

In the TUNA data, +LOC indicates the instances of the experiment in which participants were told that they were allowed to refer to the X,Y coordinates of the screen (i.e., selecting the X- and/or Y-DIMENSION attributes), whereas -LOC indicates the trials in which they were discouraged (but not prevented) to do so. In practice, references in +LOC trials are more likely to convey the X- and Y-DIMENSION attributes than those in which the -LOC condition was applied.

Our modified algorithm simply consists of computing separated frequency lists for +LOC and -LOC trial conditions, and then using the original frequency-based greedy approach with each list accordingly. In practice, descriptions are now generated in two different ways, depending on the trial condition, which may promote the X- and Y-DIMENSION attributes to higher positions in the list P when +LOC applies.

Using the TUNA Challenge 2009 development data set, the attribute selection task was performed as above. For the surface realisation task, we have reused the English language surface realisation module provided by Irene Langkilde-Geary for the TUNA Challenge 2008.

## 4 Results

The following Figure 1 shows mean sting-edit distance and BLEU-3 scores computed using the evaluation tool provided by the TUNA Challenge team. For ease of comparison with our previous work, we also present Dice and MASI scores computed as in the previous TUNA Challenge, although these scores were not required for the current competition.

The most relevant comparison with our previous work is observed in the overall string-edit distance values in Figure 1: considering that in Lucena & Paraboni (2008) we reported 6.12 edit-distance for Furniture and 7.38 for People, the overall improvement (driven by the descriptions in the Furniture domain) may be explained by the fact that the current version makes more accurate decisions as to when to use these attributes according to the instructions given to the participants of the TUNA trials (the trial condition +/-LOC. )

On the other hand, the divide between +LOC and -LOC strategies does not have a significant effect on the results based on the semantics of the description (i.e., Dice and MASI scores), which remain the same as those obtained previously. This may be explained by the fact that using location information inappropriately counts as one single error in Dice/MASI calculations, but it may have a much greater impact on the wording of the surface string (e.g., one single use of the X-DIMENSION attribute may be realized as "on the far left", adding four words to the descriptions.)

| | Overall | Furniture | People |
|---|---|---|---|
| String-edit distance | 6.03 | 4.78 | 7.50 |
| BLEU-3 | 0.19 | 0.31 | 0.04 |
| Dice | 0.74 | 0.82 | 0.65 |
| MASI | 0.53 | 0.63 | 0.41 |

Figure 1. Results (TUNA Challenge 2009 development data set)

## 5 Conclusion

We have presented a refined version of our previous frequency-based greedy attribute selection strategy. The current version takes into account the instructions given to the participants of TUNA trials regarding the use of location information (the trial condition +/-LOC.)

Results obtained using the TUNA Challenge 2009 development data set show improvements on string-edit distance, suggesting that the generated descriptions resemble more closely those seen in the TUNA corpus.

**Acknowledgments**

This work has been supported by CNPq-Brazil (484015/2007-9) and FAPESP (2006/03941-7).

## References

Lucena, Diego Jesus de, and Ivandré Paraboni (2008) *USP-EACH Frequency-based Greedy Attribute Selection for Referring Expressions Generation.* Proc. of INLG-2008 (TUNA Challenge 2008). Salt Fork, US, pp.219-220.

# A Probabilistic Model of Referring Expressions for Complex Objects

**Kotaro Funakoshi**[†] **Philipp Spanger**[‡] **Mikio Nakano**[†] **Takenobu Tokunaga**[‡]
[†]Honda Research Institute Japan Co., Ltd.
Saitama, Japan
funakoshi@jp.honda-ri.com
nakano@jp.honda-ri.com
[‡]Tokyo Institute of Technology
Tokyo, Japan
philipp@cl.cs.titech.ac.jp
take@cl.cs.titech.ac.jp

## Abstract

This paper presents a probabilistic model both for generation and understanding of referring expressions. This model introduces the concept of *parts of objects*, modelling the necessity to deal with the characteristics of separate parts of an object in the referring process. This was ignored or implicit in previous literature. Integrating this concept into a probabilistic formulation, the model captures human characteristics of visual perception and some type of pragmatic implicature in referring expressions. Developing this kind of model is critical to deal with more complex domains in the future. As a first step in our research, we validate the model with the TUNA corpus to show that it includes conventional domain modeling as a subset.

## 1 Introduction

Generation of referring expressions has been studied for the last two decades. The basic orientation of this research was pursuing an algorithm that generates a minimal description which uniquely identifies a target object from distractors. Thus the research was oriented and limited by two constraints: minimality and uniqueness.

The constraint on minimality has, however, been relaxed due to the computational complexity of generation, the perceived naturalness of redundant expressions, and the easiness of understanding them (e.g., (Dale and Reiter, 1995; Spanger et al., 2008)). On the other hand, the other constraint of uniqueness has not been paid much attention to. One major aim of our research is to relax this constraint on uniqueness because of the reason explained below.

The fundamental goal of our research is to deal with multipartite objects, which have constituents with different attribute values. Typical domain settings in previous literature use uniform objects like the table A shown in Figure 1. However, real life is not so simple. Multipartite objects such as tables B and C can be found easily. Therefore this paper introduces the concept of *parts of objects* to deal with more complex domains containing such objects. Hereby the constraint on uniqueness becomes problematic because people easily generate and understand logically ambiguous expressions in such domains.

For example, people often use an expression such as "the table with red corners" to identify table B. Logically speaking, this expression is equally applicable both to A and to B, that is, violating the constraint on uniqueness. And yet people seem to have no problem identifying the intended target correctly and have little reluctance to use such an expression (Evidence is presented in Section 3). We think that this reflects some type of pragmatic implicature arising from human characteristics of visual perception and that is important both for understanding human-produced expressions and for generating human-friendly expressions in a real environment. This paper proposes a model of referring expressions both for generation and understanding. Our model uses probabilities to solve ambiguity under the relaxed constraint on uniqueness while considering human perception.

No adequate data is currently available in order to provide a comprehensive evaluation of our model. As a first step in our research, we validate the model with the TUNA corpus to show that it includes conventional domain modeling.

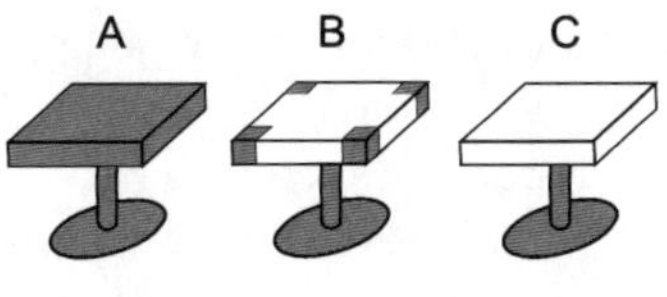


Figure 1: An example scene

*Proceedings of the 12th European Workshop on Natural Language Generation*, pages 191–194,
Athens, Greece, 30 – 31 March 2009. 

## 2 Related work

Horacek (2005) proposes to introduce probabilities to overcome uncertainties due to discrepancies in knowledge and cognition between subjects. While our model shares the same awareness of issues with Horacek's work, our focus is on rather different issues (i.e., handling multipartite objects and relaxing the constraint on uniqueness). In addition, Horacek's work is concerned only with generation while our model is available both for generation and understanding. Roy (2002) also proposes a probabilistic model for generation but presupposes uniform objects.

Horacek (2006) deals with references for structured objects such as documents. Although it considers parts of objects, the motivation and focus of the work are on quite different aspects from ours.

## 3 Evidence against logical uniqueness

We conducted two psycholinguistic experiments using the visual stimulus shown in Figure 1.

In the first experiment, thirteen Japanese subjects were presented with an expression "kado no akai tukue (the table with red corners)" and asked to choose a table from the three in the figure. Twelve out of the thirteen chose table B. Seven out of the twelve subjects answered that the given expression was not ambiguous.

In the second experiment, thirteen different Japanese subjects were asked to make a description for table B without using positional relations. Ten out of the thirteen made expressions semantically equivalent to the expression used in the first experiment. Only three subjects made logically discriminative expressions such as "asi to yotu kado dake akai tukue (the table whose four corners and leg only are red)."

These results show that people easily generate/understand logically ambiguous expressions.

## 4 Proposed model

We define $\pi = \{p^1, p^2, \ldots, p^k\}$ as the set of $k$ *parts of objects* (classes of sub-parts) that appears in a domain. Here $p^1$ is special and always means the whole of an object. In a furniture domain, $p^1$ means a piece of furniture regardless of the kind of the object (*chair*, *table*, whatever). $p^i (i \neq 1)$ means a sub-part class such as *leg*. Note that $\pi$ is defined not for each object but for a domain. Thus, objects may have no part corresponding to $p^i$ (e.g., some chairs have no leg.).

A referring expression $e$ is represented as a set of $n$ pairs of an attribute value expression $e^a_j$ and a part expression $e^p_j$ modified by $e^a_j$ as

$$e = \{(e^p_1, e^a_1), (e^p_2, e^a_2), \ldots, (e^p_n, e^a_n)\}. \quad (1)$$

For example, an expression "the white table with a red leg" is represented as

$$\{(\text{"table"}, \text{"white"}), (\text{"leg"}, \text{"red"})\}.$$

Given a set of objects $\omega$ and a referring expression $e$, the probability with which the expression $e$ refers to an object $o \in \omega$ is denoted as $Pr(O = o|E = e, \Omega = \omega)$. If we seek to provide a more realistic model, we can model a probabilistic distribution even for $\Omega$. In this paper, however, we assume that $\Omega$ is fixed to $\omega$ and it is shared by interlocutors exactly. Thus, hereafter, $Pr(o|e)$ is equal to $Pr(o|e, \omega)$.

Following the definition (1), we estimate $Pr(o|e)$ as follows:

$$Pr(o|e) \approx \mathcal{N} \prod_i Pr(o|e^p_i, e^a_i). \quad (2)$$

Here, $\mathcal{N}$ is a normalization coefficient. According to Bayes' rule,

$$Pr(o|e^p_i, e^a_i) = \frac{Pr(o)Pr(e^p_i, e^a_i|o)}{Pr(e^p_i, e^a_i)}. \quad (3)$$

Therefore,

$$Pr(o|e) \approx \mathcal{N} \prod_i \frac{Pr(o)Pr(e^p_i, e^a_i|o)}{Pr(e^p_i, e^a_i)}. \quad (4)$$

We decompose $Pr(e^p_i, e^a_i|o)$ as

$$\sum_u \sum_v Pr(e^p_i|p_u, o)Pr(e^a_i|a_v, o)Pr(p_u, a_v|o) \quad (5)$$

where $p_u$ is one of *parts of objects* that could be expressed with $e^p_i$, and $a_v$ is one of attribute values[1] that could be expressed with $e^a_i$. Under the simplifying assumption that $e^p_i$ and $e^a_i$ are not ambiguous and are single possible expressions for a part of objects and an attribute value independently of objects [2],

$$Pr(o|e) \approx \mathcal{N} \prod_i \frac{Pr(o)Pr(p_i, a_i|o)}{Pr(p_i, a_i)} \quad (6)$$

$$\approx \mathcal{N} \prod_i Pr(o|p_i, a_i) \quad (7)$$

[1]Each attribute value belongs to an attribute $\alpha$, a set of attribute values. E.g., $\alpha_{color} = \{red, white, \ldots\}$.

[2]That is, we ignore *lexical selection* matters in this paper, although our model is potentially able to handle those matters including training from corpora.

$Pr(o|p,a)$ concerns *attribute selection* in generation of referring expressions. Most attribute selection algorithms presented in past work are based on set operations over multiple attributes with discrete (i.e., symbolized) values such as colors (*red, brown, white, etc*) to find a uniquely distinguishing description. The simplest estimation of $Pr(o|p,a)$ following this conventional Boolean domain modeling is

$$Pr(o|p,a) \approx \begin{cases} |\omega'|^{-1} & (p \text{ in } o \text{ has } a) \\ 0 & (p \text{ in } o \text{ does not have } a) \end{cases} \quad (8)$$

where $\omega'$ is the subset of $\omega$, each member of which has attribute value *a* in its part of *p*.

As Horacek (2005) pointed out, however, this standard approach is problematic in a real environment because many physical attributes are non-discrete and the symbolization of these continuous attributes have uncertainties. For example, even if two objects are blue, one can be more blueish than the other. Some subjects may say it's blue but others may say it's purple. Moreover, there is the problem of logical ambiguity pointed out in Section 1. That is, even if an attribute itself is equally applicable to several objects in a logical sense, other available information (such as visual context) might influence the interpretation of a given referring expression.

Such phenomena could be captured by estimating $Pr(o|p,a)$ as

$$Pr(o|p,a) \approx \frac{Pr(a|p,o)Pr(p|o)Pr(o)}{Pr(p,a)}. \quad (9)$$

$Pr(a|p,o)$ represents the relevance of attribute value $a$ to part $p$ in object $o$. $Pr(p|o)$ represents the salience of part $p$ in object $o$. The underlying idea to deal with the problem of logical ambiguity is "If some part of an object is mentioned, it should be more salient than other parts." This is related to Grice's maxims in a different way from matters discussed in (Dale and Reiter, 1995). $Pr(p|o)$ could be computed in some manner by using the saliency map (Itti et al., 1998). $Pr(o)$ is the prior probability that object $o$ is chosen. If potential functions (such as used in (Tokunaga et al., 2005)) are used for computing $Pr(o)$, we can naturally rank objects, which are equally relevant to a given referring expression, according to distances from interlocutors.

# 5 Algorithms

## 5.1 Understanding

Understanding a referring expression $e$ is identifying the target object $\hat{o}$ from a set of objects $\omega$. This is formulated in a straightforward way as

$$\hat{o} = \operatorname*{argmax}_{o \in \omega} Pr(o|e). \quad (10)$$

## 5.2 Generation

Generation of a referring expression is choosing the best appropriate expression $\hat{e}$ to discriminate a given object $\hat{o}$ from a set of distractors. A simple formulation is

$$\hat{e} = \operatorname*{argmax}_{e \in \rho} Pr(e)Pr(\hat{o}|e). \quad (11)$$

$\rho$ is a pre-generated set of candidate expressions for $\hat{o}$. This paper does not explain how to generate a set of candidates.

$Pr(e)$ is the generation probability of an expression $e$ independent of objects. This probability can be learned from a corpus. In the evaluation described in Section 6, we estimate $Pr(e)$ as

$$Pr(e) \approx Pr(|e|) \prod_i Pr(\alpha_i). \quad (12)$$

Here, $Pr(|e|)$ is the distribution of expression length in terms of numbers of attributes used. $Pr(\alpha)$ is the selection probability of a specific attribute $\alpha$ ($SP(a)$ in (Spanger et al., 2008)).

# 6 Preliminary evaluation

As mentioned above, no adequate corpus is currently available in order to provide an initial validation of our model which we present in this paper. In this section, we validate our model using the TUNA corpus (the "Participant's Pack" available for download as part of the Generation Challenge 2009) to show that it includes traditional domain modeling. We use the training-part of the corpus for training our model and the development-part for evaluation.

We note that we here assume a homogeneous distribution of the probability $Pr(o|p,a)$, i.e., we are applying formula (8) here in order to calculate this probability. We first implemented our probabilistic model for the area of understanding. This means our algorithm took as input the user's selection of attribute–value pairs in the description and calculated the most likely target object. This was

Table 1: Initial evaluation of proposed model for generation in TUNA-domain

| | *Furniture* | *People* |
|---|---|---|
| *Total cases* | 80 | 68 |
| *Mean Dice-score* | 0.78 | 0.66 |

carried out for both the furniture and people domains. Overall, outside of exceptional cases (e.g., human error), our algorithm was able to distinguish the target object for all human descriptions (precision of 100%). This means it covers all the cases the original approach dealt with.

We then implemented our model for the case of generation. We measured the similarity of the output of our algorithm with the human-produced sets by using the Dice-coefficient (see (Belz and Gatt, 2007)). We evaluated this both for the Furniture and People domain. The results are summarized in Table 1.

Our focus was here to fundamentally show how our model includes traditional modelling as a subset, without much focus or effort on tuning in order to achieve a maximum Dice-score. However, we note that the Dice-score of our algorithm was comparable to the top 5-7 systems in the 2007 GRE-Challenge (see (Belz and Gatt, 2007)) and thus produced a relatively good result. This shows how our algorithm – providing a model of the referring process in a more complex domain – is applicable as well to the very simple TUNA-domain as a special case.

## 7 Discussion

In past work, parts of objects were ignored or implicit. In case of the TUNA corpus, while the Furniture domain ignores parts of objects, the People domain contained parts of objects such as *hair*, *glasses*, *beard*, etc. However, they were implicitly modeled by combining a pair of a part and its attribute as an attribute such as *hairColor*. One major advantage of our model is that, by explicitly modelling parts of objects, it can handle the problem of logical ambiguity that is newly reported in this paper. Although it might be possible to handle the problem by extending previously proposed algorithms in some ways, our formulation would be clearer. Moreover, our model is directly available both for generation and understanding. Referring expressions using attributes (such as discussed in this paper) and those using discourse contexts (such as "it") are separately approached in past work. Our model possibly handles both of them in a unified manner with a small extension.

This paper ignored *relations* between objects. We, however, think that it is not difficult to prepare algorithms handling relations using our model. Generation using our model is performed in a generate-and-test manner. Therefore computational complexity is a matter of concern. However, that could be controlled by limiting the numbers of attributes and parts under consideration according to relevance and salience, because our model is under the relaxed constraint of uniqueness unlike previous work.

As future work, we have to gather data to evaluate our model and to statistically train lexical selection in a new domain containing multipartite objects.

## References


Anja Belz and Albert Gatt. 2007. The attribute selection for GRE challenge: Overview and evaluation results. In *Proc. the MT Summit XI Workshop Using Corpora for Natural Language Generation: Language Generation and Machine Translation (UC-NLG+MT)*, pages 75–83.

Robert Dale and Ehud Reiter. 1995. Computational interpretations of the Gricean maxims in the generation of referring expressions. *Cognitive Science*, 18:233–263.

Helmut Horacek. 2005. Generating referential descriptions under conditions of uncertainty. In *Proc. ENLG 05*.

Helmut Horacek. 2006. Generating references to parts of recursively structured objects. In *Proc. ACL 06*.

L Itti, C. Koch, and E. Niebur. 1998. A model of saliency-based visual attention for rapid scene analysis. *IEEE Transactions on Pattern Analysis and Machine Intelligence*, 20(11):1254–1259.

Deb Roy. 2002. Learning visually-grounded words and syntax for a scene description task. *Computer Speech and Language*, 16(3).

Philipp Spanger, Takehiro Kurosawa, and Takenobu Tokunaga. 2008. On "redundancy" in selecting attributes for generating referring expressions. In *Proc. COLING 08*.

Takenobu Tokunaga, Tomonori Koyama, and Suguru Saito. 2005. Meaning of Japanese spatial nouns. In *Proc. the Second ACL-SIGSEM Workshop on The Linguistic Dimensions of Prepositions and their Use in Computational Linguistics Formalisms and Applications*, pages 93 – 100.

# Author Index

**Association for Computational Linguistics**
209 N. Eighth Street
Stroudsburg, Pennsylvania 18360

CURRAN ASSOCIATES INC
proceedings
.com